Lecture Notes in Computer Science 7190

Commenced Publication in 1973
Founding and Former Series Editors:
Gerhard Goos, Juris Hartmanis, and Jan van Leeuwen

Ngoc Thanh Nguyen (Ed.)

Transactions on Computational Collective Intelligence VI

Springer

Volume Editor

Ngoc Thanh Nguyen
Wrocław University of Technology
Wyb. Wyspiańskiego 27
50-370, Wrocław, Poland
E-mail: ngoc-thanh.nguyen@pwr.edu.pl

ISSN 0302-9743
e-ISSN 1611-3349
ISBN 978-3-642-29355-9
e-ISBN 978-3-642-29356-6
DOI 10.1007/978-3-642-29356-6

Springer Heidelberg Dordrecht London New York

Library of Congress Control Number: 2012934582

CR Subject Classification (1998): I.2, C.2.4, I.2.11, H.3-5, D.2, I.5

Typesetting: Camera-ready by author, data conversion by Scientific Publishing Services, Chennai, India

Printed on acid-free paper

Springer is part of Springer Science+Business Media (www.springer.com)

Preface

Welcome to the sixth volume of *Transactions on Computational Collective Intelligence* (TCCI). This is the first issue in 2012, the third year of TCCI activities. In 2010, the first year, TCCI published 20 papers in two issues, while in 2011 there were three issues containing 30 papers. From 2012 we are planning to keep a constant number of issues with about 35–40 papers per year. All papers included in TCCI issues contain original and advanced research results of the authors. Each of these papers constitutes a complete and comprehensive description of the contribution.

TCCI is devoted to research in computer-based methods of computational collective intelligence (CCI) and their applications in a wide range of fields such as group decision making, knowledge integration, consensus computing, Semantic Web, social networks and multiagent systems. TCCI strives to cover new computational, methodological, theoretical and practical aspects of collective intelligence understood as the form of intelligence that emerges from the collaboration and competition of many individuals (artificial and/or natural).

This volume of TCCI includes ten interesting and original papers. The first of them, entitled "On the Pattern Recognition and Classification of Stochastically Episodic Events" by Colin Bellinger and B. John Oommen, presents the frontiers of novelty detection through the introduction of a new field of problems open for analysis. In particular, the authors note that this new realm deviates from the standard set of one-class classification problems based on the presence of three characteristics, which ultimately amplify the classification challenge. In the second paper with the title "Paraconsistent Reasoning for Semantic Web Agents" the authors, Linh Anh Nguyen and Andrzej Szałas, address the problem of processing inconsistency of knowledge, which, for example, can appear in fusing knowledge from distributed sources. The authors introduce a number of paraconsistent semantics by providing a special logic named SROIQ, including three-valued and four-valued semantics. The next paper, "An Agent Model for Cognitive and Affective Empathic Understanding of Other Agents" by Zulfiqar A. Memon and Jan Treur, focuses on modelling capabilities to interpret another person's mind, taking into account both affective and cognitive states. The authors have built an agent model that describes how the empathic agent deals with another agent's cognitive states and the associated feelings. In the fourth paper entitled "Multiagent-Based Simulation as a Supply Chain Analysis Workbench" the authors, Jacek Jakieła, Paweł Litwin and Marcin Olech, present the application of multiagent-based simulation tools to the analysis of supply chain behavior. They show that the agent-oriented approach may be considered as a powerful conceptual framework for organization modeling and workbench for simulations of intra- and inter-organizational business processes. In the paper "On the Effective Distribution and Maintenance of Knowledge Represented by

Complementary Graphs" by Leszek Kotulski and Adam Sędziwy, a method for knowledge distribution and maintenance using parallel graph transformations is presented. In the next paper, entitled "Agent System for Managing Distributed Mobile Interactive Documents in Knowledge-Based Organizations," Magdalena Godlewska presents a model of knowledge-based organization and general assumptions of the mobile interactive document (MIND) architecture and selected workflow patterns applicable to knowledge-based organizations. She describes the elements of the agent system for managing distributed mobile documents and shows case studies that use the MIND architecture. In the seventh paper with the title "Agent Cooperation Within Adversarial Teams in Dynamic Environment — Key Issues and Development Trends" Bartłomiej Dzieńkowski and Urszula Markowska-Kaczmar present a comprehensive survey of multiagent systems with adversarial teams competing in dynamic environments. The next paper, "On Pricing Strategies of Boundedly Rational Telecommunication Operators" by Bogumil Kaminski and Maciej Latek, contains an analysis of a multiagent model of a pre-paid telecommunication market and illustrates how the topology of the call graph among customers influences long-run market prices. The ninth paper entitled "Reasoning About Time-Dependent Multiagents: Foundations of Theorem Proving and Model Checking," by Norihiro Kamide, presents some extensions of linear-time temporal logic and computation tree logic. The author has proved that owing to these approaches it is easier to process time-dependent knowledge in multiagent systems. In the last paper, "Learning Predictive Models for Financial Time Series by Using Agent Based Simulations," Filippo Neri presents a computational technique to model financial time series combining a learning component with a simulation one. The author also describes an agent-based model of the financial market to simulate how the market will evolve in the short term while the learning component based on evolutionary computation is used to optimize the simulation parameters.

TCCI is a peer-reviewed and authoritative journal dealing with the working potential of CCI methodologies and applications as well as with emerging issues of interest to academics and practitioners. The research area of CCI has been growing significantly in recent years and we are very thankful to everyone within the CCI research community who has supported the *Transactions on Computational Collective Intelligence* and its affiliated events including the *International Conferences on Computational Collective Intelligence* (ICCCI). The first ICCCI event was held in Wroclaw, Poland, in October 2009. ICCCI 2010 was held in Kaohsiung, Taiwan, in November 2010 and ICCCI 2011 in Gdynia, Poland, in September 2011. For ICCCI 2011 almost 300 papers from 25 countries were submitted, and only 105 papers were selected for inclusion in the proceedings published by Springer in the LNCS/LNAI series. ICCCI 2012 will be held in Ho Chi Minh city, Vietnam, in November 2012. After each ICCCI event we invite authors of selected papers to extend them and submit them for publication in TCCI.

We are very pleased that TCCI and the ICCCI conferences are strongly cemented as high-quality platforms for presenting and exchanging the most important and significant advances in CCI research and development. It is also our pleasure to announce the new Technical Committee on Computational Collective Intelligence within the Systems, Man and Cybernetics Society (SMC) of IEEE.

We would like to thank all the authors, Editorial Board members, and the reviewers for their contributions to TCCI. Finally, we would also like to express our gratitude to the LNCS editorial staff of Springer headed by Alfred Hofmann for supporting the TCCI journal.

December 2011 Ngoc Thanh Nguyen

Transactions on Computational Collective Intelligence

This Springer journal focuses on research in applications of the computer-based methods of computational collective intelligence (CCI) and their applications in a wide range of fields such as the Semantic Web, social networks and multiagent systems. It aims to provide a forum for the presentation of scientific research and technological achievements accomplished by the international community.

The topics addressed by this journal include all solutions of real-life problems for which it is necessary to use CCI technologies to achieve effective results. The emphasis of the papers is on novel and original research and technological advancements. Special features on specific topics are welcome.

Table of Contents

On the Pattern Recognition and Classification of Stochastically Episodic Events*

Colin Bellinger[1] and B. John Oommen[2]

[1] The School of Information Technology and Engineering,
University of Ottawa, Ottawa, Canada
cbell052@uottawa.ca

[2] *Chancellor's Professor*, *Fellow: IEEE* and *Fellow: IAPR*
School of Computer Science,
Carleton University, Ottawa, Canada
oommen@scs.carleton.ca

Abstract. Researchers in the field of Pattern Recognition (PR) have traditionally presumed the availability of a representative set of data drawn from the classes of interest, say ω_1 and ω_2 in a 2-class problem. These samples are typically utilized in the development of the system's discriminant function. It is, however, widely recognized that there exists a particularly challenging class of PR problems for which a representative set is not available for the second class, which has motivated a great deal of research into the so-called domain of One Class (OC) classification. In this paper, we extend the frontiers of novelty detection by the introduction of a new field of problems open for analysis. In particular, we note that this new realm deviates from the standard set of OC problems based on the presence of three characteristics, which ultimately amplify the classification challenge. They involve the *temporal* nature of the appearance of the data, the fact that the data from the classes are "interwoven", and that a labelling procedure is not merely impractical - it is almost, by definition, impossible. As a first attempt to tackle these problems, we present two specialized classification strategies denoted by Scenarios $S1$ and $S2$ respectively. In Scenarios $S1$, the data is such that standard binary and one-class classifiers can be applied. Alternatively, in Scenarios $S2$, the labelling challenge prevents the application of binary classifiers, and instead dictates the novel application of one-class classifiers. The validity of these scenarios has been demonstrated for the exemplary domain involving the Comprehensive Nuclear Test-Ban-Treaty (CTBT), for which our research endeavour has also developed a simulation model. As far as we know, our research in this field is of a pioneering sort, and the results presented here are novel.

Keywords: Pattern Recognition, Rare Events, Stochastic Events, Erroneous Data.

---

* The first author is also an *Adjunct Professor* with the University of Agder in Grimstad, Norway. Both the authors are grateful for the partial support provided by NSERC, the Natural Sciences and Engineering Research Council of Canada. A preliminary version of this paper was presented at ACIIDS'11, the 2011 Asian Conference on Intelligent Information and Database Systems, in Daegu, Korea, in April 2011.

N.T. Nguyen (Ed.): Transactions on CCI VI, LNCS 7190, pp. 1–35, 2012.

1 Introduction

1.1 Problem Formulation

A common assumption within supervised learning is that the distributions of the target classes can be learned, either parametrically or non-parametrically. Moreover, it is assumed that a representative set of data from these classes is available for the training of supervised learning algorithms; indeed, the latter implies the former.

Beyond this commonly-reported method of classification, there exists a special form of Pattern Recognition (PR), which is regularly denoted One Class (OC) classification [10,12,14,16,30,31]. This "exceptional" category of binary classification is noteworthy in lieu of the significant challenge that it presents. Escalating the difficulty, is the fact that drawing a representative set of data to compose the second class (ω_2), which is fundamental to the derivation of a binary discriminant function, is abnormally arduous, if not altogether impossible. The difficulty of acquiring a sufficiently symbolic set may arise because of:

1. The natural *imbalance* in the classification task;
2. The difficulty (due to cost, privacy, etc.) of acquiring samples from the ω_2 class;
3. The task of obtaining representative samples of the ω_2 class is overwhelming, as a result of the vastness of the distribution.

PR tasks of this nature have previously been constituted as involving outlier (or novelty) detection in lieu of the fact that the vast majority of the data takes, what is assumed to be, a well-defined form that can be learned, and that samples from the ω_2 class will appear anomalously – outside the learned distribution. Although such problems can be significantly more difficult than those that involve two well-defined classes of data, the results reported in the literature demonstrate that satisfactory results can often be obtained (see [10,12,14,16,30,31], for example).

1.2 SE Event Recognition

To expand the horizon of the field, we observe that there exists a further, and yet more challenging subset of the OC classification domain of problems, which remains unexplored. We have denoted this class of problems as Stochastically Episodic (SE) event recognition.

The problem of SE event recognition can be viewed in a manner that distinguishes it from the larger set of OC classification tasks. In particular, this category of problem has a set of characteristics that collectively distinguish it from its more general counterparts. The characteristics of this category can be best summarized as follows:

- The data presents itself as a time sequence;
- The minority class is challenging to identify, thus, adding unwarranted noise to the one-class training set;

- The state-of-nature is dominated by a single class;
- The minority class occurs both rarely and randomly *within* the data sequence.

Typically in PR solutions to so-called OC problems, the accessible class, and in particular, the data on which the OC classifier is trained, is considered to be well-defined. Thus, it is presumed that this data will enable the classifier to generalize an adequate function to discriminate between the two conceptual classes. This, for example, was demonstrated in [30], where the training set consisted exclusively of images of non-cancerous tissue. Similarly, in [12], a representative set of the target computer user's typing patterns, which are both easily accessible and verifiable, were utilized in the training processes.

The classification of SE events[1] is considerably more difficult because deriving a strong estimate of the target class's distribution is unfeasible due to the prospect of invalid instances (specifically members of the ω_2 class erroneously labelled ω_1) in the training set. In this work, we present solutions to this problem based on tradition one-class classifiers.

SE event recognition is additionally challenging because the validity of instances drawn from the target class are suspect, and the occurrences of the minority class are temporally (i.e. with respect to the time-axis) interwoven with the data from the majority class.

1.3 Characteristics of the Domain of Problems

To accentuate the difference between the problems that have been studied, and the type of problems investigated in this research, we refer the reader to Table 1. This table displays an assessment of six one-class classification problems, which, while only a small subset, cumulatively illustrate the traditional scope of the problem set. In addition, we include the problem of CTBT verification, which forms our exemplary SE event recogonition problem. The first column indicates whether the problem has traditionally been viewed as possessing an important *temporal* aspect. The three entries with an asterisk require special consideration. In particular, we note that while, traditionally, these domains have not been studied with a temporal orientation, they do indeed contain a temporal aspect. The subsequent column signals whether the manual labelling of data drawn from the application domain is a significant challenge. This is, for example, considered to be a very difficult task within the field of computer intrusion detection, where attacks are well disguised in order to subvert the system.

The following two columns quantify the presence of class imbalance. In the first of these, we apply a standard assessment of class imbalance, one which relies on the determination of the *a priori* class probabilities. Our subsequent

[1] Events of this nature are denoted stochastic because their appearances in the time-series are the results of both deterministic and non-deterministic processes. The non-deterministic triggering event could, for example, be the occurrence of an earthquake, while the transmission of the resulting p- and s-waves, which are recorded in the time-serise, are deterministic.

Table 1. A comparison of well-known One-Class (OC) classification problems. The explanation about the entries is found in the text.

Dataset	Temporal	ID Challenge	Imbalance *Type I*	Imbalance *Type II*	Interwoven
Mammogram	No	Low	Yes	Medium	No
Continuous typist recognition	No	Low	Yes	Medium	No
Password hardening	No	Low	Yes	Medium	No
Mechanical fault detection	No*	Low	Yes	Medium	No
Intrusion detection	No*	High	Yes	High	No
Oil spill	No*	High	Yes	Medium	No*
CTBT verification	Yes	High	Yes	High	Yes

judgement departs slightly from the standard view, and considers class imbalance that arises from the difficulty of acquiring measurements (due to cost, privacy, *etc.*). The final column specifies if the minority class occurs rarely, and randomly (in time and magnitude), and if it occurs within a *time sequence dominated by the majority class.*

To summarize, in this section we have (briefly) both demonstrated the novelty of this newly introduced sub-category of PR problems, and positioned the CTBT verification task within it. We additionally note that the fault detection, intrusion detection, and oil spill problems could be reformulated to meet the requirements of our proposed category. This, indeed, suggests a new angle from which these problems can be approached.

1.4 Overview of Our Solution

As previously indiated, SE event recognition composes a particular challenging problem due to the combined affect of the four characteristics that are inherent in such problems. Under these circumstances, we envision two possible techniques for discriminating between the target class and the stochastically episodic events of interest. If the incoming training data contains a sufficient quantity of accurately identifiable stochastic events, a standard clustering/PR algorithm could be applied to label both the classes appropriately. Subsequent to the labelling procedure, a standard binary classifier could be trained and utilized to achieve the classification of novel instances. In this body of work, we refer to this scenario as S1, and the subsequent scenario as S2.

Alternatively, and more applicable in scenarios in which the SE events are extremely rare, all of the training data can be assigned to the target class, and an OC classifier can be applied. The details of, and justification for, this approach are described in the subsequent sections. Our primary objective in this research is to illustrate how standard supervised learning algorithms can be applied to discriminate rare stochastic episodes, which apart being unanticipated, are random in magnitude and position within the sequence of background data.

1.5 Contributions of This Paper

The novel contributions of this paper, with respect to PR, are as follows:

- We introduce an important new category of PR, namely SE event recognition. In particular, we note that this new realm deviates from the standard set of one-class problems based on the presence of four characteristics: *(a)* the data presents itself as a time sequence; *(b)* the minority class is challenging to identify, thus, adding unwarranted noise to the OC training set; *(c)* the state-of-nature is dominated by a single class; and, *(d)* the minority class occurs both rarely and randomly within the data sequence.
- In addition, we present a first attempt at classifying SE events within the examplary verification problem suggested by the Comprehensive Test-Ban-Treaty (CTBT). Our initial approach is extremely accessible, as it is based on "off the shelf" PR solutions.
- More specifically, where the ω_2 is sufficiently large, we demonstrate how clustering/PR algorithms can be applied to label training data for the development of a sound binary classifier.
- Finally, in scenarios where training instances cannot be acquired from the second class (the so-called OC problem), and where the accessible class in known to contain noise due to labeling issues, we illustrate how, through novel means, standard OC classifiers can be applied as unsupervised learners.

We conclude this section by mentioning that our results probably represent the state-of-the-art!

1.6 Paper Organization

The rest of the paper is organized as follows. In Section 2 we presented a brief survey of the available solutions for dealing with PR. Subsequently, in Section 3, we present the application domain, and our solution to modelling SE event systems for the purpose of PR system development. Then, in Section 4 we present a brief overview of issues of PR in relation to SE event recognition. Thereafter, experimental results obtained by rigorously testing our solution on the exemplary scenarios suggested by the CTBT are presented in Section 5 and 6, and discussed in Section 7. Section 8 concludes the paper.

2 Pattern Recognition: State of the Art

This section[2] serves to present the state-of-the-art in PR. In that regard, Duda, *et al.*, in [9] describe pattern recognition as follows:

> "The act of taking in raw data and taking an action based on the 'category' of the pattern."

[2] This brief section has been included in the interest of completeness. Although these issues are considered commonplace for the general PR problem, they are still fairly non-standard for OC problems - which advocates the necessity of the section.

It is, indeed, natural that we should desire to 'teach' machines to recognize sets of patterns that are easily recognizable to humans, such as handwritten characters, speech and faces, as computers present the possibility of increased efficiency and do not become tired of mundane tasks. Furthermore, the benefits of training machines to classify complex patterns, typically left to doctors and scientists with considerable specialization in the domain, are equally apparent. Thus, researchers have continued to push the state-of-the-art in PR systems since the advent of the modern computer.

Supervised Learning. Prior to application, the PR system must be trained to discriminate between the objects of interest in its particular application domain. For multi-class problems, such as discrimination between handwritten characters, the PR system is said to learn a mapping that discriminates between the individual inputs by directing them to their corresponding categories. Alternatively, in the special scenario, which is of primary interest in this work, termed OC learning, instances of a single target category are available for the training of the PR system. As a result, the system takes a recognition-based approach, and attempts to learn a function that maps novel instances of the target category to the target class, and all others to the outlier class.

Broadly speaking, standard PR systems for supervised learning are trained on datasets drawn from their prospective application domains, in which each feature vector has been accented with its corresponding class label. The objective of the training process is the derivation of a set of models that articulate the individual characteristics of the classes. Thus, while the performance on the training set is of little interest, rather, the focus shifts to the selection of a model that will perform well on novel instances in the future. The derivation of these models is algorithm-specific, however, there exists commonalities between all learners. Generally speaking, regardless of the learning strategy, the accuracy of the derived model on novel instances will increase with the size of the training set. In addition, all learners strive to optimize the balance between specialization and generalization [18].

Under ideal circumstances, the training procedure for a binary learner is able to rely on an ample supply of data that has been uniformly drawn from both classes. As a result, increasingly accurate models of the classes in question can be constructed, and therefore, an effective classifier of novel instances is produced. Conversely, this assumption cannot be made in SE event recognition problems. Thus, particular expertise is required in order to derive an acceptable model.

OC learning problems characteristically involve scenarios in which the available class is easily acquired and exists in abundance, while the second class is exceptionally difficult to acquire, or naturally rare [31]. During extreme class imbalance, the majority class can be expected to compose as much as ninety-five percent of the data. In such scenarios, it is typical that the class we are most interested in identifying is the minority class, as is the case in automated mammogram scans and many other medical disciplines [30]. Japkowicz, in [14], and Kubat *et al.*, in [16], demonstrate scenarios in which acquiring instances is both difficult and expensive. In particular, the challenge of Kubat *et al.* requires the hand-labelling of satellite imagery, while the former involves fault detection in helicopter gearboxes, which are expensive to run. Moreover, the derivation of the outlier class would require the destruction of the gearboxes in an infinite number of ways. Alternatively, under certain conditions, the second class might be so large as to render the accumulation of a sufficient supply a seemingly insurmountable challenge. This scenario is well illustrated by the continuous typist recognition problem described by Hempstalk *et al.*, in [12]. The objective of the depicted classification challenge is to distinguish the sole legitimate terminal user from all other users. A proper training set, therefore, would be drawn uniformly from the set of all people, which is clearly infeasible.

A variety of approaches have been applied to OC classification. The more traditional of these involve extensions to existing binary classifiers or density estimations. The density estimation approach fits a statistical distribution, such as Gaussian, to the target data, and classifies novel instances based on the learned probability of their occurrences. Such a technique has been applied by the authors of [4,21,30]. Techniques that extend existing classifiers typically modify the inner structure of the classifier to fit boundaries around the target class, and classify those novel instances falling outside the boundary as outliers, as is demonstrated by [14,27]. These two approaches, in addition to some alternative approaches to one-class learning, such as the work described in [12], which is a combination of these two techniques, are discussed in the sections to follow.

Density Estimation. Density estimation is, perhaps, the most elementary of all approaches to OC classification. The fundamental idea behind this OC classification technique is the estimation of a Probability Density Function (PDF), $\hat{P}(\mathbf{x})$, based on a training set, $\mathbf{D}^n = \{\mathbf{x}_1, \mathbf{x}_2, ..., \mathbf{x}_n\}$, drawn independently and identically from the underlying distribution, $P(\mathbf{x})$, of the target class. Subsequent to the estimation of the PDF, novel instances are classified according to a predefined target threshold or by resorting to a suitable statistical test.

Under ideal circumstances, and in particular, where sufficient training data is accompanied by a substantial understanding of the background distribution, or a flexible density estimation technique, density estimation-based classifiers are known to produce strong results [31]. However, a significant quantity of training data is required to overcome the curse of dimensionality, as is described by Duda *et al*, in [9].

Bishop, in [5], discusses three approaches to PDF estimation; the first of these techniques requires the modeller to provide an initial specification of the functional form of the underlying distribution, such as Gaussian or Poisson. An iterative process based on the predefined distribution, is applied to fit the density function to the training data through the optimization of the corresponding PDF parameters. The application of the parametric method is significantly limited by the fact that, in many cases, the specified PDF may be incapable of describing the training data.

Non-parametric estimation techniques represent a more flexible approach, as they do not assume a particular functional form, and instead allow the training data to completely specify the PDF. As a result, the PDF is not limited to a small set of standard distributions, and does not have to be provided at initialization. However, the fact that the number of parameters to be optimized expands quickly as the dataset increases in size, can prove to be prohibitive.

Yeung and Chow, in [33], applied the non-parametric method for probability density estimation, introduced by Parzen, in [19], to the development of an intrusion detection system. More specifically, their approach utilized the Parzen-window estimation of $\hat{P}(\mathbf{x})$, with a Gaussian kernel, on a dataset composed of normal network activities. The generalized Parzen-window estimation of $\hat{P}(\mathbf{x})$, based on an n element dataset $\mathbf{D}$, takes the following form:

$$\hat{P}(\mathbf{x}) = \frac{1}{n} \sum_{i=1}^{i} \delta_n(\mathbf{x} - \mathbf{x}_i), \tag{1}$$

where $\delta_n(\cdot)$ is the kernel function (in this case, Gaussian in form), the exact form of which depends upon the number of instances in the training set. Subsequent to the training process, novel instances are classified based on their log-likelihood. In addition, the Parzen-window approach was previously applied by Tarassenko *et al.*, in [30], to the classification of anomalous mammograms.

A final approach, sometimes referred to as semi-parametric estimation, attempts to strike a balance between the previous two methods. This approach enables a general class of functional forms, in which the number of adaptive parameters is increased systematically to build a progressively more flexible model.

The mixture of Gaussians approach is a particular category of semi-parametric estimation schemes, which has received considerable application, as it is analytically attractive. This approach to semi-parametric estimation was applied in [22,23] to the detection of novel instances in a series of medical datasets, and as a procedure for noise removal in an image processing task. In its essence, the mixture of Gaussians method is composed of a linear combination of j Gaussian distributions, each of which is uniquely parametrized according to its particular mean, μ_j, and covariance, $\mathbf{\Sigma}_j$, such that

$$\hat{p}_{MoG}(\mathbf{x}) = \frac{1}{N_{MoG}} \sum_{j} \alpha_j \, pN(\mathbf{x}; \mu_j, \mathbf{\Sigma}_j), \tag{2}$$

where the α_js are the mixing coefficients.

2.1 One-Class Extensions to Binary Classifiers

Autoassociator. An autoassociator in an example of a feedforward Artificial Neural Network (ANN). However, unlike its more prevalent binary counterpart, the Multi-Layer Perceptron (MLP), which aims to produce a classification decision at the output layer, the autoassociator is trained to *reconstruct* the input vector at the output layer [24]. The general architectures for both forms of ANNs are illustrated in Figure 1.

The theoretical basis for the autoassociator relies on the fact that it is trained to compress and decompress instances of the concept class exclusively. Thus,

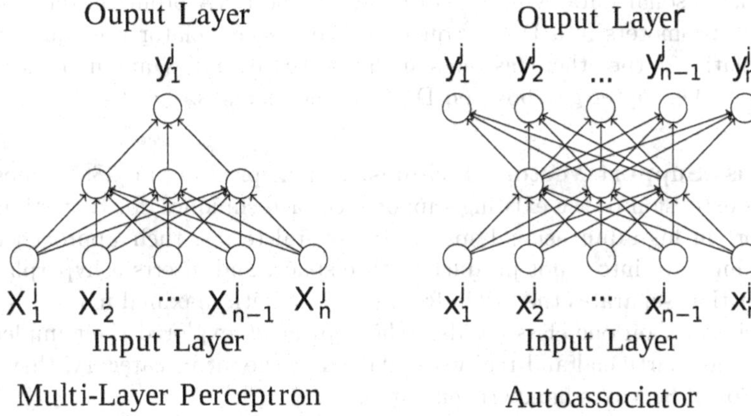

Fig. 1. This figure demonstrates two possible feedforward artificial neural network architectures. Subfigure (a) illustrates the general form of the Multi-Layer Perceptron (MPL). In Subfigure (b), the essential structure of an autoassociator is displayed.

during application, novel instances of the concept class should compress and decompress successfully. More specifically, the reconstruction error resulting from a novel member of the concept class, during application, is expected to be small. Alternatively, non-members of the target class are characterized by large reconstruction errors. Therefore, the classification procedure entails a comparison of the reconstruction error and a user-defined threshold. All instances reproduced with an error less than the threshold are considered to be members of the concept class, while the remainder are labelled as outliers, or non-members.

The OC classifiers of the above form have been applied in a number of domains with considerable success. Hanson and Kegl, in [11], introduced an autoassociator system, namely PARSNIP, developed to reconstruct syntactically correct sentences using the backpropigation procedure described by Rumelhart *et al.*, in [24]. The PARSNIP system, trained on the Brown University Corpus of Present-Day American English, in which the words of each sentence are tagged with their active syntactic category, learned to accurately identify sentences that were syntactically correct and reject those that were incorrect.

Subsequently, Petsche *et al.*, in [20], developed a system similar to a fuel gauge based on the principle of the autoassociator. The system described in that work, learned to predict the impending failure of a motor. Its intended application domain is characterized by a high cost associated with failures, such as the fire pump on navy vessels.

More recently, Japkowicz, [14], examined the performance of the autoassociator in comparison with a variety of binary learners on three domains. In particular, the case studies utilized a CH46 Helicopter gearbox dataset, with the objective of predicting the failure of the gearbox based on vibration time signals, and the sonar and DNA promoter datasets from the U.C. Irving Repository of Machine Learning. The recognition task in the former was to distinguish mines from rocks in sonar data, while the objective in the DNA promoter dataset was to classify promoters in a DNA sequence. The autoassociator was found to be robust relative to the other classifiers in all three case studies, and more accurate on both the helicopter gearbox and DNA promoter tasks.

One-Class Support Vector Machines. Schölkopf *et al.*, in [28], proposed a one-class extension to the existing support vector techniques, for the estimation of support in high-dimensional spaces. In general terms, their approach maps the training data into a dot product feature space, and inserts a hyperplane in a manner that separates the origin from the data with maximal margin.

In their work on one-class SVMs, Schölkopf *et al.* explored their implementation on both artificial and real-world data. For the latter category, they used the US Postal Service's handwritten digits.

The handwritten digits dataset was converted to facilitate two distinct sets of experiments. In the first experiment, tests were conducted that specified a random set of instances drawn from a single class that composed the target data, and left all instances from the remaining nine classes to form a large set of outliers. On this experiment, the one-class SVM was found to correctly identify the target class 91% of the time, and had a false positive rate of 7%.

In the second experiment, ten binary features were added to the handwritten digits dataset; one new feature for each of the possible digits. These features were included to identify the class to the classifier during training, with the notion that the classifier would learn to recognize what each digit should look like. For this experiment, the OC classifier was trained on instances drawn from each class, with the additional features. The authors found that the OC SVM learned to accurately identify anomalous patterns, and the erroneously labelled instances.

Similar implementations of the OC SVM have subsequently been applied to a large number of problems. Manevitz and Yousef, in [17] for example, applied the OC SVM to discover text documents of similar topics to those in the training set, and compared the results to a set of alternate OC classifiers. They concluded that, while the OC SVM is very sensitive to parametrization, with the right parameter set, it outperformed the other classifiers considered in the study, with the exception of the OC ANN.

Further examples of previous applications of OC SVMs are to classify yeast gene regulation predictors in [15], and for image retrieval in [6].

2.2 Nearest Neighbour

The standard Nearest Neighbour (NN) algorithm is a binary classifier that takes a non-parametric approach to PR. More specifically, in its simplest form, the training process involves "remembering" all of the training instances and their corresponding labels. During application, a novel instance $\mathbf{x}$ is classified according to a majority vote rule, in which the k (k is an odd number specified by the user) NNs of $\mathbf{x}$, in the training set, are polled for their respective classes.

The novel instance is subsequently assigned to the class that is occupied by the majority of its neighbours [9].

The NN algorithm has seen considerable application. Horton and Nakai, for example, compared the NN to Naïve Bayes and to decision trees, in [13], on the problem of predicting the cellular localization sites of proteins in yeast and ecoli. In their study, Horton and Nakai reported favourable results for the NN classifier.

More recently, modifications have been made to the NN classifier to facilitate OC classification. Datta, in [7], adapted the standard NN algorithm to preform OC classification through the utilization of a threshold learned during the training phases. More specifically, the algorithm searches the training set for the pair of NNs that are separated by the greatest distance, which is denoted by τ. When classifying a novel instance, the distance between it and its NN is compared to the learned parameter. If the distance is less than or equal to τ, the novel instance is assigned to the positive class. Otherwise it is assigned to the negative class.

The author applied this implementation of the OC NN (ocNN) algorithm to a number of UCI datasets and found it to be comparable with other OC classifiers. It was additionally found to be comparable with the binary C4.5 decision tree classifier on some classes of the Breast Cancer Wisconsin, Pima Indian Diabetes and Wine domains.

Tax, in [31], provided a comprehensive survey of the performance of one-class classifiers on a number of artificial domains, in which an alternate adaptation of the standard NN algorithm for one-class learning was included. Notably, he identified the OC NN algorithm to be a poor performer in a general analysis of robustness against outliers. This is, indeed, a problem that we noted when applying the ocNN to the task of SE event recognition, due to the fact that the mislabelled instances of the ω_2 class in the training set often appear as outliers, which should not be generalized into the model of the background (ω_1) class.

Scaled Nearest Neighbour. In recognition of the limitations of ocNN within the domain of SE event recognition, we propose a more suitable NN classifier [2] – which is one of the contributions of this paper. This modification was motivated by the second classification scenario, namely the one referred to earlier as S2. In particular, this scenario is characterized by a series of rare SE events where:

- The data exists as a time-series;
- The state-of-nature is dominated by a single class (the ω_1 class composes more than, for example 90% of the instances);
- The minority class is nearly impossible to manually identify. Thus, it naïvely takes the ω_1 label *even in the training set.*

In this scenario, we have stated that due to the rarity of the outlier class, and the extreme challenge of manually labelling those instances in the training set, it can be naïvely issued to a OC classifier. Moreover, this can be done with considerable confidence, provided that an estimate of the *a priori* probability of the outlier class can be acquired. This hypothesis relies on the availability

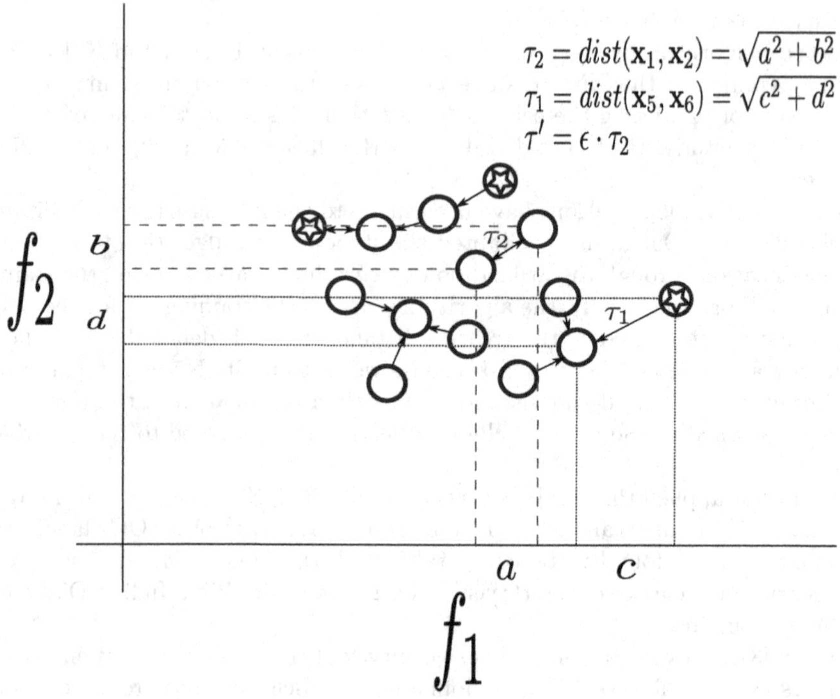

Fig. 2. This figure demonstrates the calculation of the τ parameter in the ocNN classifiers, and the effect of erroneous instances in the training set on the learned target rejection rate threshold

of a so-called rejection rate, which ensures a portion of the training set will be misclassified after the derivation of the discriminant function.

Observe that the standard ocNN algorithm is intuitively unable to learn a threshold capable of discriminating most of the erroneously labelled outliers, and is inherently ineffective in the presence of noise. The problem, which is embedded in the ocNN algorithm, is depicted in Figure 2. By definition, the naïvely labelled instances of the second class are outliers. Thus, they are expected to reside on the periphery of the "real" background distribution. Therefore, with a high probability, the learned parameter, τ, which is intended to record the variability in the background class [7], can be expected to represent the distance between a background instance and an erroneously labelled member of the outlier class. A hypothetically learned distance of this sort is illustrated in Figure 2 as τ_1. Ideally, however, the algorithm should learn the distance that is denoted as τ_2, because it is the maximum target rejection rate threshold found in the set of pure background instances (represented as empty circles).

Because this scenario creates an unsupervised learning environment, in which we cannot explicitly identify the members of the outlier class during training, we rely on a rejection rate parameter to be "engrained" in the OC classification

algorithm in order to facilitate the exclusion of these instances. However, while Datta coined τ to be the target rejection rate threshold, by definition, it does not exclude any instances in the training set. Indeed, this was not the intention. Thus, in this exceptional domain, it incorporates the erroneous information provided by the mislabelled members of the outlier class into the learned threshold, as is depicted by τ_1 in Figure 2.

As a means of accounting for the overestimate, we have added a scaling parameter, ϵ, where $0 < \epsilon \leq 1$, such that

$$\tau' = \epsilon \cdot \tau, \tag{3}$$

with the understanding that the optimal value of ϵ will enable the rejection of the majority of the outlier instances, by reducing the magnitude of the learned threshold.

2.3 Combined Density and Class Probability Estimation

Hempstalk *et al.*, in [12], introduced a technique for converting OC classification problems into binary tasks, based on a two-fold strategy. The initial phase of the strategy involves an examination of the training data for the concept class in order to determine its distribution. This knowledge is subsequently utilized in the generation of a non-concept, or outlier, class. In the second phase, a standard binary classifier is trained based on the concept class and the generated class. Most standard classification techniques are applicable here. The single limiting factor in the selection of a binary classifier is the requirement that the classifier of choice can produce a class probability estimate at prediction time. Using Bayes' rule, the authors demonstrate how the class density function can be combined with the class probability estimate to yield a description of the concept class.

The performance of the combined density and class probability estimation technique was examined on a multitude of datasets, the bulk of which result from the U.C. Irving Repository of Machine Learning. In addition, the performance was gauged on the very interesting task of recognizing a "continuous typist". This latter application required the validation of individual computer terminal users based on their learned typing patterns. With considerations founded upon these experiments, the authors concluded that the combination of the density function with a classification model can produce an improvement in accuracy beyond that which resulted from the density function or the classification model alone.

3 Modelling the Problem

To this point, we have described a novel sub-category of PR, which is characterized by the detection of a minute number of SE events interwoven in a time-series. Indeed, a number of interesting PR problems fit this form, including advanced earthquake, tsunami and machine failure warning systems, to name but a few. In this section, we present a series of experiments based on the verification of the CTBT. These experiments are designed to both illustrate the domain of SE events, and to exhibit a first attempt at SE events recognition.

3.1 Application Domain

The CTBT aims to prevent nuclear proliferation through the banning of all nuclear detonations in the environment. As a result, a number of verification strategies are currently under study, aimed at ensuring the integrity of the CTBT. The primary verification technique being explored relies on the quantity of radioxenon measured continuously at individual receptor sites, distributed throughout the globe. Radionuclide monitoring, in general, has been identified as the sole technique capable of unambiguously discriminating low yield nuclear detonations from the background emissions. More specifically, verification of the treaty based on the four radioxenon isotopes, ^{131}Xe, ^{133}Xe, ^{133m}Xe and ^{135}Xe, has been promoted due to the relatively low background levels, their ideal rates of decay, and their inert properties [25,29].

In general, the measured radioxenon levels are expected to have resulted from industrial activities, such as nuclear power generation and the production of medical isotopes. However, they are also the byproducts of low yield clandestine nuclear weapons tests, which are the subject of the CTBT.

3.2 Procuring Data: Aspects of Simulation

While it is generally beneficial to develop and study classifiers on "real" data, this is, indeed, impossible within the CTBT verification problem due to the absence of measured detonations, and the limited availability of background instances. It has, however, been demonstrated that artificial data can be utilized for PR system development, and to generate controlled experiments (generalized case-studies), in the absence of "real" measurements [1,8]. In this vein, as a means of acquiring experimental datasets for this research, we utilized the simulation framework presented by Bellinger and Oommen in [3]. Their simulation framework models SE events, such as earthquakes, nuclear explosions, etc., as they propagate through the background noise, in this case representing radioxenon emitted from the industry into the earth's atmosphere.

Simulation Scenario. In order to explore the PR of low yield clandestine nuclear tests, we devised a simulation scenario to capture the effects of a diverse set of detonation possibilities, within a realistic background scenario. In particular, and accordance with the majority of the CTBT's International Monitoring Station (IMS), the IMS in the simulated environment was impacted by a single industrial emitter. In this simulation scenario, the industrial emitter was positioned 3,000 km away from the IMS. Thus, when the atmospheric conditions transported the emitted radioxenon directly from the source to the receptor, and when the conditions were not conducive to the dispersion of the radioxenon, the background concentration could reached significant levels. However, due to the realistic atmospheric conditions that were built into the model, such as the fluctuations in wind speed and direction, along with atmospheric stability, the background levels were generally low. This fact is displayed by the histogram in Figure 3. The figure specifically demonstrates that the majority of the ^{131}Xe

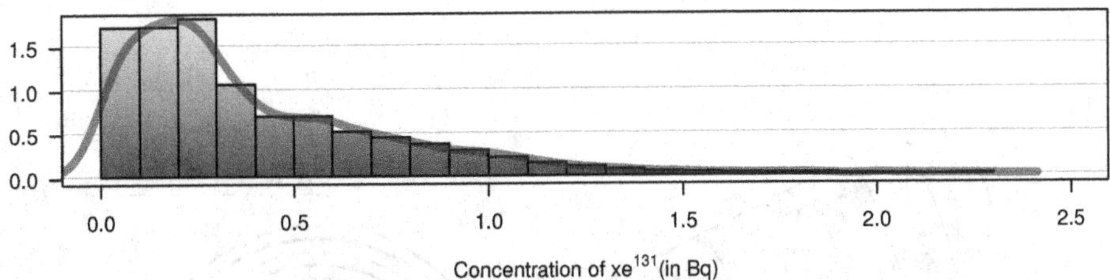

Fig. 3. This figure displays a histogram of the measured concentrations of ^{131}Xe at the IMS, resulting from the background source during the simulation

concentrations measured at the IMS site during the simulation were less than 0.5 $Bq\ m^{-3}$.

It is, however, highly probable that a clandestine detonation will occur at distances beyond the industrial source, thus, causing no, or only a minute, change in the radioxenon concentrations measured at the IMS, depending on the angular direction to the detonation site, and the prevailing meteorological conditions. Therefore, the classification of this type of SE event is extremely challenging.

With the above fact in mind, we considered the performance's of the PR systems as a function of distances. This is to specifically assess the probability of detecting detonations at various distances. In particular, 23 subcategories of datasets were generated. In each case, the modelled environment contained the same industrial source and IMS at the receptor site. As a result, for each simulation the background readings can be assumed to follow the distribution displayed in Figure 3. The 23 subsets formed a series of incremental detonation ranges, which commenced with all detonations occurring between 500 km and 1000 km, as illustrated in Figure 4.

The detonation range was iteratively increased by 500 km for each successive set. This incremental approach enabled the examination of performance as a function of distance, in addition to the more general considerations of performance.

As a binary classification problem, the generated sets were composed of two classes, in this case a background class and a detonation class. In addition to the class label, each instance was composed of the concentrations of the four isotopes measured by the IMS at the receptor site over the period of an hour. The simulation system contains two phases, the first phase simulates the effect of the background emission source on the receptor sites, thereby producing instances of the background class (labelled 0). Thus, an instance measured over hour i, takes the following form:

$$\mathbf{x}_{i,0} = {}^{131}Xe_{i,0},\ {}^{133}Xe_{i,0},\ {}^{133m}Xe_{i,0},\ {}^{135}Xe_{i,0},\ 0. \tag{4}$$

The second phase generates the data for the detonation class (labelled 1). This is done by generating random (in time, space and magnitude) low yield explosions, and measuring their impact on the receptor site. Subsequently, the effect of the detonation is combined with that of the background source over the appropriate

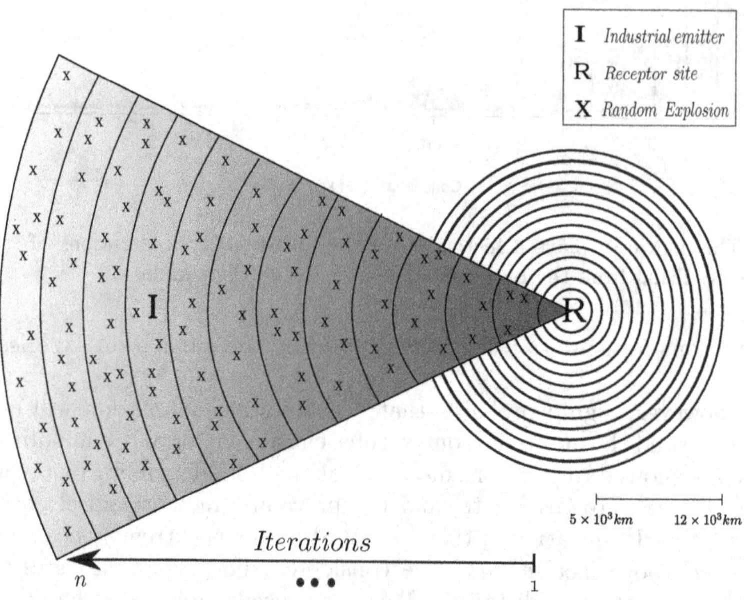

Fig. 4. This figure demonstrates the iterative composition of the simulated domain. In each iteration of the simulation, a fixed number of explosions are probabilistically generated as uniform, random events in time, space and magnitude, and dispersed according to the prevailing meteorology, which may or may not carry the pollutant cloud past the receptor site.

period of time, and written to the dataset with the detonation label. Therefore, a detonation instance measured over hour j, takes the following form:

$$\mathbf{x}_{j,1} = \mathbf{x}_{j,0} + \ {}^{131}Xe_{j,1}, {}^{133}Xe_{j,1}, {}^{133m}Xe_{j,1}, {}^{135}Xe_{j,1}, \ 1. \tag{5}$$

3.3 Generated Datasets

A total of 230 datasets were derived and applied to scenario S1 and S2, according to the simulation procedure previously described. More specifically, 10 datasets were generated for each of the 23 detonation ranges, each of which was subsequently divided into training and testing components.

Intuitively, the first scenario presents a slightly easier classification problem, because a set, albeit small, of SE events can be extracted from the application domain and applied to train and/or test the PR systems. More specifically, within this scenario, we assume that the ω_2 class is both identifiable and available in quantities that facilitate the training of binary classifiers. However, in many ways, the classification problem still presents itself as a so-called OC classification task, and thus warrants exploration on both fronts. The datasets specifically contain a 90% background data (ω_1) and 10% explosion data (ω_2).

Alternatively, each set involved in the S2 scenario is divided with 99% background data (ω_1) and 1% explosion data (ω_2). In order to simulate the challenge of manually labelling the instances drawn from class ω_2, and in accordance with the disguised nature of the SE events, all of the ω_2 training instances were erroneously labelled ω_1.

Alternatively, the test sets included appropriately labelled instances from both classes, with proportions following the predefined states-of-nature. This enabled us to assess each classifier's ability to generalize the "real" background data from the noisy training set.

4 PR Solutions

In this section, we present a series of experiments designed to both illustrate the demonstration domain, and to exhibit a first attempt at classifying this sub-category of PR problems.

4.1 Classification Scenarios

As mentioned in the introductory section, within this challenging domain of classification problems, there exist two conceivable scenarios, which we have denoted as S1 and S2. These scenarios explicitly influence the choice of the classification scheme applied to the task of recognizing the SE events.

Intuitively, the first scenario presents a slightly easier classification problem, because a set, albeit small, of SE events can be extracted from the application domain and applied to train and/or test the PR systems. More specifically, within this scenario, we assume that the outlier class is both identifiable and available in quantities that facilitate the training of binary classifiers. However, in many ways, the classification problem still presents itself as a so-called OC classification task, and thus warrants exploration on both fronts.

Alternatively, the second scenario presents itself as a much more difficult PR task, and in many ways more accurately reflects the PR problem suggested by the detection of SE events, in general, and the verification of the CTBT, in particular.

In accordance with the general domain characteristics, as they were originally defined, the data presents itself as a time-series of background measurements that are interwoven with a minute number of SE events. However, unlike the ideal scenario depicted in S1, here we attempt to assume a state-of-nature that is more appropriate for the CTBT task. In particular, we assume that there is a 1% *a priori* probability of a detonation, which, while still an overestimate, is a more accurate depiction, while it still provides insight into the behaviour of PR systems on the class of SE events.

Raising the difficulty further, is the recognition that, in practice, the clandestine nature of the SE events are such that manually identifying a distant clandestine occurrence in the acquired time-series of readings is extremely difficult, if not impossible. Thus, this prohibits the derivation of a labelled training set, which dictates that practitioners are left to utilize a training set composed largely of background instances, but with a minute number of *unidentifiable* members of the SE event class.

In the absence of a labelled training set, we propose the application of standard OC learners as unsupervised classifiers. When applying OC classifiers to an unlabelled training set, the practitioner must rely on the knowledge of a domain expert to acquire estimates of the *a priori* class probabilities.

In particular, estimates of the state-of-nature are required to appropriately specify the parameters of the OC classifiers, such as the rejection rate, or error rate. This technique aims to prevent the inclusion of the SE event instances in the generalized description of the background class. Our reliance on an error, or rejection rate, presumes that the SE events will reside on the periphery of the background class, and thus, by marginally tightening the generalization of the background class, those instances of the SE event class will no longer be included.

4.2 Classification

Standard PR problems typically assume the existence of data that was drawn independently and identically from the application domain, and that the data can be divided upon class lines into representative sets. The availability of such data facilitates the training of binary classifiers, which have been shown to be proficient at learning class distributions, and thus at labelling novel instances.

In all brevity, we mention that the binary classifiers used in this study were the Multi-layer Perceptron (MLP), the Support Vector Machine (SVM), the Nearest Neighbour (NN), the Naïve Bayes (NB) and the Decision Tree (J48), all of which are fairly well known, and so their descriptions are omitted here. However, we mention that their implementations were obtained from Weka.

Alternatively, OC classifiers rely on instances drawn from a single class in the derivation of a discriminant function. A broad set of OC classifiers exists in the literature, each of which applies a slightly different strategy to the construction of a binary discriminant function from a single class. However, in simple terms, the process can be articulated as one in which the selected classifier learns to recognize, in some general terms, novel instances that are similar to those viewed during the training process. Thus, novel instances that do not appear to fit into the learned distribution are designated to the ω_2 class.

Although these classifiers were briefly outlined earlier, to summarize:

- The autoassociator (AA), for example, applies a neural network structure to compress/decompress instances of the concept class exclusively. Thus, an unsuccessful compression/decompression results in the instance being assigned to the second class [14].
- Hempstalk *et al.*, in [12], converted the OC classification problem into binary tasks by estimating the distribution of the concept class and generating instances of the non-concept, accordingly. Finally, a standard binary classifier is trained. This process has been denoted the Combined Probability and Density Estimator (PDEN).

- Alternatively, the one-class Nearest Neighbour (ocNN) algorithm [7] learns a *target rejection rate*, τ, where τ is the distance between the two nearest neighbours with the greatest separation in the training data. Subsequently, all novel instances whose nearest neighbours are at greater distances than τ are classified as outliers.
- We have additionally implemented a modified version of the ocNN in Weka, and denoted it as the scaled ocNN (socNN). Contrary to the ocNN, the socNN classifier is capable of learning a model that accounts for the noise in the training set.
- Subsequent research also explored the performance of the often extolled one-class SVM [28]. However, due to the poor results which were generally equivalent to those yielded by the ocNN, it is not included in the present discussion.

4.3 Classifier Assessment Criteria

As discussed in the previous section, this research considers the performance of the classifier within two distinct scenarios. Within each of the scenarios, namely S1 and S2, we considered the performance of the classifier according to a set of criteria. These criteria are discussed in greater detail.

In particular, we examined the general performance of the classifiers across all of the simulated detonation ranges. Performance in this category is particularly important, as, in practice, the detonation ranges are largely unpredictable. The results of this assessment are presented in Sections 5.1 and 6.1. In addition, we explored the performance of the classifier within two shorter detonation ranges, the result of which is presented in Sections 5.2 and 6.2.

The performance of the classifier, as a function of distance, was also examined. The results of this comparison are detailed in Sections 5.3 and 6.3.

Finally, in light of the inherent challenge of distinguishing these two very similar classes according to the four radioxenon isotopes, we were motivated to explore an expanded CTBT feature space. Based on the significant role held by meteorology in affecting the pollutant levels at the receptor site, we surmised that the inclusion of meteorological features would improve the performance of the classifiers. The results of our experiments with an expanded feature space are provided in Sections 5.4 and 6.4.

5 Results: Scenario 1

In this section, we present the results that were obtained according to the four assessment criteria that were motivated in the previous section, on the first classification scenario, S1. We commence our exploration of PR performance by examining the Area Under the ROC Curve (AUC) scores produced by each classifier over the 23 detonation ranges.

5.1 General Performance

In this section, we present a general overview of the performance levels of each of the considered classifiers on the simulated CTBT domain. More specifically, we

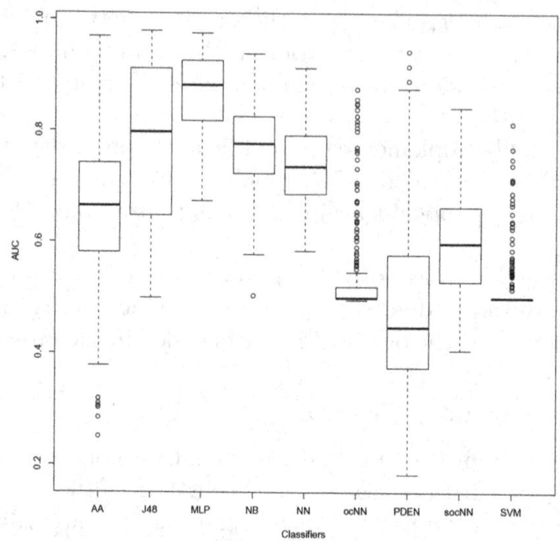

Fig. 5. This figure displays the performance of the nine classifiers, in terms of their AUC scores on the 230 generated CTBT datasets, in the form of a series of boxplots

present an assessment of the five binary classifiers and the four one-class classifiers, in terms of their AUC scores averaged over the 230 datasets that spanned the 23 detonation ranges. In light of the fact that the SE events, which are to be identified, will, in practice, occur at random and unpredictable distances, these results are a particularly insightful overview of the general performance levels.

The results depicted in Figure 5 were compiled as a series of boxplots; one for each classifier.

The solid lines that bisect the boxes represent the median AUC score produced by the particular classifier. The box itself indicates the distribution of the middle half of the AUC scores produced by the classifier. Thus, it stretches from the 25th percentile (at the lower hinge) to the 75th percentile (at the upper hinge). The boxes that are evenly divided indicate that the classifier's scores are evenly distributed throughout the central region. This is, indeed, the case for AA and NB.

The fact that there is no box around the median indicator for the SVM, suggests that nearly all of the AUC results were equivalent, and in this case, approximately 0.5. The relatively large number of circles extending up from the median, individually identify outliers. This suggests that, in general, the SVM classifier performed poorly, but that it occasionally produced anomalously strong results, which stretched slightly beyond 0.8.

Alternatively, the scenario where the median does not produce an even bisection of the box indicates that the distribution of the inter-quartile range is skewed. This is the case, for example, with PDEN, where the upper-quartile is large, indicating that the points composing the upper-quartile are spread over a larger distance.

The dashed lines, or whiskers, stretch to either the maximum and minimum values, where outliers do not exist, or to 1.5 times the range of the inter-quartile region in scenarios with outliers, such as in the case with the SVM classification results.

The SVM classifier is, surprisingly, by far the worst-performing classifier on this data, and in spite of its bias, it is, on average, worse than the OC classifiers, AA and socNN. This is reiterated in Table 2, which contrasts the mean AUC scores of AA and socNN as 0.656 and 0.603, respectively, with the mean value for the SVM classifier being 0.528. Moreover, all four OC classifiers appear to be superior to the SVM when considered in terms of their maximum AUC scores.

When assessing the classifiers according to the boxplot, the median value provides a good indication of their performances, in general. However, most interesting are the ranges of the inter- and outer-quartiles along with the presence of the outliers, when combined with a high median value, as these components provide a strong indication of how likely it is that the classifiers will reproduce the median result.

In these terms, the binary classifier, the MLP, stands out as the superior classifier, with J48, NN, and NB contending for the intermediate positions. The results posted in Table 2 confirm that the MLP is the strongest of the classifiers considered here. Furthermore, it indicates that the J48 and NB are very similar, and that the NN is the fourth-ranking binary classifier according to the mean and maximum scores. However, the NN is second when ranked according to the minimum AUC scores.

Table 2. This table displays the general classification results, in terms of AUC

	Mean	Max	Min	STDV
NB	0.772	0.939	0.504	0.074
MLP	0.869	0.976	0.674	0.067
NN	0.741	0.913	0.584	0.071
J48	0.774	0.98	0.500	0.148
SVM	0.528	0.813	0.500	0.065
ocNN	0.540	0.875	0.496	0.087
PDEN	0.487	0.943	0.182	0.156
socNN	0.603	0.842	0.405	0.094
AA	0.656	0.970	0.251	0.140

Notably, of the set of OC classifiers, the PDEN produced the most variable range of the AUC scores. It is our suspicion that this variability resulted from the PDEN's generation of an artificial second class in its training process. However, further exploration of this matter is required.

In general, the AA classifier is identified as the strongest OC classifier, both with respect to its mean and median values. While the socNN classifier achieved the second highest mean, it is more stable than the AA, and does not produce any anomalous results. Indeed, the socNN has a lower standard deviation, and furthermore, its boxplot spans a smaller range.

5.2 Performance on Short- and Long-Range Detonations

In Figure 6, we present the AUC results produced over two detonation ranges of particular interest. The Boxplot on the left in this figure contains the results for the datasets that included detonations ranging from 1,000 km and 5,500 km, while the Boxplot on the right has those with detonations between 5,500 km and 10,000 km. Together, these plots contrast the performance of the individual classifiers in the various detonation ranges. This experimental setup demonstrates one technique through which the performance of various receptor network topologies can be examined. For example, if PR within the second range is found to be a considerable challenge, the shorter range may, perhaps, be considered an upper bound on the acceptable distance between receptors.

There are two factors at play when hypothesizing about classifier performance within these ranges. Intuitively, detonations closer to the receptor site will be more visible at the receptor site, provided the meteorological conditions are such that the emissions are advected in the direction of the receptor. Conversely, detonations that occur farther afield are likely to have a smaller influence on the pollutant levels at the receptor site, leading to a more challenging classification problem. On the surface, then, it appears that nearby detonations should be easier to detect. Indeed, the very near detonations are often easily identifiable. However, the scenario is made more complex by the fact that during the simulation, the industrial

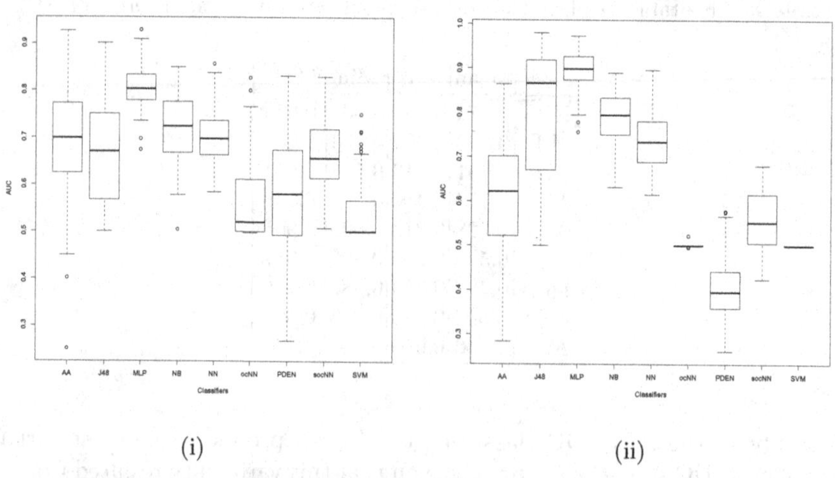

Fig. 6. In this figure, Boxplot (i) displays the performance of the nine classifiers, in terms of their AUC scores for detonations occurring between the distances of 1,000 km and 5,500 km, and Boxplot (ii) displays their performances for detonations between the distances of 5,500 km and 10,000 km

source was positioned approximately in the middle of the shorter range. Thus, there was, in a sense, a great deal of competing background noise to distort the signal.

Indeed, Figure 6 demonstrates that within this scenario it is possible for the performance of the classifiers to improve when detonations occur at greater distances. However, the fact that this only occurred for the binary classifiers, highlights the importance of the second class in the learning process. It turns out that the majority of the binary classifiers are able to, through the training process, utilize the low concentration instances of the detonation class, which resulted from explosions at great distances, to specialize their models to the counter-intuitive point where many of the instances with low concentrations were correctly identified as explosions.

Alternatively, the figure suggests that neither the one-class classifiers, nor the SVM, were able learn a model with this characteristic. Moreover, the SVM exclusively produces AUC scores of 0.5 within the second range, and the ocNN's performance was nearly equivalent. Finally, at greater distances, the PDEN's performance fell even further, with only a minute number of instances exceeding an AUC of 0.5.

Within the shorter range, it is notable that the stronger OC classifiers, namely the AA and socNN, are very comparable with most of the binary classifiers. However, the distinction in favour of the binary learners is emphasized for the larger detonation range.

5.3 Performance as a Function of Distance

In this sub-section, we present the performance of the classifier as a function of distance, where the performance is assessed both according to the AUC and the False Positive Rate (FPR).

A *false positive* occurs when the classifier mislabels a novel instance as a member of the positive class (in this case, a member of the background class), when it is, in fact, a member of the negative class (specifically, a member of the SE event class). Thus, the FPR is the total number of false positives over the total number of negative instances. As a metric, the FPR provides insight into whether the model is overly biased towards the positive class, which is a significant risk when the problem is extremely imbalanced.

These results are particularly interesting, as they provide greater insight into performance trends. Moreover, these suggest a performance scale for successively sparser receptor networks, and enable the interested parties to weigh the cost of receptor stations against the probability of detection.

The performance plots depicted both in Figure 7 and Figure 8 were produced by calculating the ensemble mean of each classifier's performance at the 23 detonation ranges, and then through the extrapolation of a performance function.

Within Figure 7, the MLP classifier is identifiably the superior classifier when compared to the remaining four binary learners in terms of the AUC, across the range of detonation distances. In addition, it is not subject to the abrupt fluctuations that J48, and to a lesser extent, NB, incur.

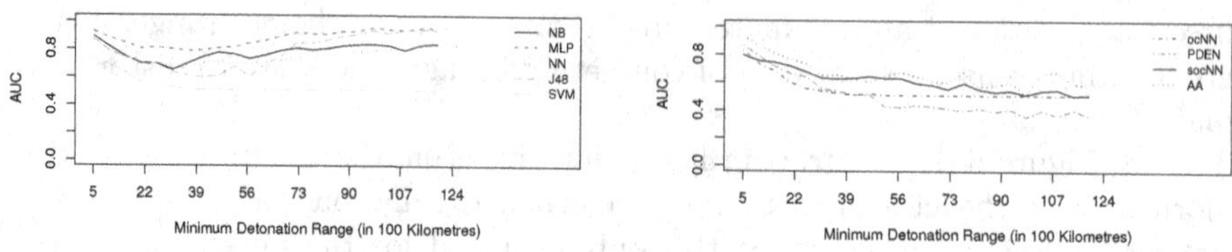

Fig. 7. In this figure, the plot on the left displays the performance of the five binary classifiers, in terms of their AUC scores, as a function of distance. Similarly, the plot on the right displays the performances of the four one-class classifiers as a function of distance, according to their AUC scores.

All of the classifiers, with the SVM appearing as the sole exception, have notable hulls in their performance curves that extend over varying distances and to distinct depths. In each case, a slow descent begins immediately, and is subsequently accompanied by a slow ascent. Alternatively, the SVM classifier suffers from a similar initial decline. However, it fails to recover from the degradation at greater distances.

In each case, the position of the performance hull roughly corresponds to the radial distance between the industrial source of radioxenon and the receptor site. Thus, this suggests that detonations occurring at approximately the same radial distance as that of the primary background emitter are a significant challenge for the detection systems.

The plot on the left in Figure 7 confirms our previous findings, which identified the MLP as the top classifier in this domain, the SVM as the worst, and the remaining three classifiers as contenders for the inner rankings. Indeed, while there are notable differences in the AUC plots for the J48, the NB, and the NN, the fact that their functions cross at numerous points, prohibits the derivation of a general ranking over the entire range of distances.

The plot on the right in Figure 7 presents the performance of the one-class learners as a function of distance. In general, the plot demonstrates that all of the one-class classifiers follow a similar downward trend from their initial peaks, which occurred between 0.8 and 0.9, towards, or beyond in the case of the PDEN, an AUC of 0.5.

Moreover, the performance functions are broadly divisible into two categories. Both the ocNN and the PDEN descend relatively quickly, while the AA and the socNN degrade in a slower, more linear fashion. Therefore, the AA and the socNN are the more suitable of the four one-class learners, with the AA appearing generally superior to the socNN.

The performance of the nine classifiers, measured in terms of the FPR metric, are plotted as a function of distance in Figure 8. In this figure, the plot on the left emphasizes the significant challenge incurred by the binary learners when the detonations occur at a distance similar to the noise source. Although we previously identified the MLP as the strongest binary classifier on this domain, for a relatively broad range (roughly between 25,000 km and 65,000 km), the vast majority of instances, which are truly of the detonation class, were assigned

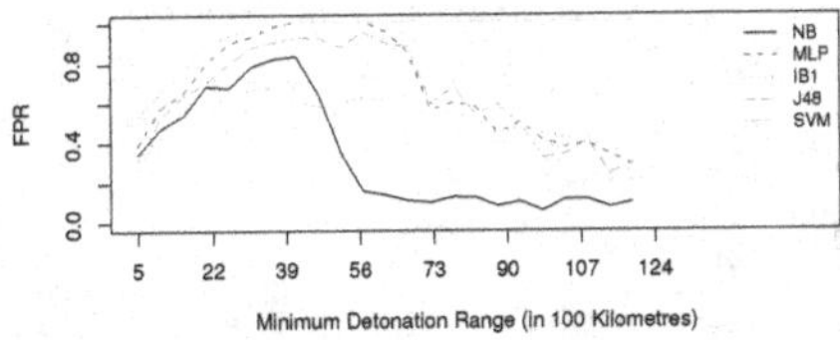

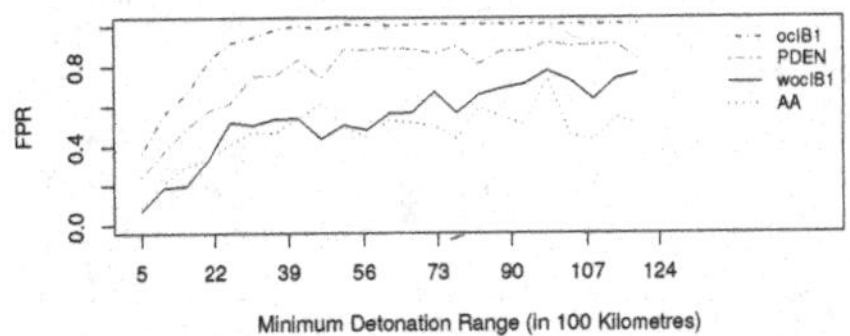

Fig. 8. In this figure, the plot on the left displays the performance of the five binary classifiers, in terms of their FPR scores, as a function of distance. Similarly, the plot on the right displays the performances of the four one-class classifiers as a function of distance, according to their FPR scores.

to the background class. The results are similar for J48. Interestingly, NB has the smallest area under its FPR curve. Thus, it least often identified members of the SE event class as background noise. While we do not consider the FPR results to be individually sufficient for model selection, they do provide some very intriguing insight into the behaviour of the classifiers.

The trends for the one-class classifiers in the plot on the left follow much the same trends previously seen in Figure 7. In particular, the AA and the socNN are superior to the PDEN and the ocNN. However, the distinction between the AA and the socNN is less clear.

5.4 Expanded Feature-Space

Through our exploration of this most interesting of classification problems, we recognized both the inherent challenge presented in the classification of SE events that are interwoven in background noise, and the role of meteorology in effecting the very noise levels that make the task so difficult. Our extensive consideration of this application domain has led us to identify the particularly strong relationship between the wind direction and pollutant levels at the receptor, which suggests a possibly informative feature.

By expanding the standard CTBT feature space to include wind direction, we have produced a significant increase in the AUC. In particular, the top classifiers (MLP, AA, socNN), now demonstrate the ability to detect detonations that, when considered solely on the basis of the four radioxenon measurements, fit into the background distribution with a high probability. This fact is, indeed, depicted for many of the binary and one-class classifiers in Figure 9 and Figure 10.

In particular, while the depth to the hull in the performance of the MLP decreases only slightly, the J48's hull is entirely removed when the wind direction feature is added. Thus, the J48 classification ceases to be affected by the detonation distance when the new feature is included. In addition, its mean AUC is significantly improved.

The NN and SVM classifiers also benefit from the inclusion of the wind direction feature. However, the new feature has a slightly negative effect on the NB. It has been noted in the literature, that many of the PR algorithms, including the MLP, SVM and NB may benefit from normalization of the features [9,32].

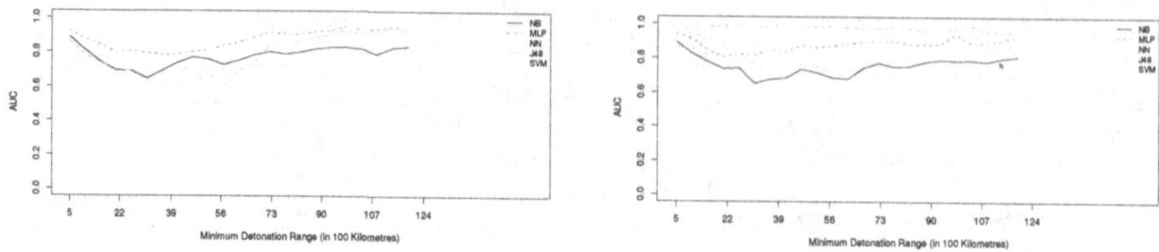

Fig. 9. This figure contrasts the performance of the binary classifiers, in terms of the AUC as a function of distance, on the standard feature-space (see the plot on the left), and when the feature-space is extended to include an assessment of the wind direction (see the plot on the right)

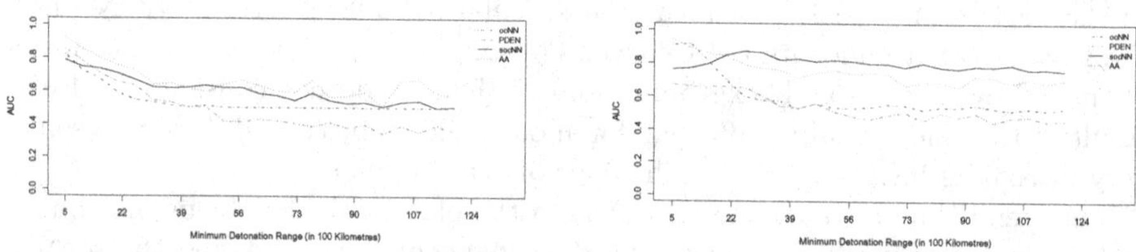

Fig. 10. This figure contrasts the performance of the one-class classifiers, in terms of the AUC as a function of distance, on the standard feature-space (see the plot on the left), and when the feature-space in extended to include an assessment of the wind direction (see the plot on the right)

Thus, it is conceivable that the performance of these classifier may be improved to some degree. However, these results provide a good baseline from which the individual classifiers can be compared.

By expanding the feature-space to include the wind direction, the OC learner, socNN, improves significantly, and becomes, in general, the top learner amongst its peers. The classifier, AA, also improves as a result of the new feature. However, its AUC scores do not increase to the same extent as the socNN.

Similar to the socNN, the PDEN's initial performance is lower in the newly expanded feature-space. However, the majority of its performance function is elevated. Finally, the ocNN benefits the least from the new feature, although, its initial performance is improved.

Thus, in the worst case, the wind direction feature produces marginal improvements in the performance of the four OC learners. However, it significantly improves both the AA and the socNN's ability to perform in scenarios where the detonations occur at distances equivalent to, and beyond the radial distance to the background source.

In Figure 11, a series of boxplots are utilized to facilitate the comparison of classifier performance in the two feature-spaces. Indeed, these results confirm the trends that we have previously identified. Particularly noteworthy is the depiction of J48's performance; this plot emphasizes both the significant increase in the J48's median AUC score, and the impressive stabilization of its classification

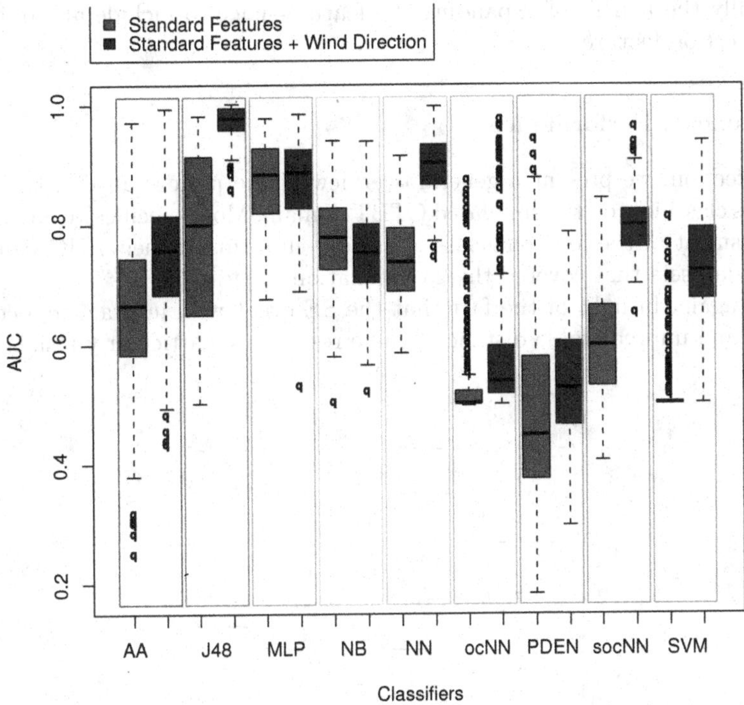

Fig. 11. This figure utilizes a series of boxplots to compare the performance of the nine classifiers and the standard feature-space, and with the extended feature-space, which is augmented by a wind direction indicator

results when the wind direction feature is added. The benefits to the SVM are also well visualized in this figure.

It is, indeed, well demonstrated in Figure 9, Figure 10, and Figure 11 that the additional information has assisted many of the classifiers to overcome the significant challenges inherent in identifying SE events within the field of background noise.

6 Results: Scenario 2

In this section, we present the results that were produced on the four assessment criteria that were motivated, and utilized in the previous sections. In this section, however, we explore the very intriguing classification scenario, which we previously denoted S2. This exploration follows the same structure that was previously applied in the exploration of the first classification scenario. Thus, we begin by examining the AUC scores produced by each of the one-class classifiers over the 23 detonation ranges; we then proceed to consider the performance over the two successive, smaller distances, the performance as a function of distance, and finally the benefit of expanding the feature-space to include an additional wind direction feature.

6.1 General Performance

In this section, we present a general overview of the performance of the set of one-class classifiers on the simulated CTBT domain. More specifically, we present an assessment of the four one-class classifiers, in terms of their AUC scores on the 230 datasets that covered the 23 detonation ranges.

Once again, in light of the fact that the SE event will, in practice, occur at random and unpredictable distances, these results are particularly insightful.

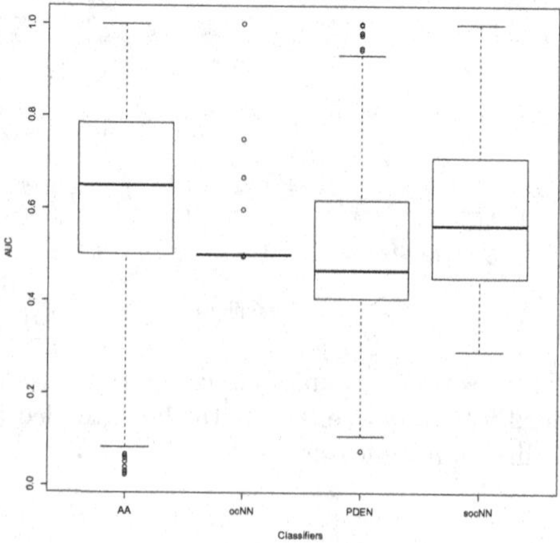

Fig. 12. This figure displays the performance of the four classifiers, in terms of their AUC scores on the 230 generated CTBT datasets, in the form of a series of boxplots

The results that are depicted in Figure 12 were compiled as a series of boxplots; one for each classifier. In addition, Table 3 contains a compilation of the mean, maximum, minimum and standard deviation of the each classifier's overall results.

Table 3. This table displays the general classification results, in terms of AUC

	Mean	Max	Min	STDV
ocNN	0.505	1	0.496	0.042
PDEN	0.507	1	0.075	0.185
socNN	0.587	1	0.292	0.171
AA	0.621	1	0.024	0.225

Our assessments of both Figure 12 and Table 3 reveal that, similar to our findings on the S1 scenario, the AA classifier is superior, in terms of its mean, and median scores, to the other OC classifiers. Indeed, on this, which is a more challenging task, its mean and median values are only slightly lower than in the previous task. However, within this second scenario, it has the lowest minimum AUC scores, which appear as outliers in the boxplot. In addition, it is extremely unstable, with results ranging from perfect to near zero.

The socNN classifier ranks second after the AA according to its median and mean, and was considerably more stable, while the ocNN and PDEN classifiers produced values that were near or below 0.5.

6.2 Performance on Short- and Long-Range Detonations

In Figure 13, we present the results produced over two detonation ranges of particular interest. Specifically, the Boxplot on the left in the figure contains the results for the datasets that include detonations between the distances of 1,000 km and 5,500 km, while the Boxplot on the right has those with detonations between 5,500 km and 10,000 km. Together, these plots demonstrate, contrary to the previous results, that there is little change in performance at greater distances.

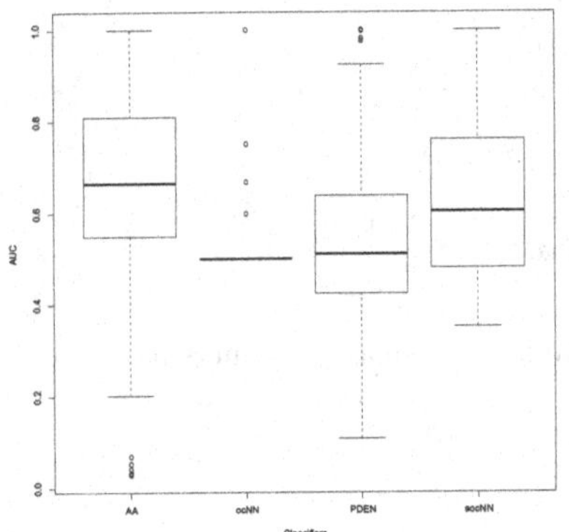

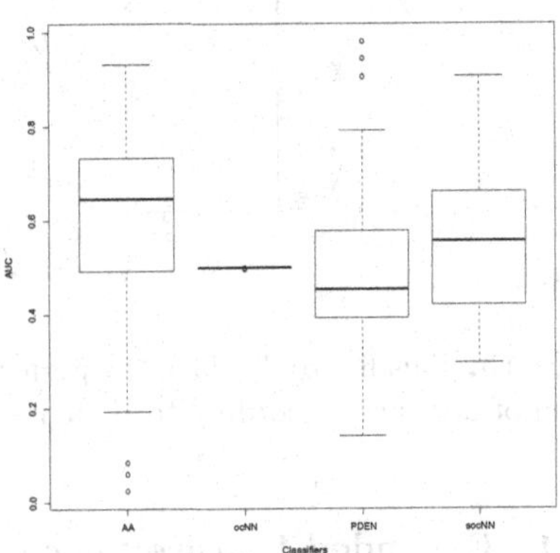

Fig. 13. In this figure, Boxplot on the left displays the performance of the four classifiers, in terms of their AUC scores for detonations occurring between the distances of 1,000 km and 5,500 km, and the Boxplot on the right displays their performances for detonations between the distances of 5,500 km and 10,000 km

6.3 Performance as a Function of Distance

In this sub-section, we present classifier performance as a function of distance. As in the previous section, performance is assessed both according to the AUC and the FPR.

The AA and socNN are, once again, roughly identifiable as the best of the four classifiers in Figure 14 and Figure 15. However, all of the classifiers, with the exception of ocNN, which rapidly converges to 0.5, suffer from significant and essentially random fluctuations. These fluctuations in performance suggest that the classifiers' results were as dependent on the nature of the SE events in the 230 datasets, as on the distance at which the events originally occurred.

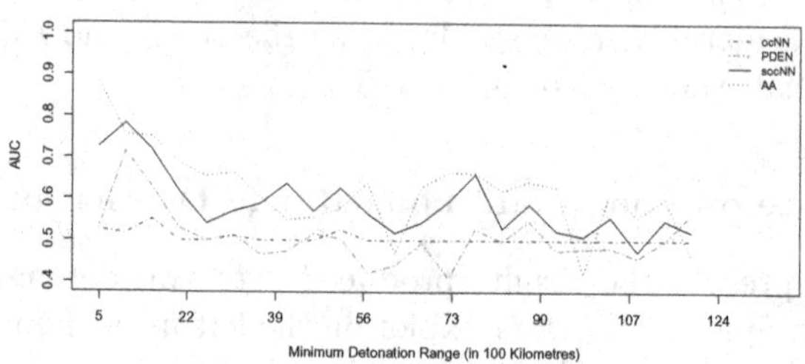

Fig. 14. This figure displays the performance of the four one-class classifiers as a function of distance, according to their AUC scores

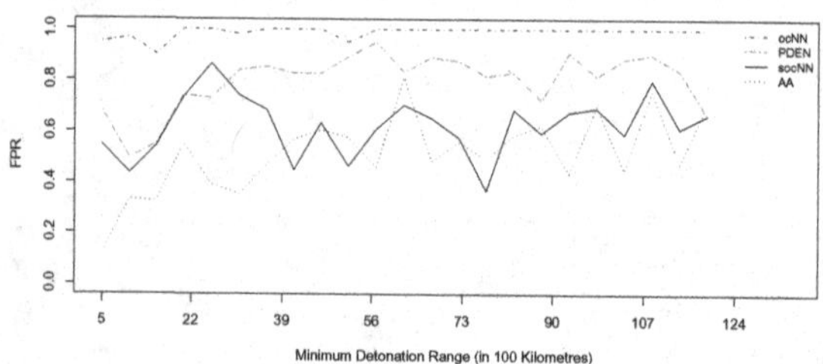

Fig. 15. This figure displays the performance of the four one-class classifiers as a function of distance, according to their FPR scores

6.4 Expanded Feature-Space

In this final section, we consider the benefits of extending the feature space to include a wind direction indicator. In Figure 16, both the original plot of the four classifiers' performances as a function of distance, and their performances on the extended feature-space are plotted. For an alternate view, the comparison is composed of a series of boxplots in Figure 17.

These figures illustrate that both the AA and the socNN significantly benefit from the expanded feature-space. Indeed, the socNN benefits the most, as it becomes superior to the AA for the vast majority of distances, and the variability in its results are significantly dampened.

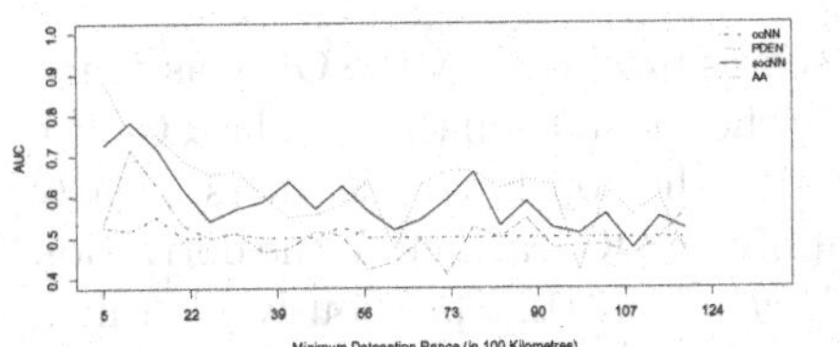

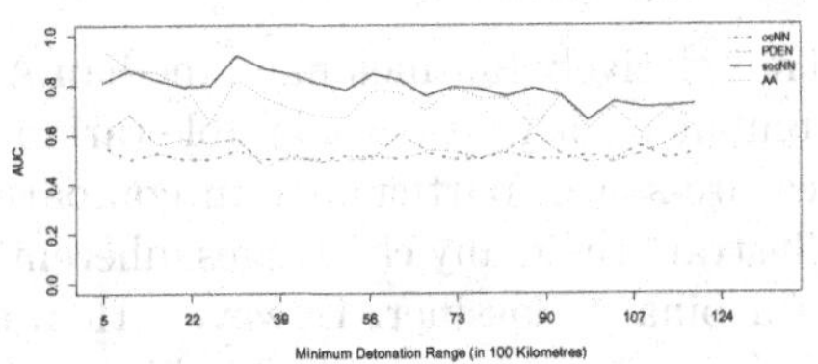

Fig. 16. This figure contrasts the performance of the one-class classifiers, in terms of the AUC as a function of distance, on the standard feature-space (see the plot on the left), and when the feature-space is extended to include an assessment of the wind direction (see the plot on the right)

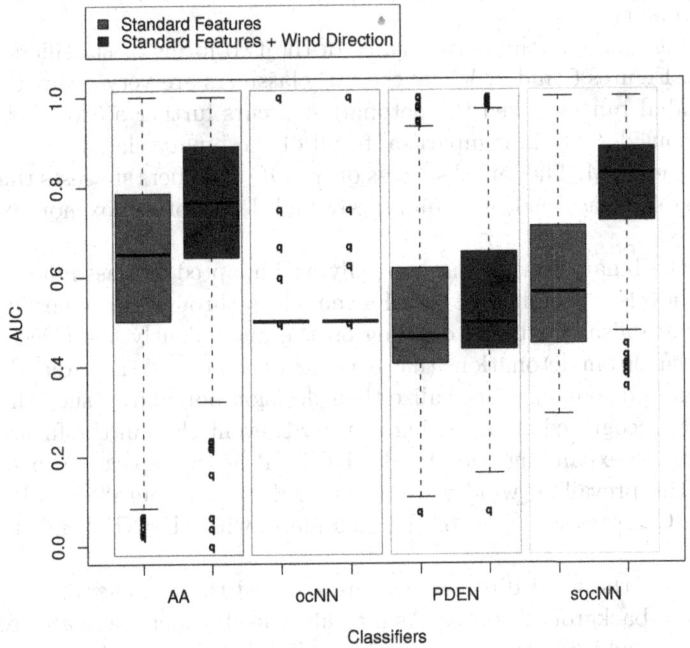

Fig. 17. This figure utilizes a series of boxplots to compare the performance of the four classifiers and the standard feature-space, and with the extended feature-space, which is augmented by a wind direction indicator

7 Discussion

In this section, we consider the results previously reported for the OC classifiers in comparison to those reported for the binary learners. In particular, Section 7.1 compares the two classification strategies within the first scenario, namely S1. Alternatively, the OC classifiers are considered in comparison to the set of standard binary classifiers on scenario S2 in Section 7.2.

7.1 Results: S1

The relatively low mean and median AUC scores produced by the OC classifiers, combined with the considerable variability in their results on the standard CTBT feature-space, particularly in comparison with the top binary learners, clearly illustrate the many challenges inherent in applying OC learning to the derivation of a binary classifier. However, Hempstalk *et al.*, in [12], previously identified similar comparisons between binary and OC learners as "naïve" comparisons, when applied to scenarios that are accurately identifiable as OC problems.

In particular, in so-called OC problems, such as the detection of SE events, the second class is inherently ill-understood due to the fact that a characteristic set cannot be drawn from it. Thus, training and testing a binary learner as if one could draw a representative set from the second class, which is generally assumed when training a binary classifier, provides an upper bound on the classifier's future performance.

The key differences in the performance of the two forms of classifiers is well illustrated in Figures 6 and 7. While the OC classifiers are very competitive on the initial radial ranges, when the detonation occurs further afield, their AUC scores drop considerably in comparison to all of the binary classifiers, with the exception of the SVM. The initial success of the OC classifiers suggests that they are very capable of associating anomalously high levels of radioxenon with the SE event class.

However, the binary learners are not only well adapted to classifying anomalously highly levels as members of the SE event class, through the binary learning process they are also capable of drawing on the anomalously low levels, which commonly result from detonations that occurred well beyond the radial distance to the background source, to specialize their decision boundaries such that similar events are recognized as belonging to the SE event class in the future.

The results of expanding the standard CTBT feature-space to include an indicator of the prevailing wind were, in general, very favourable, and lead to improved AUC scores for most of the classifiers, with the NB being the sole exception.

In its essence, the wind direction feature enabled the classifiers to learn the direction of the background source. As a result, the classifiers were able to identify detonations, which occurred at similar radial distances to the receptor site as the background emissions, and thus, had signatures that were similar to the background levels, but were transported from a different direction. This result is identified very clearly in Figure 9, and suggests that the further expansion of the feature-space might additionally improve performance.

7.2 Results: S2

A considerable portion of the previous analysis is applicable to this second, more challenging, classification scenario. Most importantly, the benefits of the extended feature-space were witnessed within S2 as well. However, due to the nature of the problem, only the OC classifiers were applied to this first attempt at performing PR within this new domain.

As a result of the formulation of the problem, we proposed the use of standard OC classifiers as unsupervised learners, and relied on inner mechanisms of the individual classifiers to facilitate the derivation of a model that segregated those instances of the training set that were accurately of the background class from the naïvely/erroneously labelled instances of the outlier class.

It is clear that the instability in performance that is depicted with respect to distance, and which is significantly more apparent in S2 than S1, results both from the erroneous instances in the training sets of S2, and the variability in classification challenges presented by the few members of the SE event class in the test sets. Indeed, the generation of random SE events over a domain as vast as the simulated CTBT domain, will inevitably produce both very easy, and nearly impossible classification tasks. Thus, when randomly including only a minute number of these events in the test sets, it is probable that performance on the SE event class will fluctuate significantly. This is, of course, why a large number of receptors are required in the global receptor network.

However, while the ensemble mean performance fluctuates considerably over the successive radial ranges, when considered in terms of the overall means, or medians, the performance of the OC classifiers on the S2 task is only slightly lower than on the S1 task. In addition, this is true if in Figures 7 and 14, we were to conduct our analysis according to a series of best-fit lines.

Finally, as is depicted in Figure 16, in addition to elevating the performance of the top classifiers, the inclusion of the wind direction in the feature-space significantly dampens the variability in their performance. Moreover, Saey, in an extensive study of background radioxenon concentrations in Europe and North America, found that a few outliers representing significant increases in the background concentrations can be expected [26]. These outliers are attributed to alternate background sources, and can be assumed to have arrived at the receptor site via short-lived, and anomalous alterations in meteorology. Based on the standard CTBT feature space, such events, undoubtedly, suggest the detonation of a nuclear weapon. However, provided a sufficient quantity of training data is available, it is conceivable that PR systems functioning with the wind direction feature may appropriately identify outliers of the background class.

8 Conclusions

In this research, we extend the frontiers of novelty detection through the introduction of a new field of problems open for analysis. In particular, we note that this new realm deviates from the standard set of one-class problems based on the presence of three characteristics, which ultimately amplify the classification challenge. They involve the *temporal* nature of the appearance of the data, the fact that the data from the classes are "interwoven", and that a labelling procedure is not merely impractical - it is almost, by definition, impossible.

As a first attempt to tackle these problems, we presented two specialized classification strategies as demonstrated within the exemplary scenario intended for the verification of the CTBT. More specifically, we applied the simulation framework presented in [3], to generate CTBT inspired datasets, and demonstrated these classification strategies within the most challenging classification domain. More specifically, we have shown that OC classifiers can be successfully applied to classify SE events, which are unknown, although present, at the time of training.

Finally, we have added a weighting parameter to the OC nearest neighbour algorithm, thereby significantly increasing its performance on our experimental domain. We have also demonstrated that the expansion of the CTBT feature space significantly improves classifier performance on our simulated data, thus, motivating further exploration of the expansion of the standard CTBT feature space to include meteorological measurements.

References

1. Aha, D.W.: Generalizing from case studies: A case study. In: Proceedings of the Ninth International Conference on Machine Learning, pp. 1–10 (1992)
2. Bellinger, C.: Modelling and Classifying Stochastically Episodic Events. Master's thesis, Carleton University, Ottawa, Ontario (2010)
3. Bellinger, C., Oommen, B.J.: On simulating episodic events against a background of noise-like non-episodic events. In: Proceedings of 42nd Summer Computer Simulation Conference, SCSC 2010, Ottawa, Canada, July 11-14 (2010)
4. Bishop, C.M.: Novelty detection and neural network validation. IEEE Proceedings-Vision Image and Signal Processing 141(4), 217–222 (1994)
5. Bishop, C.M.: Neural networks for pattern recognition. Oxford University Press, Walton Street (1995)
6. Chen, Y., Zhou, X., Huang, T.S.: One-class svm for learning in image retrieval. In: IEEE International Conference on Image Processing, pp. 34–37 (2001)
7. Datta, P.: Characteristic concept representations. Ph.D. thesis, Irvine, CA, USA (1997)
8. Dietterich, T.G., Lathrop, R.H., Lozano-Pérez, T.: Solving the multiple instance problem with axis-parallel rectangles. Artificial Intelligence 89(1-2), 31–71 (1997)
9. Duda, R.O., Hart, P.E., Stork, D.G.: Pattern Classification, 2nd edn. Wiley, New York (2001)
10. Ghosh, A.K., Schwartzbard, A., Schatz, M.: Learning program behavior profiles for intrusion detection. In: Proceedings of the Workshop on Intrusion Detection and Network Monitoring, vol. 1, pp. 51–62 (1999)
11. Hanson, S.J., Kegl, J.: PARSNIP: A connectionist network that learns natural language grammar from exposure to natural language sentences. In: Ninth Annual Conference of the Cognitive Science Society, pp. 106–119 (1987)
12. Hempstalk, K., Frank, E., Witten, I.H.: One-Class Classification by Combining Density and Class Probability Estimation. In: Daelemans, W., Goethals, B., Morik, K. (eds.) ECML PKDD 2008, Part I. LNCS (LNAI), vol. 5211, pp. 505–519. Springer, Heidelberg (2008)
13. Horton, P., Nakai, K.: Better prediction of protein cellular localization sites with the k nearest neighbors classifier. In: International Conference on Intelligent Systems for Molecular Biology, vol. 5, pp. 147–152 (1997)
14. Japkowicz, N.: Concept-Learning in the Absence of Counter-Examples: An Autoassociation-Based Approach to Classication. Ph.D. thesis, Rutgers University (1999)

15. Kowalczyk, A., Raskutti, B.: One class SVM for yeast regulation prediction. SIGKDD Explorations Newsletter 4(2), 99–100 (2002)
16. Kubat, M., Holte, R.C., Matwin, S.: Machine learning for the detection of oil spills in satellite radarimages. Machine Learning 30(2), 195–215 (1998)
17. Manevitz, L.M., Yousef, M.: One-class svms for document classification. Journal Machine Learning Research 2, 139–154 (2002)
18. Mitchell, T.: Machine learning. McGraw-Hill (1997)
19. Parzen, E.: On estimation of a probability density function and mode. The Annals of Mathematical Statistics 33(3), 1065–1076 (1962), http://www.jstor.org/stable/2237880
20. Petsche, T., Marcantonio, A., Darken, C., Hanson, S.J., Kuhn, G.M., Santoso, I.: A neural network autoassociator for induction motor failure prediction. Advances in Neural Information Processing Systems, 924–930 (1996)
21. Ritter, G., Gallegos, M.T.: Outliers in statistical pattern recognition and an application to automatic chromosome classification. Pattern Recognition Letters 18(6), 525–539 (1997)
22. Roberts, S., Tarassenko, L.: A probabilistic resource allocating network for novelty detection. Neural Computation 6(2), 270–284 (1994), http://www.mitpressjournals.org/doi/abs/10.1162/neco.1994.6.2.270
23. Roberts, S.J.: Novelty detection using extreme value statistics. IEE Proceedings - Vision, Image, and Signal Processing 146(3), 124–129 (1999), http://link.aip.org/link/?IVI/146/124/1
24. Rumelhart, D.E., Hinton, G.E., Williams, R.J.: Learning internal representations by error propagation, pp. 318–362 (1986)
25. Saey, P.R.J., Bowyer, T.W., Ringbom, A.: Isotopic noble gas signatures released from medical isotope production facilities – Simulation and measurements. Applied Radiation and Isotpes (2010)
26. Saey, P.R.: The influence of radiopharmaceutical isotope production on the global radioxenon background. Journal of Environmental Radioactivity 100(5), 396–406 (2009), http://www.sciencedirect.com/science/article/B6VB2-4VP1CRK-1/2/ac5135ae3e61e80e9145e24cf1405efd
27. Schölkopf, B., Platt, J.C., Shawe-Taylor, J., Smola, A.J., Williamson, R.C.: Estimating the support of a high-dimensional distribution. Neural Computation 13(7), 1443–1471 (2001)
28. Schölkopf, B., Williamson, R.C., Smola, A.J., Shawe-Taylor, J., Platt, J.: Support vector method for novelty detection. Advances in Neural Information Processing Systems, 12, 582–588 (2000)
29. Stocki, T.J., Japkowicz, N., Li, G., Ungar, R.K., Hoffman, I., Yi, J.: Summary of the data mining contest for the IEEE International Conference on Data Mining, Pisa, Italy (2008)
30. Tarassenko, L., Hayton, P., Cerneaz, N., Brady, M.: Novelty detection for the identification of masses in mammograms. IEE Conference Publications 1995(CP409), 442–447 (1995), http://link.aip.org/link/abstract/IEECPS/v1995/iCP409/p442/s1
31. Tax, D.M.J.: One-class classification; Concept-learning in the absence of counter-examples. Ph.D. thesis, Technische Universiteit Delft, Netherlands (2001)
32. Witten, I.H., Frank, E.: Data Mining: Practical machine learning tools and techniques, 2nd edn. Morgan Kaufmann Publishers (2005)
33. Yeung, D., Chow, C.: Parzen-window network intrusion detectors. In: International Conference on Pattern Recognition, vol. 4, p. 40385 (2002)

Paraconsistent Reasoning for Semantic Web Agents

Linh Anh Nguyen[1] and Andrzej Szałas[1,2]

[1] Institute of Informatics, University of Warsaw
Banacha 2, 02-097 Warsaw, Poland
{nguyen,andsz}@mimuw.edu.pl

[2] Dept. of Computer and Information Science, Linköping University
SE-581 83 Linköping, Sweden

Abstract. Description logics refer to a family of formalisms concentrated around concepts, roles and individuals. They are used in many multiagent and Semantic Web applications as a foundation for specifying knowledge bases and reasoning about them. Among them, one of the most important logics is $\mathcal{SROIQ}$, providing the logical foundation for the OWL 2 Web Ontology Language recommended by W3C in October 2009.

In the current paper we address the problem of inconsistent knowledge. Inconsistencies may naturally appear in the considered application domains, for example as a result of fusing knowledge from distributed sources. We introduce a number of paraconsistent semantics for $\mathcal{SROIQ}$, including three-valued and four-valued semantics. The four-valued semantics reflects the well-known approach introduced in [5,4] and is considered here for comparison reasons only. We also study the relationship between the semantics and paraconsistent reasoning in $\mathcal{SROIQ}$ through a translation into the traditional two-valued semantics. Such a translation allows one to use existing tools and reasoners to deal with inconsistent knowledge.

1 Introduction

The Web Ontology Language (OWL) is a family of knowledge representation languages for designing ontologies. It is considered one of the fundamental technologies underpinning the Semantic Web, and has attracted both academic and commercial interest. OWL has a formal semantics based on description logics (DLs), which are formalisms concentrated around concepts (classes of individuals) and roles (binary relations between individuals), and aim to specify concepts and concept hierarchies and to reason about them.[1] DLs belong to the most frequently used knowledge representation formalisms and provide a logical basis to a variety of well known paradigms, including frame-based systems, semantic networks and Semantic Web ontologies and reasoners. The extension OWL 2

[1] There is a rich literature on DLs. For good surveys consult [2], in particular papers [20,3] as well as the bibliography provided there.

N.T. Nguyen (Ed.): Transactions on CCI VI, LNCS 7190, pp. 36–55, 2012.

of OWL, based on the DL $\mathcal{SROIQ}$ [10], became a W3C recommendation in October 2009.

Description logics have usually been considered as syntactic variants of restricted versions of classical first-order logic. On the other hand, in Semantic Web and multiagent applications, knowledge/ontology fusion frequently leads to inconsistencies. When inconsistencies occur in facts provided by different sites of a distributed system (e.g., in the ABox of a combined ontology), the consensus-based method proposed by N.T. Nguyen [23,24,25,26] is an advanced approach that can be used to solve conflicts. When inconsistencies are caused through ontological knowledge (e.g., a TBox) rather than by direct conflicts in facts, one can adapt paraconsistent reasoning approaches. For example, consider an ontology KB_1 reflecting the typical relationship between concepts $Bird$ and Fly, $Bird \sqsubseteq Fly$, an ontology KB_2 extending KB_1 with axioms $Penguin \sqsubseteq Bird$ and $Penguin \sqsubseteq \neg Fly$, and an ontology KB_3 extending KB_2 with facts $Bird(a)$ and $Penguin(tweety)$. Then, using paraconsistent reasoning we would like to draw from KB_3 facts $Fly(a)$ and $Bird(tweety)$. Also, both $Fly(tweety)$ and $\neg Fly(tweety)$ can be derived, so $Fly(tweety)$ is inconsistent w.r.t. KB_3. However, we do not want to draw $\neg Fly(a)$ from KB_3. This example will be continued in Section 6.

There is a rich literature on paraconsistent logics (see, e.g., [7] and references there). In general, paraconsistent reasoning relies on weakening the traditional reasoning methods in order to avoid trivialization (which allows to draw any conclusion from an inconsistent knowledge base). In [11] Hunter listed a few approaches for dealing with paraconsistent reasoning in classical propositional logic:

1. restricting to a consistent subset of the knowledge base
2. forbidding some inference rules
3. using four-valued semantics
4. using quasi-classical semantics
5. using argumentation-based reasoning.

All of these approaches can be applied for paraconsistent reasoning in DLs. The first approach involves knowledge maintenance and will not be addressed in this paper. The second approach lacks semantics and usually leads to non-intuitive consequences [11], and hence not received much attention from the DL community. The fifth approach has recently been applied for the basic DL $\mathcal{ALC}$ by Zhang et al. [32,33]. However, they did not provide adequate reasoning methods. The third and fourth approaches will be addressed in more detail for DLs and compared with our approaches presented in this paper.

A number of researchers have extended description logics with paraconsistent semantics and adequate reasoning methods [19,28,27,15,14,31,30,22,21]. The work [27] studies a constructive version of the basic description logic $\mathcal{ALC}$, but it is not clear how to extend the semantics provided in this work to other description logics. Papers [19,28,15,14] are based on the well-known Belnap's four-valued logic [5,4]. Truth values in this logic represent truth ($\mathfrak{t}$), falsity ($\mathfrak{f}$), the lack of knowledge ($\mathfrak{u}$) and inconsistency ($\mathfrak{i}$). However, there are serious problems with using Belnap's logic for the Semantic Web. Some of these problems are considered in the general context, e.g., in [18,29]. We give here some others, more directly related to description logics (see also Sections 3 and 4):

- According to the semantics considered in [19,28,15,14], if $(x \in C^{\mathcal{I}}) = \mathfrak{i}$ and $(x \in D^{\mathcal{I}}) = \mathfrak{u}$ then $(x \in (C \sqcap D)^{\mathcal{I}}) = \mathfrak{f}$ and $(x \in (C \sqcup D)^{\mathcal{I}}) = \mathfrak{t}$ which, in our opinion, is not intuitive.
- A knowledge base, as a theory, may be incomplete in the sense that truth value of a formula given as a query to the knowledge base may be not determined using the theory. In such cases, we have a meta-unknown value. If the semantics uses the truth value $\mathfrak{u}$, one can raise the question about the relationship between $\mathfrak{u}$ and the meta-unknown value. This problem was not addressed in the mentioned works.
- One of the most common approaches is to use paraconsistent reasoning for knowledge bases specified in the traditional way without explicit truth values $\mathfrak{t}$, $\mathfrak{f}$, $\mathfrak{i}$, $\mathfrak{u}$. The reason is that, if we allow explicit uses of $\mathfrak{t}$, $\mathfrak{f}$, $\mathfrak{i}$, $\mathfrak{u}$ then, for example, two facts $C(a) : \mathfrak{t}$ and $C(a) : \mathfrak{u}$ in a knowledge base form a clash. With this approach, as used in [19,28,15,14], $\mathfrak{u}$ is not used for knowledge representation but only for the semantics. On the other hand, in many cases allowing the value $\mathfrak{u}$ by excluding the axioms $\top \sqsubseteq A \sqcup \neg A$ weakens the logic too much.

In [31] Zhang et al. gave a quasi-classical semantics for the DL $\mathcal{SHIQ}$, which is a sublogic of $\mathcal{SHOIQ}$ used for OWL 1. The semantics is based on both Belnap's four-valued logic and the quasi-classical logic of Besnard and Hunter [6,12]. In [30] Zhang et al. also gave a paradoxical semantics for the basic DL $\mathcal{ALC}$, which is based on a three-valued semantics.[2]

Independently from [30], in the conference paper [22] we modeled inconsistency using only three truth values $\mathfrak{t}$, $\mathfrak{f}$, $\mathfrak{i}$ (as in Kleene's three-valued logic [13,8]) for the DL $\mathcal{SHIQ}$, which is more expressive than $\mathcal{ALC}$. In a sense, we identified inconsistency with the lack of knowledge. There are many good reasons for such an identification (see, e.g., [9]). Assuming that the objective reality is consistent, the value $\mathfrak{i}$ reflects a sort of lack of knowledge. Namely, inconsistent information often reflects differences in subjective realities of agents resulting, for example, from their different perceptual capabilities. Inconsistency appears, when different information sources do not agree with one another and one cannot decide which of them is right. Also, in many multiagent and Semantic Web scenarios one has contradictory evidence as to a given fact. In [22] we also gave a faithful translation of our formalism into a suitable version of a two-valued description logic. Such a translation allows one to use existing tools and reasoners to deal with inconsistent knowledge in $\mathcal{SHIQ}$.

In [21] Nguyen extended the method and results of [22] for the expressive DL $\mathcal{SROIQ}$. He introduced a number of different paraconsistent semantics for

[2] Theorems 3, 5, 6 of [30] are wrong. For Theorem 3 of [30], take $\top \sqsubseteq \bot$ as an ontological axiom. For Theorems 5 and 6 of [30], take $\phi = (A \sqcap \neg A \sqsubseteq \bot)$.

$\mathcal{SROIQ}$ and studied the relationship between them. He also addressed paraconsistent reasoning in $\mathcal{SROIQ}$ w.r.t. some of such semantics through a translation into the traditional semantics. His paraconsistent semantics for $\mathcal{SROIQ}$ are characterized by four parameters for:

- using two-, three-, or four-valued semantics for concept names
- using two-, three-, or four-valued semantics for role names
- considering two kinds of interpretation of concepts of the form $\forall R.C$ or $\exists R.C$
- using weak, moderate, or strong semantics for terminological axioms.

Due to the lack of space, the results of [21] were given without proofs. Furthermore, the definition of $\mathfrak{s} \sqsubseteq \mathfrak{s}'$ given in Section 5 of that paper is not entirely correct.

This work is a revised and extended version of the conference papers [22,21]. The main contributions of the current paper comparing to [22,21] are a correction for the mentioned definition of [21] and full proofs for the results listed in that paper. Also, new discussions and examples are provided. As $\mathcal{SROIQ}$ and its simpler versions are used for specifying Web ontologies, our semantics and method are useful for paraconsistent reasoning for Semantic Web agents.

Let us emphasize that the four-valued semantics is considered in our paper for comparisons only. It reflects the approach based on Belnap's logic which we found inadequate for Semantic Web applications (see Sections 3 and 4). A logic which seems to behave much better in this context is provided in [18,29]. We do not consider it here as its adaptation to Semantic Web applications is not obvious and requires further investigations, especially in the light of new developments in the field of paraconsistent rule languages [17,16].

Note that, in the context of description logics, three-valued semantics has been studied earlier only for $\mathcal{ALC}$ [30] and $\mathcal{SHIQ}$ [22]. Also note that, studying four-valued semantics for DLs, Ma and Hitzler [14] did not consider all features of $\mathcal{SROIQ}$. For example, they did not consider concepts of the form $\exists R.\mathtt{Self}$ and individual assertions of the form $\neg S(a, b)$.

The rest of this paper is structured as follows. In Section 2 we recall notations and semantics of $\mathcal{SROIQ}$. We present our paraconsistent semantics for $\mathcal{SROIQ}$ in Section 3 and study the relationship between them in Section 4. Comparison with other authors' paraconsistent semantics of $\mathcal{SROIQ}$ and $\mathcal{SHIQ}$ is given in Section 5. In Section 6 we give a faithful translation of the problem of conjunctive query answering w.r.t. some of the considered paraconsistent semantics into a version that uses the traditional semantics. Section 7 concludes this work.

2 The Two-Valued Description Logic $\mathcal{SROIQ}$

In this section we recall notations and semantics of the DL $\mathcal{SROIQ}$ [10]. Assume that our language uses a finite set $\mathbf{C}$ of *concept names*, a subset $\mathbf{N} \subseteq \mathbf{C}$ of *nominals*, a finite set $\mathbf{R}$ of role names including the universal role U, and a finite set $\mathbf{I}$ of individual names. Let $\mathbf{R}^- \stackrel{\text{def}}{=} \{r^- \mid r \in \mathbf{R} \setminus \{U\}\}$ be the set of *inverse roles*. A *role* is any member of $\mathbf{R} \cup \mathbf{R}^-$. We use letters like R and S for roles.

An *interpretation* $\mathcal{I} = \langle \Delta^\mathcal{I}, \cdot^\mathcal{I} \rangle$ consists of a non-empty set $\Delta^\mathcal{I}$, called the *domain* of $\mathcal{I}$, and a function $\cdot^\mathcal{I}$, called the *interpretation function* of $\mathcal{I}$, which maps every concept name A to a subset $A^\mathcal{I}$ of $\Delta^\mathcal{I}$, where $A^\mathcal{I}$ is a singleton set if $A \in \mathbf{N}$, and maps every role name r to a binary relation $r^\mathcal{I}$ on $\Delta^\mathcal{I}$, with $U^\mathcal{I} = \Delta^\mathcal{I} \times \Delta^\mathcal{I}$, and maps every individual name a to an element $a^\mathcal{I} \in \Delta^\mathcal{I}$. Inverse roles are interpreted as usual, i.e., for $r \in \mathbf{R}$, we define

$$(r^-)^\mathcal{I} \stackrel{\text{def}}{=} (r^\mathcal{I})^{-1} = \{\langle x, y\rangle \mid \langle y, x\rangle \in r^\mathcal{I}\}.$$

A *role inclusion axiom* is an expression of the form $R_1 \circ \ldots \circ R_k \sqsubseteq S$. A *role assertion* is an expression of the form $\mathtt{Ref}(R)$, $\mathtt{Irr}(R)$, $\mathtt{Sym}(R)$, $\mathtt{Tra}(R)$, or $\mathtt{Dis}(R, S)$, where $R, S \neq U$. Given an interpretation $\mathcal{I}$, define that:

$$\begin{array}{lll}
\mathcal{I} \models R_1 \circ \ldots \circ R_k \sqsubseteq S & \text{if} & R_1^\mathcal{I} \circ \ldots \circ R_k^\mathcal{I} \subseteq S^\mathcal{I} \\
\mathcal{I} \models \mathtt{Ref}(R) & \text{if} & R^\mathcal{I} \text{ is reflexive} \\
\mathcal{I} \models \mathtt{Irr}(R) & \text{if} & R^\mathcal{I} \text{ is irreflexive} \\
\mathcal{I} \models \mathtt{Sym}(R) & \text{if} & R^\mathcal{I} \text{ is symmetric} \\
\mathcal{I} \models \mathtt{Tra}(R) & \text{if} & R^\mathcal{I} \text{ is transitive} \\
\mathcal{I} \models \mathtt{Dis}(R, S) & \text{if} & R^\mathcal{I} \text{ and } S^\mathcal{I} \text{ are disjoint,}
\end{array}$$

where the operator $\circ$ stands for the composition of relations. By a *role axiom* we mean either a role inclusion axiom or a role assertion. We say that a role axiom φ is *valid* in $\mathcal{I}$ (or $\mathcal{I}$ *validates* φ) if $\mathcal{I} \models \varphi$.

An *RBox* is a set $\mathcal{R} = \mathcal{R}_h \cup \mathcal{R}_a$, where $\mathcal{R}_h$ is a finite set of role inclusion axioms and $\mathcal{R}_a$ is a finite set of role assertions. It is required that $\mathcal{R}_h$ is *regular* and $\mathcal{R}_a$ is *simple*. In particular, $\mathcal{R}_a$ is simple if all roles R, S appearing in role assertions of the form $\mathtt{Irr}(R)$ or $\mathtt{Dis}(R, S)$ are *simple roles* w.r.t. $\mathcal{R}_h$. These notions (of regularity and simplicity) will not be exploited in this paper and we refer the reader to [10] for their definitions. An interpretation $\mathcal{I}$ is a *model* of an RBox $\mathcal{R}$, denoted by $\mathcal{I} \models \mathcal{R}$, if it validates all role axioms of $\mathcal{R}$.

The set of *concepts* is the smallest set such that:

- all concept names (including nominals) and $\top$, $\bot$ are concepts
- if C, D are concepts, R is a role, S is a simple role and n is a non-negative integer, then $\neg C$, $C \sqcap D$, $C \sqcup D$, $\forall R.C$, $\exists R.C$, $\exists S.\mathtt{Self}$, $\geq n S.C$, and $\leq n S.C$ are also concepts.

We use letters like A, B to denote concept names, and letters like C, D to denote concepts.

Given an interpretation $\mathcal{I}$, the interpretation function $\cdot^\mathcal{I}$ is extended to complex concepts as follows, where $\#\Gamma$ stands for the number of elements in the set Γ:

$$\begin{aligned}
\top^\mathcal{I} &\stackrel{\text{def}}{=} \Delta^\mathcal{I} \\
\bot^\mathcal{I} &\stackrel{\text{def}}{=} \emptyset \\
(\neg C)^\mathcal{I} &\stackrel{\text{def}}{=} \Delta^\mathcal{I} \setminus C^\mathcal{I} \\
(C \sqcap D)^\mathcal{I} &\stackrel{\text{def}}{=} C^\mathcal{I} \cap D^\mathcal{I}
\end{aligned}$$

$$
\begin{aligned}
(C \sqcup D)^{\mathcal{I}} &\stackrel{\text{def}}{=} C^{\mathcal{I}} \cup D^{\mathcal{I}} \\
(\forall R.C)^{\mathcal{I}} &\stackrel{\text{def}}{=} \{x \in \Delta^{\mathcal{I}} \mid \forall y[\langle x, y\rangle \in R^{\mathcal{I}} \text{ implies } y \in C^{\mathcal{I}}]\} \\
(\exists R.C)^{\mathcal{I}} &\stackrel{\text{def}}{=} \{x \in \Delta^{\mathcal{I}} \mid \exists y[\langle x, y\rangle \in R^{\mathcal{I}} \text{ and } y \in C^{\mathcal{I}}]\} \\
(\exists S.\mathtt{Self})^{\mathcal{I}} &\stackrel{\text{def}}{=} \{x \in \Delta^{\mathcal{I}} \mid \langle x, x\rangle \in S^{\mathcal{I}}\} \\
(\geq n\, S.C)^{\mathcal{I}} &\stackrel{\text{def}}{=} \{x \in \Delta^{\mathcal{I}} \mid \#\{y \mid \langle x, y\rangle \in S^{\mathcal{I}} \text{ and } y \in C^{\mathcal{I}}\} \geq n\} \\
(\leq n\, S.C)^{\mathcal{I}} &\stackrel{\text{def}}{=} \{x \in \Delta^{\mathcal{I}} \mid \#\{y \mid \langle x, y\rangle \in S^{\mathcal{I}} \text{ and } y \in C^{\mathcal{I}}\} \leq n\}.
\end{aligned}
$$

A *terminological axiom*, also called a *general concept inclusion* (GCI), is an expression of the form $C \sqsubseteq D$. A *TBox* is a finite set of terminological axioms. An interpretation $\mathcal{I}$ validates an axiom $C \sqsubseteq D$, denoted by $\mathcal{I} \models C \sqsubseteq D$, if $C^{\mathcal{I}} \subseteq D^{\mathcal{I}}$. We say that $\mathcal{I}$ is a *model* of a TBox $\mathcal{T}$, denoted by $\mathcal{I} \models \mathcal{T}$, if it validates all axioms of $\mathcal{T}$.

We use letters like a and b to denote individual names. An *individual assertion* is an expression of the form $a \neq b$, $C(a)$, $R(a,b)$, or $\neg S(a,b)$, where S is a simple role and $R, S \neq U$. Given an interpretation $\mathcal{I}$, define that:

$$
\begin{array}{ll}
\mathcal{I} \models a \neq b & \text{if } a^{\mathcal{I}} \neq b^{\mathcal{I}} \\
\mathcal{I} \models C(a) & \text{if } a^{\mathcal{I}} \in C^{\mathcal{I}} \\
\mathcal{I} \models R(a,b) & \text{if } \langle a^{\mathcal{I}}, b^{\mathcal{I}}\rangle \in R^{\mathcal{I}} \\
\mathcal{I} \models \neg S(a,b) & \text{if } \langle a^{\mathcal{I}}, b^{\mathcal{I}}\rangle \notin S^{\mathcal{I}}.
\end{array}
$$

We say that $\mathcal{I}$ *satisfies* an individual assertion φ if $\mathcal{I} \models \varphi$. An *ABox* is a finite set of individual assertions. An interpretation $\mathcal{I}$ is a *model* of an ABox $\mathcal{A}$, denoted by $\mathcal{I} \models \mathcal{A}$, if it satisfies all assertions of $\mathcal{A}$.

A *knowledge base* is a tuple $\langle \mathcal{R}, \mathcal{T}, \mathcal{A}\rangle$, where $\mathcal{R}$ is an RBox, $\mathcal{T}$ is a TBox, and $\mathcal{A}$ is an ABox. An interpretation $\mathcal{I}$ is a *model* of a knowledge base $\langle \mathcal{R}, \mathcal{T}, \mathcal{A}\rangle$ if it is model of all $\mathcal{R}$, $\mathcal{T}$, and $\mathcal{A}$. A knowledge base is *satisfiable* if it has a model.

A (*conjunctive*) *query* is an expression of the form $\varphi_1 \wedge \ldots \wedge \varphi_k$, where each φ_i is an individual assertion. An interpretation $\mathcal{I}$ satisfies a query $\varphi = \varphi_1 \wedge \ldots \wedge \varphi_k$, denoted by $\mathcal{I} \models \varphi$, if $\mathcal{I} \models \varphi_i$ for all $1 \leq i \leq k$. We say that a query φ is a *logical consequence* of a knowledge base $\langle \mathcal{R}, \mathcal{T}, \mathcal{A}\rangle$, denoted by $\langle \mathcal{R}, \mathcal{T}, \mathcal{A}\rangle \models \varphi$, if every model of $\langle \mathcal{R}, \mathcal{T}, \mathcal{A}\rangle$ satisfies φ.

Note that, queries are defined to be "ground". In a more general context, queries may contain variables for individuals. However, one of the approaches to deal with such queries is to instantiate variables by individuals occurring in the knowledge base or the query.

3 Paraconsistent Semantics for $\mathcal{SROIQ}$

3.1 Discussion and Definitions

Recall that, using the traditional semantics, every query is a logical consequence of an inconsistent knowledge base. A knowledge base may be inconsistent, for example, when it contains both individual assertions $A(a)$ and $\neg A(a)$ for some

$A \in \mathbf{C}$ and $a \in \mathbf{I}$. Paraconsistent reasoning is inconsistency-tolerant and aims to derive (only) meaningful logical consequences even when the knowledge base is inconsistent. Following the recommendation of W3C for OWL, we use the traditional syntax of DLs and only change its semantics to cover paraconsistency. The general approach is to define a semantics $\mathfrak{s}$ such that, given a knowledge base KB, the set $Cons_{\mathfrak{s}}(KB)$ of logical consequences of KB w.r.t. semantics $\mathfrak{s}$ is a subset of the set $Cons(KB)$ of logical consequences of KB w.r.t. the traditional semantics, with the property that $Cons_{\mathfrak{s}}(KB)$ contains mainly only meaningful logical consequences of KB and $Cons_{\mathfrak{s}}(KB)$ approximates $Cons(KB)$ as much as possible.

In this paper, we introduce a number of paraconsistent semantics for the DL $\mathcal{SROIQ}$. Each of them, let's say $\mathfrak{s}$, is characterized by four parameters, denoted by $\mathfrak{s}_C$, $\mathfrak{s}_R$, $\mathfrak{s}_{\forall\exists}$, $\mathfrak{s}_{GCI}$, with the following intuitive meanings:

- $\mathfrak{s}_C \in \{2,3,4\}$ specifies the number of possible truth values of assertions of the form $x \in A^{\mathcal{I}}$, where A is a concept name not being a nominal and $\mathcal{I}$ is an interpretation. In the case $\mathfrak{s}_C = 2$, the truth values are $\mathfrak{t}$ (true) and $\mathfrak{f}$ (false). In the case $\mathfrak{s}_C = 3$, the third truth value is $\mathfrak{i}$ (inconsistent). In the case $\mathfrak{s}_C = 4$, the additional truth value is $\mathfrak{u}$ (unknown). When $\mathfrak{s}_C = 3$, one can identify inconsistency with the lack of knowledge, and the third value $\mathfrak{i}$ can be read either as inconsistent or as unknown.
- $\mathfrak{s}_R \in \{2,3,4\}$ specifies the number of possible truth values of assertions of the form $\langle x,y\rangle \in r^{\mathcal{I}}$, where r is a role name different from the universal role U and $\mathcal{I}$ is an interpretation. The truth values are as in the case of $\mathfrak{s}_C$.
- $\mathfrak{s}_{\forall\exists} \in \{+,\pm\}$ specifies which of the two semantics studied by Straccia [28] for concepts of the form $\forall R.C$ or $\exists R.C$ is used.
- $\mathfrak{s}_{GCI} \in \{w,m,s\}$ specifies one of the three semantics for general concept inclusions: weak (w), moderate (m), strong (s).

For simplicity, we use the same value of $\mathfrak{s}_C$ for all concept names of $\mathbf{C} \setminus \mathbf{N}$ and use the same value of $\mathfrak{s}_R$ for all role names of $\mathbf{R} \setminus \{U\}$. One may want to consider different values of $\mathfrak{s}_C$ for different concept names, and different values of $\mathfrak{s}_R$ for different role names. The methods and results of this paper can be generalized for that case in a straightforward way.

We identify $\mathfrak{s}$ with the tuple $\langle \mathfrak{s}_C, \mathfrak{s}_R, \mathfrak{s}_{\forall\exists}, \mathfrak{s}_{GCI}\rangle$. The set $\mathfrak{S}$ of considered paraconsistent semantics is thus $\{2,3,4\} \times \{2,3,4\} \times \{+,\pm\} \times \{w,m,s\}$.

For $\mathfrak{s} \in \mathfrak{S}$, an *$\mathfrak{s}$-interpretation* $\mathcal{I} = \langle \Delta^{\mathcal{I}}, \cdot^{\mathcal{I}}\rangle$ is similar to a traditional interpretation except that the interpretation function maps every concept name A to a pair $A^{\mathcal{I}} = \langle A^{\mathcal{I}}_+, A^{\mathcal{I}}_-\rangle$ of subsets of $\Delta^{\mathcal{I}}$ and maps every role name r to a pair $r^{\mathcal{I}} = \langle r^{\mathcal{I}}_+, r^{\mathcal{I}}_-\rangle$ of binary relations on $\Delta^{\mathcal{I}}$ such that:

- if $\mathfrak{s}_C = 2$ then $A^{\mathcal{I}}_+ = \Delta^{\mathcal{I}} \setminus A^{\mathcal{I}}_-$
- if $\mathfrak{s}_C = 3$ then $A^{\mathcal{I}}_+ \cup A^{\mathcal{I}}_- = \Delta^{\mathcal{I}}$
- if $\mathfrak{s}_R = 2$ then $r^{\mathcal{I}}_+ = (\Delta^{\mathcal{I}} \times \Delta^{\mathcal{I}}) \setminus r^{\mathcal{I}}_-$
- if $\mathfrak{s}_R = 3$ then $r^{\mathcal{I}}_+ \cup r^{\mathcal{I}}_- = \Delta^{\mathcal{I}} \times \Delta^{\mathcal{I}}$
- if A is a nominal then $A^{\mathcal{I}}_+$ is a singleton set and $A^{\mathcal{I}}_- = \Delta^{\mathcal{I}} \setminus A^{\mathcal{I}}_+$
- $U^{\mathcal{I}}_+ = \Delta^{\mathcal{I}} \times \Delta^{\mathcal{I}}$ and $U^{\mathcal{I}}_- = \emptyset$.

Remark 3.1. The intuition behind $A^{\mathcal{I}} = \langle A^{\mathcal{I}}_+, A^{\mathcal{I}}_- \rangle$ is that $A^{\mathcal{I}}_+$ gathers positive evidence about A, while $A^{\mathcal{I}}_-$ gathers negative evidence about A. Thus, $A^{\mathcal{I}}$ can be treated as the function from $\Delta^{\mathcal{I}}$ to $\{\mathfrak{t}, \mathfrak{f}, \mathfrak{i}, \mathfrak{u}\}$ defined below:

$$A^{\mathcal{I}}(x) \stackrel{\text{def}}{=} \begin{cases} \mathfrak{t} \text{ for } x \in A^{\mathcal{I}}_+ \text{ and } x \notin A^{\mathcal{I}}_- \\ \mathfrak{f} \text{ for } x \in A^{\mathcal{I}}_- \text{ and } x \notin A^{\mathcal{I}}_+ \\ \mathfrak{i} \text{ for } x \in A^{\mathcal{I}}_+ \text{ and } x \in A^{\mathcal{I}}_- \\ \mathfrak{u} \text{ for } x \notin A^{\mathcal{I}}_+ \text{ and } x \notin A^{\mathcal{I}}_- \end{cases} \tag{1}$$

Informally, $A^{\mathcal{I}}(x)$ can be thought of as the truth value of $x \in A^{\mathcal{I}}$. Note that $A^{\mathcal{I}}(x) \in \{\mathfrak{t}, \mathfrak{f}\}$ if $\mathfrak{s}_{\mathsf{C}} = 2$ or A is a nominal, and $A^{\mathcal{I}}(x) \in \{\mathfrak{t}, \mathfrak{f}, \mathfrak{i}\}$ if $\mathfrak{s}_{\mathsf{C}} = 3$. The intuition behind $r^{\mathcal{I}} = \langle r^{\mathcal{I}}_+, r^{\mathcal{I}}_- \rangle$ is similar, and under which $r^{\mathcal{I}}(x,y) \in \{\mathfrak{t}, \mathfrak{f}\}$ if $\mathfrak{s}_{\mathsf{R}} = 2$ or $r = U$, and $r^{\mathcal{I}}(x,y) \in \{\mathfrak{t}, \mathfrak{f}, \mathfrak{i}\}$ if $\mathfrak{s}_{\mathsf{R}} = 3$. ◁

The interpretation function $\cdot^{\mathcal{I}}$ maps an inverse role R to a pair $R^{\mathcal{I}} = \langle R^{\mathcal{I}}_+, R^{\mathcal{I}}_- \rangle$ defined by $(r^-)^{\mathcal{I}} \stackrel{\text{def}}{=} \langle (r^{\mathcal{I}}_+)^{-1}, (r^{\mathcal{I}}_-)^{-1} \rangle$. It maps a complex concept C to a pair $C^{\mathcal{I}} = \langle C^{\mathcal{I}}_+, C^{\mathcal{I}}_- \rangle$ of subsets of $\Delta^{\mathcal{I}}$ defined as follows:

$$\begin{aligned}
\top^{\mathcal{I}} &\stackrel{\text{def}}{=} \langle \Delta^{\mathcal{I}}, \emptyset \rangle \\
\bot^{\mathcal{I}} &\stackrel{\text{def}}{=} \langle \emptyset, \Delta^{\mathcal{I}} \rangle \\
(\neg C)^{\mathcal{I}} &\stackrel{\text{def}}{=} \langle C^{\mathcal{I}}_-, C^{\mathcal{I}}_+ \rangle \\
(C \sqcap D)^{\mathcal{I}} &\stackrel{\text{def}}{=} \langle C^{\mathcal{I}}_+ \cap D^{\mathcal{I}}_+, C^{\mathcal{I}}_- \cup D^{\mathcal{I}}_- \rangle \\
(C \sqcup D)^{\mathcal{I}} &\stackrel{\text{def}}{=} \langle C^{\mathcal{I}}_+ \cup D^{\mathcal{I}}_+, C^{\mathcal{I}}_- \cap D^{\mathcal{I}}_- \rangle \\
(\exists R.\mathtt{Self})^{\mathcal{I}} &\stackrel{\text{def}}{=} \langle \{x \in \Delta^{\mathcal{I}} \mid \langle x,x \rangle \in R^{\mathcal{I}}_+\}, \{x \in \Delta^{\mathcal{I}} \mid \langle x,x \rangle \in R^{\mathcal{I}}_-\} \rangle \\
(\geq n\, R.C)^{\mathcal{I}} &\stackrel{\text{def}}{=} \langle \{x \in \Delta^{\mathcal{I}} \mid \#\{y \mid \langle x,y \rangle \in R^{\mathcal{I}}_+ \text{ and } y \in C^{\mathcal{I}}_+\} \geq n\}, \\
&\qquad \{x \in \Delta^{\mathcal{I}} \mid \#\{y \mid \langle x,y \rangle \in R^{\mathcal{I}}_+ \text{ and } y \notin C^{\mathcal{I}}_-\} < n\} \rangle \\
(\leq n\, R.C)^{\mathcal{I}} &\stackrel{\text{def}}{=} \langle \{x \in \Delta^{\mathcal{I}} \mid \#\{y \mid \langle x,y \rangle \in R^{\mathcal{I}}_+ \text{ and } y \notin C^{\mathcal{I}}_-\} \leq n\}, \\
&\qquad \{x \in \Delta^{\mathcal{I}} \mid \#\{y \mid \langle x,y \rangle \in R^{\mathcal{I}}_+ \text{ and } y \in C^{\mathcal{I}}_+\} > n\} \rangle;
\end{aligned}$$

if $\mathfrak{s}_{\forall\exists} = +$ then

$$\begin{aligned}
(\forall R.C)^{\mathcal{I}} &\stackrel{\text{def}}{=} \langle \{x \in \Delta^{\mathcal{I}} \mid \forall y (\langle x,y \rangle \in R^{\mathcal{I}}_+ \text{ implies } y \in C^{\mathcal{I}}_+)\}, \\
&\qquad \{x \in \Delta^{\mathcal{I}} \mid \exists y (\langle x,y \rangle \in R^{\mathcal{I}}_+ \text{ and } y \in C^{\mathcal{I}}_-)\} \rangle \\
(\exists R.C)^{\mathcal{I}} &\stackrel{\text{def}}{=} \langle \{x \in \Delta^{\mathcal{I}} \mid \exists y (\langle x,y \rangle \in R^{\mathcal{I}}_+ \text{ and } y \in C^{\mathcal{I}}_+)\}, \\
&\qquad \{x \in \Delta^{\mathcal{I}} \mid \forall y (\langle x,y \rangle \in R^{\mathcal{I}}_+ \text{ implies } y \in C^{\mathcal{I}}_-)\} \rangle;
\end{aligned}$$

if $\mathfrak{s}_{\forall\exists} = \pm$ then

$$\begin{aligned}
(\forall R.C)^{\mathcal{I}} &\stackrel{\text{def}}{=} \langle \{x \in \Delta^{\mathcal{I}} \mid \forall y (\langle x,y \rangle \in R^{\mathcal{I}}_- \text{ or } y \in C^{\mathcal{I}}_+)\}, \\
&\qquad \{x \in \Delta^{\mathcal{I}} \mid \exists y (\langle x,y \rangle \in R^{\mathcal{I}}_+ \text{ and } y \in C^{\mathcal{I}}_-)\} \rangle \\
(\exists R.C)^{\mathcal{I}} &\stackrel{\text{def}}{=} \langle \{x \in \Delta^{\mathcal{I}} \mid \exists y (\langle x,y \rangle \in R^{\mathcal{I}}_+ \text{ and } y \in C^{\mathcal{I}}_+)\}, \\
&\qquad \{x \in \Delta^{\mathcal{I}} \mid \forall y (\langle x,y \rangle \in R^{\mathcal{I}}_- \text{ or } y \in C^{\mathcal{I}}_-)\} \rangle.
\end{aligned}$$

Remark 3.1 applies also to complex concepts. For example, we say that $C^{\mathcal{I}}(x) = \mathfrak{i}$ if $x \in C^{\mathcal{I}}_{+}$ and $x \in C^{\mathcal{I}}_{-}$. Note that $C^{\mathcal{I}}$ is computed in the standard way [15,14,31,22] for the case C is of the form $\top$, $\bot$, $\neg D$, $D \sqcap D'$, $D \sqcup D'$, $\geq n\, R.D$ or $\leq n\, R.D$. When $\mathfrak{s}_{\forall\exists} = +$, $(\forall R.C)^{\mathcal{I}}$ and $(\exists R.C)^{\mathcal{I}}$ are computed as in [15,14,31,22] and as using semantics A of [28]. When $\mathfrak{s}_{\forall\exists} = \pm$, $(\forall R.C)^{\mathcal{I}}$ and $(\exists R.C)^{\mathcal{I}}$ are computed as using semantics B of [28].

3.2 Example

The following example illustrates the above definitions.

Consider a Semantic Web service supplying information about stocks. Assume that a web agent looks for low risk stocks, promising big gain. The agent's query can be expressed by

$$(LR \sqcap BG)(x), \tag{2}$$

where LR and BG stand for "low risk" and "big gain", respectively.

For simplicity, assume that the service has a knowledge base consisting only of the following concept assertions (perhaps provided by different experts/agents):

$$LR(s_1), \neg LR(s_1), \neg LR(s_2), \neg BG(s_2), LR(s_3), BG(s_3).$$

We then consider the interpretation $\mathcal{I}$ with:

$$LR^{\mathcal{I}} = \langle \{s_1, s_3\}, \{s_1, s_2\} \rangle \text{ and } BG^{\mathcal{I}} = \langle \{s_1, s_3\}, \{s_2\} \rangle. \tag{3}$$

The query (2) looks for stocks x that are instances of $LR \sqcap BG$ w.r.t. $\mathcal{I}$.

In the case of the traditional (two-valued) semantics, the knowledge base has no models, and hence all of s_1, s_2, s_3 are answers to the query, despite the fact that s_2 is of high risk and low gain.

Using any semantics $\mathfrak{s} \in \mathfrak{S}$ with $\mathfrak{s}_C = 3$, we have that

$$(LR \sqcap BG)^{\mathcal{I}} = \langle LR^{\mathcal{I}}_{+} \cap BG^{\mathcal{I}}_{+}, LR^{\mathcal{I}}_{-} \cup BG^{\mathcal{I}}_{-} \rangle = \langle \{s_1, s_3\}, \{s_1, s_2\} \rangle,$$

meaning that (according to (1)):

$$(LR \sqcap BG)^{\mathcal{I}}(s_1) = \mathfrak{i}, \;\; (LR \sqcap BG)^{\mathcal{I}}(s_2) = \mathfrak{f} \text{ and } (LR \sqcap BG)^{\mathcal{I}}(s_3) = \mathfrak{t},$$

which is well-justified. Namely, there is both positive and negative evidence that s_1 satisfies (2), there is only negative evidence that s_2 satisfies (2) and there is only positive evidence that s_3 satisfies (2).

Consider now the four-valued semantics and let $\mathcal{I}'$ differ from $\mathcal{I}$ given by (3) in that $BG^{\mathcal{I}'} = \langle \{s_3\}, \{s_2\} \rangle$. Notice that $BG^{\mathcal{I}'}_{+} \cup BG^{\mathcal{I}'}_{-} \neq \Delta^{\mathcal{I}'}$. In this case, according to (1), we have that $BG^{\mathcal{I}'}(s_1) = \mathfrak{u}$. Now

$$(LR \sqcap BG)^{\mathcal{I}'} = \langle \{s_3\}, \{s_1, s_2\} \rangle,$$

that is,

$$(LR \sqcap BG)^{\mathcal{I}'}(s_1) = \mathfrak{f}, \;\; (LR \sqcap BG)^{\mathcal{I}'}(s_2) = \mathfrak{f} \text{ and } (LR \sqcap BG)^{\mathcal{I}'}(s_3) = \mathfrak{t}.$$

The result that $(LR \sqcap BG)^{\mathcal{I}'}(s_1) = \mathfrak{f}$ is not intuitive. Namely, we have inconsistent information that s_1 is low risk and have no information whether it promises big gain and still we have the result that the conjunction of both is false.

Observe also that

$$(LR \sqcup BG)^{\mathcal{I}'} = \langle LR_+^{\mathcal{I}'} \cup BG_+^{\mathcal{I}'}, LR_-^{\mathcal{I}'} \cap BG_-^{\mathcal{I}'} \rangle = \langle \{s_1, s_3\}, \{s_2\} \rangle.$$

This means that the disjunction

$$\underbrace{s_1 \text{ is of low risk}}_{\mathfrak{i}} \text{ or } \underbrace{s_1 \text{ promises big gain}}_{\mathfrak{u}}$$

is $\mathbf{t}$, which is again not intuitive.

In fact, the definitions of $\sqcap$ and $\sqcup$ in the four-valued context reflect the truth ordering proposed by Belnap [5,4] and used in the Semantic Web context, e.g., in [14,15]. The use of Belnap's knowledge ordering also provides non-intuitive results in many other cases. Therefore we advocate for using three-valued logic, as proposed in [22] in the case of complete knowledge. In the case of incomplete knowledge the use of truth ordering proposed independently in [1] and [18,29] provides much more intuitive results ($\mathfrak{i}$ for the disjunction and $\mathfrak{u}$ for the conjunction).

3.3 Properties of Paraconsistent Semantics

We write $C \equiv_{\mathfrak{s}} D$ and say that C and D are *equivalent w.r.t.* $\mathfrak{s}$ if $C^{\mathcal{I}} = D^{\mathcal{I}}$ for every $\mathfrak{s}$-interpretation $\mathcal{I}$. The following proposition states that De Morgan laws hold for our constructors w.r.t. any semantics from $\mathfrak{S}$. Its proof is straight forward.

Proposition 3.2. *The following equivalences hold for every* $\mathfrak{s} \in \mathfrak{S}$ *:*

$$\begin{aligned}
(\neg\neg C)^{\mathcal{I}} &\equiv_{\mathfrak{s}} C^{\mathcal{I}} \\
(\neg\top)^{\mathcal{I}} &\equiv_{\mathfrak{s}} \bot^{\mathcal{I}} \\
(\neg(C \sqcap D))^{\mathcal{I}} &\equiv_{\mathfrak{s}} (\neg C \sqcup \neg D)^{\mathcal{I}} \\
(\neg\forall R.C)^{\mathcal{I}} &\equiv_{\mathfrak{s}} (\exists R.\neg C)^{\mathcal{I}} \\
(\neg(\geq 0\, R.C))^{\mathcal{I}} &\equiv_{\mathfrak{s}} \bot^{\mathcal{I}} \\
(\neg(\geq (n+1)\, R.C))^{\mathcal{I}} &\equiv_{\mathfrak{s}} (\leq n\, R.C)^{\mathcal{I}} \\
(\neg(\leq n\, R.C))^{\mathcal{I}} &\equiv_{\mathfrak{s}} (\geq (n+1)\, R.C)^{\mathcal{I}}
\end{aligned}$$

◁

The following proposition means that: if $\mathfrak{s}_{\mathrm{C}} \in \{2,3\}$ and $\mathfrak{s}_{\mathrm{R}} \in \{2,3\}$ then $\mathfrak{s}$ is a three-valued semantics; if $\mathfrak{s}_{\mathrm{C}} = 2$ and $\mathfrak{s}_{\mathrm{R}} = 2$ then $\mathfrak{s}$ is a two-valued semantics. Its proof is straightforward via induction on the structure of C and R.

Proposition 3.3. *Let* $\mathfrak{s} \in \mathfrak{S}$ *be a semantics such that* $\mathfrak{s}_{\mathrm{C}} \in \{2,3\}$ *and* $\mathfrak{s}_{\mathrm{R}} \in \{2,3\}$. *Let* $\mathcal{I}$ *be an* $\mathfrak{s}$*-interpretation,* C *be a concept, and* R *be a role. Then* $C_+^{\mathcal{I}} \cup C_-^{\mathcal{I}} = \Delta^{\mathcal{I}}$ *and* $R_+^{\mathcal{I}} \cup R_-^{\mathcal{I}} = \Delta^{\mathcal{I}} \times \Delta^{\mathcal{I}}$. *Furthermore, if* $\mathfrak{s}_{\mathrm{C}} = 2$ *and* $\mathfrak{s}_{\mathrm{R}} = 2$ *then* $C_+^{\mathcal{I}} = \Delta^{\mathcal{I}} \setminus C_-^{\mathcal{I}}$ *and* $R_+^{\mathcal{I}} = (\Delta^{\mathcal{I}} \times \Delta^{\mathcal{I}}) \setminus R_-^{\mathcal{I}}$. ◁

Let $\mathfrak{s} \in \mathfrak{S}$ and let $\mathcal{I}$ be an $\mathfrak{s}$-interpretation. We say that:

- $\mathcal{I}$ $\mathfrak{s}$-*validates* a role axiom $R_1 \circ \ldots \circ R_k \sqsubseteq S$ if $R_{1+}^{\mathcal{I}} \circ \ldots \circ R_{k+}^{\mathcal{I}} \subseteq S_+^{\mathcal{I}}$
- $\mathcal{I}$ $\mathfrak{s}$-*validates* a role assertion $\mathtt{Ref}(R)$ (resp. $\mathtt{Irr}(R)$, $\mathtt{Sym}(R)$, $\mathtt{Tra}(R)$) if $R_+^{\mathcal{I}}$ is reflexive (resp. irreflexive, symmetric, transitive)
- $\mathcal{I}$ $\mathfrak{s}$-*validates* a role assertion $\mathtt{Dis}(R, S)$ if $R_+^{\mathcal{I}}$ and $S_+^{\mathcal{I}}$ are disjoint
- $\mathcal{I}$ is an $\mathfrak{s}$-*model* of an RBox $\mathcal{R}$, denoted by $\mathcal{I} \models_{\mathfrak{s}} \mathcal{R}$, if it $\mathfrak{s}$-validates all axioms of $\mathcal{R}$

- $\mathcal{I}$ $\mathfrak{s}$-*validates* $C \sqsubseteq D$, denoted by $\mathcal{I} \models_{\mathfrak{s}} C \sqsubseteq D$, if:
  - case $\mathfrak{s}_{\mathtt{GCI}} = w : C_-^{\mathcal{I}} \cup D_+^{\mathcal{I}} = \Delta^{\mathcal{I}}$
  - case $\mathfrak{s}_{\mathtt{GCI}} = m : C_+^{\mathcal{I}} \subseteq D_+^{\mathcal{I}}$
  - case $\mathfrak{s}_{\mathtt{GCI}} = s : C_+^{\mathcal{I}} \subseteq D_+^{\mathcal{I}}$ and $D_-^{\mathcal{I}} \subseteq C_-^{\mathcal{I}}$
- $\mathcal{I}$ is an $\mathfrak{s}$-*model* of a TBox $\mathcal{T}$, denoted by $\mathcal{I} \models_{\mathfrak{s}} \mathcal{T}$, if it $\mathfrak{s}$-validates all axioms of $\mathcal{T}$

- $\mathcal{I}$ $\mathfrak{s}$-*satisfies* an individual assertion φ if $\mathcal{I} \models_{\mathfrak{s}} \varphi$, where
  $\mathcal{I} \models_{\mathfrak{s}} a \neq b$ if $a^{\mathcal{I}} \neq b^{\mathcal{I}}$
  $\mathcal{I} \models_{\mathfrak{s}} C(a)$ if $a^{\mathcal{I}} \in C_+^{\mathcal{I}}$
  $\mathcal{I} \models_{\mathfrak{s}} R(a,b)$ if $\langle a^{\mathcal{I}}, b^{\mathcal{I}} \rangle \in R_+^{\mathcal{I}}$
  $\mathcal{I} \models_{\mathfrak{s}} \neg S(a,b)$ if $\langle a^{\mathcal{I}}, b^{\mathcal{I}} \rangle \in S_-^{\mathcal{I}}$
- $\mathcal{I}$ is an $\mathfrak{s}$-*model* of an ABox $\mathcal{A}$, denoted by $\mathcal{I} \models_{\mathfrak{s}} \mathcal{A}$, if it $\mathfrak{s}$-satisfies all assertions of $\mathcal{A}$

- $\mathcal{I}$ is an $\mathfrak{s}$-*model* of a knowledge base $\langle \mathcal{R}, \mathcal{T}, \mathcal{A} \rangle$ if it is an $\mathfrak{s}$-model of all $\mathcal{R}$, $\mathcal{T}$ and $\mathcal{A}$
- a knowledge base $\langle \mathcal{R}, \mathcal{T}, \mathcal{A} \rangle$ is $\mathfrak{s}$-*satisfiable* if it has an $\mathfrak{s}$-model
- $\mathcal{I}$ $\mathfrak{s}$-*satisfies* a query $\varphi = \varphi_1 \wedge \ldots \wedge \varphi_k$, denoted by $\mathcal{I} \models_{\mathfrak{s}} \varphi$, if $\mathcal{I} \models_{\mathfrak{s}} \varphi_i$ for all $1 \leq i \leq k$
- φ is an $\mathfrak{s}$-*logical consequence* of a knowledge base $\langle \mathcal{R}, \mathcal{T}, \mathcal{A} \rangle$, denoted by $\langle \mathcal{R}, \mathcal{T}, \mathcal{A} \rangle \models_{\mathfrak{s}} \varphi$, if every $\mathfrak{s}$-model of $\langle \mathcal{R}, \mathcal{T}, \mathcal{A} \rangle$ $\mathfrak{s}$-satisfies φ.

4 The Relationship between the Semantics

The following proposition states that if $\mathfrak{s} \in \mathfrak{S}$ is a semantics such that $\mathfrak{s}_{\mathtt{C}} = 2$ and $\mathfrak{s}_{\mathtt{R}} = 2$ then $\mathfrak{s}$ coincides with the traditional semantics.

Proposition 4.1. *Let $\mathfrak{s} \in \mathfrak{S}$ be a semantics such that $\mathfrak{s}_{\mathtt{C}} = 2$ and $\mathfrak{s}_{\mathtt{R}} = 2$, let $\langle \mathcal{R}, \mathcal{T}, \mathcal{A} \rangle$ be a knowledge base, and φ be a query. Then $\langle \mathcal{R}, \mathcal{T}, \mathcal{A} \rangle \models_{\mathfrak{s}} \varphi$ iff $\langle \mathcal{R}, \mathcal{T}, \mathcal{A} \rangle \models \varphi$.*

Proof. Consider the "if" direction. Suppose that $\langle \mathcal{R}, \mathcal{T}, \mathcal{A} \rangle \models \varphi$. We show that $\langle \mathcal{R}, \mathcal{T}, \mathcal{A} \rangle \models_{\mathfrak{s}} \varphi$. Let $\mathcal{I}$ be an $\mathfrak{s}$-model of $\langle \mathcal{R}, \mathcal{T}, \mathcal{A} \rangle$. We show that $\mathcal{I} \models_{\mathfrak{s}} \varphi$.

Let $\mathcal{I}'$ be the traditional interpretation specified by $\Delta^{\mathcal{I}'} = \Delta^{\mathcal{I}}$, $A^{\mathcal{I}'} = A_+^{\mathcal{I}}$ for $A \in \mathbf{C}$, $r^{\mathcal{I}'} = r_+^{\mathcal{I}}$ for $r \in \mathbf{R}$, and $a^{\mathcal{I}'} = a^{\mathcal{I}}$ for $a \in \mathbf{I}$. It can be proved by induction (on the structure of C) that, for any concept C, $C^{\mathcal{I}'} = C_+^{\mathcal{I}}$. Clearly, we also have that $R^{\mathcal{I}'} = R_+^{\mathcal{I}}$ for any role R.

Since $\mathcal{I} \models_{\mathfrak{s}} \mathcal{R}$, it follows that $\mathcal{I}' \models \mathcal{R}$. By Proposition 3.3, for any concept C, $C^{\mathcal{I}}_{-} = \Delta^{\mathcal{I}} \setminus C^{\mathcal{I}}_{+}$. Hence, for any terminological axiom $C \sqsubseteq D$, $\mathcal{I} \models_{\mathfrak{s}} C \sqsubseteq D$ iff $C^{\mathcal{I}}_{+} \subseteq D^{\mathcal{I}}_{+}$. Since $\mathcal{I} \models_{\mathfrak{s}} \mathcal{T}$, it follows that $\mathcal{I}' \models \mathcal{T}$. By Proposition 3.3, we also have that $R^{\mathcal{I}}_{-} = (\Delta^{\mathcal{I}} \times \Delta^{\mathcal{I}}) \setminus R^{\mathcal{I}}_{+}$ for any role R. Hence, for any individual assertion ψ, $\mathcal{I} \models_{\mathfrak{s}} \psi$ iff $\mathcal{I}' \models \psi$. Since $\mathcal{I} \models_{\mathfrak{s}} \mathcal{A}$, it follows that $\mathcal{I}' \models \mathcal{A}$.

Therefore, $\mathcal{I}'$ is a model of $\langle \mathcal{R}, \mathcal{T}, \mathcal{A} \rangle$. Since $\langle \mathcal{R}, \mathcal{T}, \mathcal{A} \rangle \models \varphi$, it follows that $\mathcal{I}' \models \varphi$, which implies that $\mathcal{I} \models_{\mathfrak{s}} \varphi$. This completes the proof of the "if" direction. The "only if" direction can be proved analogously. ◁

Proposition 4.2. *Let $\mathfrak{s}, \mathfrak{s}' \in \mathfrak{S}$ be semantics such that $\mathfrak{s}_{\mathrm{R}} = \mathfrak{s}'_{\mathrm{R}} = 2$, $\mathfrak{s}_{\mathrm{C}} = \mathfrak{s}'_{\mathrm{C}}$, $\mathfrak{s}_{\mathrm{GCI}} = \mathfrak{s}'_{\mathrm{GCI}}$, but $\mathfrak{s}_{\forall\exists} \neq \mathfrak{s}'_{\forall\exists}$. Then $\mathfrak{s}$ and $\mathfrak{s}'$ are equivalent in the sense that, for every knowledge base $\langle \mathcal{R}, \mathcal{T}, \mathcal{A} \rangle$ and every query φ, $\langle \mathcal{R}, \mathcal{T}, \mathcal{A} \rangle \models_{\mathfrak{s}} \varphi$ iff $\langle \mathcal{R}, \mathcal{T}, \mathcal{A} \rangle \models_{\mathfrak{s}'} \varphi$.* ◁

The proof of this lemma is straightforward.

Let $\mathfrak{s}, \mathfrak{s}' \in \mathfrak{S}$. We say that $\mathfrak{s}$ is *weaker than or equal to* $\mathfrak{s}'$ (and $\mathfrak{s}'$ is *stronger than or equal to* $\mathfrak{s}$) if for any knowledge base KB, $Cons_{\mathfrak{s}}(KB) \subseteq Cons_{\mathfrak{s}'}(KB)$. (Recall that $Cons_{\mathfrak{s}}(KB)$ stands for the set of $\mathfrak{s}$-logical consequences of KB.)

Define $\mathfrak{s}_{\mathrm{GCI}} \sqsubseteq \mathfrak{s}'_{\mathrm{GCI}}$ according to $w \sqsubseteq m \sqsubseteq s$, where $\sqsubseteq$ is transitive. Define that $\mathfrak{s} \sqsubseteq \mathfrak{s}'$ if:[3]

$$\mathfrak{s}'_{\mathrm{C}} \leq \mathfrak{s}_{\mathrm{C}} \leq 3,\ \mathfrak{s}'_{\mathrm{R}} \leq \mathfrak{s}_{\mathrm{R}} \leq 3,\ \mathfrak{s}_{\forall\exists} = \mathfrak{s}'_{\forall\exists},\ \text{and } \mathfrak{s}_{\mathrm{GCI}} \sqsubseteq \mathfrak{s}'_{\mathrm{GCI}};\ \text{or} \tag{4}$$

$$\mathfrak{s}'_{\mathrm{C}} \leq \mathfrak{s}_{\mathrm{C}},\ \mathfrak{s}'_{\mathrm{R}} \leq \mathfrak{s}_{\mathrm{R}},\ \mathfrak{s}_{\forall\exists} = \mathfrak{s}'_{\forall\exists},\ \text{and } m \sqsubseteq \mathfrak{s}_{\mathrm{GCI}} \sqsubseteq \mathfrak{s}'_{\mathrm{GCI}};\ \text{or} \tag{5}$$

$$\mathfrak{s}'_{\mathrm{C}} \leq \mathfrak{s}_{\mathrm{C}} \leq 3,\ \mathfrak{s}_{\mathrm{R}} = \mathfrak{s}'_{\mathrm{R}} = 2,\ \text{and } \mathfrak{s}_{\mathrm{GCI}} \sqsubseteq \mathfrak{s}'_{\mathrm{GCI}};\ \text{or} \tag{6}$$

$$\mathfrak{s}'_{\mathrm{C}} \leq \mathfrak{s}_{\mathrm{C}},\ \mathfrak{s}_{\mathrm{R}} = \mathfrak{s}'_{\mathrm{R}} = 2,\ \text{and } m \sqsubseteq \mathfrak{s}_{\mathrm{GCI}} \sqsubseteq \mathfrak{s}'_{\mathrm{GCI}};\ \text{or} \tag{7}$$

$$\mathfrak{s}_{\mathrm{C}} = \mathfrak{s}'_{\mathrm{C}} = 2 \text{ and } \mathfrak{s}_{\mathrm{R}} = \mathfrak{s}'_{\mathrm{R}} = 2. \tag{8}$$

Theorem 4.3. *Let $\mathfrak{s}, \mathfrak{s}' \in \mathfrak{S}$ be semantics such that $\mathfrak{s} \sqsubseteq \mathfrak{s}'$. Then $\mathfrak{s}$ is weaker than or equal to $\mathfrak{s}'$ (i.e., for any knowledge base KB, $Cons_{\mathfrak{s}}(KB) \subseteq Cons_{\mathfrak{s}'}(KB)$).*

Proof. The assertion for the case (8) follows from Proposition 4.1. By using Proposition 4.2, the cases (6) and (7) are reduced to the cases (4) and (5), respectively. Consider the cases (4) and (5), and assume that one of them holds. Let $\mathfrak{s}'' = \langle \mathfrak{s}'_{\mathrm{C}}, \mathfrak{s}'_{\mathrm{R}}, \mathfrak{s}_{\forall\exists}, \mathfrak{s}_{\mathrm{GCI}} \rangle$. We show that $\mathfrak{s}$ is weaker than or equal to $\mathfrak{s}''$, and $\mathfrak{s}''$ is weaker than or equal to $\mathfrak{s}'$, which together imply the assertion of the theorem.

Observe that every $\mathfrak{s}''$-interpretation is an $\mathfrak{s}$-interpretation. Furthermore, since $\mathfrak{s}''_{\forall\exists} = \mathfrak{s}_{\forall\exists}$ and $\mathfrak{s}''_{\mathrm{GCI}} = \mathfrak{s}_{\mathrm{GCI}}$, if $\mathcal{I}$ is an $\mathfrak{s}''$-interpretation then, for every knowledge base KB and every query φ, $\mathcal{I} \models_{\mathfrak{s}''} KB$ iff $\mathcal{I} \models_{\mathfrak{s}} KB$, and $\mathcal{I} \models_{\mathfrak{s}''} \varphi$ iff $\mathcal{I} \models_{\mathfrak{s}} \varphi$. Hence, for every knowledge base KB and every query φ, $KB \models_{\mathfrak{s}} \varphi$ implies $KB \models_{\mathfrak{s}''} \varphi$. That is, $\mathfrak{s}$ is weaker than or equal to $\mathfrak{s}''$.

Semantics $\mathfrak{s}''$ may differ from $\mathfrak{s}'$ only by the pair $\mathfrak{s}''_{\mathrm{GCI}}$ and $\mathfrak{s}'_{\mathrm{GCI}}$, with $\mathfrak{s}''_{\mathrm{GCI}} \sqsubseteq \mathfrak{s}'_{\mathrm{GCI}}$. Every $\mathfrak{s}''$-interpretation is an $\mathfrak{s}'$-interpretation, and vice versa. Let $\mathcal{I}$ be an arbitrary $\mathfrak{s}''$-interpretation. Observe that, for any terminological axiom $C \sqsubseteq D$, if $\mathcal{I} \models_{\mathfrak{s}'} C \sqsubseteq D$ then $\mathcal{I} \models_{\mathfrak{s}''} C \sqsubseteq D$ (for the case (4), note that $C^{\mathcal{I}}_{+} \subseteq D^{\mathcal{I}}_{+}$ implies

[3] This corrects the corresponding definition given in [21].

$C_-^{\mathcal{I}} \cup C_+^{\mathcal{I}} \subseteq C_-^{\mathcal{I}} \cup D_+^{\mathcal{I}}$ and hence $C_-^{\mathcal{I}} \cup D_+^{\mathcal{I}} = \Delta^{\mathcal{I}}$). Hence, for every knowledge base KB, if $\mathcal{I} \models_{\mathfrak{s}'} KB$ then $\mathcal{I} \models_{\mathfrak{s}''} KB$. Clearly, for every query φ, $\mathcal{I} \models_{\mathfrak{s}'} \varphi$ iff $\mathcal{I} \models_{\mathfrak{s}''} \varphi$. Hence, for every knowledge base KB and every query φ, $KB \models_{\mathfrak{s}''} \varphi$ implies $KB \models_{\mathfrak{s}'} \varphi$. That is, $\mathfrak{s}''$ is weaker than or equal to $\mathfrak{s}'$. $\lhd$

We give below a revised version of a corollary of [21] stating which semantics from $\mathfrak{S}$ give only correct answers. It follows immediately from the above theorem and Proposition 4.1.

Corollary 4.4. *Let $\mathfrak{s} \in \mathfrak{S}$ be a semantics such that $\mathfrak{s}_{\mathtt{GCI}} \neq w$ or $\mathfrak{s}_{\mathtt{C}} \leq 3$ and $\mathfrak{s}_{\mathtt{R}} \leq 3$, and let $\langle \mathcal{R}, \mathcal{T}, \mathcal{A} \rangle$ be a knowledge base and φ be a query. Then $\langle \mathcal{R}, \mathcal{T}, \mathcal{A} \rangle \models_{\mathfrak{s}} \varphi$ implies $\langle \mathcal{R}, \mathcal{T}, \mathcal{A} \rangle \models \varphi$.* $\lhd$

5 Comparison with Existing Paraconsistent Semantics

Here, we restrict only to many-valued semantics and quasi-classical semantics for DLs. Other paraconsistent semantics have been discussed in the introduction.

In [14,15] Ma et al. use non-traditional inclusion axioms $C \mapsto D$, $C \sqsubset D$ and $C \to D$, which correspond to our inclusion $C \sqsubseteq D$ w.r.t. semantics $\mathfrak{s}$ with $\mathfrak{s}_{\mathtt{GCI}} = w$, m, s, respectively. The work [15] concerns paraconsistent reasoning in the DL $\mathcal{SHIQ}$, which is later extended in [14] for paraconsistent reasoning in the DL $\mathcal{SROIQ}$. Defining a four-valued semantics for $\mathcal{SROIQ}$, Ma and Hitzler [14] did not consider all features of $\mathcal{SROIQ}$. For example, they did not consider concepts of the form $\exists R.\mathtt{Self}$ and individual assertions of the form $\neg S(a, b)$. Ignoring such detailed differences, their four-valued semantics for $\mathcal{SROIQ}$ can be characterized using the traditional language (with $\sqsubseteq$ instead of $\mapsto$, $\sqsubset$, $\to$), when $\sqsubseteq$ is interpreted as:

$\mapsto$: their semantics is equivalent to our semantics $\langle 4, 2, +, w \rangle$
$\sqsubset$: their semantics is equivalent to our semantics $\langle 4, 2, +, m \rangle$
$\to$: their semantics is equivalent to our semantics $\langle 4, 2, +, s \rangle$.

By Theorem 4.3, their semantics is weaker than our semantics $\langle 3, 2, +, \mathfrak{s}_{\mathtt{GCI}} \rangle$, where $\mathfrak{s}_{\mathtt{GCI}} \in \{w, m, s\}$ when $\sqsubseteq$ is interpreted as $\mapsto$, $\sqsubset$, $\to$, respectively.

Recall also that in Section 3.2 we have shown that approaches based on Belnap's four-valued logic, like [14,15], sometimes lead to counter-intuitive results.

In [31], Zhang et al. define weak and strong quasi-classical semantics for $\mathcal{SHIQ}$, which will be denoted here by $\models_4^w$ and $\models_4^s$. These semantics are four-valued semantics and are based on the quasi-classical semantics of Besnard and Hunter [6,12]. For the conjunctive query answering in $\mathcal{SHIQ}$, the weak quasi-classical semantics is weaker than our semantics $\langle 3, 2, +, w \rangle$. Comparing our semantics $\langle 3, 2, +, s \rangle$ with $\models_4^s$, neither of them is stronger than the other. The relationship between these semantics (for $\mathcal{SHIQ}$) can be characterized as follows. First, axioms of the form $C \sqsubseteq C$ is not valid w.r.t. the semantics $\models_4^s$, which is quite unusual. Second, extending $\models_4^s$ with axioms $A \sqsubseteq A$ for all atomic concepts A results in a three-valued semantics that differs from our three-valued semantics in that it assumes $\mathfrak{t} \wedge \mathfrak{i} = \mathfrak{t}$ and $\mathfrak{f} \vee \mathfrak{i} = \mathfrak{f}$, while our three-valued semantics assume $\mathfrak{t} \wedge \mathfrak{i} = \mathfrak{i}$ and $\mathfrak{f} \vee \mathfrak{i} = \mathfrak{i}$. Moreover, the same problem as indicated in Section 3.2, applies to both weak and strong semantics proposed in [31].

Recall that the paradoxical semantics for $\mathcal{ALC}$ by Zhang et al. [30] is based on a three-valued semantics and was developed independently from our three-valued semantics for $\mathcal{SHIQ}$ [22]. It is equivalent to our semantics $\langle 3, 2, +, w\rangle$ when restricted to $\mathcal{ALC}$ (and the case without negative individual assertions of the form $\neg S(a, b)$).

6 A Translation into the Traditional Semantics

In this section we give a linear translation $\pi_{\mathfrak{s}}$, for $\mathfrak{s} \in \mathfrak{S}$ with $\mathfrak{s}_\mathrm{C} \in \{3, 4\}$, $\mathfrak{s}_\mathrm{R} \in \{2, 4\}$ and $\mathfrak{s}_{\forall\exists} = +$, such that, for every knowledge base KB and every query φ, $KB \models_{\mathfrak{s}} \varphi$ iff $\pi_{\mathfrak{s}}(KB) \models \pi_{\mathfrak{s}}(\varphi)$. In this section, if not otherwise stated, we assume that $\mathfrak{s}$ satisfies the mentioned conditions.

For $A \in \mathbf{C} \setminus \mathbf{N}$, let A_+ and A_- be new concept names. For $r \in \mathbf{R} \setminus \{U\}$, let r_+ and r_- be new role names. In accordance to the semantics $\mathfrak{s}$, let $\mathbf{C}' = \{A_+, A_- \mid A \in \mathbf{C} \setminus \mathbf{N}\} \cup \mathbf{N}$, and

$$\mathbf{R}' = \begin{cases} \mathbf{R} & \text{for } \mathfrak{s}_\mathrm{R} = 2 \\ \{r_+, r_- \mid r \in \mathbf{R} \setminus \{U\}\} \cup \{U\} & \text{for } \mathfrak{s}_\mathrm{R} = 4. \end{cases}$$

We also define two auxiliary translations $\pi_{\mathfrak{s}+}$ and $\pi_{\mathfrak{s}-}$. In the following, if not otherwise stated, r, R, S, A, C, D, a, b, $\mathcal{R}$, $\mathcal{T}$, $\mathcal{A}$ are arbitrary elements of their appropriate types (according to the used convention) in the language using $\mathbf{C}$ and $\mathbf{R}$.

If $\mathfrak{s}_\mathrm{R} = 2$ then:

- $\pi_{\mathfrak{s}+}(R) \stackrel{\text{def}}{=} R$ and $\pi_{\mathfrak{s}}(\mathcal{R}) \stackrel{\text{def}}{=} \mathcal{R}$
- $\pi_{\mathfrak{s}}(R(a, b)) \stackrel{\text{def}}{=} R(a, b)$ and $\pi_{\mathfrak{s}}(\neg S(a, b)) \stackrel{\text{def}}{=} \neg S(a, b)$
- $\pi_{\mathfrak{s}+}(\exists R.\mathtt{Self}) \stackrel{\text{def}}{=} \exists R.\mathtt{Self}$ and $\pi_{\mathfrak{s}-}(\exists R.\mathtt{Self}) \stackrel{\text{def}}{=} \neg\exists R.\mathtt{Self}$.

If $\mathfrak{s}_\mathrm{R} = 4$ then:

- $\pi_{\mathfrak{s}+}(U) \stackrel{\text{def}}{=} U$
- $\pi_{\mathfrak{s}+}(r) \stackrel{\text{def}}{=} r_+$ and $\pi_{\mathfrak{s}-}(r) \stackrel{\text{def}}{=} r_-$, where $r \neq U$
- $\pi_{\mathfrak{s}+}(r^-) \stackrel{\text{def}}{=} (r_+)^-$ and $\pi_{\mathfrak{s}-}(r^-) \stackrel{\text{def}}{=} (r_-)^-$, where $r \neq U$
- for every role axiom φ, $\pi_{\mathfrak{s}}(\varphi) \stackrel{\text{def}}{=} \varphi'$, where φ' is the role axiom obtained from φ by replacing each role R by $\pi_{\mathfrak{s}+}(R)$
- $\pi_{\mathfrak{s}}(\mathcal{R}) \stackrel{\text{def}}{=} \{\pi_{\mathfrak{s}}(\varphi) \mid \varphi \in \mathcal{R}\}$
- $\pi_{\mathfrak{s}}(R(a, b)) \stackrel{\text{def}}{=} \pi_{\mathfrak{s}+}(R)(a, b)$ and $\pi_{\mathfrak{s}}(\neg S(a, b)) \stackrel{\text{def}}{=} \pi_{\mathfrak{s}-}(S)(a, b)$, for $R, S \neq U$
- $\pi_{\mathfrak{s}+}(\exists R.\mathtt{Self}) \stackrel{\text{def}}{=} \exists \pi_{\mathfrak{s}+}(R).\mathtt{Self}$ and $\pi_{\mathfrak{s}-}(\exists R.\mathtt{Self}) \stackrel{\text{def}}{=} \exists \pi_{\mathfrak{s}-}(R).\mathtt{Self}$.

$$
\begin{array}{ll}
\pi_{\mathfrak{s}+}(\top) \stackrel{\text{def}}{=} \top & \pi_{\mathfrak{s}-}(\top) \stackrel{\text{def}}{=} \bot \\
\pi_{\mathfrak{s}+}(\bot) \stackrel{\text{def}}{=} \bot & \pi_{\mathfrak{s}-}(\bot) \stackrel{\text{def}}{=} \top \\
\pi_{\mathfrak{s}+}(\neg C) \stackrel{\text{def}}{=} \pi_{\mathfrak{s}-}(C) & \pi_{\mathfrak{s}-}(\neg C) \stackrel{\text{def}}{=} \pi_{\mathfrak{s}+}(C) \\
\pi_{\mathfrak{s}+}(C \sqcap D) \stackrel{\text{def}}{=} \pi_{\mathfrak{s}+}(C) \sqcap \pi_{\mathfrak{s}+}(D) & \pi_{\mathfrak{s}-}(C \sqcap D) \stackrel{\text{def}}{=} \pi_{\mathfrak{s}-}(C) \sqcup \pi_{\mathfrak{s}-}(D) \\
\pi_{\mathfrak{s}+}(C \sqcup D) \stackrel{\text{def}}{=} \pi_{\mathfrak{s}+}(C) \sqcup \pi_{\mathfrak{s}+}(D) & \pi_{\mathfrak{s}-}(C \sqcup D) \stackrel{\text{def}}{=} \pi_{\mathfrak{s}-}(C) \sqcap \pi_{\mathfrak{s}-}(D) \\
\pi_{\mathfrak{s}+}(\forall R.C) \stackrel{\text{def}}{=} \forall \pi_{\mathfrak{s}+}(R).\pi_{\mathfrak{s}+}(C) & \pi_{\mathfrak{s}-}(\forall R.C) \stackrel{\text{def}}{=} \exists \pi_{\mathfrak{s}+}(R).\pi_{\mathfrak{s}-}(C) \\
\pi_{\mathfrak{s}+}(\exists R.C) \stackrel{\text{def}}{=} \exists \pi_{\mathfrak{s}+}(R).\pi_{\mathfrak{s}+}(C) & \pi_{\mathfrak{s}-}(\exists R.C) \stackrel{\text{def}}{=} \forall \pi_{\mathfrak{s}+}(R).\pi_{\mathfrak{s}-}(C)
\end{array}
$$

$$
\begin{aligned}
\pi_{\mathfrak{s}+}(\geq n\, R.C) &\stackrel{\text{def}}{=} \geq n\, \pi_{\mathfrak{s}+}(R).\pi_{\mathfrak{s}+}(C) \\
\pi_{\mathfrak{s}-}(\geq (n+1)\, R.C) &\stackrel{\text{def}}{=} \leq n\, \pi_{\mathfrak{s}+}(R).\neg\pi_{\mathfrak{s}-}(C) \\
\pi_{\mathfrak{s}-}(\geq 0\, R.C) &\stackrel{\text{def}}{=} \bot \\
\pi_{\mathfrak{s}+}(\leq n\, R.C) &\stackrel{\text{def}}{=} \leq n\, \pi_{\mathfrak{s}+}(R).\neg\pi_{\mathfrak{s}-}(C) \\
\pi_{\mathfrak{s}-}(\leq n\, R.C) &\stackrel{\text{def}}{=} \geq (n+1)\, \pi_{\mathfrak{s}+}(R).\pi_{\mathfrak{s}+}(C)
\end{aligned}
$$

Fig. 1. A partial specification of $\pi_{\mathfrak{s}+}$ and $\pi_{\mathfrak{s}-}$

If A is a nominal then $\pi_{\mathfrak{s}+}(A) \stackrel{\text{def}}{=} A$ and $\pi_{\mathfrak{s}-}(A) \stackrel{\text{def}}{=} \neg A$. If A is a concept name but not a nominal then $\pi_{\mathfrak{s}+}(A) \stackrel{\text{def}}{=} A_+$ and $\pi_{\mathfrak{s}-}(A) \stackrel{\text{def}}{=} A_-$.

The translations $\pi_{\mathfrak{s}+}(C)$ and $\pi_{\mathfrak{s}-}(C)$ for the case C is not of the form A or $\exists R.\texttt{Self}$ are defined as in Figure 1.

Define $\pi_{\mathfrak{s}}(C \sqsubseteq D)$ and $\pi_{\mathfrak{s}}(\mathcal{T})$ as follows:

- case $\mathfrak{s}_{\texttt{GCI}} = w$: $\pi_{\mathfrak{s}}(C \sqsubseteq D) \stackrel{\text{def}}{=} \{\top \sqsubseteq \pi_{\mathfrak{s}-}(C) \sqcup \pi_{\mathfrak{s}+}(D)\}$
- case $\mathfrak{s}_{\texttt{GCI}} = m$: $\pi_{\mathfrak{s}}(C \sqsubseteq D) \stackrel{\text{def}}{=} \{\pi_{\mathfrak{s}+}(C) \sqsubseteq \pi_{\mathfrak{s}+}(D)\}$
- case $\mathfrak{s}_{\texttt{GCI}} = s$: $\pi_{\mathfrak{s}}(C \sqsubseteq D) \stackrel{\text{def}}{=} \{\pi_{\mathfrak{s}+}(C) \sqsubseteq \pi_{\mathfrak{s}+}(D),\ \pi_{\mathfrak{s}-}(D) \sqsubseteq \pi_{\mathfrak{s}-}(C)\}$
- case $\mathfrak{s}_{\texttt{C}} = 3$: $\pi_{\mathfrak{s}}(\mathcal{T}) \stackrel{\text{def}}{=} \bigcup_{\varphi \in \mathcal{T}} \pi_{\mathfrak{s}}(\varphi) \cup \{\top \sqsubseteq A_+ \sqcup A_- \mid A \in \mathbf{C} \setminus \mathbf{N}\}$
- case $\mathfrak{s}_{\texttt{C}} = 4$: $\pi_{\mathfrak{s}}(\mathcal{T}) \stackrel{\text{def}}{=} \bigcup_{\varphi \in \mathcal{T}} \pi_{\mathfrak{s}}(\varphi)$.

Define that:

- $\pi_{\mathfrak{s}}(a \neq b) \stackrel{\text{def}}{=} a \neq b$ and $\pi_{\mathfrak{s}}(C(a)) \stackrel{\text{def}}{=} \pi_{\mathfrak{s}+}(C)(a)$
- $\pi_{\mathfrak{s}}(\mathcal{A}) \stackrel{\text{def}}{=} \{\pi_{\mathfrak{s}}(\varphi) \mid \varphi \in \mathcal{A}\}$
- $\pi_{\mathfrak{s}}(\langle \mathcal{R}, \mathcal{T}, \mathcal{A} \rangle) \stackrel{\text{def}}{=} \langle \pi_{\mathfrak{s}}(\mathcal{R}), \pi_{\mathfrak{s}}(\mathcal{T}), \pi_{\mathfrak{s}}(\mathcal{A}) \rangle$
- for a query $\varphi = \varphi_1 \wedge \ldots \wedge \varphi_k$, define $\pi_{\mathfrak{s}}(\varphi) \stackrel{\text{def}}{=} \pi_{\mathfrak{s}}(\varphi_1) \wedge \ldots \wedge \pi_{\mathfrak{s}}(\varphi_k)$.

Note that, if $\langle \mathcal{R}, \mathcal{T}, \mathcal{A} \rangle$ is a knowledge base and φ is a query in $\mathcal{SROIQ}$ using $\mathbf{C}$ and $\mathbf{R}$, then $\pi_{\mathfrak{s}}(\langle \mathcal{R}, \mathcal{T}, \mathcal{A} \rangle)$ is a knowledge base and $\pi_{\mathfrak{s}}(\varphi)$ is a query in $\mathcal{SROIQ}$ using $\mathbf{C}'$ and $\mathbf{R}'$, with the property that:

- the length of $\pi_{\mathfrak{s}}(\varphi)$ is linear in the length of φ
- the size of $\pi_{\mathfrak{s}}(\langle \mathcal{R}, \mathcal{T}, \mathcal{A}\rangle)$ is linear in the size of $\langle \mathcal{R}, \mathcal{T}, \mathcal{A}\rangle$ in the case $\mathfrak{s}_{\mathrm{C}} = 4$, and linear in the sizes of $\langle \mathcal{R}, \mathcal{T}, \mathcal{A}\rangle$ and $\mathbf{C} \setminus \mathbf{N}$ in the case $\mathfrak{s}_{\mathrm{C}} = 3$.[4]

To have a translation for the case $\mathfrak{s}_{\mathrm{R}} = 3$ one would have to allow role axioms of the form $U \sqsubseteq r \cup r'$ (for expressing $U \sqsubseteq s_+ \cup s_-$). To have a translation for the case $\mathfrak{s}_{\forall\exists} = \pm$ one would have to allow concepts of the form $\forall(\neg r).C$ (for expressing $\forall(\neg s_-).D_+$). These features fall out of $\mathcal{SROIQ}$ and that is why we do not present translation for the case $\mathfrak{s}_{\mathrm{R}} = 3$ or $\mathfrak{s}_{\forall\exists} = \pm$.

Theorem 6.1. *Let $\mathfrak{s} \in \mathfrak{S}$ be a semantics such that $\mathfrak{s}_{\mathrm{C}} \in \{3, 4\}$, $\mathfrak{s}_{\mathrm{R}} \in \{2, 4\}$ and $\mathfrak{s}_{\forall\exists} = +$. Let $\langle \mathcal{R}, \mathcal{T}, \mathcal{A}\rangle$ be a knowledge base and φ be a query in the language using $\mathbf{C}$ and $\mathbf{R}$. Then $\langle \mathcal{R}, \mathcal{T}, \mathcal{A}\rangle \models_{\mathfrak{s}} \varphi$ iff $\pi_{\mathfrak{s}}(\langle \mathcal{R}, \mathcal{T}, \mathcal{A}\rangle) \models \pi_{\mathfrak{s}}(\varphi)$.*

Proof. Consider the left to right implication and suppose that $\langle \mathcal{R}, \mathcal{T}, \mathcal{A}\rangle \models_{\mathfrak{s}} \varphi$. Let $\mathcal{I}'$ be a traditional model of $\pi_{\mathfrak{s}}(\langle \mathcal{R}, \mathcal{T}, \mathcal{A}\rangle)$ in the language using $\mathbf{C}'$ and $\mathbf{R}'$. We show that $\mathcal{I}' \models \pi_{\mathfrak{s}}(\varphi)$. Let $\mathcal{I}$ be the $\mathfrak{s}$-interpretation in the language using $\mathbf{C}$ and $\mathbf{R}$ specified as follows:

- $\Delta^{\mathcal{I}} = \Delta^{\mathcal{I}'}$
- for $A \in \mathbf{C} \setminus \mathbf{N}$, $A^{\mathcal{I}}_{+} = (A_+)^{\mathcal{I}'}$ and $A^{\mathcal{I}}_{-} = (A_-)^{\mathcal{I}'}$
- for $A \in \mathbf{N}$, $A^{\mathcal{I}}_{+} = A^{\mathcal{I}'}$ and $A^{\mathcal{I}}_{-} = \Delta^{\mathcal{I}} \setminus A^{\mathcal{I}}_{+}$
- if $\mathfrak{s}_{\mathrm{R}} = 2$ then, for $r \in \mathbf{R}$, $r^{\mathcal{I}}_{+} = r^{\mathcal{I}'}$ and $r^{\mathcal{I}}_{-} = (\Delta^{\mathcal{I}} \times \Delta^{\mathcal{I}}) \setminus r^{\mathcal{I}}_{+}$
- if $\mathfrak{s}_{\mathrm{R}} = 4$ then
  - for $r \in \mathbf{R} \setminus \{U\}$, $r^{\mathcal{I}}_{+} = (r_+)^{\mathcal{I}'}$ and $r^{\mathcal{I}}_{-} = (r_-)^{\mathcal{I}'}$
  - $U^{\mathcal{I}}_{+} = \Delta^{\mathcal{I}} \times \Delta^{\mathcal{I}}$ and $U^{\mathcal{I}}_{-} = \emptyset$
- for $a \in \mathbf{I}$, $a^{\mathcal{I}} = a^{\mathcal{I}'}$.

Observe that $\mathcal{I}$ is indeed an $\mathfrak{s}$-interpretation. It can be proved by induction on the structure of C and R that, for any concept C and role R :

- $C^{\mathcal{I}} = \langle (\pi_{\mathfrak{s}+}(C))^{\mathcal{I}'}, (\pi_{\mathfrak{s}-}(C))^{\mathcal{I}'}\rangle$
- if $\mathfrak{s}_{\mathrm{R}} = 2$ then $R^{\mathcal{I}} = \langle R^{\mathcal{I}'}, (\Delta^{\mathcal{I}} \times \Delta^{\mathcal{I}}) \setminus R^{\mathcal{I}'}\rangle$
- if $\mathfrak{s}_{\mathrm{R}} = 4$ and $R \neq U$ then $R^{\mathcal{I}} = \langle (\pi_{\mathfrak{s}+}(R))^{\mathcal{I}'}, (\pi_{\mathfrak{s}-}(R))^{\mathcal{I}'}\rangle$.

Using this and the assumption that $\mathcal{I}' \models \pi_{\mathfrak{s}}(\langle \mathcal{R}, \mathcal{T}, \mathcal{A}\rangle)$, we derive that $\mathcal{I} \models_{\mathfrak{s}} \langle \mathcal{R}, \mathcal{T}, \mathcal{A}\rangle$. Hence $\mathcal{I} \models_{\mathfrak{s}} \varphi$, and it follows that $\mathcal{I}' \models \pi_{\mathfrak{s}}(\varphi)$.

The right to left implication can be proved analogously. ◁

To check whether $\pi_{\mathfrak{s}}(\langle \mathcal{R}, \mathcal{T}, \mathcal{A}\rangle) \models \pi_{\mathfrak{s}}(\varphi)$ one can use, e.g., the tableau method given in [10]. We have the following corollary of Theorem 6.1 by taking $\varphi = \bot$.

Corollary 6.2. *Let $\mathfrak{s} \in \mathfrak{S}$ be a semantics such that $\mathfrak{s}_{\mathrm{C}} \in \{3, 4\}$, $\mathfrak{s}_{\mathrm{R}} \in \{2, 4\}$ and $\mathfrak{s}_{\forall\exists} = +$, and let $\langle \mathcal{R}, \mathcal{T}, \mathcal{A}\rangle$ be a knowledge base in the language using $\mathbf{C}$ and $\mathbf{R}$. Then $\langle \mathcal{R}, \mathcal{T}, \mathcal{A}\rangle$ is $\mathfrak{s}$-satisfiable iff $\pi_{\mathfrak{s}}(\langle \mathcal{R}, \mathcal{T}, \mathcal{A}\rangle)$ is satisfiable (w.r.t. the traditional semantics).* ◁

[4] Where the notions of length and size are defined as usual.

Example 6.3. Consider the knowledge base $KB = \langle \mathcal{R}, \mathcal{T}, \mathcal{A} \rangle$, where

$$\begin{aligned}
\mathcal{R} &= \emptyset \\
\mathcal{T} &= \{Bird \sqsubseteq Fly, \\
&\quad Penguin \sqsubseteq Bird, \\
&\quad Penguin \sqsubseteq \neg Fly\} \\
\mathcal{A} &= \{Bird(a),\ Penguin(tweety)\}.
\end{aligned}$$

Let $\mathfrak{s}$ be any semantics from $\mathfrak{S}$ with $\mathfrak{s}_C = 3$ and $\mathfrak{s}_{GCI} = m$.
We have that $\pi_{\mathfrak{s}}(KB) = KB' = \langle \emptyset, \mathcal{T}', \mathcal{A}' \rangle$, where

$$\begin{aligned}
\mathcal{T}' &= \{Bird_+ \sqsubseteq Fly_+, \\
&\quad Penguin_+ \sqsubseteq Bird_+, \\
&\quad Penguin_+ \sqsubseteq Fly_-\} \\
\mathcal{A}' &= \{Bird_+(a),\ Penguin_+(tweety)\}.
\end{aligned}$$

We also have that

$$\begin{aligned}
\pi_{\mathfrak{s}}(Bird(tweety)) &= Bird_+(tweety) \\
\pi_{\mathfrak{s}}(Fly(tweety)) &= Fly_+(tweety) \\
\pi_{\mathfrak{s}}(\neg Fly(tweety)) &= Fly_-(tweety) \\
\pi_{\mathfrak{s}}(Fly(a)) &= Fly_+(a) \\
\pi_{\mathfrak{s}}(\neg Fly(a)) &= Fly_-(a).
\end{aligned}$$

Observe that $\pi_{\mathfrak{s}}(Bird(tweety))$, $\pi_{\mathfrak{s}}(Fly(tweety))$, $\pi_{\mathfrak{s}}(\neg Fly(tweety))$ and $\pi_{\mathfrak{s}}(Fly(a))$ are logical consequences of KB' using the the traditional two-valued semantics, but $\pi_{\mathfrak{s}}(\neg Fly(a))$ is not. This implies that $Bird(tweety)$, $Fly(tweety)$, $\neg Fly(tweety)$ and $Fly(a)$ are $\mathfrak{s}$-logical consequences of KB, but $\neg Fly(a)$ is not. $\triangleleft$

7 Conclusions

$\mathcal{SROIQ}$ is a powerful DL used as the logical foundation of OWL 2. In this work, we introduced and studied a number of different paraconsistent semantics for $\mathcal{SROIQ}$ in a uniform way. We gave a translation of the problem of conjunctive query answering w.r.t. some of the considered paraconsistent semantics into a version that uses the traditional semantics. This allows one to directly use existing tools and reasoners of $\mathcal{SROIQ}$ for paraconsistent reasoning.

Note that answering queries that contain negative individual assertions of the form $\neg S(a, b)$ using a paraconsistent semantics is first studied in this work. Also note that only a four-valued paraconsistent semantics has previously been introduced for $\mathcal{SROIQ}$ [14] (without considering some important features of $\mathcal{SROIQ}$ and having conceptual problems, as shown in Section 3.2). If $\mathfrak{s}, \mathfrak{s}' \in \mathfrak{S}$ are semantics such that $\mathfrak{s} \sqsubseteq \mathfrak{s}'$ and $\mathfrak{s}'$ is weaker than the traditional semantics then, by Theorem 4.3, for the conjunctive query answering problem, $KB \models_{\mathfrak{s}'} \varphi$

approximates $KB \models \varphi$ better than $KB \models_{\mathfrak{s}} \varphi$ does. Our postulate is that, if $\mathfrak{s} \sqsubseteq \mathfrak{s}'$ and KB is $\mathfrak{s}'$-satisfiable, then it is better to use $\mathfrak{s}'$ than $\mathfrak{s}$. In particular, one should use a four-valued semantics only when the considered knowledge base is $\mathfrak{s}'$-unsatisfiable in semantics $\mathfrak{s}'$ with $\mathfrak{s}'_C = 3$. In such cases the four-valued semantics based on truth ordering proposed in [1,18,29] appears to be a better choice than the four valued semantics based on Belnap's logic [5,4]. Its adaptation to paraconsistent reasoning in the Semantic Web is, however, left for future work.

The approach of this work and [19,28,15,14,31,22] does not guarantee that all knowledge bases are satisfiable in the considered paraconsistent logic. The reason is that axioms like $\top \sqsubseteq \bot$ are not valid in any $\mathfrak{s}$-interpretation, where $\mathfrak{s} \in \mathfrak{S}$. Due to the specific meanings of the universal role U and nominals, we do not propose three- and four-semantics for them.[5] This may also cause a knowledge base KB $\mathfrak{s}$-unsatisfiable, e.g., when KB contains both individual assertions $A(a)$ and $\neg A(a)$ with $A \in \mathbf{N}$. In [22], we provided a quite general syntactic condition of safeness guaranteeing satisfiability of a knowledge base in $\mathcal{SHIQ}$ w.r.t. three-valued semantics.

To overcome the above mentioned problems one may want to define and use constructive DLs in a similar way as Odintsov and Wansing did for their constructive version of the basic DL $\mathcal{ALC}$. Extending such an approach to dealing with number restrictions $\geq nS.C$ and $\leq nS.C$ is not obvious. We leave this for future work.

Acknowledgements. This work was supported by the Polish MNiSW under Grant No. N N206 399334. The first author was supported by the National Centre for Research and Development (NCBiR) under Grant No. SP/I/1/77065/10 by the strategic scientific research and experimental development program: "Interdisciplinary System for Interactive Scientific and Scientific-Technical Information". The second author was supported by Polish National Science Centre grant 2011/01/B/ST6/02769.

References

1. Amo, S., Pais, M.S.: A paraconsistent logic approach for querying inconsistent databases. International Journal of Approximate Reasoning 46, 366–386 (2007)
2. Baader, F., Calvanese, D., McGuinness, D.L., Nardi, D., Patel-Schneider, P.F. (eds.): Description Logic Handbook. Cambridge University Press (2002)
3. Baader, F., Nutt, W.: Basic description logics. In: Baader, et al. (eds.) [2], pp. 47–100
4. Belnap, N.D.: How a computer should think. In: Ryle, G. (ed.) Contemporary Aspects of Philosophy, pp. 30–55. Oriel Press, Stocksfield (1977)
5. Belnap, N.D.: A useful four-valued logic. In: Eptein, G., Dunn, J.M. (eds.) Modern Uses of Many Valued Logic, pp. 8–37. Reidel (1977)
6. Besnard, P., Hunter, A.: Quasi-Classical Logic: Non-Trivializable Classical Reasoning from Incosistent Information. In: Froidevaux, C., Kohlas, J. (eds.) ECSQARU 1995. LNCS, vol. 946, pp. 44–51. Springer, Heidelberg (1995)

[5] The way of dealing with nominals in [14] is not appropriate.

7. Béziau, J.-Y., Carnielli, W., Gabbay, D.M. (eds.): Handbook of Paraconsistency. Logic and Cognitive Systems, vol. 9. College Publications (2007)
8. Bloesch, A.: A tableau style proof system for two paraconsistent logics. Notre Dame Journal of Formal Logic 34(2), 295–301 (1993)
9. Doherty, P., Łukaszewicz, W., Skowron, A., Szałas, A.: Knowledge Representation Techniques. A Rough Set Approach. Studies in Fuziness and Soft Computing, vol. 202. Springer, Heidelberg (2006)
10. Horrocks, I., Kutz, O., Sattler, U.: The even more irresistible $\mathcal{SROIQ}$. In: Doherty, P., Mylopoulos, J., Welty, C.A. (eds.) Proceedings of KR 2006, pp. 57–67. AAAI Press (2006)
11. Hunter, A.: Paraconsistent logics. In: Gabbay, D., Smets, P. (eds.) Handbook of Defeasible Reasoning and Uncertain Information, pp. 11–36. Kluwer (1998)
12. Hunter, A.: Reasoning with contradictory information using quasi-classical logic. J. Log. Comput. 10(5), 677–703 (2000)
13. Kleene, S.C.: Introduction to Metamathematics. D. Van Nostrand, Princeton (1952)
14. Ma, Y., Hitzler, P.: Paraconsistent Reasoning for OWL 2. In: Polleres, A., Swift, T. (eds.) RR 2009. LNCS, vol. 5837, pp. 197–211. Springer, Heidelberg (2009)
15. Ma, Y., Hitzler, P., Lin, Z.: Paraconsistent reasoning for expressive and tractable description logics. In: Proceedings of Description Logics (2008)
16. Małuszyński, J., Szałas, A.: Computational aspects of paraconsistent query language 4QL. Journal of Applied Non-classical Logics 21(2), 211–232 (2011)
17. Małuszyński, J., Szałas, A.: Living with Inconsistency and Taming Nonmonotonicity. In: Furche, T. (ed.) Datalog 2010. LNCS, vol. 6702, pp. 384–398. Springer, Heidelberg (2011)
18. Małuszyński, J., Szałas, A., Vitória, A.: Paraconsistent Logic Programs with Four-Valued Rough Sets. In: Chan, C.-C., Grzymala-Busse, J.W., Ziarko, W.P. (eds.) RSCTC 2008. LNCS (LNAI), vol. 5306, pp. 41–51. Springer, Heidelberg (2008)
19. Meghini, C., Straccia, U.: A relevance terminological logic for information retrieval. In: Proceedings of SIGIR 1996, pp. 197–205. ACM (1996)
20. Nardi, D., Brachman, R.J.: An introduction to description logics. In: Baader, et al. (eds.) [2], pp. 5–44
21. Nguyen, L.A.: Paraconsistent and Approximate Semantics for the OWL 2 Web Ontology Language. In: Szczuka, M., Kryszkiewicz, M., Ramanna, S., Jensen, R., Hu, Q. (eds.) RSCTC 2010. LNCS (LNAI), vol. 6086, pp. 710–720. Springer, Heidelberg (2010)
22. Nguyen, L.A., Szałas, A.: Three-Valued Paraconsistent Reasoning for Semantic Web Agents. In: Jędrzejowicz, P., Nguyen, N.T., Howlet, R.J., Jain, L.C. (eds.) KES-AMSTA 2010, Part I. LNCS, vol. 6070, pp. 152–162. Springer, Heidelberg (2010)
23. Nguyen, N.T.: Using distance functions to solve representation choice problems. Fundam. Inform. 48(4), 295–314 (2001)
24. Nguyen, N.T.: Consensus system for solving conflicts in distributed systems. Inf. Sci. 147(1-4), 91–122 (2002)
25. Nguyen, N.T.: Inconsistency of knowledge and collective intelligence. Cybernetics and Systems 39(6), 542–562 (2008)
26. Nguyen, N.T., Truong, H.B.: A Consensus-Based Method for Fuzzy Ontology Integration. In: Pan, J.-S., Chen, S.-M., Nguyen, N.T. (eds.) ICCCI 2010, Part II. LNCS, vol. 6422, pp. 480–489. Springer, Heidelberg (2010)
27. Odintsov, S.P., Wansing, H.: Inconsistency-tolerant description logic. part II: A tableau algorithm for $\mathrm{CACL}^{\mathrm{C}}$. Journal of Applied Logic 6(3), 343–360 (2008)

28. Straccia, U.: A Sequent Calculus for Reasoning in Four-Valued Description Logics. In: Galmiche, D. (ed.) TABLEAUX 1997. LNCS, vol. 1227, pp. 343–357. Springer, Heidelberg (1997)
29. Vitória, A., Maluszyński, J., Szałas, A.: Modeling and reasoning in paraconsistent rough sets. Fundamenta Informaticae 97(4), 405–438 (2009)
30. Zhang, X., Lin, Z., Wang, K.: Towards a Paradoxical Description Logic for the Semantic Web. In: Link, S., Prade, H. (eds.) FoIKS 2010. LNCS, vol. 5956, pp. 306–325. Springer, Heidelberg (2010)
31. Zhang, X., Qi, G., Ma, Y., Lin, Z.: Quasi-classical semantics for expressive description logics. In: Proceedings of Description Logics (2009)
32. Zhang, X., Zhang, Z., Lin, Z.: An argumentative semantics for paraconsistent reasoning in description logic ALC. In: Proceedings of Description Logics (2009)
33. Zhang, X., Zhang, Z., Xu, D., Lin, Z.: Argumentation-Based Reasoning with Inconsistent Knowledge Bases. In: Farzindar, A., Kešelj, V. (eds.) Canadian AI 2010. LNCS, vol. 6085, pp. 87–99. Springer, Heidelberg (2010)

An Agent Model for Cognitive and Affective Empathic Understanding of Other Agents*

Zulfiqar A. Memon[1,2] and Jan Treur[1]

[1] VU University Amsterdam, Agent Systems Research Group
De Boelelaan 1081, 1081 HV Amsterdam
[2] Sukkur Institute of Business Administration (Sukkur IBA)
Air Port Road Sukkur, Sindh, Pakistan
memon.zulfiqar@gmail.com, zulfiqar@iba-suk.edu.pk,
treur@few.vu.nl
http://www.iba-suk.edu.pk/ibasuk/faculty/wpZulfiqarmemon.aspx,
http://www.few.vu.nl/~treur

Abstract. This paper focuses on modelling capabilities to interpret another person's mind, taking into account both affective and cognitive states. A basic agent model to generate emotional responses and feelings in response to certain stimuli is taken as a point of departure. For the case these stimuli concern observation of another person's body state (e.g., face expressions), emotion reading is achieved, following the Simulation Theory approach to mindreading. Furthermore, by taking (internal) cognitive states instead of stimuli as a source for emotional responses, it is shown how to model the way in which a person associates feelings to cognitive states. Moreover, it is shown how another person can obtain empathic understanding of a person by simulating the way in which feelings are associated to cognitive states. The obtained agent model describes how the empathic agent deals with another agent's cognitive states and the associated feelings, thus not only understanding the other agent's cognitive state but at the same time feeling the accompanying emotion of the other agent.

Keywords: Cognitive agent model, empathic understanding, mindreading.

1 Introduction

For effective functioning within a social context, one of the most important issues is to which extent persons have a good understanding of one another. Having understanding of another person often is related to the notion of *mindreading* or having a *Theory of Mind* (ToM). This is a very wide notion, subsuming different aspects or foci of the understanding, and different methods to obtain the understanding. From an evolutionary perspective, mindreading in humans and some other kinds of animals has developed for a number of foci, for example, intention,

* Parts of the work described in this paper have been presented at the 8th IEEE/WIC/ACM International Conference on Intelligent Agent Technology (IAT'08), and at the First International Conference on Computational Collective Intelligence (ICCCI'09).

N.T. Nguyen (Ed.): Transactions on CCI VI, LNCS 7190, pp. 56–83, 2012.

attention, desire, emotion, knowing, belief; e.g., [1], [6], [9], [17], [18]). Concerning the methods used to obtain a Theory of Mind, two philosophical perspectives as described in philosophical literature are Simulation Theory and Theory Theory; e.g., [18]. In the Simulation Theory perspective it is assumed that mindreading takes place by using the facilities (for example, network of causal relations) involving the own cognitive states that are counterparts of the cognitive states attributed to the other person. In the Theory Theory perspective it is assumed that mindreading takes place by reasoning about the other person's mind without using the corresponding facilities. In [9] mindreading models from a Theory Theory perspective have been described for an agent reasoning about another agent's intentions and actions.

For humans, one of the deepest and most fundamental forms of mutual understanding is based on the notion of *empathy*; e.g., [30], [26], [41], [14], [34], [28], [29]. Originally (cf. [35]) the notion of empathy was named by the German word 'einfühlung' which could be translated as 'feeling into'; e.g., [41]. As this word indicates more explicitly, the notion has a strong relation to feeling: *empathic understanding* is a form of understanding which includes (but is not limited to) feeling what the other person feels. This paper not only addresses how a person can be modelled that is able to perform mindreading, but also to have empathic understanding of other persons. A particular challenge here is how to enrich understanding of any cognitive state (such as an attention, belief, desire or intention state) of another person to a form of understanding of this state which includes feeling the same associated emotion as the other person.

One ingredient of the approach developed is a generalisation of Damasio's concept of *body loop* as put forward in [12], [13] and formalised in [8]. This perspective distinguishes the (bodily) emotional response to a stimulus from feeling the emotion, which is caused by sensing the own bodily response. An extension of this idea was obtained by assuming that the body loop is not processed once, as a linear causal chain starting with the stimulus and via the body loop ending up in the feeling, as assumed in [12], [13], [8]. Instead, in [37] a *recursive body loop* was introduced: a converging positive feedback loop based on reciprocal causation between feeling state (with gradually more feeling) and preparation for a body state (with gradually stronger expression). Triggered by a stimulus, after a number of rounds this loop ends up in an equilibrium for both states. Such a recursive loop resolves the wellknown dilemma whether emotions felt cause the prepared response, or, the other way around, the prepared response cause emotions felt. The agent model based on a recursive body loop takes a dynamical system perspective (e.g., [40]) and assumes reciprocal causation.

Two other ingredients that were adopted are the *Simulation Theory* perspective on mindreading (e.g., [18]), and recent neurological findings on preparation neurons with a *mirroring function* (e.g., [27], [39], [45], [43], [44], [46], [48]). As already pointed out above, the Simulation Theory perspective on mindreading assumes that mindreading that focuses on certain mental states and causal network of an observed agent makes use of the same mental states and causal network within the observing agent. The mirroring function of preparation neurons is that they are not only active when a person performs some specific action, but also when he or she observes another person performing the same action.

A nontrivial obstacle for the Simulation Theory perspective on mindreading is what can be called the *reverse causation paradox*. This paradox originates from the often made assumption that the causal relations used by the observed person flow from mental states to actions and body states, whereas the latter is what the observing agent observes. As within the observing agent this observation is the starting point for the simulation process to determine the observed person's mental states, this would be against the direction of the causal relations used. In [18], [21] this paradox was one of the issues encountered. It turns out that to resolve this paradox, a recursive body loop model as exploited here, with its underlying circular causal network involving both the observable body states and the mental states, is an appropriate basis. It provides models for emotion reading and empathic understanding from the Simulation Theory perspective, using the same causal relations in both the observed and observing agent.

In this paper, first the notions of mindreading and empathic understanding are clarified and positioned (Section 2), and the three main ingredients used as a point of departure are briefly introduced: recursive body loops, the Simulation Theory perspective on mindreading, and the mirroring function of preparation neurons (Section 3). In Section 4 the basic agent model for emotion generation based on a recursive body loop, used as a point of departure, is described. Incorporating a mirroring function in preparation states it is shown how this model can be used to model emotion reading from the Simulation Theory perspective. In Section 5 the agent model for empathic understanding is introduced and as an illustration some simulation results for a relatively simple case study are discussed. Section 6 presents a mathematical analysis of the equilibria of the model, which confirms the outcomes of the simulations. Finally, Section 7 is a discussion.

2 On Empathic Understanding

An observed agent's states can have different types of impact on an observing agent's states. In the literature some of these are called empathy. Other examples of such mutual impact are (emotion) contagion and mindreading. In this section the positioning of such types of impact is clarified, and a conceptualisation of empathy as a specific type of impact is provided. In the literature, empathy is described in different manners:

- The ability to put oneself into the mental shoes of another person to understand his or her emotions and feelings [19]
- A complex form of psychological inference in which observation, memory, knowledge, and reasoning are combined to yield insights into the thoughts and feelings of others [30]
- An affective response more appropriate to someone else's situation than to one's own [26]
- An affective response that stems from the apprehension or comprehension of another's emotional state or condition, and which is similar to what the other person is feeling or would be expected to feel in the given situation [16]

- Four criteria of empathy are: (1) presence of an affective state in a person, (2) isomorphism of the person's own and the other person's affective state, (3) elicitation of the person's affective state upon observation or imagination of the other person's affective state, (4) knowledge of the person that the other person's affective state is the source of the person's own affective state ([15], p. 435; [47], p. 974)

Recurring aspects in such descriptions are on the one hand understanding, knowing, having insight in, apprehension or comprehension, and on the other hand feeling the feeling state of the other person. Here the state of the other person may involve emotions felt and/or cognitive states of the person. For the sake of simplicity, below notions such as understanding, having insight in, apprehension, comprehension, are indicated as *understanding*. For example, a person may understand but not feel an emotion felt by another person, or a person may feel but not understand an emotion felt by another person. The latter case means that the person has an emotional activation but does not recognize or label it, like it may happen with the person's own emotional responses (this is a form of emotion contagion). This use of the word understanding (or lack thereof) does not refer to 'knowing why', i.e., the reasons or causes, which is a more enhanced form of understanding.

These distinctions can be used more generally to obtain a form of classification of different types of mindreading that are possible. More specifically, mindreading can address three types of states of an observed person:

(a) Emotions felt by the person
(b) Cognitive states (e.g., attention states, desire, intention, belief states)
(c) Both emotion states and cognitive states

Moreover, this not only applies to a person who is observed but also to a person performing the observing. In particular, a person can understand or feel another person's state, or both. Given this, mindreading of another person's state can take three forms:

(1) Feeling the state of another person without understanding it
(2) Understanding the state of another person without feeling it
(3) Both understanding and feeling the state of another person

As the other person's state may involve emotions felt and/or cognitive states, the combination of these provides the matrix of possibilities as shown in Table 1.

Here row (1) covers *contagion* cases in which by the observed agent feelings within the observing agent are generated, but the observing agent only feels them and has no understanding of the states of the observed agent and their relation to the observing agent's feelings. For example, the possibility indicated as type (1a), 'feeling but not understanding another person's emotion', is a case of *emotion contagion* as often occurs in the interaction between persons (e.g., [23]). Here the emotion felt by one person is only mirrored in the emotion felt in the other person. Some may describe this as a form of (emotional) empathy, but below the standard for the concept empathy will be put a bit higher.

Table 1. Different types of mutual impact of agent states

Observed person ***Observing person***	*Other person's emotions felt* (a)	*Other person's cognitive states* (b)	*Other person's emotions felt and cognitive states* (c)
Feeling but not understanding (1)	Feeling but not understanding another person's emotion	Feeling but not understanding another person's belief, desire, intention, attention, …	Feeling but not understanding another person's emotions and cognitive states
Understanding but not feeling (2)	Understanding but not feeling another person's emotion	Understanding but not feeling another person's belief, desire, intention, attention, …	Understanding but not feeling another person's emotions and cognitive states
Both understanding and feeling (3)	Understanding and feeling another person's emotion	Understanding and feeling another person's belief, desire, intention, attention, …	Understanding and feeling another person's emotions and cognitive states

In Table 1, row (2) covers cases where the observing person understands certain states of the observed person but does not feel anything in relation to that. These can be considered cases of *mindreading*. A specific case is type (2c): 'understanding but not feeling another person's emotions and cognitive states'. This is a case that is often assumed to occur in psychopaths who have well-developed skills in mindreading and apply them to their victims thereby serving their own interest, but do not mirror the feelings of their victims (cf. [42], pp. 159-165; [5]). Yet other specific cases are type (2b) which subsumes classicical cases described by the Theory Theory perspective on mindreading (e.g., [18], [9]), and type (2a) that subsumes approaches based on dedicated emotion recognition methods, for example, from facial expressions; e.g., [38].

Within the literature, cases that fall in row (3) of Table 1 are often related to empathy; therefore this row (3) is considered here as a most general or *weak notion of empathy*. Some of the descriptions of the notion of empathy (e.g., in the informal approaches from [19], [26], [16], quoted above) concentrate on feelings and mirroring them, which can be described as being of type (3a), although sometimes more emphasis is on feeling than on understanding; without understanding it would be of type (1a) which in fact is considered here emotion contagion and not empathy. In ([15], p. 435), and ([47], p. 974) four criteria of empathy are used: (1) presence of an affective state in a person, (2) isomorphism of the person's own and the other person's affective state, (3) elicitation of the person's affective state upon observation or imagination of the other person's affective state, (4) knowledge of the person that the other person's affective state is the source of the person's own affective state. As only affective states are considered, this also classifies as type (3a), or emotional empathy. The basic agent model for emotion reading from a Simulation Theory perspective described in Section 4 and used as a starting point for the agent model introduced in Section 5 is also of type (3a).

In addition to feelings, other descriptions in the literature explicitly involve thoughts as well, of both the observed and observing person (e.g., [30]), which makes them subsumed by type (3c). This type (3c) can be considered as the *strong notion of empathy*. In Section 5 below this more extended (and challenging) notion of empathy is taken as the aim for the agent model introduced. Here an extra aspect is that feelings and cognitive states are interrelated: usually any cognitive state of a person (for example, a belief, desire, intention or attention state) induces or goes together with a certain emotion state. For example, a belief that something bad is to happen, may relate to feeling fear, or the belief that something good has happened may relate to feeling happiness. Another example of such a relationship is the role of cognitive elements (for example, certain thoughts) in the development, persistence and recurrence of mood disorders such as depressions; e.g., [31].

3 Recursive Body Loops, Mirroring and Simulation Theory

In this section the three main ingredients used are briefly introduced: recursive body loops, the mirroring function of preparation states, and the Simulation Theory perspective on mindreading.

3.1 Recursive Body Loops

The approach developed here adopts from [12], [13] the idea of a 'body loop' and 'as if body loop', in a recursive form. According to the original idea, a body loop roughly proceeds according to the following causal chain; see [12], [13], [8]:

> sensing a stimulus → sensory representation of stimulus → preparation for bodily response → sensing the body modification → sensory representation of the body modification → feeling

In the approach taken as a point of departure here (adopted from [37]) an essential addition is that the body loop (or as if body loop) is extended to a *recursive body loop* (or *recursive as if body loop*) by assuming that the preparation of the bodily response is also affected by the state of feeling:

> feeling → preparation for bodily response

as an additional causal relation. Such recursiveness is also assumed by [13], as he notices that what is felt by sensing is actually a body state which is an internal object, under control of the person:

> 'The brain has a direct means to respond to the object as feelings unfold because the object at the origin is inside the body, rather than external to it. The brain can act directly on the very object it is perceiving. It can do so by modifying the state of the object, or by altering the transmission of signals from it. The object at the origin on the one hand, and the brain map of that object on the other, can influence each other in a sort of reverberative process that is not to be found, for example, in the perception of an external object.' (...) 'In other words, feelings are not a passive perception or a flash in time, especially not in the case of feelings of joy and sorrow. For a while after an occasion of such feelings begins – for seconds or for minutes – there is a dynamic

engagement of the body, almost certainly in a repeated fashion, and a subsequent dynamic variation of the perception. We perceive a series of transitions. We sense an interplay, a give and take.' ([13], pp. 91-92)

Thus the obtained model is based on reciprocal causation relations between feeling and (preparations for) body states, as roughly shown in Fig. 1.

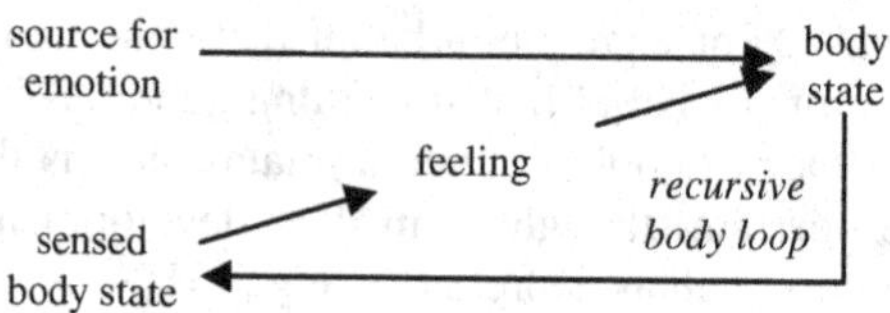

Fig. 1. Recursive body loop induced by a source for emotion (external stimulus or internal cognitive state)

Here the source of the emotion can be an external stimulus as in the causal chain described above, but, as further discussed below, also any internal cognitive state. In the approach presented here both the bodily response and the feeling are assigned a level or gradation, expressed by a number, which is assumed dynamic. The causal cycle is modelled as a positive feedback loop, triggered by the stimulus and converging to a certain level of feeling and body state preparation. Here in each round of the cycle the next body state preparation has a level that is affected by both the levels of the stimulus and the feeling state, and the next level of the feeling is based on the level of the body state preparation. In the more detailed model described in Sections 4 and 5 below, the combined effect of the levels of the stimulus and the emotional state on the body state is modelled as a weighted sum (with equal weights).

A question that may arise from the distinctions made in Section 2 is whether it is possible to feel a state of another person which by itself is not a feeling, for example, a belief state. An answer to this involves the way in which any cognitive state in a person induces emotions felt within this person, as described by Damasio ([12], [13]); e.g.:

'Even when we somewhat misuse the notion of feeling – as in "I feel I am right about this" or "I feel I cannot agree with you" – we are referring, at least vaguely, to the feeling that accompanies the idea of believing a certain fact or endorsing a certain view. This is because believing and endorsing *cause* a certain emotion to happen. As far as I can fathom, few if any exceptions of any object or event, actually present or recalled from memory, are ever neutral in emotional terms. Through either innate design or by learning, we react to most, perhaps all, objects with emotions, however weak, and subsequent feelings, however feeble.' ([13], p. 93)

From this perspective, if any cognitive state of an observed person is mirrored within an observing person, by an (assumingly) similar mechanism the feeling associated to that cognitive state can be generated within the observing person as well. In principle, this can even happen for the case where the observed person has a damaged neural structure causing that this associated feeling is not generated. In this case the observing person can feel the other person's state, whereas the person him or herself does not feel it. For example, if such a person believes he or she has won a lottery, he or she may not feel happiness about it, whereas an observing agent may mirror such a belief and based on that may generate the accompanying feeling of happiness. In some more detail, for this situation emotion generation via a body loop roughly proceeds according to the following causal chain; see [12], [13]:

having a cognitive state → preparation for the induced bodily response → induced body modification → sensing the body modification → sensory representation of the body modification → feeling

Again, as a variation, an 'as if body loop' uses a direct causal relation from preparation to sensory representation of body state, as a shortcut in the causal chain, and the body loop (or as if body loop) is extended to a recursive (as if) body loop by adding an additional causal relation from the state of feeling to the preparation of the bodily response.

3.2 The Mirroring Function of Preparation States

The idea of a recursive body loop combines quite well with recent neurological findings on mirror neurons (e.g., [27], [39], [43], [46]). Mirror neurons are preparation neurons with a special additional function, called a *mirroring function*: they are active not only when a person performs a specific action, but also when the person observes somebody else performing this action. For example, there is strong evidence that (already from an age of 1 hour) sensing somebody else's face expression leads (within about 300 milliseconds) to preparing for and showing the same face expression ([18], pp. 129-130).

The idea is that these neurons play an important role in social functioning and in (empathic) understanding of others; (e.g., [27], [46]). The discovery of mirror neurons is considered a crucial step for the further development of the discipline of social cognition, comparable to the role the discovery of DNA has played for biology, as it provides a neurological basis for many social phenomena; cf. [27].

Combined with the perspective of a recursive body loop, the mirroring function of preparation neurons provides an additional ingredient that explains how an observed emotional response of another person (via the person's body state; e.g., a face expression), via the activation of preparation for the same response within the observing person due to its mirroring function, triggers the recursive body loop which subsequently leads to a corresponding feeling within the observing person.

3.3 The Simulation Theory Perspective on Mindreading

The idea of a body loop together with the mindreading function of preparation states forms an adequate basis for modelling mindreading from the Simulation Theory perspective in philosophy (e.g., [18]). The Simulation Theory perspective assumes that mindreading uses the network of causal relations involving the own cognitive states that are counterparts of the cognitive states attributed to the other person. For example, the state of feeling pain oneself is used in the process to determine whether the other person has pain. This means that the own network is used to simulate the process of the other person; a similar simulation perspective can be used to explain imagination; see [24].

In contrast, the Theory Theory perspective is based on reasoning using knowledge about relationships between cognitive states and observed behaviour. An example of such a pattern based on causal knowledge of the observing person about the observed person is: 'I hear that she says 'ouch!'. I know that having pain causes saying 'ouch!'. Therefore she has pain'.

In ([18], pp. 124-132), a number of possible informal emotion reading models from the Simulation Theory perspective are sketched and discussed. When a mental state is assumed to cause the observed person's body states and actions, and observing the latter is the starting point, a main challenge to be addressed is to solve what can be called the *paradox of reverse causation*: how to simulate a process which in principle has the reverse order compared to the causal relations used in the simulation.

For his model 1, to resolve this paradox, a 'generate and test process' for emotional states was assumed, where on the basis of a hypothesized emotional state an own facial expression is generated, and this is compared to the observed facial expression of the other person. In the assessment of this model, the unspecified hypothesis generation process for a given observed face was considered as a less satisfactory aspect. Models 2 and 3 discussed in [18] are based on a notion of what he called 'reverse simulation'. This means that for the causal relation from emotional state to (the preparation of) a facial expression which is used to generate the own facial expressions, also a reverse relation from prepared own facial expression to emotional state is assumed, which is used for the mind reading process. A point of discussion concerning these two models is that it is difficult to fit them to the Simulation Theory perspective: whereas the emotional states and facial expression (preparation) states used for mindreading are the same as used for the own emotions and facial expressions, the causal relations between them used in the two cases are not the same. Model 4 is based on a so-called 'mirroring process', where a correlation between the emotional state of the other person and the corresponding own emotional state is assumed, based on a certain causal chain between the two. However, the relation of such a causal chain with the causal relations used to generate the own emotional states and facial expressions is not made clear, so it is still hard to claim that it fits in the Simulation Theory perspective.

The approach adopted from [37] in the current paper has drawn some inspiration from the four models sketched (but not formalised) in [18], as briefly discussed above. The recursive body loop (or as if body loop) introduced here addresses the problems of model 1, as it can be viewed as an efficient and converging way of generating and testing hypotheses for the emotional states, where the (as if) body loop takes care of the generation process. Moreover, it solves the problems of models 2 and 3, as the causal chain used from facial expression to emotional state is not a reverse simulation, but just the circular causal chain (body loop) via the body state which is used for generating the own responses and feeling states as well. Finally, compared to model 4, the models put forward here can be viewed as an efficient manner to obtain a mirroring process between the emotional state of the other person on the own emotional state, based on the machinery available for the own emotional states.

A mental process within the observing person based on a recursive body loop and a mirroring function of preparation states can be used as a form of simulation of the mental process within the observed person, and therefore coheres well with the Simulation Theory perspective on mindreading. Thus the combination of ideas briefly discussed in this section (recursive body loop, mirroring function of preparation neurons, and Simulation Theory) fits together quite well and forms the basis of the modelling approach presented here.

4 A Basic Agent Model for Emotion Generation and Imputation

In this section a basic agent model to generate emotions and feeling for a given stimulus is introduced. This model is a dynamical system style model (e.g., Port and van Gelder, 1995) and was adopted from [37] and can be classified as being of type (3a) in Table 1. The agent model is based on the Simulation Theory perspective (e.g., [18]), and is inspired by recent neurological findings on mirror neurons (e.g., [27]). It is shown how in this model the emotion felt by an observed person is mirrored in the observing person and can be imputed by the observing person to the observed person.

In the description of the detailed agent model the temporal relation a → b denotes that when a state property a occurs, then after a certain time delay (which for each relation instance can be specified as any positive real number), state property b will occur. In this hybrid dynamical modelling language (called LEADSTO) both logical and numerical (dynamical systems) calculations can be specified, and a dedicated software environment is available to support specification and simulation; for more details see [7]).

First a general agent model is discussed of the case where any stimulus leads to an induced emotional response which is felt, and imputed to the stimulus. Next it is discussed how, when this stimulus is an observed body state (for example, a face expression) of another person expressing that person's emotion, then the same emotion is felt by the observing person and imputed to this person.

4.1 Generating Emotional Responses and Feelings by a Recursive Body Loop

The specification (both informally and formally) of the model for emotion generation based on a recursive body loop is as follows, as also shown by arrows between nodes in Fig. 2; here labels LP1, … at the arrows refer to local properties specified below in detail. Capitals are used for variables and lower case letters for instances. First a general pattern from world states to sensory representations of them is described. Note that it is assumed that only the observable part of the world is included in the model.

LP1 Sensing a world state
If world state property *W* occurs of level *V*
then a sensor state for *W* of level *V* will occur.
world_state(W, V) ↠ sensor_state(W, V)

LP2 Generating a sensory representation for a sensed world state
If a sensor state for world state property *W* with level *V* occurs,
then a sensory representation for *W* with level *V* will occur.
sensor_state(W, V) ↠ srs(W, V)

The above two properties are assumed to hold for all instances of the variables *W* and *V*. In contrast, note that the following property applies to a specific instance *s* and a specific instance *b*, which indicates the emotional response to this specific *s*.

LP3 From sensory representation and feeling to preparation
If a sensory representation for *s* occurs with level *1*
and body state *b* is felt with level *V*,
then preparation state for body state *b* will occur with level *(1+V)/2*.
srs(s, 1) & feeling(b, V) ↠ preparation_state(b, (1+V)/2)

Note that here the impact of the sensory representation of s (assumed to have level *1*) and the feeling of b (level *V*) is combined, expressed as *(1+V)/2*. Next the general recursive body loop is modelled, by properties LP4 to LP8 as follows. These properties are assumed to hold for all instances of the variables *B* and *V*.

LP4 From preparation to body modification
If preparation state for body state *B* occurs with level *V*,
then the body state is modified to express *B* with level *V*.
preparation_state(B, V) ↠ effector_state(B, V)

LP5 From body modification to modified body
If the body state is modified to express *B* with level *V*,
then the body state will have expression *B* with level *V*.
effector_state(B, V) ↠ body_state(B, V)

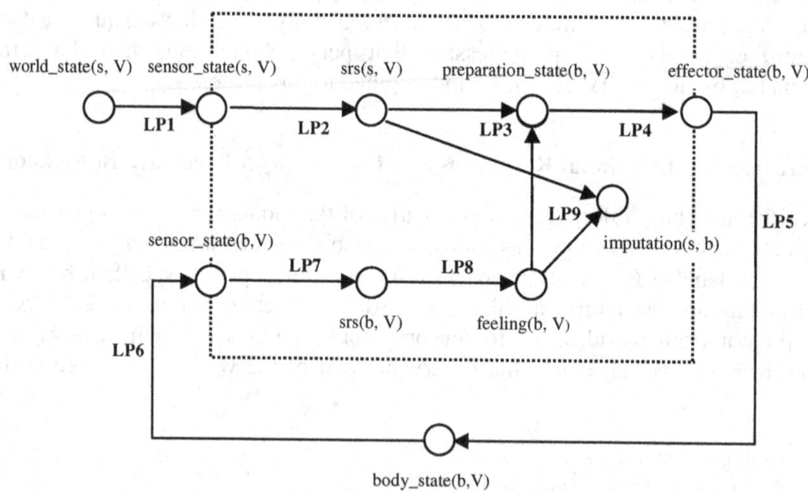

Fig. 2. Agent model for emotion generation and imputation

LP6 Sensing a body state
If body state *B* with level V occurs,
then this body state is sensed.
body_state(B, V) → sensor_state(B, V)

LP7 Generating a sensory representation of a body state
If body state *B* of level *V* is sensed,
then a sensory representation for body state *B* with level *V* will occur.
sensor_state(B, V) → srs(B, V)

LP8 From sensory representation of body state to feeling
If a sensory representation for body state *B* with level *V* occurs,
then *B* is felt with level *V*.
srs(B, V) → feeling(B, V)

In the imputation state, the emotion b felt, is related to the stimulus s, that triggered the emotion generation process. Note that this state makes sense in general, for any type of stimulus s, as usually a person does not only feel an emotion, but also has an awareness of what causes an emotion; what in (Damasio, 1999) is called a state of conscious feeling also plays this role.

LP9 Imputation
If a certain emotion *b* is felt, with level $V \geq 0.5$ and a sensory representation for *s* occurs,
then emotion *b* will imputed to *s*.
srs(s, 1) & feeling(Bb, V) & V≥0.5 → imputation(s, b)

4.2 Incorporating a Mirroring Function to Enable Simulation and Mindreading

An agent model for emotion reading from the Simulation Theory perspective should essentially be based on a model to generate the own emotions. Indeed, the model presented in the previous section can be used in a quite straightforward manner to enable emotion reading. The main step is that the stimulus s that triggers the emotional process, which until now was left open, is instantiated with the body state of another person, to make it specific, a face expression f of another person is considered: s = othersface(f). Based on the assumption that a preparation state (for a similar own face expression) exists that by some connection is triggered by this observation, the model described above will immediately start to perform simulation of the observed person's internal process, and through this performs mindreading. The assumption that such a connection between an observed face expression and preparation for a similar own face expression exists (either innate or resulting from learning) has found a wide support in the literature, starting, for example, from very young children responding to a smile of their parents by their own smile; see also (Iacoboni, 2008).

Using the model, a number of simulations have been performed; for an example, see Fig. 3 (here the time delays within the temporal LEADSTO relations were taken 1 time unit). In this figure, where time is on the horizontal axis, the upper part shows the time periods in which the binary logical state properties world_state(s), sensor_state(s), srs(s), imputation(s, f) hold (indicated by the dark lines): respectively from time point 0, 1, 2 and 9. Below this part for the other state properties values for the different time periods are shown (by the dark lines). For example, the preparation state for f has value *0.5* at time point 3, which is increased to *0.75* and further at time point 9 and further. The graphs show how the recursive body loop approximates converging states both for feeling and face expression: value *1* for both.

The model extended by the above two temporal relations in LEADSTO format, was used for simulation as well. An example simulation trace was obtained that for a large part coincides with the one shown in Fig. 2 (with the other person's face expression f as the stimulus), with an extension as shown in Fig. 4. Here also the time delays within the additional temporal LEADSTO relations were taken one time unit. Where relevant, initial values were taken *0*.

Furthermore, for the sake of illustration, following the emotion imputation, a communication about it is prepared and performed. This extension is not essential for the emotion reading capability, but shows an example of behavior based on emotion reading.

LP10 Communication preparation
If emotion *B* is imputed to *S*,
then a related communication is prepared
imputation(B, S) →→ preparation_state(say(your emotion is B))

LP11 Communication
If a communication is prepared,
then this communication will be performed.
preparation_state(say(your emotion is B)) →→ effector_state(say(your emotion is B))

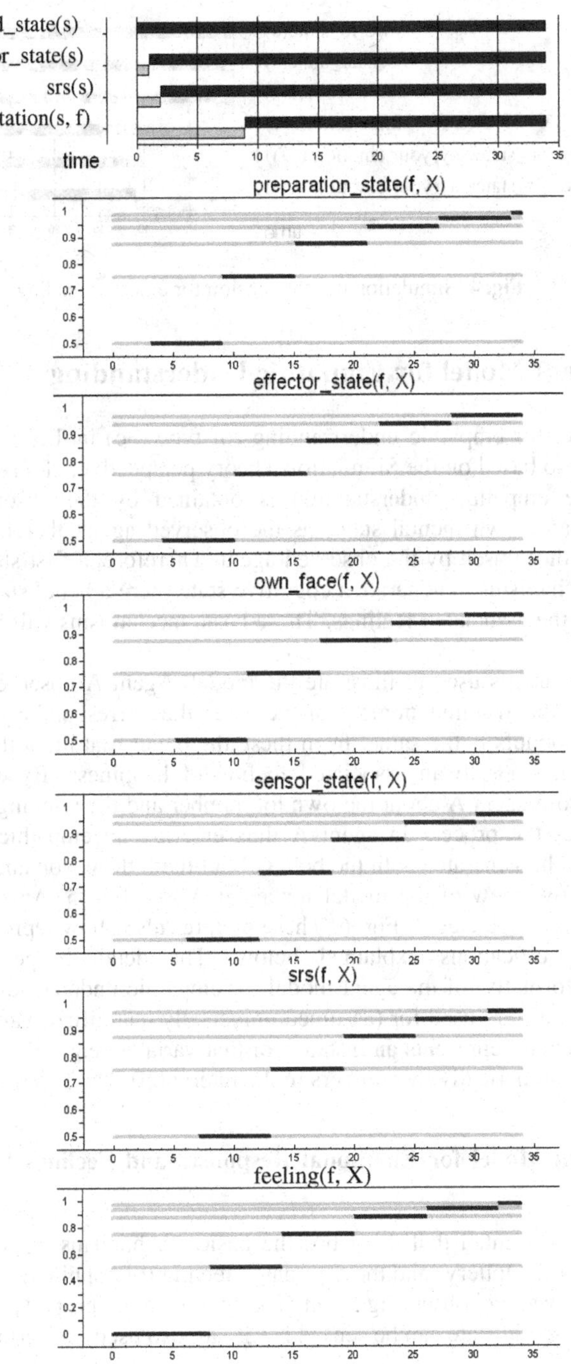

Fig. 3. Simulation trace for emotional responses and feelings based on a recursive body loop

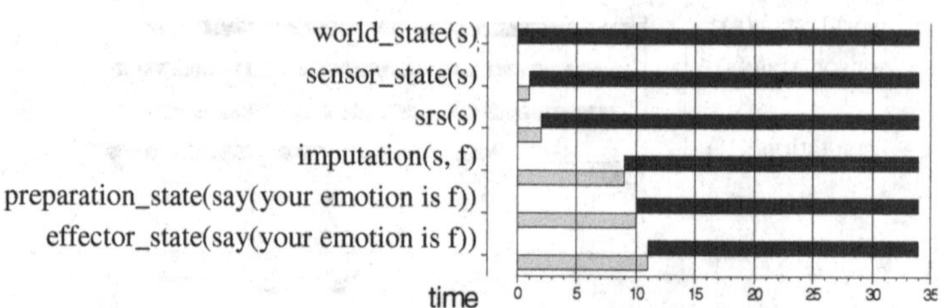

Fig. 4. Simulation trace extension for emotion reading

5 An Agent Model for Empathic Understanding

The agent model for empathic understanding (of type (3c) in Table 1) presented in this section is also based on the Simulation Theory perspective; cf. [18]. According to this perspective empathic understanding is obtained by the observing agent by activating the same own mental states as the observed agent, thereby using similar mechanisms as those used by the observed agent. Therefore, a first step is the design of the basic mechanisms to generate a cognitive state (here a belief state was chosen), and to generate the associated feelings. These basic mechanisms will be used by both agents.

A lottery scenario is used to illustrate the model. Agent A observes both his own lot number and the winning number and creates the corresponding beliefs; as the number in both beliefs is the same, from these the belief that the lottery was won is generated, which leads to an associated feeling of happiness. By communication, agent B hears from agent A about the own lot number and the winning number. From this he simulates the process in agent A thus entering an empathic understanding process in which he generates both the belief about the lottery won and the associated feeling. For an overview of the model for agent A, see Fig. 5. An overview of the model of agent B is depicted in Fig. 6. These pictures also show representations from the detailed specifications explained below. The detailed specification (both informally and formally) of the agent model for empathic understanding is presented below. Here capitals are used for (assumed universally quantified) variables, e.g. 'B', whereas small letters represents an instance of that variable, e.g. 'b'. All aspects have been formalized numerically by numbers in the interval [0, 1].

5.1 An Agent Model for Emotional Responses and Feelings for the Lottery Case

First the part is presented that describes the basic mechanisms to generate a belief state (on winning the lottery) and the associated feeling (of happiness). These are used by both the observed and observing agent. The first dynamic property addressing how properties of the world state can be sensed is LP1 as also used in Section 4.

LP1 Sensing a world state
If world state property *W* occurs of level *V*
then a sensor state for *W* of level *V* will occur.
world_state(W, V) →→ sensor_state(W, V)

For this case this dynamic property is used by agent A to observe both the own number and the winning number (see Fig. 5); to this end the variable W is instantiated by own_number(x) and winning_number(x). Note that communications are also considered world facts; LP1 is used by agent B by instantiating W for communications indicated as communicated_by_to(I, agentA, agentB). From this sensory representations and beliefs are generated according to the next two dynamic properties LP2 and LP3. Note that also for these the variable W is instantiated as before. By LP2 a sensory representation is created.

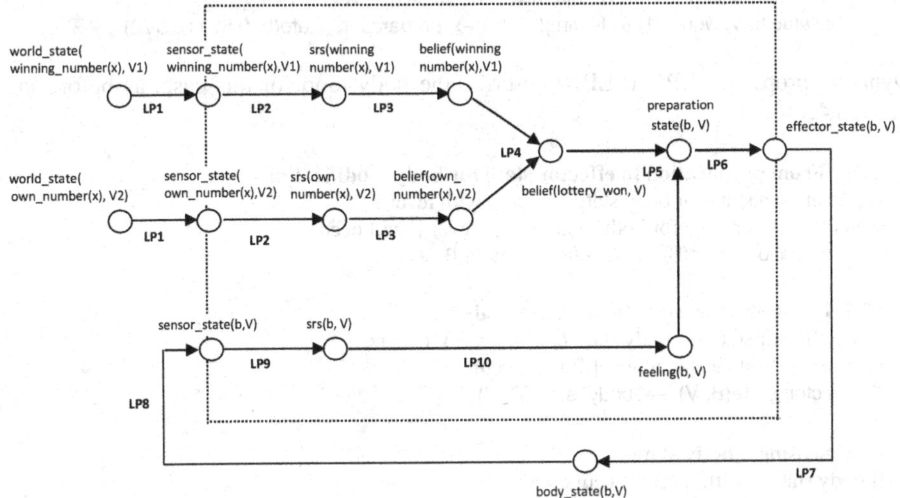

Fig. 5. Overview of the agent model for the observed person A

The generation of beliefs based on observations goes via a sensory representation as follows.

LP2 Generating a sensory representation for a sensed world state
If a sensor state for world state property *W* with level *V* occurs,
then a sensory representation for *W* with level *V* will occur.
sensor_state(W, V) →→ srs(W, V)

LP3 Generating a belief state for a sensory representation
If a sensory representation for *W* with level *V* occurs,
then a belief for *W* with level *V* will occur.
srs(W, V) →→ belief(W, V)

Dynamic property LP4 describes how the beliefs based on observations are used to infer a belief that the lottery was won.

LP4 Generating a belief on winning the lottery
If a belief with level *V1* occurs that *X* is the main price winning number of the lottery and a belief with level *V2* occurs that *X* is the number of the own lot then a belief with level *0.5V1+0.5V2* will occur that the main price of the lottery was won
belief(winning_number(X), V1) & belief(own_number(X), V2) → belief(lottery_won, 0.5V1+0.5V2)

The emotional response to this belief is the preparation for a specific bodily reaction b, as expressed in dynamic property LP5.

LP5 From belief that lottery was won and feeling to preparation of a specific body state
If a belief that the lottery was won with level *V1* occurs and feeling body state b has level *V2*, then preparation state for body state *b* will occur with level *0.5V1+0.5V2*.
belief(lottery_won, V1) & feeling(b, V2) → preparation_state(b, 0.5V1+0.5V2)

Dynamic properties LP6 to LP10 describe the body loop for this case, as before in Section 4.

LP6 From preparation to effector state for body modification
If preparation state for body state *B* occurs with level *V*,
then the effector state for body state *B* with level *V* will occur.
preparation_state(B, V) → effector_state(B, V)

LP7 From effector state to modified body
If the effector state for body state *B* with level *V* occurs,
then the body state *B* with level *V* will occur.
effector_state(B, V) → body_state(B, V)

LP8 Sensing a body state
If body state *B* with level *V* occurs,
then this body state *B* with level *V* will be sensed.
body_state(B, V) → sensor_state(B, V)

LP9 Generating a sensory representation of a body state
If body state *B* with level *V* is sensed,
then a sensory representation for body state *B* with level *V* will occur.
sensor_state(B, V) → srs(B, V)

LP10 From sensory representation of body state to feeling
If a sensory representation for body state *B* with level *V* occurs,
then *B* is felt with level *V*.
srs(B, V) → feeling(B, V)

5.2 An Agent Model for Empathic Understanding for the Lottery Case

Above the part of the model was shown that is used by both the observed and observing agent. Next the part of the model is discussed that is particularly involved in the empathic understanding process. This part of the model is used within the observing agent; see Fig. 6. First the communication from the other agent is related to the own beliefs.

LP11 Affecting own beliefs by communicated information
If in agent B a sensory representation with level *V* occurs that agent A communicated world fact *W*, then a belief with level *V* for this world fact will occur.

srs(communicated_by_to (W, agentA, agentB), V) → belief(W, V)

Next it is shown how the imputation process takes place for a belief. Here, *th* is a (constant) threshold for imputation. In the simulations shown, th is assumed 0.95 as an example.

LP12 Imputation of a belief
If a belief that the lottery was won with level $V1 \geq th$ occurs
and a belief occurs with level $V2 \geq th$ that the own number was communicated by agentA,
and a belief occurs with level $V3 \geq th$ that the winning number was communicated by agentA,
then the belief that the lottery was won will imputed.

belief(lottery_won, V1) &
belief(communicated_by_to(own_number(X1), agentA, agentB), V2) &
belief(communicated_by_to(winning_number(X2), agentA, agentB), V3) &
V1≥th & V2≥th & V3≥th
→ imputation(belief(lottery_won), agentA)

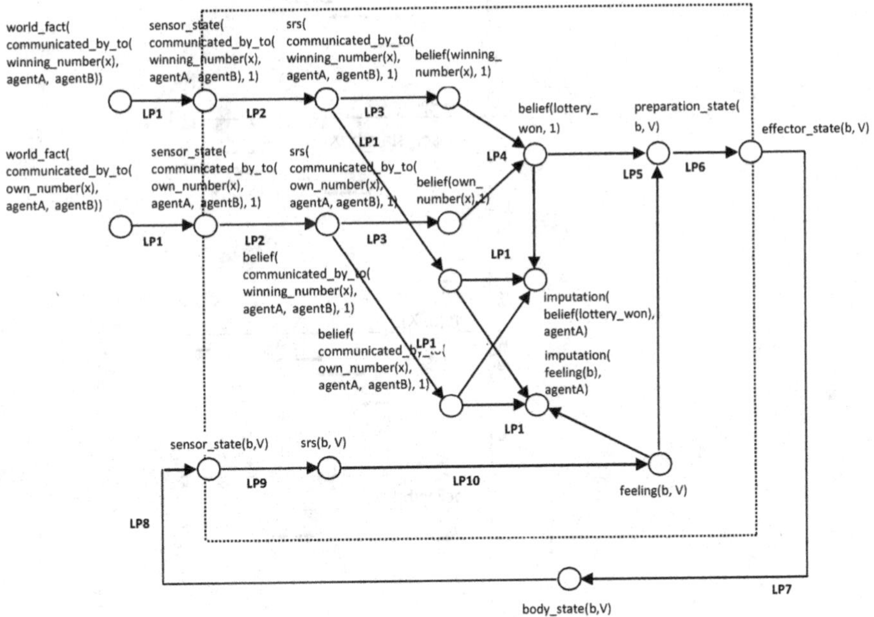

Fig. 6. Overview of the agent model for empathic understanding by the observing person B

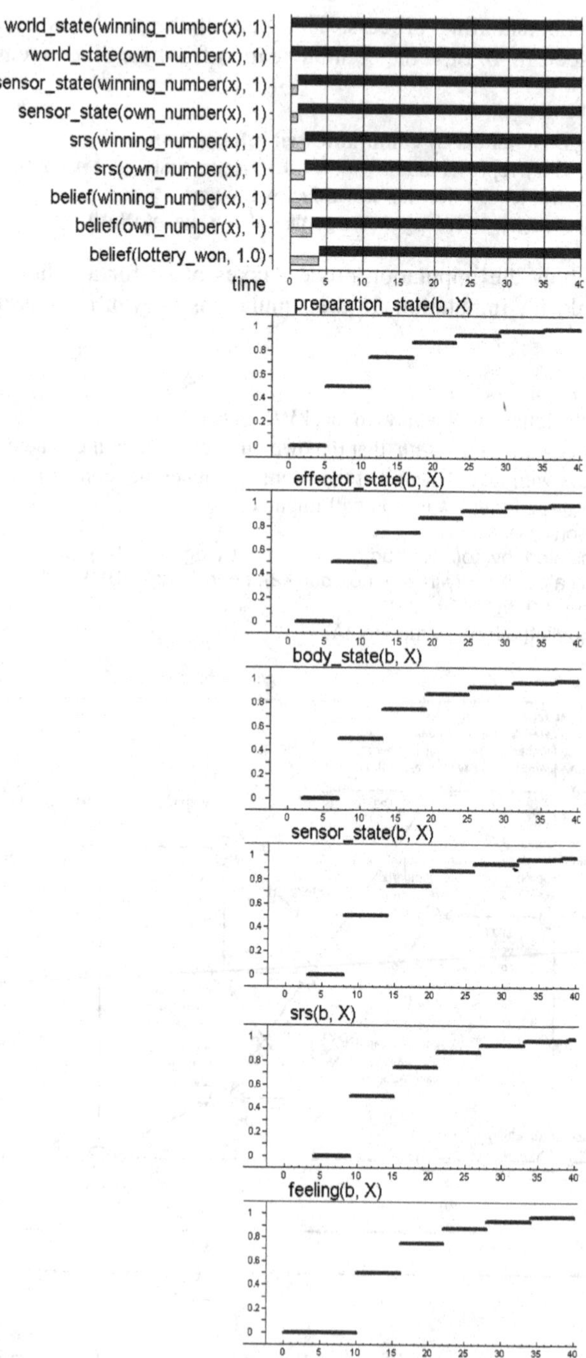

Fig. 7. Example simulation trace for the observed person

Finally, feelings are imputed in the following manner.

LP13 Imputation of a feeling
If a certain body state *B* is felt, with level *V1*≥ *th*
and a belief occurs with level *V2*≥*th* that the own number was communicated by agentA,
and a belief occurs with level *V3*≥*th* that the winning number was communicated by agentA,
then feeling *B* will imputed.

```
feeling(B, V1) &
belief(communicated_by_to(own_number(X1), agentA, agentB), V2) &
belief(communicated_by_to(winning_number(X2), agentA, agentB), V3) &
V1≥th & V2≥th & V3≥th
  → imputation(feeling(B), agentA)
```

5.3 Example Simulation Results for Empathic Understanding in the Lottery Case

Based on the model described in the previous section, a number of simulations have been performed. Some example simulation traces are included in this section as an illustration; see Fig. 7 and Fig. 8 (here the time delays within the temporal LEADSTO relations were taken 1 time unit). In all of these figures, where time is on the horizontal axis, the upper part shows the time periods, in which the binary logical state properties hold (indicated by the dark lines); for example,

```
world_state(winning_number(X), 1)
belief(lottery_won, 1.0)
imputation(feeling(b), agentA)
```

Below this part, quantitative information for the other state properties values for the different time periods are shown (by the dark lines). For example, in Fig. 7, the preparation state for b has value 0.5 at time point 6 which increased to 0.75 at time point 12 and so forth. The graphs show how the recursive body loop approximates a state for feeling with value 1. Notice that in all lower 6 traces i.e. from preparation state to feeling state, the states are activated based on temporal delay between them, i.e. preparation state has activation level '0' at time point 0, the successor state effector state has activation level '0' at time point 1 and so on.

Fig. 7 shows the simulation for the observed agent based on the basic mechanisms to generate a belief state and to generate the associated feeling as described in the previous section (from LP1 to LP10). As shown in Fig. 7 (upper part), the observed agent A notices his own number and the winning number from the world state, shown by the state properties

```
sensor_state(own_number(X), 1)
sensor_state(winning_number(X), 1)
```

respectively. It then generates the belief that he has won the lottery by comparing the two numbers shown by the state property

```
belief(lottery_won(X), 1.0)
```

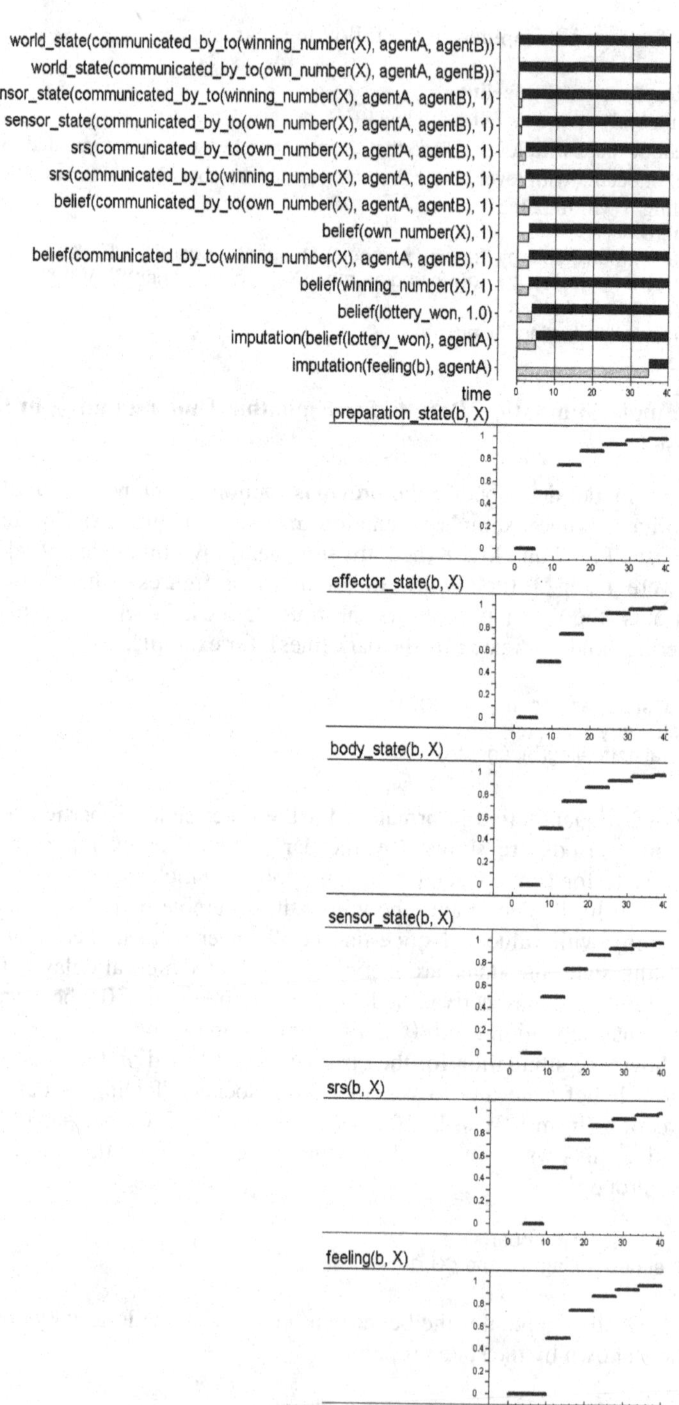

Fig. 8. Example simulation trace for the observing agent

The lower part of Fig. 7 shows the values of the various activation levels over time. Here it is shown that the recursive body loop results in an approximation of convergent activation levels for the states that relate to the feeling and the body state, among others.

Fig. 8 shows a simulation trace for the observing agent, depicting the empathic understanding process described in the previous section (in particular using LP11 to LP13, but also using LP1 to LP10 for the underlying basic mechanism). Here it is shown (in the upper part of the Fig. 8) that agent A (observed agent) communicates his own number and winning number to the agent B (observing agent), shown by the state properties

```
sensor_state(communicated_by_to(own_number(X), agentA, agentB), 1)
sensor_state(communicated_by_to(winning_number(X), agentA, agentB), 1)
```

respectively. Stepping in the shoes of agent A, then agent B (the observing agent) generates its own beliefs about the lot numbers and about winning lottery belief (which mirror the beliefs of agent A), as shown by the state property

```
belief(lottery_won, 1.0)
```

Later agent B imputes this belief (at time point 5) to agent A as shown by state property

```
imputation(belief(lottery_won), agentA).
```

As shown in the figure, after generating the associated feeling, agent B also imputes this feeling to agent A, shown by the state property

```
imputation(feeling(b), agentA)
```

at time point 35.

6 Mathematical Analysis

In this section it is analysed what the equibria of the proposed model are. The following equilibrium equations ELP1 to ELP13 can be obtained from the dynamic properties LP1 to LP13. Here, for example, *sensor_state(W)* denotes the equilibrium value for the sensor state for *W*, and the same for the other states; moreover, for binary logical states expressions such as

imputation(belief(lottery_won), agentA)

have the value *1* indicating that it is true and *0* that it is false. With these notations, the equilibrium equations are:

ELP1 *sensor_state(W) = world_state(W)*

ELP2 *srs(W) = sensor_state(W)*

ELP3 *belief(W) = srs(W)*

ELP4 *belief(lottery_won) = 0.5 belief(winning_number(X)) + 0.5 belief(own_number(X))*

ELP5 $preparation\_state(b) = 0.5\ belief(lottery\_won) + 0.5\ feeling(b)$

ELP6 $effector\_state(B) = preparation\_state(B)$

ELP7 $body\_state(B) = effector\_state(B)$

ELP8 $sensor\_state(B) = body\_state(B)$

ELP9 $srs(B) = sensor\_state(B)$

ELP10 $feeling(B) = srs(B)$

ELP11 $belief(W) = srs(communicated\_by\_to\ (W, agentA, agentB))$

ELP12 $belief(lottery\_won) \geq th$ &
$belief(communicated\_by\_to(own\_number(X1), agentA, agentB)) \geq th$ &
$belief(communicated\_by\_to(winning\_number(X2), agentA, agentB)) \geq th$
$\Rightarrow\ imputation(belief(lottery\_won), agentA) = 1$

ELP13 $feeling(B) \geq th$ &
$belief(communicated\_by\_to(own\_number(X1), agentA, agentB)) \geq th$ &
$belief(communicated\_by\_to(winning\_number(X2), agentA, agentB)) \geq th$
$\Rightarrow\ imputation(feeling(B), agentA) = 1$

Moreover, the environment context provides:

EC $world\_state(communicated\_by\_to(own\_number(X), agentA, agentB)) = 1$
$world\_state(communicated\_by\_to(winning\_number(X), agentA, agentB)) = 1$

From this via ELP1 to ELP3 and ELP11 it follows that

$belief(communicated\_by\_to(own\_number(X), agentA, agentB)) = 1$
$belief(communicated\_by\_to(winning\_number(X), agentA, agentB)) = 1$
$belief(own\_number(X)) = 1$
$belief(winning\_number(X)) = 1$

By LP4 it follows

$belief(lottery\_won) = 1$

and by ELP5 this provides

ELP14 $preparation\_state(b) = 0.5 + 0.5\ feeling(b)$

From ELP6 to ELP10 it follows

ELP15 $preparation\_state(b) = effector\_state(b) = body\_state(b) =$
$sensor\_state(b) = srs(b) = feeling(b)$

From ELP14 and ELP the following equation in $feeling(b)$ is obtained (which corresponds to the loop in the model):

$feeling(b) = 0.5 + 0.5\ feeling(b)$

From this it follows

$feeling(b) = 1$

and by ELP15, the other values in ELP15 are *1* too.

Finally, from ELP12 and ELP13 it follows

imputation(belief(lottery_won), agentA) = 1

imputation(feeling(B), agentA) = 1

This mathematical analysis confirms the outcomes of the simulations in the previous section.

7 Discussion

In the literature on automated emotion recognition, a person's observations of another person's body state, for example, facial expressions, are used as a basis. Here, a specific emotion recognition process can be modelled in the form of a classification process of facial expressions in terms of a set of possible emotions; see, for example, [38]. Indeed, a model based on such a classification procedure is able to perform emotion recognition. However, within such an approach the imputed emotions will not have any relationship to a person's own emotions. The basic agent model for emotion reading used in the current paper as a point of departure (adopted from [37]; see also the extended [11] combines the person's own emotion generation with the emotion reading process as also claimed by the Simulation Theory perspective on mindreading, e.g., [18], [21]. According to this perspective mindreading is performed by the observing agent in a simulative manner by activating the same mental states as the observed agent; see also [24]. This assumption is recently getting more and more support by empirical results, for example, concerning the discovery of the mirror neuron system; e.g., [43], [29], [27], [28], [20], [39].

For an agent observing another agent, having an empathic understanding of the observed agent is considered different from just mindreading. Mindreading as such can focus on certain aspects such as emotion, desire, belief, intention, or attention states (e.g., [17]). A characteristic of an empathic response is that the response does not only include that the observing agent understands the mental state of the observed agent, but also feels the associated feeling. In this paper it was shown how the presented agent model is capable of understanding other agents in an empathic way. The dynamical systems style (cf. [40]) agent model describes how the empathic agent does not only understand another agent's mental state but at the same time feels the accompanying emotion. This agent model for empathic understanding proposed was based on two main assumptions:

(1) The observing agent performs mindreading using the same mental states as the observed agent
(2) Both agents have a similar mechanism to associate feelings to a given mental state

Concerning assumption (1), to obtain a form of mindreading for which the observing agent generates the same mental state, the Simulation Theory perspective was followed; cf. [18]. Concerning assumption (2), to this end a computational model of Damasio [12], [13]'s informal theory about the generation of emotion and feeling was exploited. This theory assumes a neural mechanism that involves changes in an agent's sensed body state, triggered by a certain mental state. Assuming that the observed agent and the observing agent indeed have a similar mechanism for this, makes it possible that for a given mental state the observing agent generates the same feeling as the observed agent.

Especially in relation to assumption (2) it can be questioned to which extent the mechanisms to associate feelings to a given mental state are always the same for two persons. As it may be considered plausible that basically the mechanisms are similar, it is not difficult to imagine that both due to innate and learned individual differences, the empathic reaction may be limited in extent. Indeed, it is often reported that identical twins have a much higher level of mutual empathy than any two persons which are not identical twins. Moreover, it is also often considered that more empathy is shown between two persons when they have had similar experiences in life. Nevertheless, a certain extent of empathy still seems possible between persons which are not genetically identical and have not exactly the same experiences. It is an interesting challenge for future research to develop the introduced model for empathy further by introducing parameters by which such individual differences can be expressed, and for which some notion of extent to which empathy occurs can be defined.

In a wide literature, the role of emotions in virtual agents in general is addressed; e.g., [2], [22], [49]. Usually these approaches are not specifically related to empathic responses, and often use body or face expressions as a way of presentation, and not as a more biologically grounded basis for the emotion as in the neurological perspective of [12], [13], which was adopted in the current paper. The importance of computational models for 'caring' agents in a virtual context showing empathy has also been recognized in the literature; see, for example [33], [3], [4], [36]. The presented cognitive agent model differs from such existing models in that it is grounded in recent insights from neuroscience, especially the theories of Damasio [12], [13]. Other models described in the literature related to empathy usually only address more limited forms of empathy (see Section 2 and Table 1), for example:

- emotion recognition (e.g., [38], [18]), or
- recognition of some cognitive state (e.g., [9]), or
- contagion of emotions; (e.g., [23]).

As far as the authors know the model proposed here is unique in the sense that it combines both understanding and (associated) feeling of another person's states, and takes into account the way in which (other) mental states induce feelings both for the observing and the observed person in an isomorphic manner.

A limitation of the approach adopted in the current paper, is the mechanism by which it deals with 'imputation' state. In this paper, the imputation state has been worked out in a simplified manner, by using an executable rule. The current paper did not discuss about the issue of what will happen if 'imputation' did not occur or what will be the result of the 'imputation' state based on the available psychological literature. These issues have been left to future work. Future work will also address a more extensive evaluation and assessment of the models and thereby will explore more variations, for example, of different scenarios with different extents of similarity between the persons, and different values of its parameters such as the threshold value and the weight factors, for example in the generation of the preparation and the belief which were now taken *0.95* and *0.5* respectively.

References

1. Baron-Cohen, S.: Mindblindness. MIT Press (1995)
2. Bates, J., Loyall, A.B., Reilly, W.S.: An Architecture for Action, Emotion, and Social Behavior. In: Castelfranchi, C., Werner, E. (eds.) MAAMAW 1992. LNCS, vol. 830, pp. 55–68. Springer, Heidelberg (1994)
3. Bickmore, T., Fernando, R., Ring, L., Schulman, D.: Empathic Touch by Relational Agents. IEEE Trans. on Affective Computing 1, 60–71 (2010)
4. Bickmore, T.W., Picard, R.W.: Towards Caring Machines. In: Dykstra-Erickson, E., Tscheligi, M. (eds.) Proceedings of the ACM SIGCHI Conference on Human Factors in Computing Systems (CHI), pp. 1489–1492 (2004)
5. Blair, R.J.R.: Responding to the emotions of others: dissociating forms of empathy through the study of typical and psychiatric populations. Consciousness and Cognition 14, 698–718 (2005)
6. Bogdan, R.J.: Interpreting Minds. MIT Press (1997)
7. Bosse, T., Jonker, C.M., van der Meij, L., Treur, J.: A Language and Environment for Analysis of Dynamics by Simulation. International Journal of Artificial Intelligence Tools 16, 435–464 (2007)
8. Bosse, T., Jonker, C.M., Treur, J.: Formalisation of Damasio's Theory of Emotion, Feeling and Core Consciousness. Consciousness and Cognition Journal 17, 94–113 (2008)
9. Bosse, T., Memon, Z.A., Treur, J.: A Recursive BDI-Agent Model for Theory of Mind and its Applications. Applied Artificial Intelligence Journal 24, 953–996 (2010)
10. Bosse, T., Memon, Z.A., Treur, J.: An Adaptive Emotion Reading Model. In: Taatgen, N.A., van Rijn, H. (eds.) Proc. of the 31st Annual Conference of the Cognitive Science Society, CogSci 2009, pp. 1006–1011. Cognitive Science Society, Austin (2009)
11. Bosse, T., Memon, Z.A., Treur, J.: A Cognitive and Neural Model for Adaptive Emotion Reading by Mirroring Preparation States and Hebbian Learning. Cognitive Systems Research Journal 12, 39–58 (2012)
12. Damasio, A.: The Feeling of What Happens. Body and Emotion in the Making of Consciousness. Harcourt Brace, New York (1999)
13. Damasio, A.: Looking for Spinoza: Joy, Sorrow, and the Feeling Brain. Vintage books, London (2004)
14. Decety, J., Jackson, P.L.: The functional architecture of human empathy. Behav. Cogn. Neurosci. Rev. 3, 71–100 (2004)
15. De Vignemont, F., Singer, T.: The empathic brain: how, when and why? Trends in Cogn. Science 10, 437–443 (2006)
16. Eisenberg, N.: Emotion, regulation, and moral development. Annu. Rev. Psychol. 51, 665–697 (2000)
17. Gärdenfors, P.: How Homo Became Sapiens: on the Evolution of Thinking. Oxford University Press (2003)
18. Goldman, A.I.: Simulating Minds: The Philosophy, Psychology, and Neuroscience of Mindreading. Oxford Univ. Press, New York (2006)
19. Goldman, A.I.: Ethics and cognitive science. Ethics 103, 337–360 (1993)
20. Goldman, A.I.: Mirroring, Mindreading, and Simulation. In: Pineda, J.A. (ed.) Mirror Neuron Systems: The Role of Mirroring Processesi in Social Cognition, pp. 311–330. Humana Press Inc. (2009)
21. Goldman, A.I., Sripada, C.S.: Simulationist models of face-based emotion recognition. Cognition 94, 193–213 (2004)

22. Gratch, J., Marsella, S., Petta, P.: Modeling the Antecedents and Consequences of Emotion. Cognitive Systems Research 10, 1–5 (2009)
23. Hatfield, E., Cacioppo, J.T., Rapson, R.L.: Emotional contagion. Cambridge University Press, New York (1994)
24. Hesslow, G.: Conscious thought as simulation of behavior and perception. Trends Cogn. Sci. 6, 242–247 (2002)
25. Hoffman, M.L.: Empathy and Moral Development. Cambridge University Press, New York (2000)
26. Hoffman, M.L.: Development of prosocial motivation: empathy and guilt. In: Eisenberg, N. (ed.) The Development of Prosocial Behavior, pp. 281–313. Academic Press, New York (1982)
27. Iacoboni, M.: Mirroring People: the New Science of How We Connect with Others. Farrar, Straus & Giroux, New York (2008)
28. Iacoboni, M.: Understanding others: imitation, language, empathy. In: Hurley, S., Chater, N. (eds.) Perspectives on Imitation: From Cognitive Neuroscience to Social Science, vol. 1, pp. 77–100. MIT Press (2005)
29. Iacoboni, M., Molnar-Szakacs, I., Gallese, V., Buccino, G., Mazziotta, J.C., Rizzolatti, G.: Grasping the intentions of others with one's own mirror neuron system. PLoS Biol. 3, e79 (2005)
30. Ickes, W.: Empathic Accuracy. The Guilford Press, New York (1997)
31. Ingram, R.E., Miranda, J., Segal, Z.V.: Cognitive vulnerability to depression. Guilford Press, New York (1998)
32. Kim, J.: Physicalism, or Something Near Enough. Princeton University Press, Princeton (2005)
33. Klein, J., Moon, Y., Picard, R.: This Computer Responds to User Frustration: Theory, Design, Results, and Implications. Interacting with Computers 14, 119–140 (2002)
34. Lamm, C., Batson, C.D., Decety, J.: The neural basis of human empathy – effects of perspective-taking and cognitive appraisal. J. Cogn. Neurosci. 19, 42–58 (2007)
35. Lipps, T.: Einfühlung, innere Nachahmung und Organempfindung. Archiv Für Die Gesamte Psychologie 1, 465–519 (1903)
36. McQuiggan, S., Robison, J., Phillips, R., Lester, J.: Modeling Parallel and Reactive Empathy in Virtual Agents: An Inductive Approach. In: Proc. of the 7th Int. Joint Conf. on Autonomous Agents and Multi-Agent Systems, pp. 167–174
37. Memon, Z.A., Treur, J.: Cognitive and Biological Agent Models for Emotion Reading. In: Jain, L., Gini, M., Faltings, B.B., Terano, T., Zhang, C., Cercone, N., Cao, L. (eds.) Proceedings of the 8th IEEE/WIC/ACM International Conference on Intelligent Agent Technology, IAT 2008, pp. 308–313. IEEE Computer Society Press (2008)
38. Pantic, M., Rothkrantz, L.J.M.: Expert System for Automatic Analysis of Facial Expressions. Image and Vision Computing Journal 18, 881–905 (2000)
39. Pineda, J.A. (ed.): Neuron Systems: the Role of Mirroring Processes in Social Cognition. Humana Press Inc. (2009)
40. Port, R.F., van Gelder, T. (eds.): Mind as Motion: Explorations in the Dynamics of Cognition. MIT Press, Cambridge (1995)
41. Preston, S.D., de Waal, F.B.M.: Empathy: its ultimate and proximate bases. Behav. Brain Sci. 25, 1–72 (2002)
42. Raine, A.: The Psychopathology of Crime: Criminal Behaviors as a Clinical Disorder. Guilford Publications, New York (1993)
43. Rizzolatti, G., Craighero, L.: The mirror-neuron system. Annu. Rev. Neurosci. 27, 169–192 (2004)

44. Rizzolatti, G., Fogassi, L., Gallese, V.: Neuro-physiological mechanisms underlying the understanding and imitation of action. Nature Rev. Neurosci. 2, 661–670 (2001)
45. Rizzolatti, G.: The mirror-neuron system and imitation. In: Hurley, S., Chater, N. (eds.) Perspectives on Imitation: From Cognitive Neuroscience to Social Science, vol. 1, pp. 55–76. MIT Press (2005)
46. Rizzolatti, G., Sinigaglia, C.: Mirrors in the Brain: How Our Minds Share Actions and Emotions. Oxford Univsersity Press (2008)
47. Singer, T., Leiberg, S.: Sharing the Emotions of Others: The Neural Bases of Empathy. In: Gazzaniga, M.S. (ed.) The Cognitive Neurosciences, 4th edn., pp. 973–986. MIT Press (2009)
48. Wohlschlager, A., Bekkering, H.: Is human imitation based on a mirror-neurone system? Some behavioural evidence. Exp. Brain Res. 143, 335–341 (2002)
49. Yang, H., Pan, Z., Zhang, M., Ju, C.: Modeling emotional action for social characters. The Knowledge Engineering Review 23, 321–337 (2008)

Multiagent Based Simulation as a Supply Chain Analysis Workbench

Jacek Jakieła, Paweł Litwin, and Marcin Olech

Rzeszow University of Technology, Faculty of Mechanical Engineering and Aeronautics, Department of Computer Science,
Powstancow Warszawy Avenue 8, 35-959 Rzeszow, Poland
{jjakiela,plitwin,molech}@prz.edu.pl

Abstract. The paper presents the application of Multiagent Based Simulation to analysis of supply chain behavior. As has been shown in the paper, agent oriented approach may be considered as a powerful conceptual framework for organization modeling and workbench for simulations of intra- and inter-organizational business processes. All of these theses have gradually been proved in the subsequent sections of the article. Firstly the agent paradigm has been presented as a toolbox for business modeling and complexity management. Then the classical model of supply chain simulation has been transformed to its agent-based version. Finally the case study presents how the agent model of the supply chain may be used in the process of bullwhip effect analysis based on the simulation experiment.

Keywords: agent-oriented modeling, agent-oriented simulation, business modeling, supply chain modeling, extended enterprise simulation.

1 Introduction

Nowadays, more often than ever, organizations are facing problems related to fragmented consumer markets, interwoven industrial supply chains, sophisticated transportation systems and growing interdependency of infrastructures [1]. As a consequence the complexity of business models has been increasing constantly. Sometimes it leads to completely new business structures [2]. In order to survive, firms have to develop flexibility of these structures, mainly in terms of fast responses to market changes related to competitors' moves and customers' preferences. To this end, companies decide on which activities they can perform best and integrate their value chains with business models of their partners. As a result the extended enterprise is created, where each of its components should act in the optimal way, and therefore the whole value net is able to maximize efficiency and effectiveness. The core of such extended enterprises is their supply chain. The main problem is that even the simplest supply chains can behave in an unpredictable way and it is very hard to make accurate decisions. Sometimes demand for single merchandise or level of stock starts to change randomly and the behavior of whole supply chain becomes extremely

N.T. Nguyen (Ed.): Transactions on CCI VI, LNCS 7190, pp. 84–104, 2012.

complex. Well known phenomenon occurring in supply chains is *bullwhip effect* consisting in an amplification of the order variability what makes demand (i.e. orders) more unpredictable. The main consequences, among others, are: higher inventory levels, supply chain agility reduction and decrease of customer service levels.

Because of the specificity of the extended enterprise, only way to be prepared for such risky situations and make informed decisions is to use the simulation model, which becomes the workbench for analysis. In that case simulation model is used in the process of analyzing the characteristics of the real system.

The purpose of this paper is to show how an agent paradigm may be used as business modeling and simulation approach to describing and analyzing supply chain behavior in the context of bullwhip effect. The agent oriented model has been based on [3], where conceptual basis for simulation experiment is presented in detail. It describes the model of supply chain for traditional simulations. The research results presented in this paper may be considered as an extension of work published in [4] in the area of new metrics defined and simulations experiments conducted. It may also be regarded as an application of framework developed by authors and introduced in [5].

2 Multiagent System as a Simulation Workbench

2.1 Using Agents in Simulations

Multiagent-based simulation (MABS) can be defined as the modeling and simulating real world system or phenomena where the model consists of agents cooperating with one another in carrying out tasks and achieving collective goals. The advent of multi-agent based modeling has introduced an important innovation: behavior of complex systems with many active entities can be simulated by modeling individual entities and their interactions. Importantly, the operation of the system doesn't need to be defined a priori as set of equations, terms or logical statements, but the whole behavior emerges from individual objects behaviors, their interactions and impact of the environment.

The MABS approach has been becoming more and more popular; its models as well as their advantages have been widely described in [1], [6]. Contributions to the MABS domain are periodically published among others in Springer's LNAI series. According to AgentLink Roadmap [7] "agent-based simulation is characterized by the intersection of three scientific fields, namely, Agent-Based Computing, the Social Sciences and Computer Simulation" (Figure 1).

Location of MABS at the intersection of agent-based computing and computer simulation can be accepted if we consider the application of MABS in simulation of manufacturing systems and business processes. Due to the fact that vast majority of cases requires the inclusion of human factor in simulation of real world system or phenomena (for example manufacturing systems, supply chain management), it is assumed that social science also affects the MABS.

The complexity of simulation experiment building process as well as semantic gap related to simulation model may be significantly reduced when agent orientation is used as modeling paradigm. Next section refers to work that explains why agent is intuitive modeling metaphor as well as why agent paradigm is especially well suited for managing complexity of problem domain.

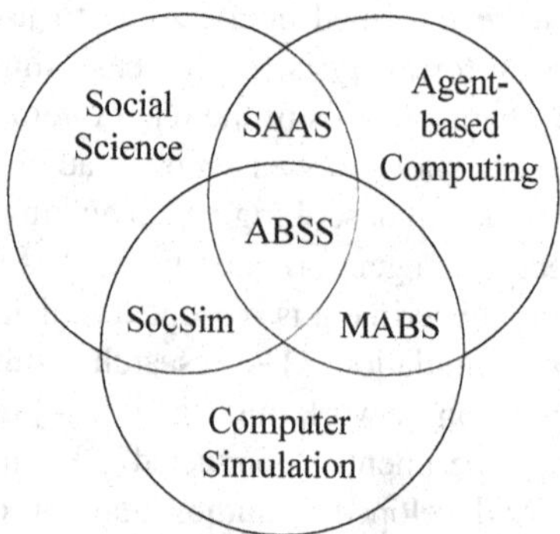

Fig. 1. Map of the agent oriented research areas [8]

2.2 Using Agent as a Modeling Metaphor and Complexity Management Tool

Main assumption for this paper is that organization modeling process is based on multi-agent system metaphor that leads to perceiving and understanding of firm in the way typical for multi-agent systems software engineering, but also takes under consideration business aspects along with basic organization characteristics.

The use of a metaphor during the process of organizational analysis and understanding is of great significance. Morgan [9] says that metaphor is frequently understood as a way to make an argument more appealing, however its meaning is much more important. The use of a metaphor is a consequence of a way one thinks and perceives which penetrate our understanding of the world that surrounds us. We use metaphor when we try to understand some problem domain using portion of reality or conceptual framework. Thus we formulate a theorem that "A is B" or that "A is similar to B". Concerning this paper, an assumption has been made that in qualitative terms the characteristics of modern organizations are really close to the characteristics of multi-agent systems both in structure and in behavior. The appearance of obvious similarities between multi-agent systems and business organizations is particularly visible in the case of extended enterprises which adopted such strategies as decentralization of operations and process orientation. Table 1 shows observed similarities. In the first column are basic structural and behavioral characteristics of multi-agent systems, and in the second characteristics of modern organizations extracted from key titles which deal with organization design and process orientation were presented.

As it can be seen, similarities presented enable to significantly reduce the semantic gap between the problem domain and the model built for simulation purposes. Thank to this, the whole modeling process is very intuitive and natural.

Table 1. Similarities between structural and behavioral characteristics of modern organizations and multi-agent systems [10]

Multi-agent system	Business organization
Multi-agent system is a set of *decentralized* software components.	Centralized model and functional decomposition reflect precisely decomposition of workload into smaller tasks, that are distributed among particular company departments and are accomplished in sequences [11]. Modern organizations operate according to decentralized business process patterns which are accomplished by distributed organizational actors. Decentralization causes that these processes are moved from companies' headquarters to local offices. The operational model of modern companies is a highly decentralized.
Multi-agent system is a set of *autonomous* software components.	Decentralization requires in turn autonomy delegation that has drastically changed the role of organizational actors, because "controlled positions" have been replaced by positions which give full competence [12]. This trend is really similar to that which takes place in software engineering due to control encapsulation in distributed components, which therefore possess operational autonomy. According to Champy and Hammer people working within processes that are being reengineered must be equipped with delegations. As members of a process team they are both allowed and obliged to make decisions [13]. In case of process orientation it is impossible to avoid situation when organizational actors, who perform process oriented jobs, are fully autonomous entities.
Multi-agent system is a set of *goal-oriented* software components.	In modern organizations functional departments have been replaced by process teams. A set of organizational actors, who cooperate in order to achieve particular goals of certain process is a natural form of modern firm's organization [14].
Multi-agent system is a set of software components, which *may carry out tasks in parallel manner.*	In the company organized around processes, subsequent work-stages are performed in natural order. Instead of artificial operations order, natural operation order is used. Processes' de-linearization allows task performance acceleration due to two factors. Firstly, lots of tasks are performed in the same time. Secondly, shrinking of time between initial and final stages of processes causes that the necessity for serious changes, which can undermine or make incoherent work done so far is less probable [13].

2.3 Managing Business Models Complexity with Agents

Agent paradigm has also more inherent features that can be used in complexity management process which is a serious problem in case of contemporary organizations modeling. Taking under consideration basic characteristics of complex systems defined by Simon [15] as well as analysis related to agent oriented software engineering provided by Jennings and Wooldridge [16], it's possible to easily prove advantages of agent approach in the context organization modeling process and complexity management.

As the first argument it can be noticed, that agent oriented decomposition of a problem domain is an effective way to divide the problem space, while modeling contemporary organizations. It can be concluded from a number of factors.

Firstly, hierarchical structure of complex systems causes, that modularization of organization components in terms of its goals, that are to be achieved is very intuitive solution. As Jennings and Wooldridge claim hierarchical organization of complex systems causes that at each level of the hierarchy the purpose of the cooperation between sub-systems is achieving a functionally of higher level. Whereas within sub-systems components, which these sub-systems are composed of, cooperate in order to achieve total functionality of a sub-system. As a consequence, decomposition oriented on goals that are to be reached is very natural division. Applying this schema to an organization the situation emerges when organization actors cooperate in order to achieve goals of the process, in turn processes are realized to achieve the goal of the organization, and organizations combine their inherent competences to achieve goals of the extended enterprise. It is worth to remember that goal orientation is one of the main characteristics of an agent and thus agent concept can be used without any additional effort.

Another vital issue is presentation of such characteristic of an extended enterprise as decentralization in the area of information processing and control. In this case agent oriented decomposition seems to be an optimal solution due to such characteristics of an agent as thread of control encapsulation in the form of autonomy property. The distributed organizational components may be thus modeled with autonomous agents as a basic modeling constructs.

Agent oriented approach allows also to solve problems connected with the design of interactions taking place between system components. It is a serious issue due to the dynamics of interactions between organization components and organizations that constitute extended enterprise. It is really frequent, that organization components enter an interaction in difficult to predict time and for unknown at the stage of design reasons. As a consequence it's really challenging to determine in advance the parameters of such interactions. The solution to this problem is existence of system components with characteristics thank to which they can make decisions concerning the type and range of interaction during the runtime.

Next argument for an agent oriented approach is that it allows to eliminate semantic gap between agent abstraction used during the simulation model design phase and structures used during organization modeling. It is directly connected with similarities which appear between structural and behavioral characteristics of a multi-agent system and organization (see Table 1).

Additional benefits connected with agent oriented approach during computational models development have been analyzed in detail in [17]. As it is claimed, agent oriented approach should lead to improvement and enrichment of such characteristics of computational representation as flexibility, reliability, ability to combine functions of various systems flexibly, as well as ability to create new properties such as self-organization or self-adaptation.

Next section shows the application of MABS to Supply Chain modeling and simulation.

3 Supply Chain Simulation Structure and Implementation

3.1 The Concept of Supply Chain Management

There are many definitions and interpretations of the term "supply chain". According to Muckstadt *et al.* [18], a supply chain may be defined as "the set of firms acting to design, engineer, market, manufacture, and distribute products and services to end-consumers". In general, this set of firms is structured as a network, as illustrated in Figure 2.

Common knowledge is that even small fluctuation of one supply chain parameter (for example demand) may lead to the unpredictable behavior of the whole supply chain system. It is also worth to mention that executing experiments on the real system is rather impossible. These are the reasons why simulation approach has been adopted. The simulation experiment building process has been based on multi-agent approach according to the scenario described in the section 4.1. The structure of the simulation process is presented in next section.

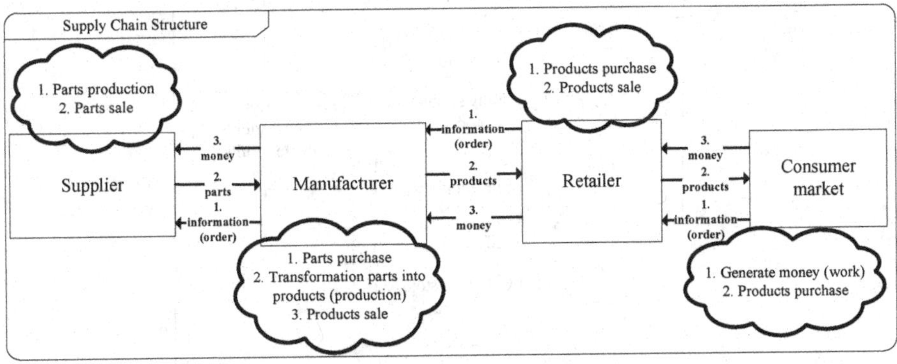

Fig. 2. The supply chain structure [2]

3.2 The Simulation Structure

The generic model of the simulation process is presented in the figure 3. The B connector comes from the environment preparation section (Warm-up Section) which is responsible for creating basic simulation model components (e.g. agents) and setting their initial parameters. It is specific to modeling and simulation environment selected. How it has been solved for the model under consideration is presented in the next section entitled Implementation of Multi-Agent Simulation.

The first decision node checks if the stop condition has been met – if not, simulation proceeds. Simulation runs in the loops. Every loop constitutes the simulation cycle. Every simulation cycle has its own unique number assigned, which is automatically incremented by *Go to Next Simulation's Cycle* procedure.

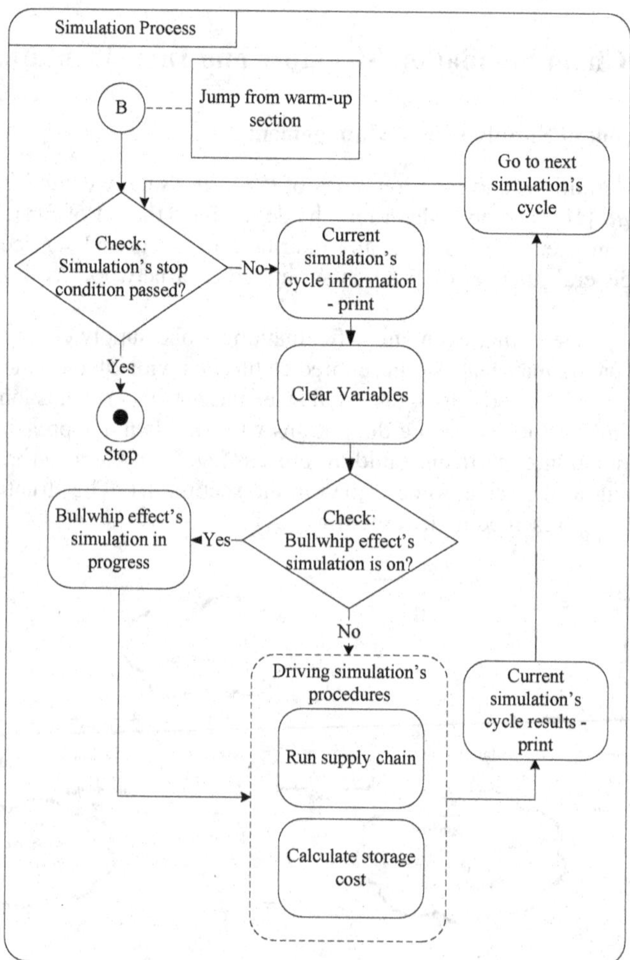

Fig. 3. Model of simulation process

The number of simulation cycles may vary and lies in range from 1 to 1000. After next cycle starts, data related to it are printed on the system's console out. Just before Supply Chain procedures are run, variables values are set to initial states.

Next decision node checks if the cycle should include bullwhip effect phenomenon. After this decision is made, the procedures responsible for supply chain operation simulation are executed. The final procedure prints the results of current simulation cycle out. The core of the simulation process is section responsible for Supply Chain operation. It consists of two main elements which are called *Generate Market's Order* and *Fulfill the Order with Supply Chain*.

The procedure entitled *Generate Market's Order* includes several decision nodes that check parameters such as demand level and market financial resources (money) level. If all conditions are met, the procedure *Try to place an order* is executed; otherwise the procedure called *Lack of an order in current cycle* is run. After the order is generated by the market, its fulfillment is driven by the procedure *Fulfill the Order with Supply Chain*. The first step in this procedure is responsible for saving the fact that order has been placed. It supports the results' analysis because one can easily determine if the products have been delivered (or not) in the current cycle. Checking if Retailer Agent has enough level of stock is done according to agents' behavioral rules. The full description of reference model, the simulation has been based on may be found in [5].

3.3 Implementation of the Multi-agent Simulation

Although one can implement model with a conventional programming language this is usually hard way to start. Some modeling environments provide complete systems in which models can be created, executed and visualized. As was shown in analysis conducted in [19] the best known are AgentSheets and NetLogo.

The simulation model presented in the paper has been implemented in NetLogo, which is considered as the very popular simulation environment [19]. It includes several facilities such as tools for building user interface or system dynamics modeler.

The Multi-Agent simulations implemented in NetLogo Integrated Development Environment consists of three following parts:

1. Definitional part.
2. Preparatory part (to setup, "warm-up section").
3. Simulation definition part (to go).

Definitional part includes definitions of agents' types ("breed"), global variables ("globals") and variables related to every agent (e.g. agent's name). In the model presented, this part defines four types of agents: Market Agent, Retailer Agent, Manufacturer Agent and Supplier Agent. Every agent has associated set of variables.

Preparatory part defines procedures setting up the environment for simulation.

Simulation definition part is composed of procedures definitions that set up and drive the core of the simulation process. *Clear simulation* procedure is predefined in NetLogo environment and is used to clear the memory for storing new simulation results data. Procedures that instantiate agents are responsible for setting up initial values for variables defined in definitional section. Next procedure creates visual connections between communicating agents. Finally presentation layer procedures prepare the simulation window and write down simulation initial values as well as simulation results what helps in results analysis process. The final step of this stage was implementation of simulation procedures according to agent behavioral rules and simulation structure.

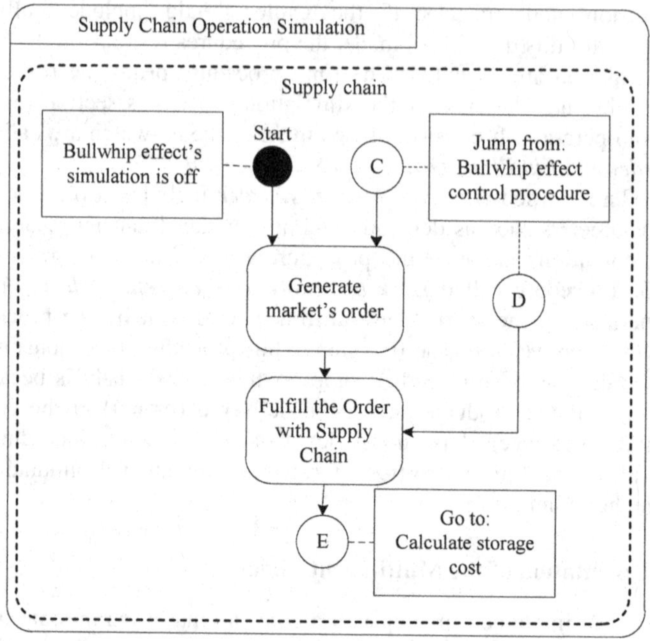

Fig. 4. Supply Chain Operation Simulation Procedure

4 The Scenario of Simulation Experiment

4.1 Experimental Procedure

When using simulation, the experiment creation process is of great significance. The case study presented in the next sections has been built according to steps listed below. The scenario has been based on [20].

1. **Identify and formulate a problem that is to be solved with simulation experiment.** It is important to have the list of questions articulated, which are supposed to be answered with the use of simulation runs.
2. **Create the model.** Definition of the real system model, which should provide a compromise between the detailed mapping of real system (impeding its implementation and validation), and simplification that suppresses the similarity between the model and real system, but making model easier to build.
3. **Choose the metrics.** After the problem is formulated it is important to have set of indicators to monitor the state of the modeled system and to draw conclusions as well as to find hidden rules or laws.
4. **Set the initial values for simulation parameters.** The sample parameter is duration of simulation or number of simulation cycles. During every cycle all necessary tasks will be done, of course, only if their preconditions are met. The example of other parameters may be demand distribution (Normal,

Poisson or Exponential distribution), parts and products prices or stock levels.

5. **Run the simulation.** After model is fully elaborated, and all variables are set up, the simulation may start and operate the predefined number of cycles during which values of variables are captured and saved.
6. **Calculate the metrics.** Metrics enable to better understand modeled object or process. Based on this data the simulation analysis is done.
7. **Interpret simulation results.** The last phase is related to the careful analysis of simulations results and calculated values of variables. It may lead to discovering new rules or dependencies that may be used in the real system management process.
8. **Validate the model.** It is based on a comparison of real system results and results of simulation, carried out with parameters corresponding to the actual operation of the system. The model can be considered valid (verified positive) if it (repetitively) reflects the behavior of real system.

4.2 Simulation Experiment

The simulation experiment has been developed and will be presented according to the steps listed in the previous section. Description of each step reveals the design decisions which have been made with regard to Supply Chain modeling and simulation processes.

1. **Identify and formulate a problem that is to be solved with simulation experiment.** As has been mentioned in Introduction section, this research is an extension of work presented in [4]. To this end, the main goal of the multi-agent simulation is broader than this one set in [4], and may be formulated as *analysis of how the bullwhip effect may influence the performance of supply chain.* In order to achieve the goal, set of new metrics has been defined and described in the step number 3.

2. **Create the model**. The process of supply chain model development has been conducted according to the framework presented in [5]. The analysis of the problem domain has led to the following model elements:
   - consumer market agent – this element is responsible for buying and consuming products,
   - retailer agent – its mission is to buy products from manufacturer and to sell them to consumers,
   - manufacturer agent – it is obliged to purchase materials from supplier, process them to final products and sell final products to retailer,
   - supplier agent – this element produces materials and sells them to manufacturer.

   Very important part of the model is the logic of agents' operation which has been formalized in behavioral rules according to patterns showed in [5]. During runtime agents communicate using the following flows

- goods flow – in the direction from the supplier through manufacturer and retailer to consumers.
- orders (information) flow – from consumers through retailer and manufacturer to supplier,
- money flow – shows how money circulates in supply chain.

After the model was built, the following most important simulation parameters have carefully been selected: duration of simulation (number of cycles), part's price, demand distributions and associated parameters (mean, standard deviation), safety parts' stock level (supplier's side), safety parts' stock level (manufacturer's side), strength of bullwhip effect.

In order to better understand the impact of bullwhip effect on supply chain performance, four versions (including two runs without bullwhip effect simulation – bullwhip effect strength = 0%) for every of two simulation experiments have been planned. Each version is related to the percentage value describing how often the bullwhip effect will occur in simulation runs. Related data are presented in the Table 2. To draw the number of cycle, bullwhip effect should take place in, the random variable generator with uniform distribution has been used.

Table 2. Initial conditions for simulation experiments

No. of Simulation experiment	% of cycles affected by bullwhip effect	No. of cycles affected by bullwhip effect
First Experiment (300 cycles)	5%	15
	15%	45
	25%	75
Second Experiment (500 cycles)	5%	25
	15%	75
	25%	125

3. **Choose the metrics.** In order to better assess the impact of bullwhip effect on supply chain performance, several metrics have been defined. They are presented below.

   1. Average total delivery time. The equation (1) describes total delivery time measured from the moment when the retailer has ordered products up to the moment when products have arrived to retailer. This metric has already been presented in [5].

$$T_T = T_D + T_P + T_{DC} + T_{PC} \tag{1}$$

where:
T_T – total delivery time, T_D – delivery time between manufacturer and retailer, T_P – production time at manufacturer's floor (it's skipped if manufacturer has products' stock greater than the order lot), T_{DC} – delivery time between supplier and manufacturer (included only if manufacturer product's stock is smaller than order lot, what is more, supplier has enough part's stock to meet manufacturer's order), T_{PC} – part's production time at supplier (included only if supplier part's stock is not sufficient to meet manufacturer's order).

2. Variations in the orders and production levels at supplier's side.
3. Variations in the total number of products in whole supply chain (based on metrics published in [3]).
4. OTIF (On Time in Full), which informs how often the products ordered were available off-hand (Based on metrics published in [21]).

The algorithms realizing these functions have been implemented in the main part of the simulation process. All metrics' values are calculated at a runtime.

4. **Set the initial values for simulation parameters.** Because the goal of the simulation experiment is to compare how the bullwhip effect may influence the performance of the supply chain, two simulation experiments and four runs in each of them have been conducted. Each run presents predefined strength of the bullwhip effect. Initial conditions of simulation experiments are provided in Table 3.

5. **Run the simulation.** The simulation has been run with parameters values as presented in Table 3. The results have been saved in text files and used in the process of metrics calculations.

Table 3. Initial values of simulation parameters

Parameters	**Parameters values**	
	First experiment	Second experiment
Duration of simulation	300	500
Part's price	2.50	2.00
Demand distribution	Normal	Poisson
Mean of distribution	6.0	5
Standard deviation of distribution	1.5	N/A
Safety part's stock at supplier	25	25
Safety part's stock at manufacturer	20	20
Strength of the bullwhip effect	20	20

6. **Calculate the metrics.** The calculated metrics have been presented in the following tables and graphs.

   Deliveries have been split into three categories named A, B and C. The logic of each category is explained as follows. Category A denotes direct delivery between manufacturer and retailer (products). Category B delivery consists of three phases: 1st delivery between supplier and manufacturer (parts), 2nd production at manufacturer's plant (parts → products), 3rd delivery between manufacturer and retailer (products). Delivery of category C has four phases: 1st production at supplier's (parts), 2nd delivery between supplier and manufacturer (parts), 3rd production at manufacturer's (parts → products), 4th delivery between manufacturer and retailer (products).

7. **Interpret simulation results.** The interpretation of calculated metrics has been divided into several sections related to metrics defined.

1. **Average delivery time and number of deliveries.** Table 4 presents the results of both experiments with regard to delivery type as well as the bullwhip effect strength (denoted by 0%, 5%, 15% and 25%).

Table 4. Delivery time and number of deliveries

Experiment	Type of delivery	Metric	0%	5%	15%	25%
First experiment (300 cycles)	Total	Average time	6,94	7,19	7,66	8,02
		Number of deliveries	265	245	214	193
	A type	Average time	4,00	4,05	3,95	4,10
		Number of deliveries	156	161	152	145
	B type	Average time	9,11	8,93	9,95	10,12
		Number of deliveries	49	43	30	15
	C type	Average time	12,82	17,74	23,16	24,32
		Number of deliveries	60	41	32	33
Second experiment (500 cycles)	Total	Average time	6,80	7,08	7,85	8,41
		Number of deliveries	365	344	288	259
	A type	Average time	4,07	3,94	4,06	4,11
		Number of deliveries	245	246	204	188
	B type	Average time	9,32	9,47	9,88	10,91
		Number of deliveries	53	43	39	22
	C type	Average time	14,81	19,26	23,29	23,80
		Number of deliveries	67	55	45	49
Total number of market's orders (1st / 2nd experiment)			281/ 451	280/ 461	283/ 470	284/ 462

It is easy to notice that the number of deliveries decreases if the bullwhip effect occurs more often. The reason for such situation can easily be inferred – more frequently bullwhip effect occurs, higher level of products safety stock is established by the firm. Even if the number of customers' requests does not change, the stock level is getting higher and higher and the number of deliveries decreases. Such situation may seem favorable because of the delivery costs, but as the analysis of the average times of delivery shows, it isn't. If we drill the results down it turns out that time of direct deliveries between manufacturer and retailer (A category) is in all cases almost the same. The problem appears in B and C type deliveries and is caused by decrease in number of deliveries mentioned previously as well as dynamic changes in production levels at supply chain partners. The results have been visualized in Figure 5 and Figure 6.

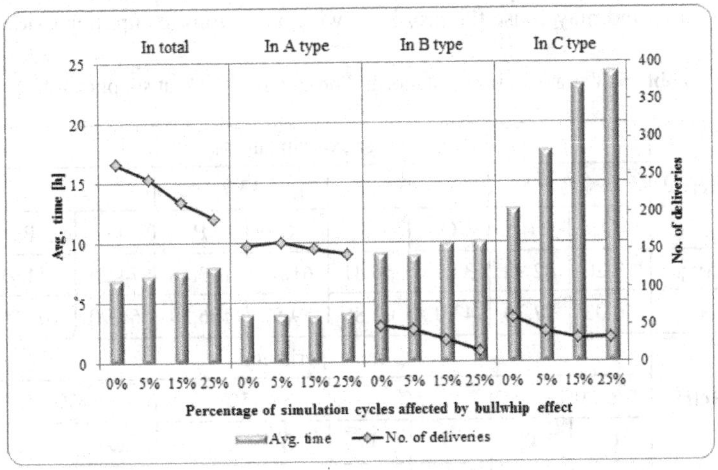

Fig. 5. Average time and number of deliveries (1st experiment)

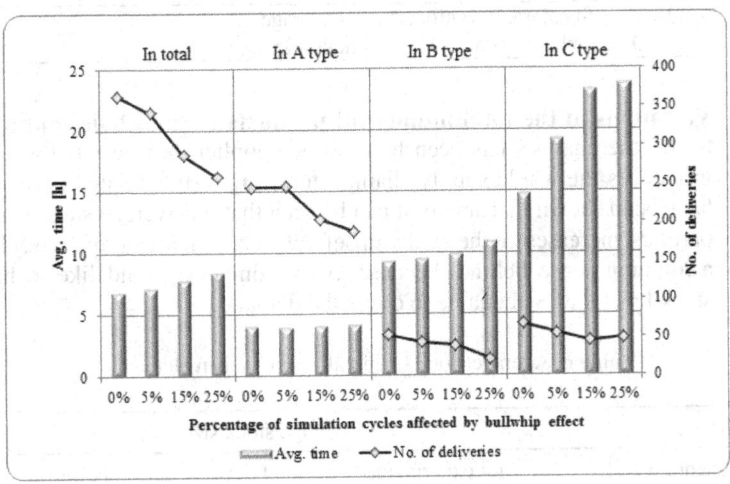

Fig. 6. Average time and number of deliveries (2nd experiment)

2. **Variations in the orders and production levels at supplier's side.** Supplier is the final element of the supply chain and therefore bullwhip effect strikes mainly this stage. In order to check how the bullwhip effect influences the supplier, the average and standard deviation of orders received by supplier and production levels at supplier's side have been calculated. The results are presented in the Table 5.

As it can be seen if the bullwhip effect occurs more often, the average of orders and production levels are increasing. The higher values of standard deviation mean that orders size and production levels are becoming more variable. Although standard deviation value stabilizes at a certain level, it is quite high in comparison to the case when bullwhip effect was not taking place and may cause the problems with operations at supplier's side.

Table 5. Variations in the orders and production levels at supplier side

Metric	1st experiment							
	0%		5%		15%		25%	
	O	P	O	P	O	P	O	P
Avg.	27,20	32,98	34,99	56,31	61,05	113,48	74,26	144,91
SD	16,02	27,73	43,02	93,86	59,52	106,59	61,90	104,20
Metric	2nd experiment							
	0%		5%		15%		25%	
	O	P	O	P	O	P	O	P
Avg.	29,61	39,97	43,58	81,72	67,52	115,63	81,66	132,77
SD	22,02	39,24	50,08	99,35	60,81	100,88	57,71	99,89
Legend: SD – Standard Deviation, Avg. – average O – number of orders; P – production level								

3. **Variations in the total number of products in the whole supply chain.** So far the analysis has been focused on supplier; however bullwhip effect influences the whole supply chain. Interesting results related to this impact have been shown in Table 6. It can be seen that the average stock level at all partners increases if the bullwhip effect occurs more frequently. There is a common sense behind, because every company would like to have the stock level that will enable to cover the demand.

Table 6. Average stock size in all supply chain elements

Metric:	Average stock size							
Experiment no.:	1st experiment				2nd experiment			
bullwhip effect strength	0%	5%	15%	25%	0%	5%	15%	25%
Retailer (products)	6,24	7,45	9,57	11,39	5,44	6,97	9,75	12,11
Manufacturer								
- parts	19,91	19,85	19,94	19,88	19,94	19,99	19,87	20,00
- products	7,51	12,75	19,14	21,20	8,39	14,88	20,67	23,55
Supplier (parts)	36,88	87,45	117,00	119,10	45,57	99,04	113,6	111,60

Interesting insight is that the parts' stock level at manufacturer is constant. After we will go back to Table 3 we will see that it is related to safety parts stock level.

As a final element in current section, few graphs have been presented to show fluctuations of products and parts stock levels in different simulation cycles and runs (See Fig.7.). It gives the opportunity to see how the bullwhip effect is changing the production routines. Figures 7a and 7e show that fluctuations of total quantity of goods in this case (bullwhip effect strengths – 0%) are rather constant. Values are in the range 50-200 pcs. In other cases (figures 7b-7d and 7f-7h) the changes have much more dynamic nature and is hard to find periods with small fluctuations in levels of goods in supply chain. The conclusion is that more often bullwhip effect occurs, the total quantity of products in supply chain becomes more random.

4. OTIF (On Time in Full). As has already been mentioned this indicator informs how often the products ordered were available off-hand. The OTIF values have been calculated according to the formula (2).

$$OTIF = \frac{D_d}{D_t} \cdot 100 \qquad (2)$$

where: D_d - number of direct deliveries performed by analyzing stage
D_t - total number of deliveries performed by analyzing stage

Calculated metric values show the percentage of deliveries with products that have been taken directly from the stock, without having to wait for production or even deliveries from other supply chain partners because there was a lack of production resources. Table 7 presents the values of OTIF indicator related to experiments conducted.

As may be observed (See Table 7) stages at the beginning of supply chain (retailer and manufacturer) have much better performance according to the OTIF indicator in case the bullwhip effect occurs, than in cases without bullwhip effect. Such situation is caused by higher inventory levels stored by all partners in supply chain what enables to base deliveries on reserve. This situation seems favorable for customers – order is fulfilled just after it has been placed, however from the firm's perspective it is a cost driver. When Fast Moving Consumer Goods and goods which storage cost is high will be taken into consideration, the conclusion is that bullwhip effect has negative impact on the cost structures of business partners in supply chain.

There is no doubt that the bullwhip effect causes longer delivery time, higher levels of stocks and random behavior of the total level of goods in the whole supply chain. The more frequently the bullwhip effect occurs the bigger impact it causes.

Of course, there are several other interesting questions to ask in this context such as: how bullwhip effect influences money resources; however this short case study was elaborated to show how an agent based simulation can be used as workbench for business simulations and does not pretend to be the full-blown analysis of all of the bullwhip effect problems.

Table 7. OTIF values

Supply Chain Stage	Indicator	1st experiment				2nd experiment			
		0%	5%	15%	25%	0%	5%	15%	25%
Retailer	Total deliveries	282	281	284	285	452	462	470	463
	Direct deliveries	163	182	205	235	277	320	374	400
	OTIF [%]	57,80	64,77	72,18	82,46	61,28	69,26	79,57	86,39
Manufacturer	Total deliveries	265	245	214	193	365	344	288	259
	Direct deliveries	156	161	152	145	245	246	204	188
	OTIF [%]	58,87	65,71	71,03	75,13	67,12	71,51	70,83	72,59
Supplier	Total deliveries	192	163	116	110	230	188	159	154
	Direct deliveries	132	122	84	75	163	133	114	103
	OTIF [%]	68,75	74,85	72,41	68,18	70,87	70,74	71,70	66,88

As a final point it is worth to mention that the simulations of supply chain are often based on traditional approach which has been carefully described in [3]. The model presented in this paper is an agent based scenario for Supply Chain simulation which provides, among others, the following benefits:

- The problem space of supply chain (or whole extended enterprise if needed) may be effectively divided with an agent modeling concept.
- Because each model element component is autonomous and proactive, it's quite easy to model decentralization which is inherent characteristic of extended enterprises.
- The model is easily scalable – one can add additional agents playing particular roles when needed, or new instances of existing agents.
- The business goals can be seamlessly encapsulated in the simulation model elements – goal orientation is the basic characteristic of an agent paradigm.
- The supply chain could be very intuitively modeled as a society of cooperating and goal oriented agents carrying out the business processes' tasks which enable to achieve the goals of the whole extended enterprise.

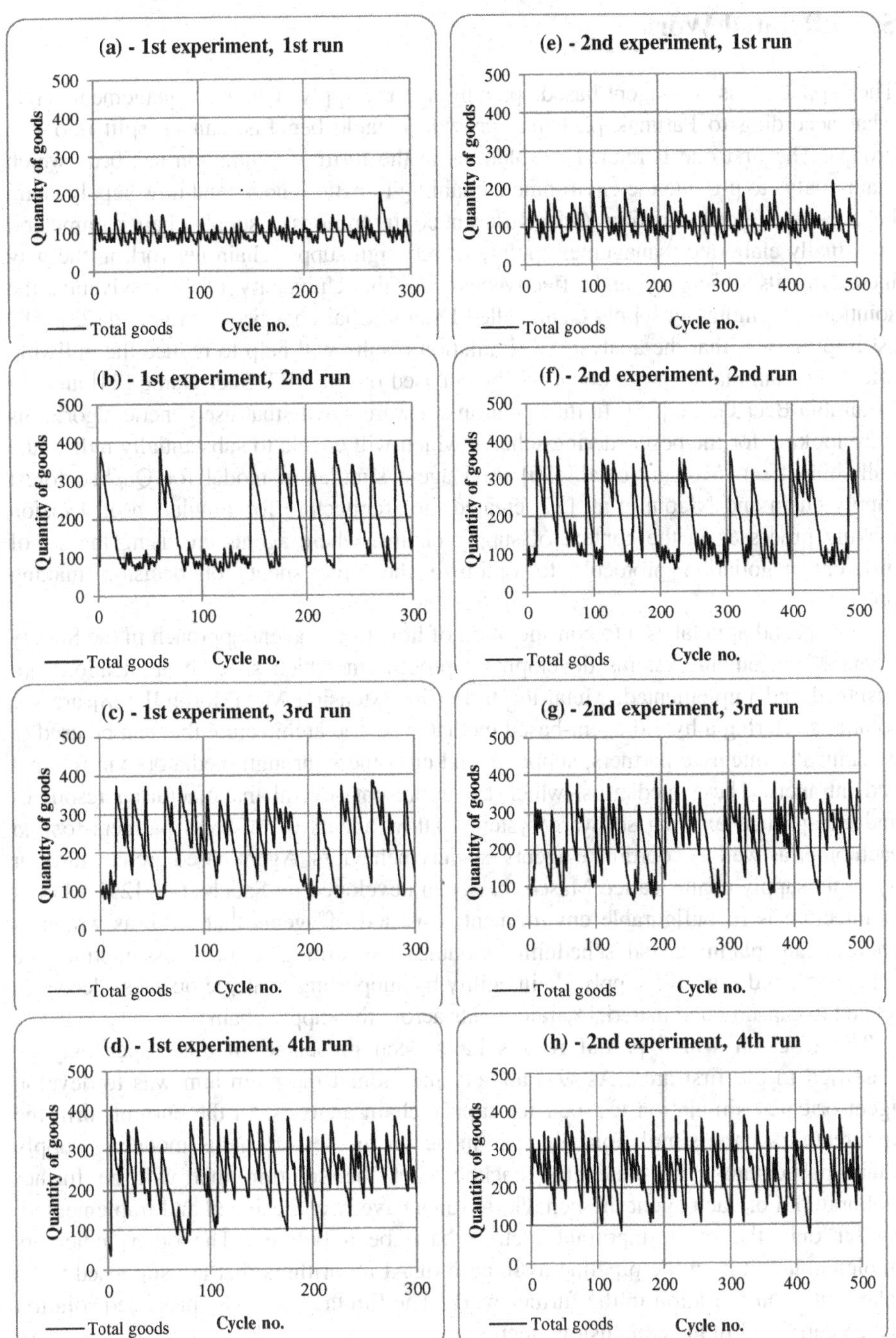

Fig. 7. Fluctuations of level of goods in whole supply chain

5 Related Work

The applications of agent-based paradigm to Supply Chain Management area, what according to Parunak [22] may provide notable benefits, can be split into two groups. The first one is related to solutions in the form of simulation test-beds which main goal is to provide the environment enabling to better understand how supply chain behaves in different situations (with different configurations of supply chain parameters) and finally elaborate management policy or redesign supply chain network in the way increasing its efficiency and effectiveness. At the University of Pennsylvania, the solution for simulating supply chain called Dragon Chain has been developed [23]. The assumption was that the analysis of simulation results will help to reduce the bullwhip effect. The simulation experiment has been based on the MIT Beer Game [24] and the Columbia Beer Game [25]. In this solution software agents that use genetic algorithms were looking for the best ordering scheme which will enable to substantially reduce the bullwhip effect. Moyaux et al. [26] used agent simulation model for Québec forest supply chain and Nfaoui et al. [27] created the architecture for simulation of decision making processes in the context of supply chains, where agents are using the set of different negotiation protocols to optimize the time spent for decision making process.

The second area takes into consideration of how to use agent approach in the Supply Chain Management systems development process in which specific applications are designed and implemented. MetaMorph and its extension MetaMorph II [28] are the solutions offering a hybrid agent-based mediator centric architecture that can be used to dynamically integrate partners, suppliers and customers through mediators via Internet and intranets. These mediators, which can represent several manufacturing resources and encapsulate existing software systems, allow agents of business partners to find each other as well as coordinate agents' society behaviors. Agent based architecture for dynamic supply chains called Mascot has been developed by Sadeh et al. [29]. Mascot architecture is reconfigurable environment consisted of agents that work as wrappers coordinating planning and scheduling modules. According to main assumption, the solution should improve supply chain agility by supporting strategic business decisions related to capacity and material requirements across the supply chain.

The research which partial results have been presented in this paper may be classified to the first area. As was already mentioned the main aim was to develop agent-oriented simulation test-bed for supply chain analysis. In the current form the architecture of the simulation which is made on the set of agents modeling supply chain participants constitutes the backbone of the solution that will be further elaborated. For each agent the behavioral rules have been designed and implemented. So far only the most important metrics have been defined. The other indicators implementation is in the pipeline as in case of AI algorithms that are supposed to be taken into consideration in the further work. The limitations of the proposed solution have been listed in the conclusions section.

6 Conclusions

Contemporary business models are so complex that there is a need for more advanced tools enabling understanding and management of firms' sophisticated structures and processes. The goal of the paper was to show how Multiagent Based Simulation may be applied in a form of a workbench for extended enterprise modeling and analysis. The case study presented how an agent-oriented mindset is used in the scenario of creating and running simulation experiments related to supply chain analysis from the bullwhip effect perspective.

It is also worth to mention that the modeling process has several simplifications. Firstly the time flow when demand occurs and order is placed has not been included. Minimal order lot calculation has been skipped. Minimal production size has not been taken into consideration as well as some inner operations such as production task planning, capacity requirements planning, demand planning and forecasting.

Looking critically at the solution from the development perspective will reveal some additional ways of future improvements. First idea that comes is to migrate the framework to more sophisticated agent development platform e.g. Jason with AgentSpeak. This would enable to implement the model using pure agent paradigm and make the solution more sensitive, flexible and scalable.

Finally it is worth to keep in mind, paraphrasing Simon [13], that every complex system that works has not been built in one fell swoop. It is usually created by developing several intermediate versions that are stable. Therefore in spite of all drawbacks listed above, the presented framework may be considered as the stable basis for further development.

References

1. North, M.J., Macal, C.M.: Managing Business Complexity. Discovering Strategic Solutions with Agent-Based Modeling and Simulation. Oxford University Press (2007)
2. Tapscott, D., Ticoll, D., Lowy, A.: Digital Capital: Harnessing the Power of Business Webs. Harvard Business Press (2000)
3. Vieira, G.E., Cesar Jr., O.: A conceptual model for the creation of supply chains models. In: Proceedings of the 37th conference on Winter simulation, Orlando, Florida, pp. 2619–2627 (2005)
4. Jakieła, J., Litwin, P., Olech, M.: MAS Approach to Business Models Simulations: Supply Chain Management Case Study. In: Jędrzejowicz, P., Nguyen, N.T., Howlet, R.J., Jain, L.C. (eds.) KES-AMSTA 2010, Part II. LNCS (LNAI), vol. 6071, pp. 32–41. Springer, Heidelberg (2010)
5. Jakieła, J., Litwin, P., Olech, M.: Toward the Reference Model for Agent-based Simulation of Extended Enterprises. In: Setlak, G., Markov, K. (eds.) Methods and Instruments of Artificial Intelligence, pp. 34–66 (2010)
6. Weyns, D., Uhrmacher, A.M. (eds.): Multi-Agent Systems Simulation and Applications. Computational Analysis, Synthesis, and Design of Dynamic Models Series. CRC Press, Florida (2009)
7. Luck, M., McBurney, P., Preist, C.: Agent technology: enabling next generation computing. A Roadmap for Agent Based Computing (2003), http://www.agentlink.org

8. Davidsson, P.: Agent based social simulation: a computer science view. J. Artif. Soc. Social Simulation 5 (2002)
9. Morgan, G.: Images of organizations. Sage Publications (2006)
10. Jakieła, J.: AROMA – Agentowo zoRientowana metOdologia Modelowania orgAnizacji. WAEiI, Politechnika Slaska, Gliwice (2006)
11. Peppard, J., Rowland, P.: Reengineering, Gebethner i S-ka. Warszawa (1997)
12. Drucker P. F.: Zarządzanie w XXI wieku. Muza S.A (2000)
13. Hammer M., Champy J.: Reengineering w przedsiębiorstwie. Neumann Management Institute, Warszawa (1996)
14. Hammer. M.: Reinzynieria i jej następstwa. PWN, Warszawa (1999)
15. Simon, H.: The Sciences of Artificial. MIT Press (1996)
16. Jennings, N.R., Wooldridge, M.: Agent-Oriented Software Engineering. In: Garijo, F.J., Boman, M. (eds.) MAAMAW 1999. LNCS, vol. 1647, pp. 1–7. Springer, Heidelberg (1999)
17. Cetnarowicz, K.: Problemy projektowania i realizacji systemów wielo-agentowych. Uczelniane Wydawnictwa Naukowo-dydaktyczne, AGH, Krakow (1999)
18. Muckstadt, J., Murray, D., Rappold, J., Collins, D.: Guidelines for collaborative supply chain system design and operation. Information Systems Frontiers 3, 427–435 (2001)
19. Gilbert, N.: Agent-Based Models. Sage Publications (2007)
20. Paolucci, M., Sacile, R.: Agent-Based Manufacturing and Control Systems. New Agile Manufacturing Solutions for Achieving Peak Performance. CRC Press (2005)
21. Byrne, P.J., Heavey, C.: Simulation, a Framework for analyzing SME supply chains. In: Proceedings of the 2004 Winter Simulation Conference (Winter 2005)
22. Van Dyke Parunak, H.: Applications of distributed artificial intelligence in industry. In: O'Hare, G.M.P., Jennings, N. (eds.) Foundations of Distributed Artificial Intelligence, pp. 71–76. John Wiley and Sons (1996)
23. Kimbrough, S.O., Wu, D., Zhong, F.: Computers play the Beer Game: Can artificial agents manage supply chains? Decision Support Systems 33, 323–333 (2002)
24. Sterman, J.D.: Modeling managerial behavior: Misperceptions of feedback in a dynamic decision making experiment. Management Science 35, 321–339 (1989)
25. Chen, F.: Decentralized supply chains subject to information delays. Management Science 45, 1076–1090 (1999)
26. Moyaux, T., Chaib-draa, B., D'Amours, S.: An Agent Simulation Model for the Quebec Forest Supply Chain. In: Klusch, M., Ossowski, S., Kashyap, V., Unland, R. (eds.) CIA 2004. LNCS (LNAI), vol. 3191, pp. 226–241. Springer, Heidelberg (2004)
27. Nfaoui, E.H., Ouzrout, Y., El Beqqali, O.: An approach of agent-based distributed simulation for supply chains: Negotiation protocols between collaborative agents. In: Proceedings of the 20th annual European Simulation and Modeling Conference, EUROSIS, Toulouse, France, pp. 290–295 (2006)
28. Maturana, F., Shen, W., Norrie, D.: Metamorph: an adaptive agent-based architecture for intelligent manufacturing. International Journal of Production Research 37, 2159–2173 (1999)
29. Sadeh, N.M., Hildum, D.W., Kjenstad, D.: MASCOT: an agent-based architecture for dynamic supply chain creation and coordination in the Internet economy. Prod. Plan. Control 12(3), 212–223 (2001)

On the Effective Distribution and Maintenance of Knowledge Represented by Complementary Graphs

Leszek Kotulski and Adam Sędziwy

AGH University of Sciences and Technology, Institute of Automatics, al. Mickiewicza 30, 30-059 Kraków, Poland
{kotulski,sedziwy}@agh.edu.pl

Abstract. Graph transformations are a powerful tool enabling the formal description of the behavior of software systems. In most cases, however, this tool fails due to its low efficiency. This can be overcome by introducing parallel graph transformations. The concept of complementary graphs enables two things: the decomposition of a centralized graph into many cooperating subgraphs, and their parallel transformations. Such a model is very useful in an agent environment, where subgraphs represent an individual knowledge of particular agents; this knowledge may be partially replicated and exchanged between the agents. The rules of a cooperation and an implicit synchronization of a knowledge, represented in this way, have been already defined in [10]. The second very important issue is the way of an initial graph distribution assuming the size criterion: the heuristic method proposed previously succeeds in 60% (i.e. 60% of subgraphs is consistent with the criterion). The method presented in this paper gives over 90% fit.

1 Introduction

Distributed computing paradigm enables cooperation of geographically distributed software components. Usually such systems are more effective and dependable (if their data and functions are replicated). Let us note that parallel computations paradigm enables an effective solving of NP-complete problems if the formalism describing such a problem supports parallelism and is implemented effectively. Kreowski shows [15] that complex problems (e.g. the Hamiltonian paths) described with the help of graph multiset transformations can be solved in a polynomial time (i.e. $NP_{GraphTransf} = P_{ParallelGraphTransf}$). Currently, we have not a polynomial implementation of graph multiset transformations, but this theoretical result encourages us to develop the tools supporting effectively the parallelization of graph transformations algorithms. In [16] there is presented the formal specification of autonomous units basing on multiset graph transformation rules in the concurrent case.

Developing environments capable of parallel (distributed) graph transformations is only the first aspect of the considered problem. It should be also remarked

N.T. Nguyen (Ed.): Transactions on CCI VI, LNCS 7190, pp. 105–120, 2012.

that designing programs working in a distributed environment is more difficult than in a sequential case. The main reason is a lack of a common data structure supporting cooperation of all processes. Instead of this data are split and replicated into a number of parts that are maintained by the local entities that cooperate to achieve a common goal. This cooperation should be synchronized to avoid time dependent errors and deadlocks. The explicit synchronization (using synchronous messages) enlarges significantly the algorithmic complexity of programs so there are required methods enabling an implicit synchronization (that need not to be supported by programmers). The complementary graphs concept [7,8] (reviewed in the Section 2) allows us to design a system in a centralized form (using a graph formalism) and its automatic translation to a distributed environment. The synchronization of an exchange of informations among agents, necessary for applying graph transformation rules, is the implicit one. This concept can be useful in practice as it was shown for both, the algebraic (single [2] and double [1] pushout graph grammars) [10,13] and algorithmic (ETPL(k) graph grammar [3]) graph transformation approaches [9].

In this paper we will consider the last approach with respect to both polynomial complexity of the membership problem [3] and the possibility of automatic generation of the graph grammar basing on the set of samples (inference of graph grammars [5]).

The correct synchronization and the support for a system design process is only one aspect of a distributed system design. The second issue is the proper distribution of software components and a knowledge maintained by a system (here represented by distributed graphs). It's obvious that we are unable to check all possible distributions to find the best one. We have to use some heuristic algorithms instead. An optimal distribution depends on a criterion assumed for a given problem. Here we consider one of the most intuitive: we would like to assure that the local environments will maintain the same part of a global knowledge. In terms of graph formalism it means the decomposition of a global graph into the equally sized subgraphs. The method proposed in the earlier articles [9,13] allowed to achieve a decomposition with about 59% of subgraphs having an assumed size. IE-graphs (generated and maintained by ETPL(k) graph grammar) are used to test new distribution algorithm. In the relaxation algorithm presented in this paper over 90% of subgraphs hit the demanded size range. Also an average subgraph size is closer to the assumed value compared to the previous method.

2 Replicated Complementary Graphs

As it was mentioned before, the replicated complementary graphs (RCGs) concept extends functionality of many graph transformation approaches. For testing the effectiveness of splitting algorithm however, we have to select the $ETPL(k)$ [3] graph grammar. There are two reasons for doing it. First of them is related to the computational complexity of the graph transformations (parsing, membership problem etc.). Since a graph grammar describing a system has to be applicable (from practical point of view), we are limited to the graph grammars with the polynomial parsing time. Second demand concerns the expressive power of the used grammar. It has to be powerful enough to describe a modeled system. Since the above requirements are mutually exclusive one has to assume the weaker properties of the used grammars. The graph structures being transformed by the graph grammar $ETPL(k)$ are called the indexed edge-unambiguous graphs (IE-graphs). That has been successfully applied for the syntactic patter recognition by Flasiński [3]. Their transformation and membership problem can be solved with quadratic time complexity[9]. In this paper we analyze the behavior of an agent system which knowledge is represented by IE-graphs.

Definition 1. *An indexed edge-unambiguous graph (IE-graph) over Σ and Γ is a quintuple $H = (V, E, \Sigma, \Gamma, \delta)$, where*

- *V is the finite, non-empty set of graph nodes, to which unique indices are ascribed; the order in the indices set defines the order within V,*
- *Σ is the set of attributed node labels,*
- *$\Gamma = \{\gamma_1, \gamma_2, \dots \gamma_n : \gamma_1 \leq \dots \leq \gamma_n\}$ is the finite, nonempty set of attributed edge labels, ordered by the relation of simple ordering,*
- *$E \subset V \times \Gamma \times V$ is the set of edges,*
- *$\delta : V \longrightarrow \Gamma$ is the node labeling function.*

In distorted pattern analysis [3] the set of edge labels describes relations in the two-dimensional space and may be represented as the wind rose directions ordered as follows: $N \leq NE \leq E \leq SE \leq S \leq SW \leq W \leq NW$.

IE-graphs are transformed with the help of algorithmic graph transformation rules based on node labels control. The necessity of assurance the polynomial complexity of the membership problem implies certain limitations on the transformation and generation rules of corresponding graph grammars ($ETL/1$, $ETPL(k)$ [3,4]): a newly generated or an existing node can be connected by an edge with some other node in two cases:

- with its immediate parent (i.e. the with the node, which performs its generation),
- with the node that is distant one length unit from it and which has at least common predecessor with it.

In this section we will introduce the formal definition of *replicated complementary graph* (RCG).

To preserve the consistency between the centralized graph G and the set of its distributed subgraphs some nodes should be replicated and placed in the proper subgraphs. Graphically, we will mark such nodes with double circles.

We introduce the following notations:

- Replicas(G_i) is the set of all nodes of the graph G_i that are shared with another local graphs, i.e for which some replicas exist.
- Private(G_i) is the set of all nodes of the graph G_i that belong to the G_i graph only (i.e. have no replicas).
- $(v, w)_{G_i}$ denotes the pair (v, w) such that: $(v, w) \in E(G_i)$ or $(w, v) \in E(G_i)$.

- $(v, w)^+_{G_i}$ denotes the sequence of the nodes $u_1, u_2, ..., u_k \in V(G_i)$ such that $v = u_1, w = u_k$, $u_m \neq u_n$ for $m \neq n$ and $\exists (u_m, u_{m+1})_{G_i}$ for $m < k$; the sequence $(u_1, u_2, \ldots, u_k)$ will be called the *proof of an acyclic connection between* v and w.
- $\mathsf{Path}(G_i, v, w)$ is the set of all proves of an acyclic connection between v and w; the set of nodes belonging to $\mathsf{Path}(G_i, v, w)$ will be denoted as $\mathsf{PNodes}(G_i, v, w)$

For example, for the graph G presented in Fig.1(a) $\mathsf{PNodes}(G, C, I) = \{C, D, E, F, G, H, I\}$.

Definition 2. *A set of graphs $G_i = (V_i, E_i, \varphi_i), i = 1, 2, \ldots k$, is a replicated and complementary form of graph G iff there exists a set of injective homomorphisms $s_i : G_i \longrightarrow G$ such that:*

1. $\bigcup_{i=1,\ldots k} s_i(G_i) = G$
2. $\forall i, j \in \{1, \ldots k\} : s_i(V_i) \cap s_j(V_j) = s_i(\mathit{Replicas}(G_i)) \cap s_j(\mathit{Replicas}(G_j))$
3. $\forall i \in \{1, \ldots k\} \mathit{Border}(G_i) = \{v \in \mathit{Replicas}(G_i) :$ *there exists* $(v, w)_{G_i}$ *for some* $w \in \mathit{Private}(G_i)\}$; *$\mathit{Border}(G_i)$ is called a set of border nodes of G_i;*
4. $\forall w \in \mathit{Private}(V_i)\ \forall v \in \mathit{Private}(V_j)\ \forall u_1, u_2, ..., u_k \in \mathit{PNodes}(G_i, w, v) \Rightarrow \exists b \in \mathit{Border}(G_i) \exists 1 \leq p \leq k : s_i(b) = u_p$

Graph G_i is referred to as a replicated complementary graph (RCG).

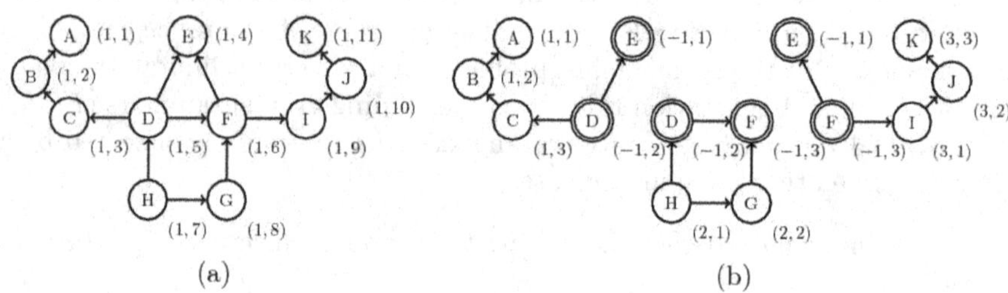

Fig. 1. (a) G in the initial, centralized form. (b) Complementary form of G, $\{G_1, G_2, G_3\}$.

Let us note, that while splitting a graph we are interested in checking whether an edge connecting two nodes crosses a border between the subgraphs i.e. at least one of its endpoints is replicated.

The example of three RCGs being the replicated complementary form of G shown in Fig.1(a) is presented in Fig. 1(b) (the replicated nodes are marked with the double circles). The indexing convention for RCG assumes that an index of each non-border node consists of two numbers: the number of its parent RCG and its local number unique within this graph. For border nodes an index is a pair of the form $(-1, j)$ where j is global border node index, and attributed by a list containing names of agents holding RCGs where other replicas of $(-1, j)$

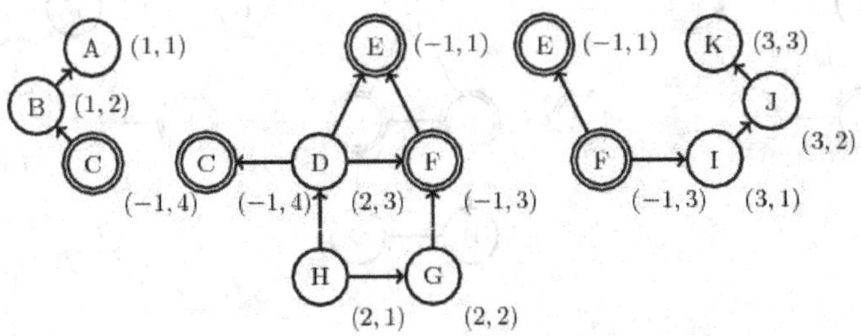

Fig. 2. Complementary form of G, $\{G_1, G_2, G_3\}$ after $\mathsf{Incorporate}((-1,2),2)$

are present. Thus each border node has an information about its all replicas so their localizations in a distributed environment can be determined immediately.

Since the formal definition of the RCG form (Definition 2) may be difficult to use in a practical construction of a set of RCGs, the effective algorithm of splitting a graph into a set of RCGs was introduced in [7]; it will be reviewed in the Section 3.

There are three operations associated with an RCG that allow to increase a number of replicas and enable local environments of RCGs to apply the graph grammar transformation rules.

$\mathsf{Expand}(v, i, Cond)$ – for the replicated node $v \in V(G_i)$ all its neighbors (and neighbors of replicas of v) satisfying the condition $Cond$ are replicated and attached to the graph G_i together with the connecting edges. Condition $Cond$ allows to restrict an extension of the graph G_i to the nodes having specific attributes or being connected with v by specifically attributed edges. This property is very useful in a practical use but this case will not be considered here: for the simplicity we assume that $Cond \equiv true$.

$\mathsf{Incorporate}(v, i)$ – for the border node $v \in \mathsf{Border}(G_i)$ replicate neighbors of all replicas v' of v (excluding v itself) and attach these replicated neighbors to G_i together with edges connecting them with v's; remove replicas of v together with adjacent edges from corresponding graphs. After this operation v becomes the private (not replicated) node of G_i. All isolated border nodes that are produced as artifacts of this procedure are additionally incorporated to G_i.

$\mathsf{Neighborhood}(v, k)$ – for the node v return the graph B consisting of the nodes distant from v not more than k (each path in B beginning in v has not more than $k+1$ vertices, including v). Finding B may require a recursive cooperation between agents maintaining particular RCGs.

Let us consider the replicated complementary graph G_2 presented in Fig.1(b). In the result of applying $\mathsf{Incorporate}((-1,2),2)$, G_2 changes to the form presented in Fig. 2. If $\mathsf{Expand}((-1,2),2,true)$ operation will be applied to G_2 from Fig.1(b) then it changes to the form shown in Fig.3. It should be remarked that in both cases G_2 graph consists of the same nodes, but node labeled by D in the incorporation case (Fig. 2) is the private one. The significant difference appears

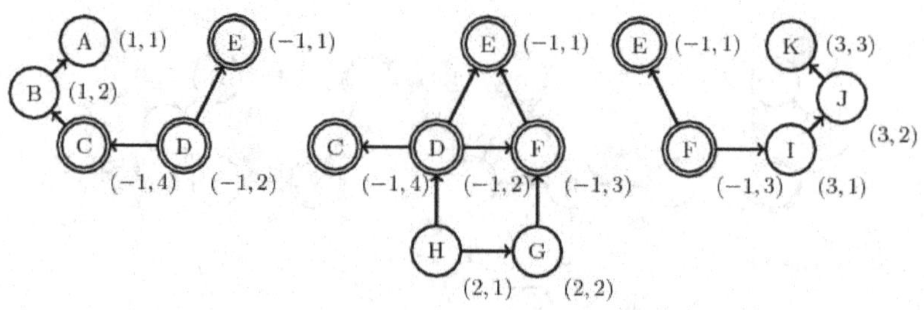

Fig. 3. Complementary form of G, $\{G_1, G_2, G_3\}$ after $\mathsf{Expand}((-1,2), 2, true)$

in the structure of the graph G_1 from which nodes are incorporated. Especially the lack of the node labeled by E in graph G_1 should be also commented: incorporation of the node $(-1,2)$ splits G_1 (from Fig.1(b)) into two subgraphs: the first that is presented in Fig. 2 and the second one that consists of a single node only (labeled by E), because this node is replicated to other graphs and any operations (using it) can be performed only in these graphs this new single node graph is removed.

The last property of the RCG environment is the possibility of a parallel application of transformation rules defined for the centralized graph. In our approach each of RCGs is managed by an associated agent. To apply the production $P : L \rightarrow R$ the agent X_i has to follow three steps:

- to determine $Priv = V(L) \cap V(G_i)$, and to find an occurrence of $V(L) - Priv$ in the distributed environment,
- incorporate $V(L) - Priv$ (if needed),
- apply locally the production P.

The finding an occurrence of L in a RCG managed by the agent X_i is supported by Expand and Neighborhood operations. In [10,13] the polynomial effective complexity of algorithms of agents cooperation was shown.

The application of a production P should be considered as an autonomous decision of an agent. On the other side the property of highly nondeterministic application of graph transformation rules is not always desirable. Thus some kind of control conditions imposed on an application of P should be introduced [16]. The parameters required for evaluating such conditions can be taken from both an agent environment (like in [6]) and complementary graphs attributes. The second case shows that the necessity of replication of some crucial parts of a graph structure is not limited to the case of an implicit synchronization.

The relation between control conditions and transformation rules creates a proper environment for maintaining of a distributed system with a knowledge represented by replicated complementary graphs. Complementary graphs concept presented here, parallel application of transformation rules or implicit synchronization of agents are supported practically by GRADIS multiagent environment [14] developed by our team. It is compliant with FIPA standards.

The crucial problem is a method of an initial partitioning and distribution of a knowledge to individual agents. That question will be considered in the next section.

3 Single Node Incorporations vs. Relaxation

The agents' common goal is to bring a system to a state where all replicated complementary graphs are (nearly) equally sized and their sizes are $\simeq S_t$. The task of optimal partitioning presented in [9] was based on moving boundaries between the RCGs i.e. by subsequent Incorporate calls (single node incorporations - SNI). The SNI algorithm presented below was used to obtain an optimal partitioning of a complementary form of a given centralized graph. Let us introduce following notations: the range of acceptable RCG size is denoted as $I = [S_t - \epsilon, S_t + \epsilon]$, where S_t is the target (optimal) value for all RCG sizes and ϵ is the size tolerance; G_i denotes a replicated complementary graph. Additionally, we ascribe in SNI algorithm the following cost function C to an agent maintaining graph G_i:

$$C(G_i) = \begin{cases} 0 & \text{for } |V(G_i)| \in I, \\ c_1(|V(G_i)| - S_t - \epsilon) & \text{for } |V(G_i)| > S_t + \epsilon, \\ c_2(-|V(G_i)| + S_t - \epsilon) & \text{for } |V(G_i)| < S_t - \epsilon, \end{cases}$$

where c_1, c_2 are positive constants.

Algorithm 1 . *SNI algorithm.*

1. *If* $|V(G_i)| > S_t + \epsilon$ *then exit, else go to the next step;*
2. *Select the neighbor RCG, say* M*, with maximal cost function value;*
3. *Let* $v \in V(G_i) \cap V(M)$*, execute* Incorporate(v).
4. *go to step 1.*

The modification introduced to the agent activity schema is made in the analogy to the relaxation method of solving the two dimensional Laplace equation, $\nabla^2 T = 0$ (boundary value problem describing the temperature distribution), in which a value of a solution $T(i,j)$ in some node (i,j) of a square lattice, in a given iteration is calculated numerically as an average of a solution values for four neighboring nodes. In the GRADIS agent environment we do similar. An agent holding a RCG being out of the optimal size range incorporates an entire neighbor RCG and next splits itself into two RCGs, H_1 and H_2, such that $V(H_1) \approx V(H_2)$ (see Fig.4). Thus the graph sizes become averaged locally. Unlike SNI method, the relaxation is achieved by "incorporating" entire RCGs.

Algorithm 2 . *Merging procedure.*

Let G *and* H *be two RCGs. Merging* G *and* H *is made in the following steps (it is assumed that* H *will be absorbed by* G*):*

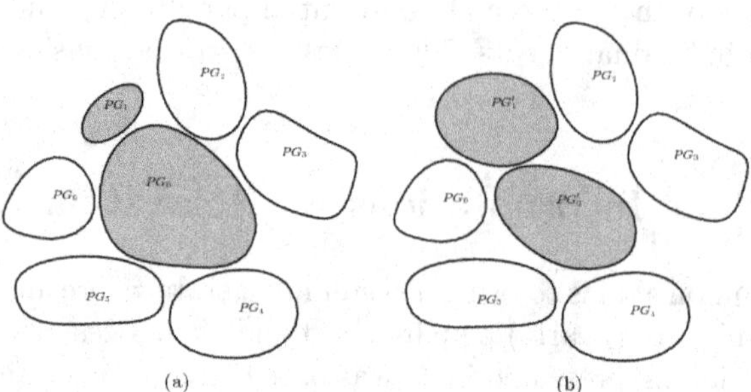

Fig. 4. Even partitioning using the relaxation method. An active agent (maintaining PG_0, shown in (a)) looks for an appropriate (i.e. satisfying a given size condition) neighbor RCG, namely PG_1, merges with it and finally splits into two halves (PG'_0, PG'_1, shown in (b)).

1. *Each* $v \in \mathsf{Private}(H)$ *becomes* $v \in \mathsf{Private}(G)$
2. *For each* $v \in \mathsf{Replicas}(H)$ *update the attribute related to the parent RCG (H changes to G) in all replicas of* v*, remove duplicates of* $v \in \mathsf{Replicas}(G)$ *(if any).*

Since the merging procedure is executed in a distributed environment there should be applied some synchronization mechanism enforcing an atomic execution of merge operation and ensuring the overall consistency of a complementary form of G.

Algorithm 3 . *Splitting procedure.*
Let H *be a subgraph of RCG* G_i*. Two RCGs,* H' *and* H''*, are created in the following steps:*

1. *Initially* $H' = H$ *and* $H'' = G_i - H$*;*
2. *For every* $v \in V(H)$ *such that there exists a node* $w \in V(G_i - H)$ *which is a neighbor of* v *in* G_i*: we replicate* v *(denoting a copy of* v *as* v'*) and: (a) We keep* v *in* H' *and mark it as a border node; (b) We attach node* v' *to* H'' *with all edges connecting* v *with* $G_i - H$ *and also mark it as a border node; (c) Proper references are added to* v *and* v'*, they allows us to determine the set of all replicas of* v *(these references are also in all its previous replicas iff* v *has been a border node before this operation);*
3. *Optionally, some reindexation of* $V_{H'}$ *and* $V_{H''}$ *can be made for optimizing local transformations.*

The relaxation algorithm being a combination of interleaving mergings an splittings has the following form:

Algorithm 4 . *Relaxation algorithm*

1. *If* $|V(G_i)| \in I$ *then return;*
2. *Let* H *be the neighbor RCG such that* $|V(H)| \notin I$*; if* H *doesn't exist then select any neighbor RCG;*
3. *Merge* G_i *and* H*;*
4. *If* $|V(G_i)| > S_t + \epsilon$ *then split* G_i *into two halves,* A *and* B*; set* $G_i = A$, $H = B$*;*
5. *Go to step 1.*

The relaxation algorithm gives a very good convergence in both aspects: the resultant sizes of the RCGs and the percentage of the optimized RCGs.

4 Tests

In this section tests and obtained results are discussed. In the first part the convergence of relaxation and its comparison with SNI are presented. In the second subsection we verify the convergence of the relaxation method against various initial conditions.

4.1 SNI and Relaxation Method. Comparison

To validate the proposed approach we compared it with the method described in [9] (*single node incorporation* - SNI) by executing the test which was intended to give comparison of the parameters describing quantitatively the base graph partitions obtained in both ways. The following basic parameters were selected for comparison:

- S_{avg} – average RCG size,
- I_{var} – range of variability of RCG sizes,
- N_{opt}, N_{rel} – number of RCGs in I, expressed as an absolute value and as a percentage of all RCGs, respectively,
- N_{RCG} – number of RCGs after a final iteration.

All those descriptors were calculated for the final complementary form of a given centralized graph G. G was generated randomly, with the fixed number of nodes $|V| = 1000$ and number of the edges $|E| \cong 1414$. Tests showed that no qualitative effects appeared for $|V| > 1000$. It should be noted that the structure of G is similar as for graphs used in syntactic pattern recognition problems [3]. This implies that $|E| = c|V|$ where c varies about 1.5. We run the test 1000 times for the subsequent G's and calculated the descriptors averaged over all 1000 runs. The following model parameters values were set: The number of nodes in the centralized graph (as mentioned above) $|V(G)| = 1000$, RCG target size $S_t = 30$ was small compared to $|V(G)|$ and its admissible deviation was assumed to be $\epsilon \approx 15\% S_t$ thus $\epsilon = 5$. Initially, the centralized graph was decomposed into the RCGs containing at last 3 nodes (i.e. $10\% S_t$). Average number of RCGs was

Table 1. The values of descriptors for SNI approach (see [9]) and for relaxation method averaged over 1,000 runs. The essential descriptors are bolded.

Descriptor	SNI	Relaxation
S_t	**30**	**30**
S_{avg}	**20.1**	**28.1**
I_{var}	[1.6,28.2]	[8.2,34.4]
N_{opt}	37.2	38.08
N_{rel}	59.0%	92.2%
N_{RCG}	63.1	41.3

$\simeq 699$. It was also assumed that an agent may execute the relaxation at last 1000 times. The obtained results are shown in the Table 1. As it can be seen the relaxation method produces significantly better results compared to the SNI, especially for two key descriptors: N_{rel} (percentage of optimized RCGs) and the average RCG size. The presented method reaches above results after 220 iterations while in SNI an average RCG size stabilizes in 70 iterations (as it was shown in Figure 5). Following results were obtained when initial RCGs were greater than S_t: S_{avg} stabilized at 20.2 and 28.6 for SNI and relaxation respectively. This behavior was similar as for the case of small RCGs. If RCGs' initial sizes were selected randomly from the range $[2, 100]$ then S_{avg} stabilized at 25.3 and 28 for SNI and relaxation respectively.

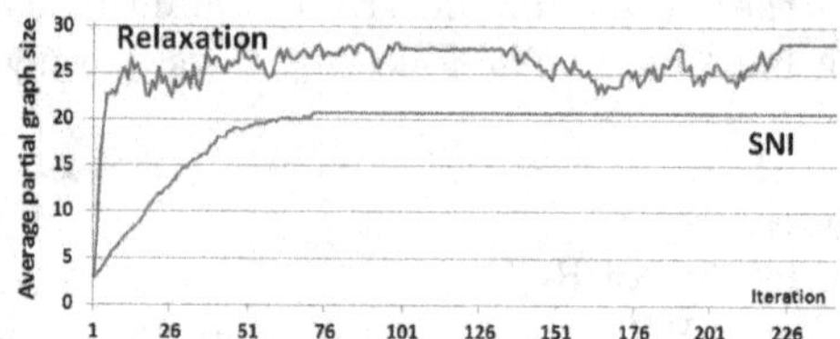

Fig. 5. Average RCG size stabilization for SNI and relaxation methods

4.2 Stability of Relaxation Method

In this subsection we aim to present properties of the relaxation method for various initial conditions in a set of RCGs. The base graph $G = (V, E, \Sigma, \Gamma, \delta)$, being a centralized representation of a problem is a randomly generated IE graph. It was assumed in the generation schema that a number of potential edges outcoming from a given node is described by the normal distribution $N(\mu, \sigma^2)$ with $\mu = 7, \sigma = 2$. For such parameters we have $|E|/|V| \simeq 1.5$.

Initially, we split G into a set of RCGs (we use greedy algorithm of decomposition) with an initial size (S_{init}) satisfying assumed conditions.

Direct simulation parameters are: the number of nodes in G, $|V(G)| = 50,000$, limitation for an initial RCG size, S_{init}, which varies dependently on a simulation type, optimal (target) RCG size $S_t = 30$, the acceptable error of an optimized RCG size $\epsilon = 5$. Total number of iterations was set to 10,000.

For a description of initial and final states of the simulation we select following characteristics of a RCGs population:

- N_{RCG} – number of RCGs,
- S_{avg} – average RCG size in a population,
- N_{opt}, N_{rel} – absolute and relative number of optimized RCGs, i.e. for which $||V(G_i)| - S_t| \leq \epsilon$ ($N_{rel} = N_{opt}/N_{RCG}$),
- I_{var} – the RCG size variability range,
- histogram of RCG sizes.

For inspecting a convergence of the relaxation method we check how the percentage of optimized RCGs and their average size change with subsequent iterations of the simulation.

Evolution form Small RCGs. In this test we impose that an initial size of a particular RCG $S_{init} \ll S_t$, namely $S_{init} \leq 3$. When setting $S_{init} \ll S_t$, we expect neighboring agents to merge their graphs in initial iterations.

Table 2. Descriptors of the set of replicated complementary graphs

Descriptor	N_{RCG}	S_{avg}	N_{opt}/N_{rel}	I_{var}
		Evolution from small RCGs		
Initial state	36180	2.8	0/0%	$[2, 3]$
Final state	2111	27.4	1946/92.2%	$[1, 40]$
		Evolution from large RCGs		
Initial state	214	237.1	0/0%	$[100, 1256]$
Final state	2131	27.3	1935 / 90.8%	$[2, 37]$
		Evolution from randomly sized RCGs		
Initial state	3003	18.0	217 / 7.2%	$[2, 100]$
Final state	2097	27.7	1993 / 95.0%	$[2, 35]$

Obtained results show that agents' activity reduced the number of RCGs by 17 times and the number of optimized subgraphs is over 92% (for details see Table 2).

Initially there were 5443 2-nodes RCGs and 30737 3-nodes ones. Figure 10 shows the final distribution of RCGs sizes. The convergence of the relaxation method is presented in Fig.6: it can be seen that the system state stabilizes about 150 (S_{avg}) and 420 iteration (N_{rel}). Next, values for both parameters fluctuate around fixed points.

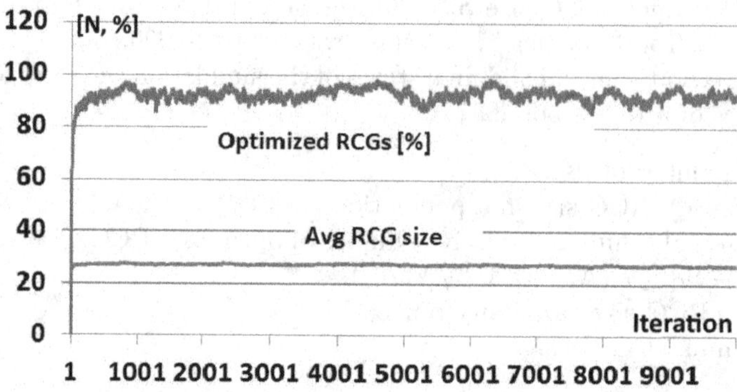

Fig. 6. Average RCG size and percentage of optimized RCGs (evolution from small RCGs)

Evolution from Large RCGs. It was assumed in this test that for each RCG $|V(G_i)| \geq S_{init} = 100$. As the greedy algorithm of an initial decomposition of G produces large amount of artifacts – small subgraphs – it was necessary to refine obtained set by merging iteratively smallest RCGs until no G_i had less than 100 nodes. By enforcing initial RCGs sizes significantly greater than their target sizes ($S_{init} \gg S_t$) we make agents split their graphs in initial iterations.

95% of initial RCGs was in the range [100, 500]. The remaining 5% of graphs had over 500 nodes. The final distributions of RCGs sizes is presented in Figure 10. Values of descriptors are presented in Table 2. The number of RCGs increased by 9 and the ratio of optimized graphs is nearly 91%.

Similarly as in the previous test it can be seen (Fig. 7) that S_{avg} and N_{rel} stabilize (at about 250 and 580 iteration respectively) around fixed values.

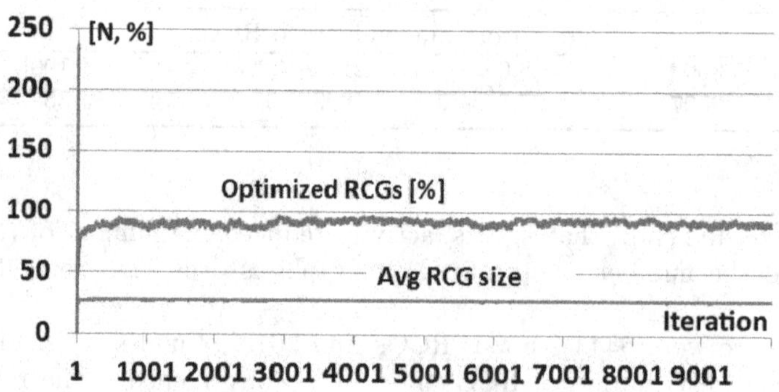

Fig. 7. Average RCG size and percentage of optimized RCGs (evolution from large RCGs)

Evolution from Random RCGs. In the third simulation we impose no limitation on RCG initial sizes besides they may vary in the range [2, 100] (see Table 2). Additionally, on the initial distribution (Fig.9) there can be seen the overrepresentation of small RCGs which is an artifact resulting from greedy algorithm of decomposition.

The characteristic of the system evolution (Fig. 8) is similar to the previous ones: with fixed stabilization points and values fluctuations. As initial RCGs sizes are variant, initial activity of agents is dominated neither by merging nor splitting their local graphs. 7.2% of initial RCGs are optimized and this ratio increases to 95% in the final state.

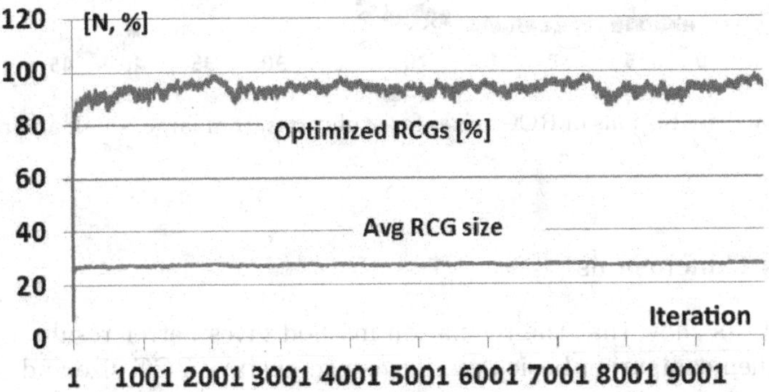

Fig. 8. Average RCG size and percentage of optimized RCGs (evolution from random RCGs)

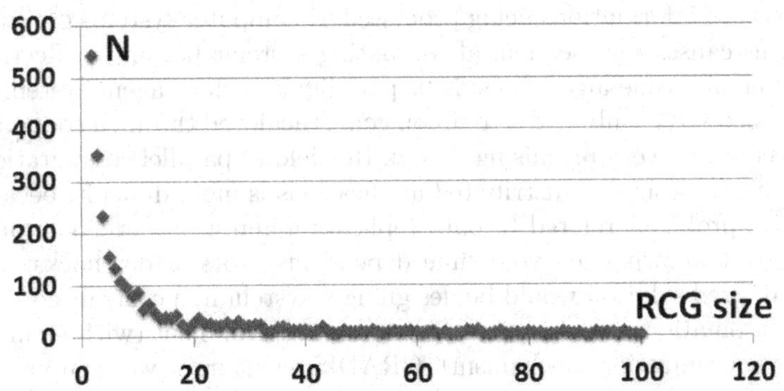

Fig. 9. Initial distribution of RCGs sizes (evolution from random RCGs)

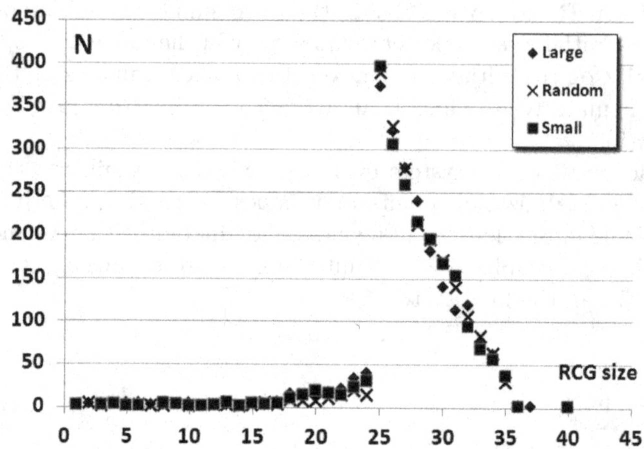

Fig. 10. Final distributions of RCGs sizes for evolutions from large, small and randomly sized RCGs

4.3 Tests Conclusions

Performed tests show that the relaxation method gives better results than SNI approach when comparing basic descriptors e.g. average RCG size and the ratio of optimized graphs. The relaxation method convergence and effectiveness were proved for various initial conditions: small, large and randomly sized RCGs.

5 Conclusion

The quantity of informations being processed by computer systems grows continuously. This causes that sequential computing systems become ineffective even using polynomial time algorithms. New paradigms such as agent systems where data are processed locally and a common goal is achieved throuh a cooperation of agents, seem to be very promising area in the field of parallel computations. On the other hand, designing distributed applications is more difficult, because one has to solve problems related to data replication and a proper synchronization of access to it allowing to avoid time dependent errors or deadlocks. Thereby the most desired solution would be designing a system in a centralized form and next, its automatic translation to a distributed environment (with assurance an implicit synchronization mechanism). GRADIS agent framework supports a co-operation of agents maintaining graphs in a replicated and complementary form in such a way that a sum of actions performed by particular agents is equivalent to a corresponding transformation made on centralized graph. Such solution is proposed for graph transformations where a centralized graph can be represented in a complementary form i.e. as a set of partial graphs [9] and rules that allow to apply "old" productions (designed for a centralized solution) in a distributed environment. This simplifies a maintenance of a knowledge represented by a distributed graph. This maintenance is, however, the second phase of a system life time, the first one is an initial graph distribution according to a given criterion. The algorithm presented in the paper seems to be enough quick (a system stabilizes in a solution within few hundred iterations) and generating results that are consistent sufficiently with the given criterion. It should be remarked that in the case of a multi-agent system one can not estimate a computational complexity in the classic way i.e. analyzing an algorithm. One can evaluate only the complexity of an individual agent's operations performed within a single iteration. It was proved [11] that both, SplitGraph and JoinGraphs, procedures have the polynomial complexity with respect to the number of agents.

References

1. Corradini, A., Montanari, U., Rossi, F., Ehrig, H., Heckel, R., Löwe, M.: Algebraic approaches to graph transformation - part i: Basic concepts and double pushout approach. In: Handbook of Graph Grammars and Computing by Graph Transformations. Foundations, vol. 1, pp. 163–246. World Scientific (1997)
2. Ehrig, H., Heckel, R., Lowe, M., Ribeiro, L., Wagner, A.: Algebraic Approaches to Graph Transformation Part II: Single Pushout and Comparison with Double Pushout Approach. In: Handbook of Graph Grammars and Computing by Graph Transformations. Foundations, vol. 1, pp. 247–312. World Scientific (1997)
3. Flasinski, M.: On the parsing of deterministic graph languages for syntactic pattern recognition. Pattern Recognition 26(1), 1–16 (1993)
4. Flasinski, M.: Power Properties of NCL Graph Grammars with a Polynomial Membership Problem. Theoretical Computer Science 201, 189–231 (1998)
5. Flasinski, M.: Inference of parsable graph grammar for syntactic pattern recognition. Fundamenta Informaticae 80, 397–412 (2007)
6. Kotulski, L.: Parallel Allocation of the Distributed Software using Node Label Controlled Graph Grammars. Automatyka 2(2), 321–338 (2008)
7. Kotulski, L.: Distributed Graphs Transformed by Multiagent System. In: Rutkowski, L., Tadeusiewicz, R., Zadeh, L.A., Zurada, J.M. (eds.) ICAISC 2008. LNCS (LNAI), vol. 5097, pp. 1234–1242. Springer, Heidelberg (2008)
8. Kotulski, L.: GRADIS - Multiagent Environment Supporting Distributed Graph Transformations. In: Bubak, M., van Albada, G.D., Dongarra, J., Sloot, P.M.A. (eds.) ICCS 2008, Part III. LNCS, vol. 5103, pp. 644–653. Springer, Heidelberg (2008)
9. Kotulski, L., Sędziwy, A.: Agent Framework For Decomposing a Graph Into the Equally Sized Subgraphs. In: WORLDCOMP 2008 Conference, Foundations of Computer Science, pp. 245–250 (2008)
10. Kotulski, L., Sędziwy, A.: Parallel Graph Transformations with Double Pushout Grammars. In: Rutkowski, L., Scherer, R., Tadeusiewicz, R., Zadeh, L.A., Zurada, J.M. (eds.) ICAISC 2010. LNCS, vol. 6114, pp. 280–288. Springer, Heidelberg (2010)
11. Kotulski, L., Sędziwy, A.: Parallel Graph Transformations Supported by Replicated Complementary Graphs. In: Dobnikar, A., Lotrič, U., Šter, B. (eds.) ICANNGA 2011, Part II. LNCS, vol. 6594, pp. 254–264. Springer, Heidelberg (2011)

12. Kotulski, L., Sędziwy, A.: Various agent strategies in the graph partioninig optimization in the GRADIS framework. In: Information systems architecture and technology: models of the organisation's risk management. Oficyna Wydawnicza Politechniki Wrocawskiej, pp. 269–279 (2008)
13. Kotulski, L., Sędziwy, A.: On the Complexity of Coordination of Parallel Graph Transformations. In: Proceedings at the Fourth International Conference on Dependability of Computer Systems DepCoS, RELCOMEX 2009, pp. 279–289. IEEE Computer Society Order Number P3674 (2009)
14. Kotulski, L., Sędziwy, A.: GRADIS - the multiagent environment supported by graph transformations. Simulation Modelling Practice and Theory 18(10), 1515–1525 (2010)
15. Kreowski, H.J., Kluske, S.: Graph Multiset Transformation as a Framework for Massive Parallel Computation. In: Ehrig, H., Heckel, R., Rozenberg, G., Taentzer, G. (eds.) ICGT 2008. LNCS, vol. 5214, pp. 351–365. Springer, Heidelberg (2008)
16. Kreowski, H.-J., Kuske, S.: Autonomous Units and Their Semantics – The Concurrent Case. In: Engels, G., Lewerentz, C., Schäfer, W., Schürr, A., Westfechtel, B. (eds.) Nagl Festschrift. LNCS, vol. 5765, pp. 102–120. Springer, Heidelberg (2010)

Agent System for Managing Distributed Mobile Interactive Documents in Knowledge-Based Organizations

Magdalena Godlewska

Gdańsk University of Technology
Faculty of Electronics, Telecommunications and Informatics
ul. Narutowicza 11/12, 80-233 Gdańsk
magdal@eti.pg.gda.pl

Abstract. The MIND architecture of distributed mobile interactive document is a new processing model defined to facilitate obtaining a proper solution in knowledge processes carried out by knowledge-based organizations. Such organizations have an established structure that defines document templates and knowledge process. The aim of the MIND architecture is to change the static document to mobile agents, which are designed to implement the structure of the organization through autonomous migration between knowledge workers in accordance with the built-in policy. An extensible functionality of the agents also extends the static document to interface unit. The prototype of the agent system, based on the MIND architecture, shows the possibility of its implementation using available technology. The case studies provide the possibility of using architecture to solve specific decision problems with external knowledge of organization's workers.

Keywords: Agent system, collaborative computing, knowledge-based organizations, policy-driven management, interactive documents, workflow patterns.

1 Introduction

MIND architecture of distributed Mobile **IN**teractive **D**ocument is a new processing model proposed by the author. Traditionally electronic documents have been treated as static objects downloaded from a server or sent by an e-mail. The MIND provides for exchange of static documents into a set of mobile agents, that can migrate between authors according to a fixed migration policy.

The MIND architecture makes possible a radical shift from *data-centric* distributed systems, with hard-coded functionality, to flexible *document-centric* ones, where only generic services are provided by local environments, while specialized functionality is embedded in migrating document components.

In order to verify the assumptions of the MIND architecture and its possible implementation with the use of available technology, a set of prototype tools was implemented. This set of tools can be defined as an environment for designing

N.T. Nguyen (Ed.): Transactions on CCI VI, LNCS 7190, pp. 121–145, 2012.

and managing document migration. Among these tools is a document editor that supports the design of documents in accordance with the assumptions of the MIND architecture and agent system that allows management components of documents.

The aim of research on this architecture is to develop a new model of object processing based on a system consisting of migrant components. Each document component is intelligent because of built-in functionality and mobile because of capabilities of migration in the system according to the inscribed policy. Workflow description language supported by the agent system will perform the workflow control-flow patterns, which are used in decision-making processes involving documents. Intelligent and mobile components form the MIND architecture that supports obtaining a proper solution by participants in collaborative computing of knowledge-based organizations. The main goal of the knowledge-based organizations is knowledge management and generation of new knowledge by knowledge workers through the documents. The documents are transferred between workers in accordance with the policy of migration.

In this paper, the author presents the model of a knowledge-based organization and general assumptions of the MIND architecture, presents also selected workflow patterns applicable to knowledge-based organizations, describes the elements of the agent system for managing distributed mobile documents and shows case studies that use the MIND architecture.

2 Related Work

The presented proposal combines existing technologies and new idea to extract some new functionality in the topics of distributed electronic document and collaborative environments. Unmarshalling and marshalling [1] allow XML documents [2] to be switched from static to dynamic form. Full distribution guarantees convenience of working in group and minimizes needs to connect with central server. Proposed solution differs from collaborative editing problem (algorithms solving that problem are introduced e.g. in [3,4,5]). Collaborative editing is the situation when users edit together the same part of document. This paper introduces problem when users work on different parts of one document, called constituent documents.

It is worth mentioning that the proposal is something different than shared workspace (e.g. BSCW - Basic Support for Cooperative Work [6]) or repository (e.g. CVS - Concurrent Versions System [7]). Those concepts are based on server. Users are able to upload and download some objects (documents, sources etc.), to communicate with other users, to be informed about some restrictions like deadlines. But most operations take place on the server. In the proposed concept, agent-objects have build-in functionality that has effect of shifting some services from server location to user location. That solution limits client-server communication. That feature distinguishes the proposal from client-server based applications like Collaboratus [8].

Full distribution and minimizing client-server communication are needed in workflow. Components of document do not have common location. They are able to migrate between users according to some policy. When there are many users in collaborative group (e.g. in court trials), the problem of too many client-server communicates appears. More independence form server allows also for implementing assumption that system managing documents should be as transparent to user as it is possible.

Workflow, based on the agent platform, is also implemented by WADE - Workflow and Agents Development Environment [9] software platform. The proposed concept differs from that implemented in WADE, because WADE is a data-centric approach and MIND is a document-centric one. In the MIND architecture, workflow (as a XPDL [10] file) is a part of the whole document. Workflow in the form of a document may be modified during the process execution. This allows the implementation of complex workflow patterns, i.e. Multiple Instances with a Priori Run-Time Knowledge or Multiple Instances without a Priori Run-time Knowledge presented in [11,12,13].

The MIND architecture proposed by the author is a completely different concept than the MIND architecture for heterogeneous multimedia federated digital libraries presented in [14,15,16]. The aim of the second architecture is integration of heterogeneous, multimedia non-co-operating digital libraries. This architecture consists of a single mediator and one proxy (composed of several proxy components) for every connected library and gives the user the impression of a single coherent system. The MIND architecture described in this paper is an abbreviation of **M**obile **IN**teractive **D**ocument. The aim of this MIND architecture is to change the static document to mobile agents, which are designed to implement the structure of the organization through autonomous migration between knowledge workers in accordance with the built-in policy. The similarity of the architecture names is coincidental.

3 Knowledge-Based Organization

Information can be defined as ordering and interpretation of data based on some patterns. The set of patterns in a certain context creates *knowledge*. New knowledge is built through the creation of new patterns. Knowledge-based organizations focus on processes based on collection, transfer and use of knowledge. Such processes are called *knowledge processes*.

Knowledge workers play an important role in the knowledge process. They generate new knowledge based on current information, their own knowledge and knowledge transfered by other workers. The purpose of the knowledge-based organization is to implement the knowledge process, in which the human mind is an important element. Knowledge is usually transferred between knowledge workers through the documents.

Tree resources of knowledge are used in the knowledge process: codified knowledge, established knowledge and personalized knowledge [17] (cf. Fig.1):

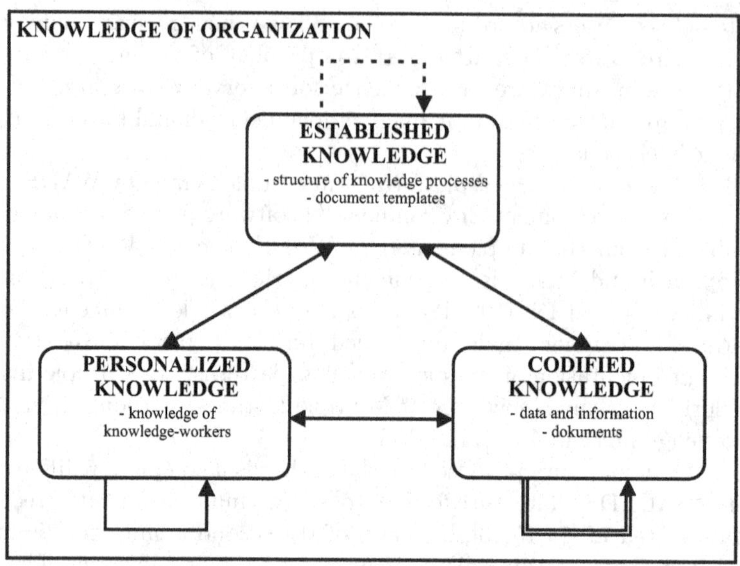

Fig. 1. Resources of knowledge in knowledge-based organizations

- *Established knowledge* includes the structure of knowledge processes. Processes are defined based on years of experience. Their aim is to ensure the execution of all necessary and sufficient activities to obtain the proper solution. The structure of the processes change rather slowly (dashed line in Fig.1) and is often conditioned by the law. Established knowledge includes also precisely defined document templates that can be used during the knowledge process.
- *Codified knowledge* includes a documentation of the process, ie information and knowledge transferred through the documents. That resource is dynamically changed during the process (double line in Fig.1).Codified knowledge is generated during the process by knowledge workers, who create new knowledge based on the data, information and knowledge contained in available documents. New knowledge is transferred to the next workers through the documents.
- *Personalized knowledge* is a knowledge of organization workers. The role of workers is creating new knowledge according to the rules of the process and based on codified knowledge. Workers collectively contribute to the proper solution of the process. Participation in the process also affects the development of knowledge workers (single line in Fig.1).

In the knowledge-based organizations, knowledge workers fill in relevant documents and transfer them to the next workers in accordance with a migration policy. In the process, the document is generally a static object, which means that: it is filled, it is sent, it is viewed, etc. In this paper the author presents a proposal to apply a distributed document, that consists of dynamic and intelligent constituent documents. The constituent documents are knowledge storages and also interface units, that facilitate the extraction of knowledge and implement the migration policy defined in the knowledge process.

Distributed document - D - is created on the basis of a template S. The template $S = \{s_1, s_2, ..., s_n\}$ is a set of templates of constituent documents that may arise during the knowledge process. The templates stem from established knowledge of organization. Document D can be composed of multiple instances of some templates s_i.

The process is defined as a set of places P and a set of transitions T. The process also stems from established knowledge of organization. This definition is based on the model of Petri nets [18,19]. Operations on documents are performed by knowledge-workers in places. Place is marked, when at least one constituent document is in this place. The constituent documents migrate between places in accordance with conditions defined in transition nodes. The process is graphically presented as a directed bigraph. The place nodes are separated by transition nodes in such a way that neither of the two places and neither of the two transitions are directly connected with each other. The transition nodes define the directed arcs between places. For example, a transition t_1 defines an arc "'form p_1 to p_2"'. It means, that there are two pairs: (p_1, t_1), (t_1, p_2) in a graph structure. The arcs in the graph form a set $A \subseteq P \times T \cup T \times P$. The conditions for transitions between places are also defined in the transition nodes.

The model of knowledge-based organization contains the sets of places and transitions that allow for defining the process and the set of constituent document templates that allows for the construction of the document D. The definition below summarizes the definition of the knowledge-based organization.

Definition 1. Knowledge-Based Organization *is a three-tuple* $KBO = (P, T, S)$, *where:*

1. P is a set of **places**.
2. T is a set of **transitions**, such that $P \cap T = \emptyset$.
3. S is a set of **constituent document templates**.

Information about the process (P, T) and the document template (S) allow for the construction of the proper document D, which task is the realization of the knowledge process. The definitions of sets and functions presented below show how to construct the document D.

Let $E = \{e_1, e_2, ..., e_n\}$ be a family of set of instances of all constituent document templates. $e_i = \{e_i^1, e_i^2, ..., e_i^k\}$ is set of instances of one constituent document template s_i. e_i^j is a constituent document, ie. specific instance of one constituent document template s_i. The constituent document is distinguished from others by the unique identifier. Let $f : S \rightarrow E$ be a function that assigns set of constituent documents to their template. Document D is a set consisting of the constituent documents, eg. $D = \{e_2^4, e_1^6, e_3^1, ..., e_3^2\}$. Functions: $pred : D \rightarrow D \cup \{nil\}$ and $succ : D \rightarrow D \cup \{nil\}$ define the order of the elements in D.

The set D is modified during the process, because the constituent documents can be deleted, copied, merged or created. The state of the document SD can be defined as a set D in a specific point in the process. The document D is distributed and mobile thus it is necessary to define the function $g : e_i \rightarrow P$ that assigns the current place to the constituent document.

4 MIND Architecture

The main goal of the MIND architecture is to implement the model of knowledge-based organization by changing the static document to mobile components, that meet their mission in the distributed agent system. After the mission, components are merged into a static final document. The concept of document life cycle is illustrated in Fig. 2.

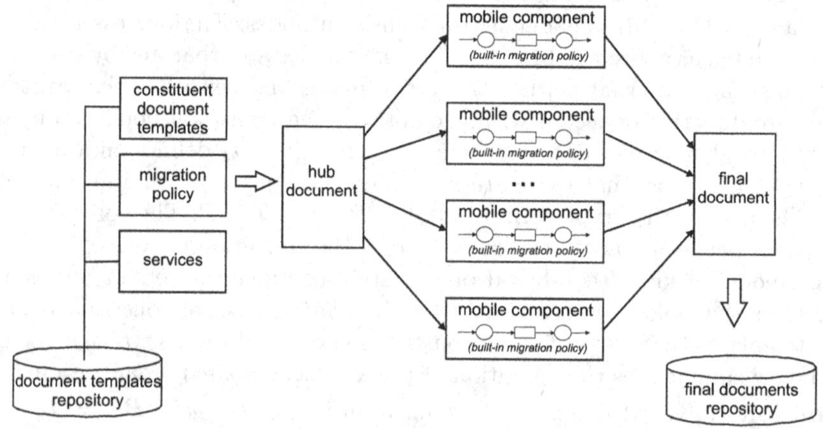

Fig. 2. The concept of MIND document life cycle

The MIND architecture has been proposed with a view of facilitating the collaboration of knowledge workers in knowledge-based organizations. In such organizations, a set of particular knowledge contributes to the final proper solution. There are some important elements in knowledge process: the structure of organization and knowledge of workers passed through the documents. In such a process the external data sources (knowledge of workers) appear. The examples of such processes are court trials, integrative bargaining, medical consultations, or crash investigations.

The MIND architecture involves the creation of a document D that contains structure of the process (sets P and T) and templates of constituent documents (set S). The constituent documents follow a defined process (migration policy) to move between their authors in the form of mobile agents and then, as the interface unit, assist in extracting knowledge from authors.

In the architecture some additional services can be defined. The purpose of these services is adaptation of the architecture to the needs of a particular organization. From the user's perspective, these services can be `local` (installed on local computer), `external` (accessible from the outside) and `embedded` (build-in in agent).

The main components of the architecture are: *HDDL* (Hub Document Description Language) [20] document template, that is defined in *XML Schema* [2] and the agent system for document managing. The document template contains the following components:

- `document.xml` - basic information about the document D in the form of a header and a specification of services.
- `authors.xml` - data about the authors (knowledge workers).
- `templates.xml` - a set S of constituent document templates.
- `parts.xml` - a definition of the document parts. Each part contains a constituent document that is an instance of one template defined in the component `templates.xml`. This component defines the structure of vector D.
- `path.xml` - a definition of the process graph. This component connects the authors with the document parts and defines workflow of constituent documents.

Main Component (`document.xml`)

Elements and attributes of the main component are presented on Fig. 3. Attributes describe identity and the basic properties of each MIND document:

- the unique identifier (`ID`) and the `title` – distinguish a specific template in the document templates repository;
- the `security` level and the ability to add new dynamic objects (components) in the document life cycle – determine the behavior of constituent documents in the form of mobile objects during interaction with knowledge workers.

The `<head>` element specifies metadata of document that is useful for searching the repositories that store documents in the static form. The following information may be contained in the `<meta>` collection: information about the tool by which the document was prepared (`name="Generator"`), basic information about the document like `version`, `keywords`, `author` and `description`, and other information defined by the user using their own names.

The `<services>` element specifies services of MIND document, that are available for each dynamic object created as a result of its conversion from a static to an object form. The services can be implemented as:

- `<embedded_service>` - services implemented with MIND application, expanding dynamically document functionality
- `<local_service>` - services acquired by document components from target hosts upon arrival
- `<external_service>` - services triggered by a document components on remote hosts

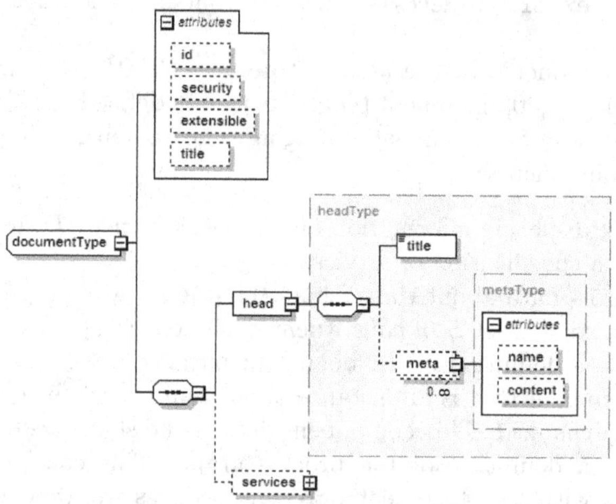

Fig. 3. Logical structure of main component

Authors Component (`authors.xml`)
Each MIND document has at least one author, who is a document originator. The document originator creates a hub document at the beginning of the life cycle (cf. Fig. 2). Constituent documents which migrate as mobile components can be assigned to other authors. This assignment is defined in the built-in migration policy of the component. During component migration, also new authors can be added to the policy path.

Elements and attributes of the <`author`> element are presented on Fig. 4. Each author is assigned a unique identifier (`ID`). The `originator` attribute pointed the document originator and the `active` attribute specifies whether the author has the right to change the constituent document.

The <`name`> element contains the first and the last name of author or the name of company, the <`position`> element specifies the author's position in the organization. The <`description`> is some additional information about the author, for example, role in the document creating. The <`contact`> element contains the contact data of the author. IP-address is especially important information for the mobile component. It specifies the host on which the constituent document should be delivered. IP address can be defined in indirect way as a persistent number that distinguishes the author. Then the appropriate service assigns the current IP address of the author to the persistent address. This solution enables work on multiple computers or on mobile devices. The <`communication`> element specifies other information necessary for communication with the author.

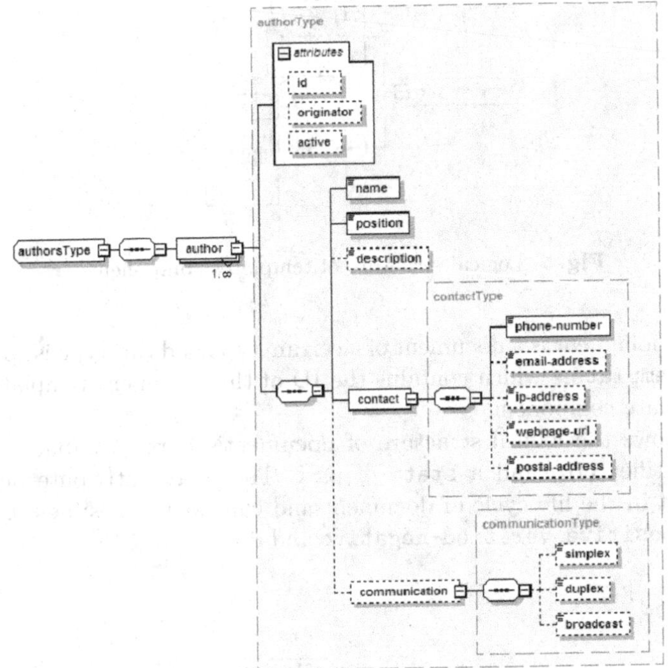

Fig. 4. Logical structure of authors component

Templates Component (`templates.xml`)
The document D consists of any number of constituent documents which are documents of a certain type. The document types are defined by a set of templates ($S = \{s_1, s_2, ..., s_n\}$). Fig. 5 shows the specification of the constituent document templates.

Each template has its own unique identifier (`ID`) and `title`. The `<mime-type>` element contains the name of a template type compatible with the standard *Multipurpose Internet Mail Extensions* (MIME) [21]. The `<content>` element represents the content of the template encoded in a format *base64* [22].

Parts Component (`parts.xml`)
The MIND document consists of constituent documents, which are converted into mobile objects. The constituent documents meet their mission of the transfer and collection of knowledge in the knowledge-based organizations. The constituent document is defined as a part in parts component. Its structure and format are defined by an appropriate template that is stored in the templates component (described earlier).

With reference to the model of knowledge-based organization, the parts component defines a vector D. The constituent documents are placed in the specific order and distinguished from others by the unique identifier (attribute `ID`). Each

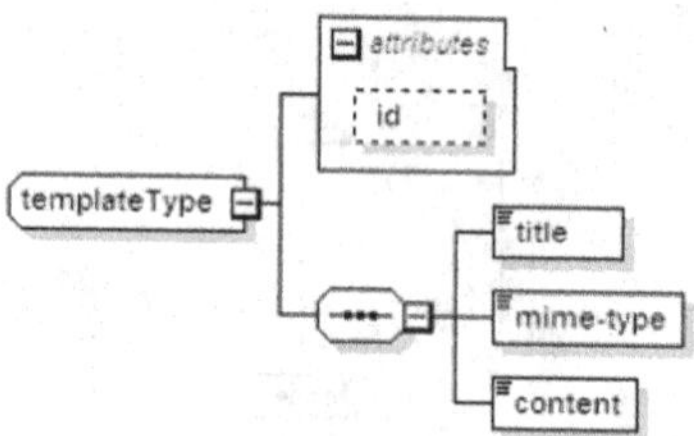

Fig. 5. Logical structure of templates component

constituent document is a document of a certain type and this type is specified by element <`template`> which contains the ID of the document template defined in the template component.

Fig. 6 shows the logical structure of document's part. Attributes specify a unique identifier (`ID`) and a `state` of part. The `state` attribute defines the state of part in the life cycle of document and can take values: `new`, `modified`, `verified-positive`, `verified-negative` and `done`.

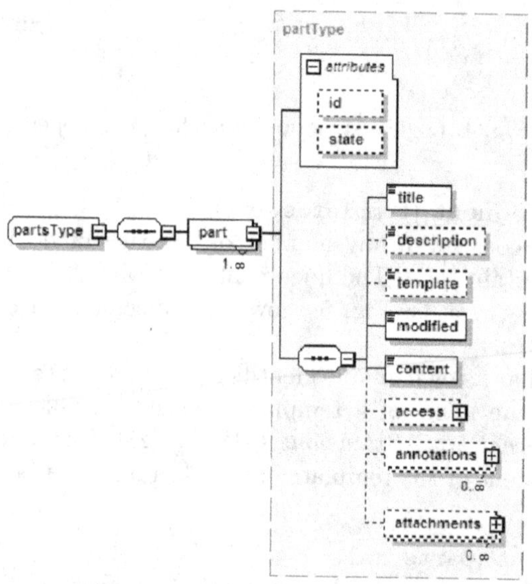

Fig. 6. Logical structure of parts component

The <`title`> element contains a title of part, the <`modified`> element contains date of last modification and the <`content`> element represents the actual content of part encoded in a format *base64*. The <`description`> element provides a full text description of the constituent document and <`template`> specifies the `ID` of document template.

The <access> element has child elements: `none`, `toc`, `read`, `write` and `print` and they specify access right of authors to the document. The access rights are: `none` - no right of access, `toc` - access to table of content, `read` - right to read the document, `write` - access to write and `print` - rigth to print. The child elements allow to assign the value of the author's `ID` attribute. `All` value of each element allows all the authors for the specified operation.

Each constituent document can have the <`annotations`> mapped dynamically at any time of the document life cycle. The <`reference`> child element of <`annotations`> allows also for putting new annotations to existing annotations. It is also possible to link some other document to MIND constituent document as an attachment.

Path Component (`path.xml`)
The migration policy is defined also as a component of the document. The `path.xml` component is a *XPDL* [10] file. XPDL (XML Process Definition Language) is a dialect of XML (Extensible Markup Language). It is a language for workflow process design.

The main element of XPDL - <`WorkflowProcesses`> - may contain any number of <`WorkflowProcess`>. The logical structure of <`WorkflowProcess`> is shown in Fig.7. Each element <`WorkflowProcess`> represents a process consisting of <`Activities`> and <`Transitions`> between them.

<`Activity`> - element of the workflow process - combines the author with the part of document that is assigned to this author. In the workflow definition, places P in a process are called activities [23]. <`Transition`> element has attributes `From` and `To` that define directed paths between activities. <`Transition`> element may also specify the conditions for transitions between activities. Construction of dynamic objects representing the components of the document is presented in Fig. 8.

5 Workflow Patterns Applicable to Knowledge-Based Organizations

In knowledge-based organizations, the process is constructed from elementary operations. These operation are called workflow patterns. This section presents sample workflow patterns that are applicable to knowledge-based organizations. These patterns are selected from the complete list (more than 40) of workflow patterns presented in [11,12,13]. Some of these are supported directly by XPDL and others may be implemented by agent systems. These workflow patterns are modules of the path component. The complete list of modules allows for construction of any process of constituent document migration.

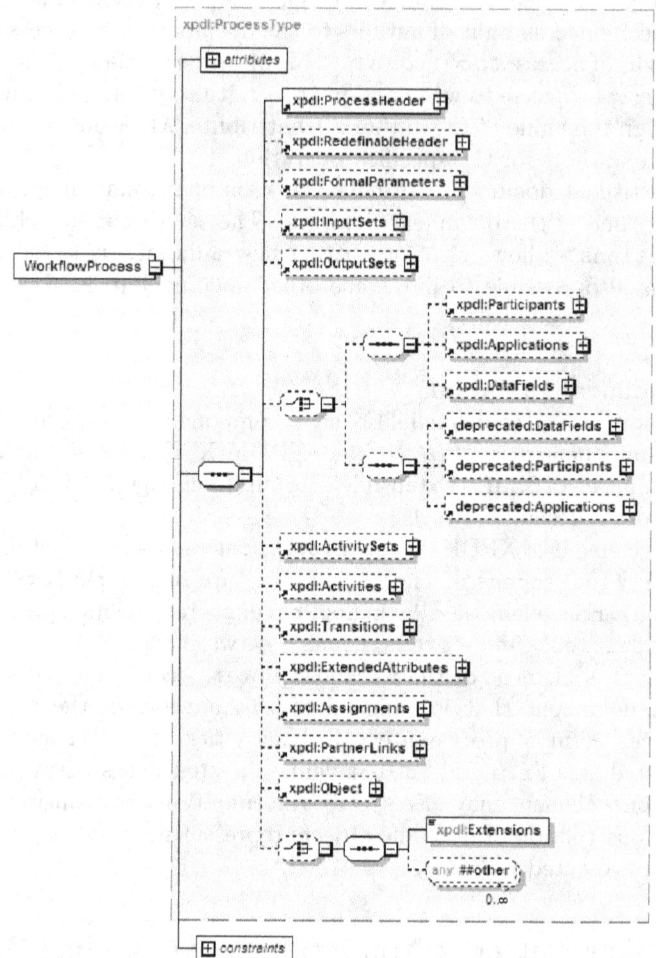

Fig. 7. Logical structure of XPDL workflow process

5.1 Basic Control-Flow Patterns

To the basic control-flow patterns include: Sequence, Parallel Split, Synchronization, Exclusive Choice and Simple Merge. All these patterns are directly supported by XPDL.

Sequence is when an activity in a workflow process is enabled after the completion of another activity in the same process. This is the basic form of transferring constituent documents in the knowledge-based organizations. When one of knowledge workers completes work on the document, this document goes to the next author, in accordance with the migration path. In MIND, agent reads, directly from the XPDL policy file, a target activity (designated by the transition)

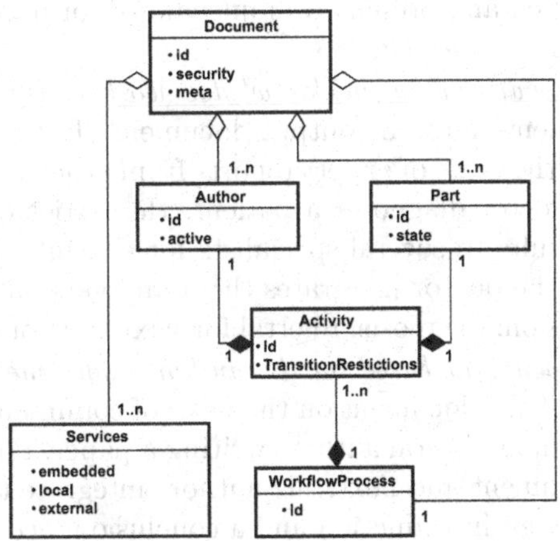

Fig. 8. MIND dynamic object

to which it has to move. Sequence is the simplest but also the most frequent form of the flow of constituent documents.

Parallel Split is a point in the process where a single thread of control splits into multiple threads of control that can be executed in parallel, thus allowing activities to be executed simultaneously or in any order. In the knowledge-based organizations, this is a case where one constituent document is copied and the copies are moved to the various knowledge workers. This places the new constituent documents in the vector D. For example, a few experts have to make independent decisions on the basis of the same research results. It is important in the parallel split, that the whole constituent document is duplicated and each of the knowledge workers get exactly the same copy.

After the Parallel Split, usually the *Synchronization* occurs in the process. This is a point in the process where multiple parallel branches converge into one single thread of control, thus synchronizing multiple threads. The merger activity is waiting for all branches to be completed. In the knowledge-based organizations, this is a case where all copies of one constituent document, that was edited by various knowledge workers are collected. A set of documents that differ from each other and containing different knowledge is appeared. The synchronization requires to wait for all copies of the document. Then the copies have to be integrated into one new constituent document. It also changes the dimension of the vector D. In the case of documents, integration does not always mean the same operation. It could be:

– *integrating into a single file*: this integration is basically gathering all copies in one document without interfering with its contents. Such situation can occur when the copy must remain unchanged. For example, in a court trial, each expert gives an independent opinion on certain evidence. These expert

reports are collected and presented in unchanged form during the trial. The particular opinion is essential.
- *integrating the document by the knowledge worker*: this is integrating the content of documents into one output document. The aggregate knowledge of one worker on the basis of expert reports from other workers is important. For instance, a doctor diagnoses a patient. He carries out a series of tests and sends the results to several specialists for consultation. After receiving all the opinions, the doctor integrates them and generates a new document containing a decision: diagnosis, referral for next tests or next consultations.
- *integrating the document based on the authors' agreement*: this is integrating the contents of the document on the basis of communication between the authors. For example, several authors writing a paper. First, everyone writes a part of the document and next, the authors integrate the whole paper together: they write an introduction and a conclusion, accept some consistent grammatical forms. In example, this is situation if few authors write one paper. First, each of them writes some section and then they establish together a common whole.
- *automatic integration*: content of the documents is automatically integrated this solution works only for simple documents with precisely specify structure, such as questionnaires.

In MIND, the merging point is defined in the policy file. This is the point where agents converge with the copies of document inside. The agents save the copies of document locally, then the copies are integrated into a single document without interfering with its contents or by the knowledge worker. Integrating the document based on the authors' agreement is more complicated. MIND architecture enables to define new applications (e.g. in services form), that facilitate and streamline the process of extracting information. In order to integrate the document, based on the authors' agreement, an application like communicator and/or an application, that allows for sharing the view and editing the document by many authors, could be used. The current version of the MIND architecture does not support directly the concept of integrating the document based on the authors' agreement. The automatic integration may also be performed by dedicated services for reading and integrating specific documents, i.e. questionnaires or tests. The aim of the MIND architecture is the support of the knowledge worker's interaction with the system, hence there is no direct support for automatic integration of documents. Regardless of the synchronization type, only one agent remains on the merging activity. This agent will continue its mission with a newly created document inside.

Exclusive Choice is a point in the process where, based on a decision or workflow control data, one of several branches is chosen. The choice is defined as a condition of the transition node. The corollary of Exclusive Choice is often a *Simple Merge* pattern. This is a point in the workflow process where two or more alternative branches come together without synchronization. It is an assumption of this pattern that none of the alternative branches is ever executed in parallel with another one. In these cases, the problem boils down to interpretation of the earlier conditions that selecting one of the options of flow. After the correct interpretation of the conditions, the flow of the agent does not differ from the normal Sequence.

5.2 Advanced Branching and Synchronization Patterns

To this group of patterns include: Multi-Choice, Synchronizing Merge, Multi-Merge and Discriminator.

Multi-Choice is a pattern similar to the Parallel Split, with the difference that there is selected a subset of threads to be executed in parallel. The corollary of the Multi-Choice is a *Synchronizing Megre* pattern, that merge the active threads. These patterns are directly supported by XPDL and in the MIND, they are connected with problems of synchronization and condition interpretation.

Multi-Merge is point in a process where two or more branches converge without synchronization, i.e. each incoming thread requires the same reaction in the activity. For example, after expert reports are received to the court, the feedback is sent. There is some workaround for this problem: the activity may be duplicated to each branch. In Together Workflow Editor (TWE) [9], there is a `WorkflowPatterns` directory, where the examples of patterns implementation can be found. There is some other solution for the Multi-Merge pattern with the use of subprocess executed asynchronously. In MIND, every agent has a built-in policy file, hence duplicating the activity is more obvious solution to this problem.

Discriminator is a point in the workflow process that waits for one (the few) of the incoming branches to complete before activating the subsequent activity. From that moment on it waits for all remaining branches to complete and ignores them. For instance, the recruitment committee is waiting for receipt of applications; when the first 20 applications arrive, the recruitment process moves to the next stage, and the rest applications are ignored. The support of this pattern in XPDL is unclear. There is some workaround solution presented in TWE. In MIND, all agents have built-in policy, so method, that counts instances of documents, is shifted from the agent to the container object, where the agents arrive with documents. So, discriminator will be implemented in the application rather than in XPDL.

5.3 Multiple Instance Patterns

This group of patterns include: Multiple Instances without Synchronization, Multiple Instances with a Priori Design-Time Knowledge, Multiple Instances with a Priori Run-Time Knowledge and Multiple Instances without a Priori Run-Time Knowledge.

Within a one process, multiple instances of an activity can be created. These instances are independent of each other and run concurrently. In the first pattern, there is no requirement synchronization upon completion and in other pattern the synchronization is required. For documents, the synchronization involves the integration of documents as in the case of Synchronization pattern.

The first three patterns can be implemented in XPDL by the LoopMultiInstance element but Multiple Instances without a Priori Run-Time Knowledge pattern can not be implemented in XPDL. In Multiple Instances without a Priori Run-Time Knowledge pattern, the number of instances to be created is not known in advance: new instances are created on demand, until no more instances are required. In the knowledge-based organizations, this is a case, when testimony of witnesses in a court trial are being collected. It is not known how many witnesses will testify and when they decide to testify. MIND allows for editing the policy file during a run time of the process. The policy file may be edited many time at each point in the process.

5.4 State-Based Patterns

This group of patterns include: Deferred Choice, Interleaved Parallel Routing and Milestone. *Deferred Choice* is a point in a process where one among several alternative branches is chosen based on information which is not necessarily available when this point is reached. The choice is not made immediately when the point is reached, but instead several alternatives are offered, and the choice between them is delayed until the occurrence of some event. *Interleaved Parallel Routing* is a pattern, when a set of activities is executed in an arbitrary order. Each activity in the set is executed exactly once. In any case, no two activities in the set can be active at the same time. *Milestone* is defined as a point in the process where a given activity has finished and another activity following it has not yet started.

These patterns use a different states of the process points. XPDL does not allow for the definition of states. Deferred Choice may fulfilled. The other patterns can be implemented by agent application. In the agent platform (e.g. JADE), agents can communicate with each other through the implemented communication protocols. They can also change some data locally and remotely. One agent ,who is in active state, may change state of other agents to inactive. So, XPDL can be extended on states by agent system.

6 Prototype System for Managing Distributed Documents

The static MIND document is designed in such way that it can be transformed into the object form, and then into a set of mobile agents. The mobile agents migrate between user's local workstations in accordance with a defined migration path. Based on the MIND architecture the prototype system for remote management of distributed components of the document has been implemented.

In the prototype system for managing distributed documents the following technologies are used. Static documents are implemented in *XML* language in accordance with the HDDL format designed for the MIND architecture. HDDL format has been specified in *XML Schema*[2]. To design workflow process *XPDL* format [10] is used. Server application [24] has been written in *Java* and *JADE* platform [25] is used for the creation, migration and tracking of agents. *XML-Beans* [1] is a technology used for accessing XML by binding it to Java types, *Java Mail* platform [26] is used for transferring agents via e-mail and *Log4j* [27] tool is used for creation of event logs.

The MIND architecture is not dependent on the chosen technologies and for its implementation different ones may be chosen. To describe the structure of documents and workflow XML language was selected. The possibility of its transformation and processing with programming languages allows to use its also in the future. The advantage of easy archiving of XML documents is particularly important in the documents, which will remain valid for many years, such as e.g. property rights.

In order to facilitate the preparation of the documents in HDDL format the following tools have been implemented: *HDDLEdit* [20] for creating and editing patterns of document and *STMPEdit* [20] for creating and editing of constituent document templates.

6.1 The Life Cycle of a Distributed Document in the Agent System

The system for managing components of the document is designed to implement the concept of converting a static form of the document to the autonomous agents that will meet their mission in the system, and then create a final document (cf. Fig.9.).

Agents have built-in migration functionality defined in the MIND policy file. According to the next stage of the document's life cycle, the agents migrate between the authors computers with a constituent document. The constituent document's content is processed by the respective authors. Organization of the agents population is involved in the agent system. The components of the system are run on the users computers. They create a platform that enables the functioning of the agents on each workstation, provides access to memory and enables the use of communication protocols. These protocols allow agents to exchange messages, and migrate independently on the network. If the author's computer is offline in terms of the agent platform, the system sends the agent by e-mail (cf. Fig. 10).

During the completion of the life cycle of the document, the agents reach different states, which, in the form of a diagram, is shown in Fig. 11.

An *active* state is a state when the agent is run on the agent platform. The agent is in a *hibernate* state in a situation when the user of the current agent's container chooses to stop work and turn off the application. The agent in this state is saved as a file on user's local computer – this operation called serialization. When the system is restarted, the agent can be rerun (transition from *hibernate* to *active* state). When the next agent's author is offline in the agent platform, the agent is sent to him by e-mail. This additional functionality moves the agent to a *sent* state. Agent is in this state, as long as the agent is stored on the mail server. The agent is received from the e-mail server and brought back

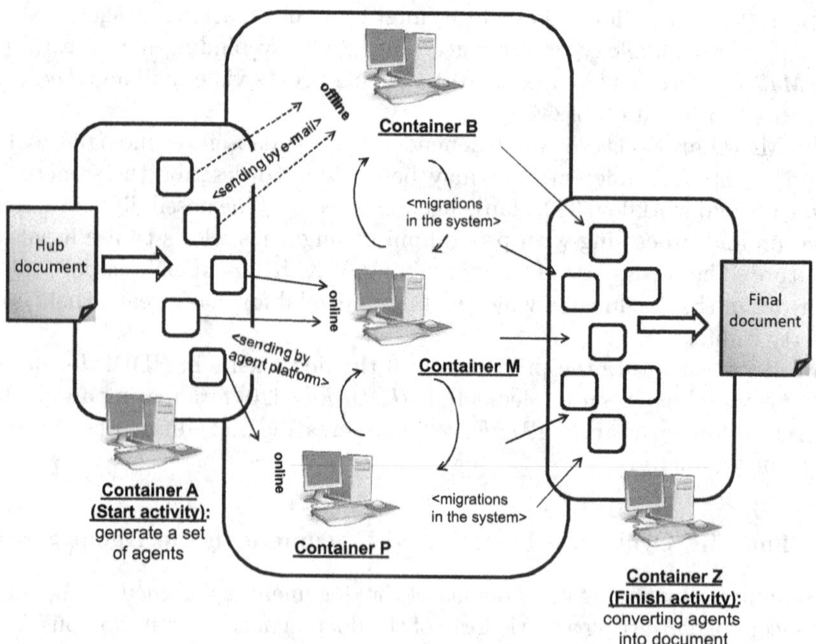

Fig. 9. The life cycle of MIND document in the implemented system

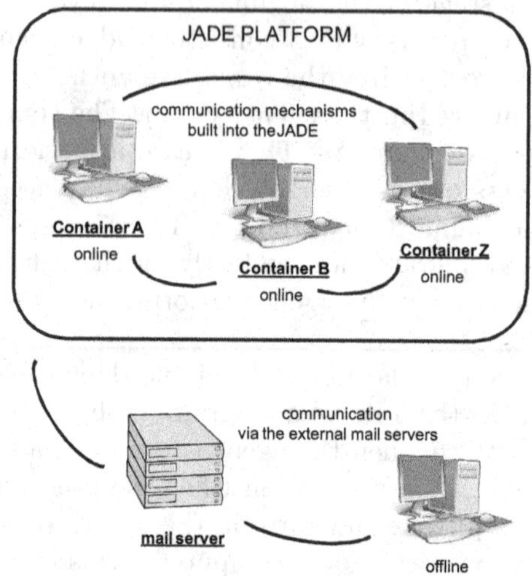

Fig. 10. The life cycle of MIND document in the implemented system

to the *active* state after restarting the application. When the agent arrives to final activity in the process, it moves to the *final* state. The agent in the final state may be *deleted* or *archived* (saved to a file).

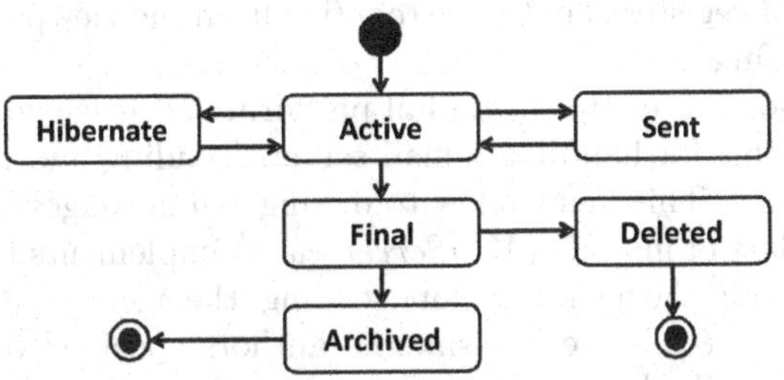

Fig. 11. Agent's states diagram

6.2 The Main Modules of the System

The application server for remote management of distributed document components consists of the following modules: agent server module, e-mail module, policy module, document module, mediator module and initial module.

Agent Server Module. The basic element in the agent server module is a *JADEServer* class. The object of this class starts JADE platform. JADE platform provides a set of containers. One of them is called a main container. The container is JADE object that allows to run the agents. In the main container, three functional agents (AMS, DF, RMA) are run. They control the JADE platform and move the agents. Any other containers must liaise with the main container in order to join the JADE platform.

The cooperation of the various computers in one agent system is possible when all containers are connected to the main container. Users of containers must enter IP address of main container to connect to the platform. A successful connection to the main container determines that the local system will work online. If connection to the main container is not possible, the user must work offline. When the JADE platform is started, the agent server module is responsible for managing agents, i.e. for creating, awakening and deleting agents.

The agent is built on the basis of the XML document conforming to the MIND architecture. The agent gets as input arguments the following information: a unique name, policy file and constituent document ID. Awakening of the agent means running it from a file and changing it state from hibernate to active or from sent to active (cf. Fig. 11).

Functionality of migration enables the agent to transfer in the JADE system. For this purpose, some parameters are determined: the name of the agent to be sent, the place of its destination after a jump and the constituent document to be forwarded.

E-mail Module. E-mails are not saved directly in a recipient's computer, but are stored on mail servers. Implementation of the e-mail module allows to transfer the serialized agent by e-mail when sending it to the JADE server is not possible. This allows the agent to reach to assigned recipient even if at the time of dispatch his container is not registered in the system (i.e. from the viewpoint of the system the recipient is offline).

The e-mail module uses the Java Mail platform and it is equipped with a set of classes responsible for handling e-mail servers, sending and receiving e-mails with a specific name. This name allow to distinguish messages with agents from others. A main class of module (*MailServer* class) implements the operations of sending and receiving the agents. Before sending, the agent is serialized to a file. To take advantage of this mechanism, the authors specified on the migration path must have e-mail addresses.

Policy Module and Document Module. The policy module is separated from the module that manages the other parts of the document, because of the very important role in the agents migration. The XPDL file defines the process of moving the agents in the system. The policy module provides a binding XPDL file to Java objects. For this purpose, XML Beans tool was used to generate *xpdl.jar* file based on XML Schema template for XPDL language. The *xpdl.jar* library allows for creation of the object representation of XPDL files within the system.

The task of the policy module is mapping a static representation of the policy file (path.xml) to the Java reference mechanism. The module opens the policy file (or files), interprets its structure and then creates Java objects.

Completion of work on a constituent document in current node triggers the movement of this document to another node. In this case, the policy server searches possible transitions. The module creates a collection of locations, which the agent must visit in the next step. In this case, the location means a container in the JADE system or e-mail address of the next user of the system.

The document module allows to load and manage other components of the MIND document. In particular, its task is to choose the appropriate constituent document in accordance with an activity element from the policy file.

This module also maps the static XML document to Java objects. XML Beans tool was used to generate *XMLHubDoc.jar* library based on XML Schema template defined for the MIND architecture.

The document module is responsible for extracting the constituent document from the agent and saving it on the local computer of the author assigned to the activity. Then the author can perform on that document some actions. After that, the document's current version is re-loaded by the agent and moved to another location. When the agent reaches the final location, the constituent documents are integrated into a final document.

Mediator Module and Initial Module. Unlike other modules, the mediator does not provide any operation. This service is implemented only to provide the communication between other modules and mediate in the running of methods. It also allows for easy implementation of subsequent modules in the evolution of the system.

The initial module runs all subsystems (modules). The task of the module is to take data from the user during the login to the system and booting the system.

6.3 Prototype Application's Performance

The system for managing of components is used to implement the life cycle of the MIND documents. The authors defined in the document should be the holders of the application, that creates the containers that forming a part of the JADE platform. After running the application, dialog box for authors authorization appears. During the login operation, the author gives the IP of the main container (unless the main container is created) and the name of the local container. The author may choose to work offline, i.e. a work without connection to the main container (cf. Fig. 12(a)).

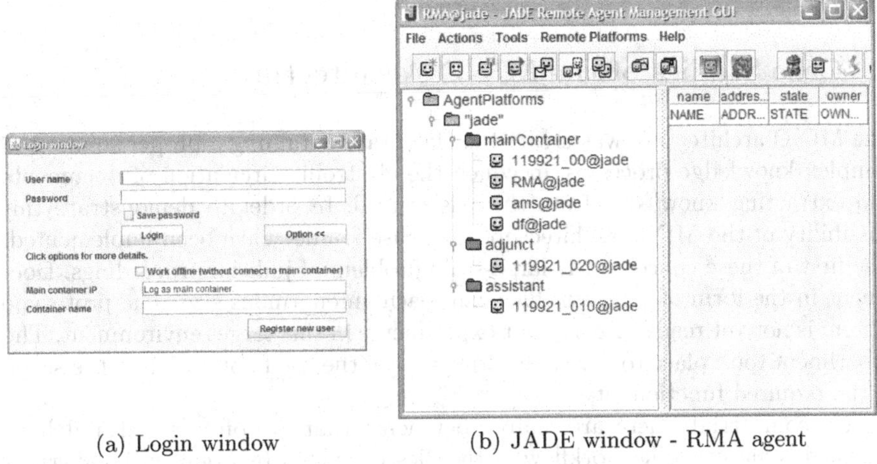

(a) Login window (b) JADE window - RMA agent

Fig. 12. Dialog box for authors authorization (a) JADE mechanism for monitoring the agents and containers (b)

After the successful authentication, the particular modules are run. That leads to join the container to the JADE platform and runs the possibility of receiving, status changing and sending agents. Launching an application as a main container causes running an additional mechanism to monitor the agents and containers on the JADE platform. For this purpose, JADE provides a tool RMA (Remote Agent Management) in the form of a dialog box (cf. Fig. 12(b)). This tool allows for monitoring the global state of the agent system.

In the next step after running, the application converts the MIND document to objects (this operation is called *unmarshalling*). The policy and document modules are responsible for that. A set of agents is created on the basis of start activities. A unique number (consistent with the activity ID) and ID number of the constituent document are assigned to each agent.

An agent interface is a simple dialog box with two possible actions: *Done* and *Exit*. The agent's GUI may be expanded depending on the system use cases. When the author finishes work on a constituent document, selects the *Done* action. The agent then reads from the policy file its next activities and moves to new locations. If the container of the target activity is present on the platform, the agent is sent by the JADE , otherwise the agent is sent by e-mail. In this way, the agent transfers the constituent document according to the defined workflow. Once the agent reaches a final location, *Done* action deletes the agent or transfers it to the archiving location. In both cases, the constituent document is saved as a file on the local computer.

If the author chooses the *Exit* action, it means that he has not finished to work on the constituent document yet. Then the agent is saved on his local computer as a file and the constituent document is also saved as a static XML document. When the system is rerun, the agent is awaken and the constituent document is upgraded in accordance with the new version from the local computer.

7 Case Studies of the MIND Architecture

The MIND architecture was created for facilitate obtaining a proper solution in complex knowledge processes, in which the electronic circulation of documents and extracting knowledge from them is crucial. In order to demonstrate this possibility of the MIND architecture, two case studies have been implemented. The first of these concerns the large-scale problem of judicial proceedings. Document in the form of complete files can reach an enormous size. The prototype system is not yet ready to carry out experiments in this target environment. The experiment took place to verify the adequacy of the used notation and the scope of the required functionality.

In a court trial, there are many documents that are often small and have specified structure. The workflow of the files is defined by organizational structure of the courts. In this case, there is a possibility to use the agent system for managing the electronic files.

The second case study involved the issue of evaluation of students in a typical university environment. This problem allows to test the mechanisms of the MIND architecture. In a teaching management system, a person, who receives a document template, is a student, and an evaluation card of one subject is a single MIND document. In the authors file, there are teachers that leads one subject for a group of students. The constituent document is transmitted from one teacher to another, according to the policy file. The teacher is responsible for the subject and the student receive the final version of the evaluation card. In the first case the agent is archived, and in the second, the agent is removed.

Fig. 13 shows the graph of one migration path of the constituent document in the agent system. AUT000 is the student's ID. The student is the author placed in the start activity (A119921_00 is a start activity ID). The constituent document is copied in the activity A119921_02 and the copies migrate to authors: AUT000 and AUT001. There are two final activities. The student is the author

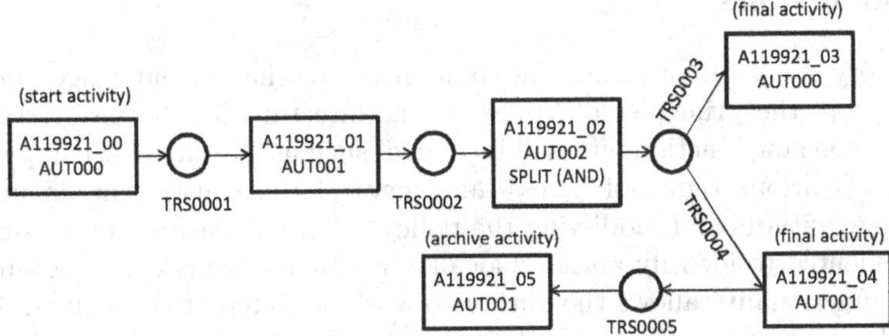

Fig. 13. Graphical representation of the policy file for one student and for one subject (constituent document ID: PAR0001)

of final activity no A119921_03. When the agent reaches this activity, the copy of constituent document is saved on the student's computer. Then the agent is deleted from the computer . The person responsible for the part of subject is the author of the final activity no A119921_04. Both the document and the agent are archived on his computer. This allows to trace the migration path of the document by the responsible author.

Teaching management system has been tested on four containers (the containers have been assigned to the authors: AUT000, AUT001, AUT002 and AUT003). The containers have been run on different computers on the same local network. Three constituent documents (PAR00001, PAR00002 and PAR00003) have migrated between the containers. The start activities have been: 119921_00, 119921_01 and 119921_02.

After the transition from the start activities to the next activities, the agent *Exit* action has been performed. Consequently, two files have been saved on the local computer: the serialized agent file and the XML constituent document file. After editing the document and running the container, the agent has brought back to the active state with modified document inside. If the author has been off-line, the agent with the document has been sent by mail. Sending agent on the mail server has proceeded quickly and without any problem. Receiving the agent from the e-mail server has proceeded successfully, but has taken a time period of few seconds. The whole process, the following the migration path and transferring the constituent documents have proceeded successfully.

The teaching management system in its current form is meeting its objectives, but it is not completely user-friendly. To edit the constituent documents on the system nodes the STMPEdit editor may be used as a local service. However, it is rather cumbersome solution. Hence, there are plans to implement tools that make the system more user-friendly. There are possibilities to implement new functionalities in the MIND architecture through a mechanism of embedded, local and remote services. Adjusting the system for this use case allows for the execution of larger scale tests. This is the nearest plan for developing the agent system.

8 Conclusions

The prototype server for managing components in the current stage does not implement all the principles of the MIND architecture. In the next version of the prototype new functionality will be added, such as: adding new components, granting of various rights of access and views of the constituent documents, adding new authors and modifying the policy files. A persistent addressing will be implemented to identify author's localization by name instead of computer's IP. This functionality allows the author to work on different computers. A control of the agent migration and edition of the document will be extended by adding conditions of transitions and checking the time of execution of the various tasks. Workflow patterns applicable to knowledge-based organizations will be implemented in order to facilitate the construction of knowledge processes.

The next stage of development of the MIND architecture is to ensure the reliability of processing and security of document. Reliability of the process refers to the possibility of self-diagnosis of distributed document in a situation where some of its component are lost or where some components are changed by unauthorized persons. Security of document concerns encryption of its the content and digital signatures.

Acknowledgments. This research work was supported by the system project Innodoktorant Scholarships for PhD students, III edition. Project is co-financed by the European Union in the frame of the European Social Fund.

References

1. The Apache XML Project, `http://xmlbeans.apache.org/sourceAndBinaries/`
2. W3C Recommendation, `http://www.w3.org/XML/Schema`
3. Mella, G., Ferrari, E., Bertino, E., Koglin, Y.: Controlled and cooperative updates of xml documents in byzantine and failure-prone distributed systems. ACM Transactions on Information and System Security 9, 421–460 (2006)
4. Oster, G., Urso, P., Molli, P., Molli, H., Imine, A.: Optimistic replication for massive collaborative editing. Technical Report 5719 (October 2005)
5. Oster, G., Urso, P., Molli, P., Molli, H., Imine, A.: Proving correctness of transformation functions incollaborative editing systems. Technical Report 5795 (December 2005)
6. OrbiTeam Software GmbH & Co. KG, Fraunhofer FIT. Bscw -basic support for cooperative work, version 4.4 (October)
7. Price, D.R.: Cvs - concurrent versions system (December 2006), `http://cvs.nongnu.org/`
8. Lowry, P.B., Albrecht, C.C., Lee, J.D., Nunamaker, J.F.: Users experiences in collaborative writing using collaboratus, an internetbased collaborative work. In: 35th Hawaii International Conference on System Sciences (2002)

9. Workflows and Agents Development Environment, http://jade.tilab.com/wade/index.html
10. WfMC. Workflow Management Coalition Workflow Standard: Process definition interface - xml process definition language. Technical Report WFMC-TC-1025, Workflow Management Coalition, Padziernik (2008)
11. Russell, N., ter Hofstede, A.H.M., van der Aalst, W.M.P., Mulyar, N.: Workflow Control-Flow Patterns: A Revised View. BPM Center Report BPM-06-22 (2006)
12. van der Aalst, W.M.P.: Patterns and xpdl: A critical evaluation of the xml process definition language. Technical Report FIT-TR-2003-06, Queensland University of Technology, Brisbane (2003)
13. Workflow Patterns Home Page, http://www.workflowpatterns.com/patterns/
14. Nottelmann, H., Fuhr, N.: MIND: an architecture for multimedia information retrieval in federated digital libraries (2001)
15. Nottelmann, H., Fuhr, N.: The MIND Architecture for Heterogeneous Multimedia Federated Digital Libraries. In: Callan, J., Crestani, F., Sanderson, M. (eds.) SIGIR 2003 Ws Distributed IR 2003. LNCS, vol. 2924, pp. 112–125. Springer, Heidelberg (2004)
16. Berretti, S., Callan, J.P., Nottelmann, H., Shou, X.M., Wu, S.: MIND: resource selection and data fusion in multimedia distributed digital libraries. In: SIGIR 2003, p. 1 (2003)
17. Mikuła, B.: Organizacje Oparte na Wiedzy. WAEK, Kraków (2006)
18. Starke, P.H.: Sieci Petri - podstawy, zastosowania, teoria. PWN, Warszawa (1987)
19. Jensen, K., Kristensen, L.M.: Coloured Petri Nets: Modelling and Validation of Concurrent Systems. Springer, Berlin (2009)
20. Siciarek, J.: Środowisko narzedziowe do wytwarzania inteligentnych dokumentów elektronicznych. Master's thesis, Faculty of Electronics, Telecommunications and Informatics, Gdańsk University of Technology (2008)
21. Internet Assigned Numbers Authority (IANA): MIME Media Types, http://www.iana.org/assignments/media-types/
22. Josefsson, S.: Base-N Encodings, RFC 4648, Network Working Group, http://tools.ietf.org/html/rfc4648
23. WfMC. Workflow Management Coalition. Terminology and glossary. Technical Report WFMC-TC-1011, Issue 3.0, Workflow Management Coalition, Winchester, United Kingdom, Luty (1999)
24. Szczepański, J.: Serwer usług bazowych do zarzdzania konfiguracj inteligentnego dokumentu elektronicznego. Master's thesis, Faculty of Electronics, Telecommunications and Informatics, Gdańsk University of Technology (2008)
25. Java Agent Development Framework, http://jade.tilab.com/
26. Java Mail: Sun Developer Network, http://java.sun.com/products/javamail/downloads
27. Apache Log4j: Logging Services, http://logging.apache.org/log4j

Agent Cooperation within Adversarial Teams in Dynamic Environment – Key Issues and Development Trends

Bartłomiej Józef Dzieńkowski and Urszula Markowska-Kaczmar

Wrocław University of Technology
{bartlomiej.dzienkowski,urszula.markowska-kaczmar}@pwr.wroc.pl

Abstract. This paper presents a survey of multi-agent systems (MAS) with adversarial teams competing in a dynamic environment. Agents within teams work together against an opposite group of agents in order to fulfill their contrary goals. The article introduces specificity of an environment and indicates fields of cooperation. It emphasizes the role of opponent analysis. Popular planning and learning methods are considered, as well. Next, possible fields of practical application are mentioned. The final part of the paper presents a summary of machine learning methods for specific problem solving and points up future development directions.

Keywords: MAS, cooperation, opponent, strategy, recognition, anticipation, prediction, planning, learning, trends, RoboCup, battlefield, combat.

1 Introduction

The idea of multi-agent systems (MAS) has gained great popularity in solving various types of problems. MAS provide a very elegant description and simplify a problem solution. They have already showed a great application potential in many distributed domains like production, communication or transportation systems in complex and rapidly changing environments [1]. In these cases the greatest impact on system performance has a quality of agent cooperation. The collaborative work requires effective task assignment and, in case of limited resources, conflict resolving methods. Work in a dangerous and unpredictable environment introduces additional requirements. Agents should forecast and avoid hazards. However, this type of environment is not tendentious and it does not act deliberatively. An appearance of an opponent changes these assumptions. A team of agents is obligated to compete with an opponent team that acts purposely.

Considering a scope of practical application, the described case is not rare. In fact, each of existing organisms participates in an endless competition. However, from the point of view presented in our survey, considered fields can be significant for military, network security or sport competition. They present a broad topic that is still insignificantly explored.

N.T. Nguyen (Ed.): Transactions on CCI VI, LNCS 7190, pp. 146–169, 2012.

The article focuses on solutions that are used in the field of MAS with adversarial teams working in uncertain and dynamic environments. The aim of the paper is to identify main challenges and directions of development of such systems. It emphasizes differences between a pure cooperation of agents and the case of cooperation against an opponent. It presents main features of systems dedicated to the considered domain and shows concepts of commonly applied solutions that improve its efficiency.

The discussion starts from the characteristics of MAS in the considered problem domain. The section distinguishes prerequisites and main features of this special group of systems. Consequently, different fields of cooperation are presented. Next, a short description of possible agent architectures provides available generic implementation frameworks with different properties. The following section emphasizes importance of opponent data mining, and includes exemplary methods of enemy action recognition and anticipation. Valuable information about opponent strategy can be very useful in planning process, which is described in the subsequent part of the paper. In the next section, commonly applied learning approaches are presented. Then, communication issue is mentioned. Subsequently, a scope of possible applications is given. Additionally, the article includes a summary of machine learning methods applied for specific problems. Finally, the article summarizes the provided description and refers to the current and further development trends.

2 Characteristics of MAS with Adversarial Teams

In contrast to many MAS that concern cooperation of agents, the domain of adversarial teams working in dynamic and uncertain environments imposes additional demanding requirements to the system. Despite the fact that a large part of existing solutions can be successfully applied in this field, there are many specific problems that require dedicated methods.

The environment is characterized by a large number of discreet world states (or continuous state in case of robotic agents) and a spatial space. It is assumed that there can be an infinite number of states, tasks have an execution duration and events occur at any time. Some of the events are nondeterministic and described by a probability of occurrence. Consequently, the practical approach requires a world state representation that allows to use algorithms operating in a discrete space. Even though, it is hardly possible the algorithms process complete information about the world or even a world state. Usually agents have an access to partial data. In addition, the calculations of the world state are performed in real time and computational resources are limited. If an agent is unable to perform action in some interval, it loses its chance. At this point, many theoretical solutions require revising before they can be applied.

The existence of an opponent is the additional adverse element of the environment. The opponent operates in a purposeful manner. An adversarial team of agents is capable of analyzing a world state and building plans. It makes elimination of an enemy negative influence very demanding. However, actions of opponent should not be treated as dynamic crises. Some dependencies can be observed. Thus, information about enemy plans can be revealed and utilized against the opponent. During a plan building process the system should observe and take into account recognized enemy plans in order to achieve goals. In practice a foe is able to do the same. In fact, because of many skirmishes, opponent's skills grow simultaneously with the development of the system. Therefore, a difficulty level of an enemy can be unlimited.

A system designed for the described domain cannot be considered in terms of a standard optimization problem. Thus, it should contain a set of robust techniques that allow to deal effectively with the opponent. In fact, the basic proof of concept is insufficient. This means that the system is required to meet the assumptions and, above all, be able to defeat an enemy. Otherwise, it cannot be successfully applied in practice.

3 Cooperation

The described dynamic environment offers many possibilities of agent's interactions in the world. Initially, an agent is able to perform actions that change the world state and in long term indirectly affect the final result of a match. Activity of a single agent should lead to benefits of the whole team. In fact, this can be achieved with a group of agents that works independently. However, there are important tasks that require assistance of organized agents. Furthermore, better results can be achieved when agents are aware of team members and benefit from support that they can provide.

There are many definitions of cooperation. Some of them does not concern competing teams. One of them says that a group of agents is cooperating when an increase of a number of agents improves system performance and agents can effectively resolve resource conflicts [14]. Other definition can be found in a brief survey on cooperation in MAS [13], in which cooperating agents work jointly towards the same end (or share the same goal).

In fact, the both cases allow for independent work of agents. For example, many independent agents work on small projects that are parts of a bigger one. This point of view on cooperation is not valid in area of adversarial teams. As an example we can provide soccer match in which each agent independently tries to shoot a goal. Game rules extend individual role of an agent and force to deeper use of cooperation possibilities.

According to the described characteristic of an environment cooperation performance should be considered as a chance of victory of a team with an opposite group of agents. We can measure a quality of cooperation by observing results of confrontations with an enemy if we assume that both teams initially have the same access to resources. Finally, cooperation determines a higher level of development of interactions in a group, which enables to gain advantage. According to different assumptions and goals that appear in an environment we can distinguish several areas of cooperation [14]:

1. Grouping and multiplication – one of the simplest approaches that involves replication of homogeneous agents, each of which performs simple operations that provide benefits for the entire group. Unfortunately it is not always possible to add new agents during a match or cost of this action is too high. Finally, sometimes it can even lead to decrease in performance of a system (e.g. large group of agents exploring a small area).
2. Communication – a form of cooperation that utilizes message exchange for knowledge sharing. It enables agents to fulfill their goals in systems based on knowledge databases [10].
3. Specialization – a process of building heterogeneous agents designated for specific tasks. In many cases it helps to accomplish difficult tasks and increases system efficiency by proper use of agents' skills [2].
4. Sharing tasks and resources – a method of cooperation that seeks for optimal tasks' assignment inside a group of agents including resource access conflict resolving [43].
5. Coordination – synchronization of actions that increases productivity [44].
6. Negotiation and arbitration – a set of rules that appoint an acceptable behaviours of agents. The rules provide a description of a negotiation protocol and conflict resolution process [43].

Looking closely at the situation inside one of adversarial teams we can see that a group of agents share compatible goals. They have to compete with an opposite team for resources and resolve resource access conflicts inside a team in the same moment. Appropriate task assignment should be provided according to agents skills, which are limited.

In order to satisfy all requirements it is effective to utilize some cooperation patterns understood as cases of effective teamwork [45]. A single cooperation pattern enables to minimize resource conflicts inside a team during execution of a complex task that takes advantage from agent specialization. Hereby, execution of these patterns leads to cooperation.

4 Agent Architecture

Agent Architecture describes an internal structure of a single system entity (an agent). Its model is an agreement between complexity, performance and scalability of the system. The topic has been frequently discussed without focusing on a particular system [14]. Most of the current solutions have a general application.

One of the earliest competitive matches in a dynamic environment has been held in RoboCup (RC) simulation [6]. Due to the real-time computations and limited resources, much emphasis was put on very short time of agent's reaction and simplicity. That is why early soccer player agents were mostly based on the reactive approach, also known as behaviour-based or situated. They were equipped with a set of predefined behaviours based on a finite state machine or a neural network. In the model, an intelligent behaviour is an emergent property without explicit representation and abstract reasoning.

However, processing of predefined behaviours causes problems of adaptation to new environments. In addition, the simplicity impedes a model extension of more sophisticated agents' behaviours. Lack of a central symbolic world model representation and mental states of an agent does not allow to build plans, which is a great limitation, because planning ability is an essence of intelligent action.

A solution to the problems that are met in the reactive architecture is the deliberative approach. A structure of the model allows to include a planner module. In many cases, a deliberative system is based on BDI (belief-desire-intention) cognitive architecture, which provides deeper reasoning for higher abilities [11]. In the approach, an agent holds functions and features similar to a human. Such agent is regarded as a knowledge-based system. It undertakes pattern matching and reasoning using symbolic manipulation.

Nevertheless, processes in the deliberative architecture can take too long. A hybrid architecture joins deliberative and reactive approaches in such manner that the advantages of the both models can be utilized [9]. In practice, because the hybrid model represents combination of two approaches, there are many different implementations of the hybrid concept. It opens new possibilities and can provide better solutions in demanding competitive environments.

5 Opponent Modeling and Anticipation

Competing teams usually have similar skills, which determine victory chances. Supremacy of a team can be gained by extraordinary information processing abilities. With no doubt the careful observation and analysis of an enemy activity in the environment can be the most deciding factor, which affects the team's victory. The recognition process of the concurrent agents' behaviours, plans and goals provides useful information, which allows predicting future actions of the enemy. With this information, the team is better prepared for the opponent's operations and has an opportunity to prevent negative situations before they occur.

In this paper, the term of low/high-level anticipation is used to separate two domains of anticipation. Forecasting at the higher level processes information about a group of agents to deliver conclusions about a plan of a team. In contrast, the low-level anticipation does not go beyond a single agent.

5.1 High-Level Anticipation

The idea of adversarial plan recognition and oppositional planning processes is described by a general framework introduced in [31], [38]. The construction of the system consists of several phases (Fig. 1). The first one operates on an set of predefined plans. The pretreatment module judges plans whether they are adversarial before they are used for building the adversarial plan library, where they are stored. The next phase involves an observation of events caused by opponent actions, which results in uncertain and partial information. Next, the data is used as the input for building the correct world state. According

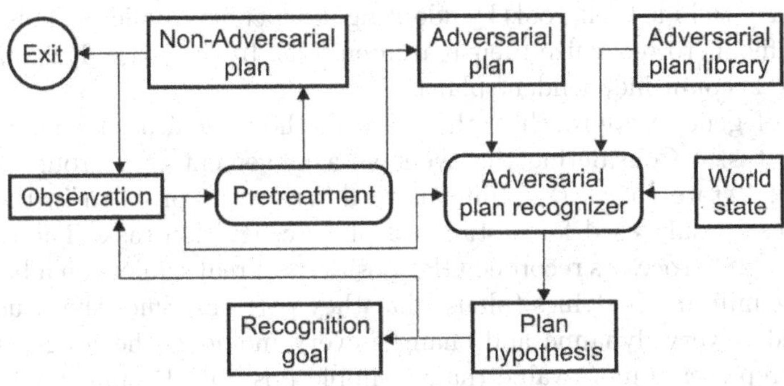

Fig. 1. Adversarial plan recognition framework [31]

to the observations, the adversarial plan library and world state the adversarial plan recognition module generates plan hypotheses. The plan hypotheses are the possible plans that are being executed – they can be updated or abandoned. The plan with the greatest reliability is used to determine the opponent goal. Finally, it is possible to apply oppositional plan, which consists of actions that oppose the enemy activity.

Plan recognition, which leads to an exposure of goals, is a well-known problem and it was considered in many works. These works in most cases propose new algorithms and methods strongly related to previous commonly applied approaches, trying to explain an observation by a plan. Solutions to the problem based on Bayesian Networks [33] or Kautz formal approach [37], [21] are facing many problems in the considered problem domain. Paper [30], which uses semantic tree-graph for knowledge representation, indicates and deals with the most of the following problems.

In contrast to article [37], original Kautz method can be used only for plan recognition, but it does not provide forecasting and generating oppositional actions. The approach processes events, but ignores the context determined by the environment state. This issue is emphasized in papers [36], [33]. Many methods lack of partial observability and missing elements support, which is crucial in practical applications. This problem is taken into account in article [32] (where algorithm based on template matching is proposed) and paper [34], which represents a hybrid approach. Methods related to Kautz algorithm do not meet temporal relationships. This means when the exact order of events does not matter (e.g. an order of wearing shoes) the quality of the method results is deteriorated. The representation of events also does not allow for processing an execution of actions that occur in the same moment. Bayesian Networks [33] deal better with these problems, but they build complex solution graphs adding redundant observations. There is an additional problem with identifying the appropriate network structure [22]. It is reasonable to use the approach based on the reconstruction of the goal-graph tree, which does not require plan library [35]. The last following problem is related to the agent action relationship, which can be unclear. Hostile agents can try to hide their goals by adopting independent policies. This activity makes it difficult to recognize their real intentions. In that case, it is important to take into account independent plans.

Instead of generic approaches, there are methods dedicated for specialized recognition tasks. Considering the event as a movement of a group of agents in the spatial state space, it is difficult to describe the problem in the terms, which are commonly used for a standard plan recognition task. The approach presented in [28] processes recorded GPS positions of real soldiers on a battlefield to recognize military doctrines (plans) that they perform. Since the situation on a battlefield is very dynamic and changes every moment, the usage of a unit movement represents more value than a simple position. Despite the fact that a movement of agents can appear very chaotic, their actions are purposeful and patterns are isolated. In fact, simple actions of agents are less important than coordinated activities of a group. In order to recognize plans or high-level goals, relationships between pairs of agents are analyzed. The comparison of two agents includes parameters like heading, velocity and distance. The algorithm computes these relationships between all pairs of agents in each step and compares with the pattern templates library. Chains of events can instantiate a pattern template. Once a pattern is recognized higher ones can still replace it. If a partial pattern cannot be satisfied until time exceeds a defined threshold, it is discarded. The described method is successfully applied in recognizing high-level behaviours.

A similar task is described in paper [27]. The authors provide a comparison of several machine learning approaches (Neural Networks, Support Vector Machines (SVM), k-Nearest Neighbor) for opponent agents' formation recognition. An input vector is represented by a set of position coordinates of a group of agents. Experiments resulted in good accuracy of formation classification (especially SVM). However, this approach does not take into account temporal dependencies and variable number of opponents (the number of inputs is fixed).

In the competitive domain repeated matches open new opportunities. In this case, a team has a chance to prepare for a specific opponent before the match. RoboCup, the soccer competition platform, includes a particular league for the coach competition [17]. The function of the coach module is to gather information about an opponent in order to identify weaknesses and behaviour patterns in the oppositional team play and finally propose an appropriate counteraction. In the considered approach, the system uses the base strategy library, which consists of a set of general strategies. Before the game starts, the coach is provided with prepared data of the opponent's past games. The first step of the data analysis is event tracking. Individual behaviours (e.g. pass, shot, dribble) form multi-agent behaviours (e.g. formation, defensive system, offensive system). Dependencies between multi-agent behaviours represent patterns. Exploited group behaviour sequences are compared with the base strategy library to identify these patterns. The phase of pattern recognition relies on statistical calculations. Chi-square test is used to find possible relations between sequences of events. The resulting set of patterns represents a model of an opponent. However, only differences between behaviours and base strategies are stored for further use. During the match, the coach module receives on-line information about the opponent and uses similar methods from previous phase to identify expected behaviour patterns.

The intense analysis of an opponent play provides beneficial knowledge [22]. The approach was tested on large amount of data mined from recorded Starcraft (computer game) matches provided by players. The method requires a set of input strategies. They represent possible tactics labeled basing on a rule set from a game expert. The work compares several algorithms used for plan recognition and provides study on common problems like imperfect information represented by lack of information, speed of recognition or exact timing of strategies that will be performed by an opponent. Instead of the fact that the game units (or agents) were controlled by a human player, the work emphasizes importance and effectiveness of forecasting enemy strategic actions.

5.2 Low-Level Anticipation

In contrast to the previous section, here the subject of interest is not a group but a single agent. This point of view is useful when an activity of one agent has a large impact on the world or the system receives signals from a physical environment and behaviours of opponent agents are described only by raw data. In this case, the low-level recognition and forecasting methods are required.

Adding anticipation to a single agent is still a great challenge, especially when it works in an environment that does not give access to complete world state. Actions appear at any time and are performed continuously as the time passes. This situation is considered in paper [29] where anticipation is added to a Quakebot. The Quakebot can be interpreted as an agent working in a first person shooter game and its goal is to gain advantage by predicting player moves. The system consists of world simulation (Quake II game), Soar module and the rules library. Soar is a general cognitive architecture for systems that exhibits intelligent behaviour. It is continually proposing, selecting, and applying operators to the world state using rules that match against the current state representation (Fig. 2). The decision procedure fires parallel actions. When a Quakebot senses an enemy it predicts behaviour of the opponent, by using its knowledge of tactics, and selects the best operator. A set of operators includes: collect powerups, attack, retreat, chase, ambush and hunt. The most interesting operator is the ambush operator. It is applied when Quakebot tries to gain predominance by setting up a favorable arrangement for itself before it meets the opponent. However, a Quakebot is unable to learn between matches because it uses predefined set of rules, operators and parameters.

Most of the anticipation procedures use information about agent's behaviours to predict next actions or plans. However, clear behaviour statements sometimes are not present. In this case, the system receives raw data and it is required to recognize behaviour depending on a low-level description. It is possible to find a solution to this problem in an application of Hidden Markov Models (HMM) [24], which are already commonly used in speech and gesture recognition. In paper [23] this approach was applied to identify a behaviour of a robot.

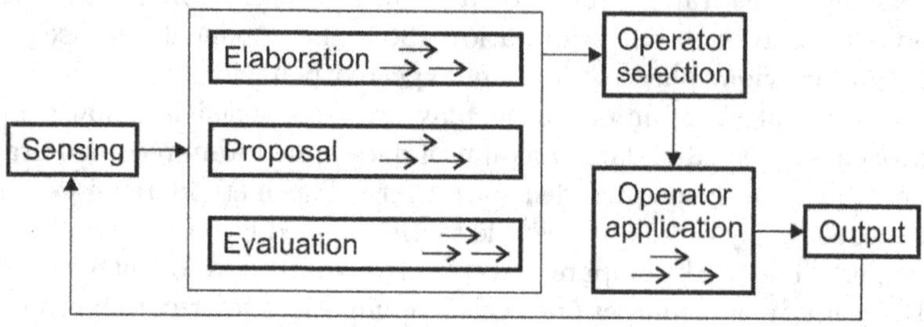

Fig. 2. Soar decision cycle [29]

One HMM is built for each behaviour. Markov states correspond to low level stages for robot control. Observations represent physical state of an agent. The feature vector consists of absolute position, relative position and dynamic properties of an object. The method calculates a probability of generating a given sequence of observations by each model and returns the model with the highest probability. It is also possible to predict future behaviours. Instead of the fact that the application of HMM is straightforward, there is a real problem with the segmentation of the continuous state. Choosing a proper time slice and dealing with missing observations is essential.

The behaviour recognition task does not belong to the lowest possible level of forecasting. Papers [19], [20] propose methods for predicting future events and states of the world. The uncertain robotic environment requires sophisticated method to predict successfulness of elementary behaviours. Robots use Neural Networks to anticipate the effect of their own actions. This approach allows learning, adaptation and generalization of the predictor module. The role of commentator (an agent responsible for forecasting) can be chosen among teammates. However, in practice standard algorithmic or heuristic approaches give likewise satisfying results.

6 Planning

Planning is an important skill of a deliberative agent. This section introduces basics of commonly used planning methods.

The description of planning process in a dynamic environment presented in [40] assumes a finite set of agents $A = \{A_1, A_2, ...A_n\}$ having knowledge Ω_i, undertaking available jobs $J(t)$ at time t, depending on limited resources $R_i(t)$ of an agent i and their cost of consumption C_i. A strategy S_{A_i} provides to an agent A_i a sequence of jobs J_i that describes world state transitions satisfying agent's goals. In fact, a goal is a final state X_f that is connected with an initial state X_0. The model of agent A_i is defined by (1):

$$A_i = \{R_i(t), C_i, \Omega_i, X_0, X_f, S_{A_i}, u_{A_i}\}, \qquad (1)$$

where $u_{A_i} : S_{A_i} \rightarrow \Re$ is an utility value that provides a numeric cost of agent's strategy, $S_{A_i} \rightarrow R_i(t) \times C_i \times \Omega_i \times X_0 \times J(t)$ defines a strategy. With this generic definition, it is possible to define planning as an optimization task, in which distribution of jobs in a group of agents minimizes summarized cost of actions in an environment. However, this formal approach does not deal with all problems that appear in a practical and distributed application. An optimal plan search space is large and a system is required to build plans faster than an opponent.

Many solutions commonly apply a strategy hierarchy [41] or Goal Oriented Behaviour Tree [42]. In these cases, a long-term goal is achieved by fulfilling sub-goals or short-term tasks. A difficult problem is defined in terms of simpler problems. An example of a task that is often used for realization of complex tasks is path finding. Nevertheless, the problem of path planning is omitted in this paper. It is connected to technical issues rather than the adversarial domain.

In many practical problems a complete set of goals is not defined, which makes it difficult to assume a strategy hierarchy. Often goals arise during interaction with an environment. Article [43] describes an example of agents working together in an uncertain environment to solve mutual goals. Members of a team are grouped by sub-coalitions with different functions. A coalition of agents shares a plan and hierarchically assigns tasks. The planning process starts from a superior agent who tries to generate a sub-plan to perform an activity. If the sub-plan generation is successful and the solution does not depend on a commitment of other agents, the agent performs its activity. Otherwise, the agent delegates sub-plan nodes to its subordinates and waits for their accomplishment. If the subordinates cannot accomplish the provided plan, the superior agent generates a new one. Finally, if the plan cannot be accomplished by neither the agent nor its subordinates, a failure notice is returned to the superior agent. Consequently, completion of tasks starts from bottom to up. In fact, effectiveness of the joint work largely depends on the agents' knowledge. It is important that agents share valid beliefs about the world state by updating information about constraints that can affect plans, or conflicts, in which two agents have different beliefs about the same fact.

Some of approaches, which build plans from scratches basing on single jobs, grapple with solution complexity and an extensive search space. This makes them much less effective in the considered problem domain. A cooperative strategy framework for team behaviours presented in [39] describes how to support planning process. The approach utilizes predefined strategies, or team plans, as a strategy base. A single strategy case consists of a problem description and the optimal solution. The problem is described by a set of conditions related to the environment in a past situation. A strategy can be considered as a long-term plan aimed at achieving a goal, while a tactics deals with short periods of time that occur during an execution of a strategy. Thus, the system searches for the most similar case and a strategy that is reasonable to apply. If conditions are not satisfied, reactive behaviour is performed. Decisions and role assignments are made by a selected leader.

Building plans from predefined elements makes the process works faster, but it also imposes additional requirements on the system design. Paper [44] proposes a framework for implementation of a *setplay*, which is described by a quick plan executed during a match. The work provides programming language and graphic tool for *setplay* definition, which consists of conditions, actions and communication commitments. Parameters of a *setplay* and agent roles are instantiated at run-time.

Unfortunately, hand-coded solutions do not provide great flexibility to the system. In the previously described approach, an effectiveness of a strategy depends on a designer's knowledge and skills. A solution proposed in [45] allows to take advantage from reducing the search space and applying more general predefined plan elements at the same moment. Pattern-Based Planning System (PBPS) uses patterns as input to generate a plan (Fig. 3a). They represent sequences of tasks that a single agent is unable to accomplish on its own. These patterns are designed by a human expert, but their general idea allows using them for automatic extraction of effective team behaviours. Each pattern executed by a team changes the environment state. It is possible to arrange patterns in a pattern tree (Fig. 3b), in which root of the tree is an initial state, edges are patterns, and nodes are environment states. PBPS generates a plan representing the best sequence of patterns in a pattern tree. When the plan is ready, tasks are assigned to agents using marked-based rules. A status of a plan execution is monitored. A failure of a task implies generation of a new plan.

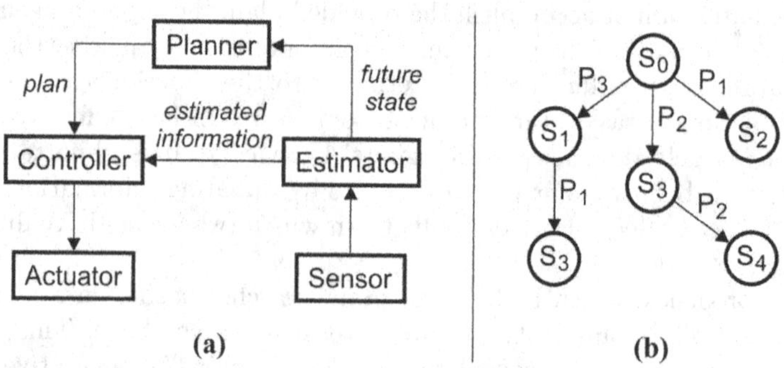

Fig. 3. PBPS model [45]: (a) module organization, (b) pattern tree consisted of states S_i connected by patterns P_i

Much emphasis was put on the speed of the algorithm (Alg. 1). It is required to generate a valid plan before the end of a defined time slice. At the beginning of the plan building process, each used pattern is adjusted to the current world state. Fitting pattern to a state modifies pattern's mutable variables (e.g. maps agent position). Only feasible patterns are used, which means there is at least one agent that can be assigned for each task in a pattern.

Sequence of patterns that joins an initial state with an end state is called *basicPlan*. Each *basicPlan* is evaluated against an Objective, which represents

Alg. 1. PBPS Planning Algorithm [45]

```
procedure planning(initialState, tasks, objectiveFunction, rawPatterns)

for all pattern in rawPatterns do
   initialize pattern for initialState
   // check pattern feasibility
   if all tasks in pattern can be assigned then
      create basicPlan
      basicPlan.addPattern(pattern)
      patternsTree.pushBack(basicPlan)
   end if
end for

BBP := Null
for all basicPlan in patternsTree do
   evaluate(basicPlan, objectiveFunction)
   if basicPlan gains the goal then
      BBP := basicPlan
      break
   end if
end for

while BBP == Null do
   expand(patternsTree, rawPatterns)
   for all basicPlan in patternsTree do
      evaluate(basicPlan, objectiveFunction)
      if basicPlan gains the goal then
         BBP := basicPlan
         break
      else
         if tree depth exceed then
            BBP := basicPlan with highest score
         end if
      end if
   end for
end while

// gather agent's bids for all tasks in BBP
plansCompos := calcBidsCompositions(BBP, bids)
for all plan in plansCompos do
   calcFitness(plan)
end for
bestPlan := plan with highest fitness in planCompos

return bestPlan
```

some world state. It is possible that the *basicPlan* does not gain the goal state. If so, it is expanded by adding additional patterns. Only patterns that can possibly follow the leaf patterns in a *basicPlan* are added. Recently added patterns are initialized with different state than the world state. They are adjusted to the estimated state at the end of a *basicPlan* path. The process is continued until the goal or the maximum number of patterns is reached. At this point the best basic plan (BBP) is returned.

In the second phase of the planning process, when the BBP is selected, agents evaluate tasks and submit bids with quality and probability of task accomplishment. Compositions of tasks assignments are collected and evaluated in order to choose a composition with the best score (Alg. 1). Finally the plan is announced to the team.

The concept was tested on several tasks: passing ball, running with ball, positioning (going to an appropriate region and waiting for pass). The described approach works well in environments with limited message passing.

7 Learning

Development of an agent and its adaptation to an environment can be achieved by utilization of learning methods. In fact, adversarial systems use some intelligent techniques. However, there are special requirements that should be satisfied. As mentioned before, system utilization largely depends on quality of applied methods. A team of agents should be prepared for the hardest opponent. Hence, not only effectiveness but also a speed of learning is crucial. Agents should learn from mistakes during a skirmish. In the perfect case, an enemy should be unable to perform the same surprising attack twice. It is required that skills of agents constantly grow. Otherwise, the usefulness period of a team is short.

Thus, a large group of training methods, which result in rigid skills (or they are simply too slow), are not interesting cases. Because the variety of commonly applied methods makes it difficult to include them all, only the most important concepts are described in this section.

7.1 Reinforcement Learning

Many of these goals can be achieved by application of reinforcement learning, which is one of the most commonly used learning methods in MAS [46], [47]. The method is appropriate for the sequential decision-making problem and is used for learning behaviours of a low abstraction level, as well as team behaviours skills. Generally, reinforcement learning algorithms are based on a computational approach to solve Markov Decision Process (MDP), which is denoted by (2):

$$M = [S, A, r, p] \, , \tag{2}$$

where S represents a set of environment states, A is a set of actions that an agent can perform, $r : S \times A \to [0;1]$ stands for the function that returns an immediate numerical reward for action a in state s, and $p : S \times A \times S \to [0;1]$ denotes probability distribution of transition from state s to state s' by performing

Alg. 2. PBPS Calculating bids compositions [45]

```
procedure calcBidsCompositions(BBP, bids)
plansCompos := Null
for all task in bids do
    if task in BBP is not assigned then
        for all plan in plansCompos do
            plan.task.responsibleAgent := bidder
        end for
    else
        // make copy of current composition
        newCompos := plansCompos
        for all plan in newCompos do
            plan.task.responsibleAgent := bidder
        end for
        plansCompos.pushBack(newCompos)
    end if
end for
return planCompos
```

action a. Since the model is stated, a state value function $V^\pi : S \rightarrow \Re$, which is used for searching the optimal behaviour, is defined by (3):

$$V^\pi(s) = E\left[\sum_{t=0}^{\infty} r(s_t, \pi(s_t)|s_0 = s)\right], \tag{3}$$

where π stands for a policy of taking actions in a particular state s, and $E(.)$ is the expected value. Thus, the optimal behaviour is described by (4):

$$\pi^*(s) = \arg\max_{a \in A} \left\{ r(s,a) + \sum_{s \in S} p(s,a,s') \cdot V^*(s') \right\} \tag{4}$$

The process of decision-making differentiates between possible successor states to choose the optimal behaviour. The procedure starts from the computation of all potentially successful actions. Next, according to the current state and the provided actions, approximate resulting states are computed. In order to select the action with the best resulting state, all the resulting states are evaluated.

An important part of the model is the state value function $V(s)$, which is used to estimate future rewards. The function is incrementally updated after each transition from s to s'. Depending on satisfaction of defined criteria, the activity is considered as successful and results in positive reward. To handle the reward approximation in a continuous states space, linear feed-forward neural networks or Gradient-Descent method can be used [47].

In practice, reinforcement learning has found an application in simple skills learning in RoboCup competition (e.g. ball kicking, ball interception). A state is described by a set of simulation parameters that can affect result of an action (e.g. ball velocity, player velocity, distance and relative angle between the ball and a player). Straightforward discretization is applied to handle real-valued action parameters. The estimation of a state value uses as the input a set of information about the arrangement of the ball, teammates and opponents. Finally, only successful experiences are recorded.

However, an application of this concept of learning is not an easy task and some problems arise. A large amount of actions and state variables has a very negative influence on problem solution complexity. In many cases, a complete world state is not known and agents face uncertainty. Because of continuous states, also complete table of rewards cannot be provided. Instead, a state reward is based on some approximations. In addition, rewards are considerably delayed. Eventually, the reward and transition function may be not known.

7.2 Case Based Learning

Another solution, which allows agents to gain experience and avoid making the same mistakes, is to build system framework based on Case Based Reasoning (CBR) [48], [50]. CBR provides decision support for problem solving and agent planning (Fig. 4a). When an agent encounters a difficult situation in the environment, the most similar case is retrieved from the case base. Retrieved information and knowledge is reused for solving the actual problem. Finally, the proposed solution is revised and new parts of experience are retained.

In paper [48] the approach is mixed with utilization of Rule Based Reasoning (RBR) and Genetic Algorithm (GA) (Fig. 4b). A case consists of features (based on pre-state parameters), suggested solution and counts of succeed and failed application of the case. A solution is a rule, presented by (5):

$$IF\ state_1\ AND\ state_2\ ...\ state_n\ THEN\ solution\ WITH\ weight \tag{5}$$

Parameters of a retrieved solution need to be matched to the world state in order to obtain an action that should be performed.

The core of the system is the indexing mechanism, which ensures that the provided cases are similar. Each case is described by a vector that consists of sequence of numeric features connected with environment state. The distance function between two cases a and b is denoted by (6):

$$d(a,b) = \sqrt{\sum_{i=1}^{N} w_i \cdot (f_i^a - f_i^b)^2} \tag{6}$$

where N is the number of features, f_i is a feature, and w_i is a weight of feature i. The weights represent the degrees of importance. Their values are optimized by GA in order to adjust the distance between cases. GA uses for evaluation the ratio of succeed to failed results of a case application.

Despite the fact that the RBR is considered as inefficient, it has an auxiliary role and proposes solutions in case CBR cannot ensure a good performance of the system. RBR is used when there are too little cases in case base or it is difficult to find a similar and useful case.

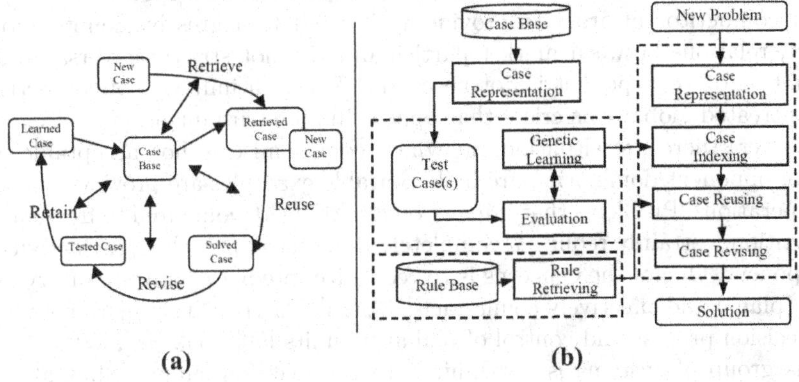

Fig. 4. CBR model: (a) case processing, (b) system architecture

Rules are easy to understand and implement. Nevertheless, the approach is not free from flaws. Knowledge extending and contradiction resolving mechanisms should be provided [49]. Small number of rules is insufficient, while huge number of rules impedes data processing.

8 Communication

How the practice shows, communication is not an issue in works related to the adversarial systems. In fact, the communication structure largely depends on a particular environment rather than the appearance of an enemy. The most popular competition environment is small-sized (RoboCup soccer players' competition) and provides immediate access to the world state (software simulation league). An exception is a field of the robot competition, but if the communication topic appears, it is related to low-level hardware issues.

According to the considered problem domain, simple broadcast is sufficient to inform agent's teammates about a current state of the world, or changes in surroundings. Agents based on the deliberative architecture require a method to distribute a set of tasks, which is a part of plan, inside a team. A task assignment is performed by a chosen leader agent. The agent arbitrarily assigns tasks to other agents or acquires bids according to marked rules [45].

9 Practical Applications

Systems with adversarial teams are much less popular subject than pure co-operating agents. Actually, many business dedicated MAS focus on production optimization and does not extend beyond the boundaries of a production line. Even though free-market competition is accounted, changes in the environment are relatively slow. This situation does not require detailed modeling of a particular competitor in order to provide an immediate aggressive counteraction. In fact, relations between market participants are not strictly adversarial and elimination of an opponent is not necessary. Thus, an influence of competitors can be treated globally as crises that appear in an environment.

However, there are situations in which compromise is not acceptable and costs of opponent domination are high. Suitable examples are provided by military operations. Problems that are met on a battlefield, compared to free-market competition, certainly require a completely different approach to the activity of an opponent. One of the concerns is to recognize, predict enemy's military doctrines (plans) and effectively counteract [28], [33]. Battlefield simulation systems aids decision process and control of real army units [59], [60], [61], [62].

This group of systems is not limited to the decision support, but also includes real-time control of agents. The idea of matches between teams of robots is applied in RoboCup simulation, which is one of the most popular test frameworks. Embodied agents require robust methods that provide efficient control in a dynamic environment. Solutions intended for the adversarial systems sometimes are utilized in other areas like rescue simulations or disaster mitigation problems. Despite the fact that these areas do not include a real opponent, an appropriate metaphor can change the meaning of events that occur in the environment. There is a group of projects that successfully uses methods derived from RoboCup competition [54], [55], [56], [57], [58]. Additionally, solutions intended for the robotic soccer teams can be transferred to the military domain. In fact, defense systems consisted of unmanned combat units are probably distant future [67]. Nevertheless, software simulations that include air, land and naval units are developed [63], [64], [65], [66], [68], [69].

Recently, the threat of virtual attacks has significantly increased. Military aggression can go hand in hand with operations that include damaging IT structure and information theft [31], [30]. The opponent can take the form of dangerous software, which is able to cooperate with other programs. In fact, the adversarial domain context remains.

The concept of adversarial teams does not need to focus on issues of security. Instead of military application, the solutions can provide fun. Recent releases of modern computer games prove how entertainment is valuable today. These productions, which are known almost only to the younger generation, already gained great popularity. The most profitable productions of all time include computer game titles. Developing artificial intelligence of a game opponent that is able to overwhelm an experienced human player team can be very profitable [42], [29]. In fact, environments in many games are quite realistic (even far more than advanced test frameworks). This gives an additional opportunity to transfer and apply some solutions in the real life.

10 Machine Learning Methods

System flexibility and adaptation to an environment are two main requirements for MAS with adversarial teams. That is why machine learning techniques are

Table 1. Machine learning methods and applications

	Machine Learning Methods					
	Q-learning	Case-Based Reasoning	Genetic Algorithm	Neural Networks	Classifier Methods	Hidden Markov Models
State-action decision	[47], [49], [53]	[48], [50]	[65], [64]	[65], [64]		
Learning rule based behaviour controller			[52]			
Learning multi-agent skill	[51]					
Learning agent skill	[46]					
Opponent strategy prediction					[22]	
Opponent behaviour recognition						[23]
Opponent behaviour prediction				[23]		
Environment next state prediction				[19], [20]		

widely applied in this area. They are used in several fields in order to increase effectiveness of team work. Table 1 shows a summary of machine learning methods applied for solving existing problems.

It is worth starting from the most common problem – choosing of an appropriate action in a specific environment state (state-action decision). The task is achieved by use of reinforcement learning methods (especially Q-learning and its modifications) for building state-action tables [47], [49], [53]. Other solutions are based on CBR [48], [50].

Genetic algorithm and neural networks are utilized to build controller for single agents in simpler environments [65], [64]. In paper [52] a rule based behaviour controller of an agent is built by applying an evolutionary approach.

An important part of development of a team is skill growth. Reinforcement learning methods are utilized for learning single agent skills (e.g. ball kicking) [46], as well as for learning multi-agent skills (e.g. ball passing) [51].

Also obtaining information about an opponent and an environment can be performed with use of machine learning methods. At the lowest level a next environment state can be predicted by simple solution based on neural network [19], [20]. An opponent behaviour is modeled by HMM in order to be recognized [23]. Subsequently, behaviour prediction is performed by neural networks [23]. Finally, paper [22] presents a comparison of several classifier methods applied for an opponent's strategy anticipation. This short survey of machine learning techniques in MAS with adversarial teams confirms that their application in this filed is very promising direction for their development.

11 Conclusions

Systems with adversarial teams represent the special case of a model with a group of cooperating agents. The appearance of an opponent adds new assumptions and increases a search space of a problem solution. Furthermore, an application of additional dedicated techniques is required.

A development of the system starts from an appropriate agent architecture selection. This choice is motivated by a particular environment and specific problem solution requirements. It usually depends on available computational resources, since system works in real time. The reactive architecture gives simple solutions that proved efficiency in robotic domain. However, much greater opportunities are provided by the deliberative architecture. The model assumes knowledge processing and planning. An evident complexity of the architecture popularizes hybrid approaches. In fact, the deliberative architecture produces slower solutions, while the reactive architecture is limited and obsolete.

Because of the fact that a team of agents acts against an enemy, mining information about an opponent team is crucial. Building a model of an enemy greatly supports strategy selection and decision-making. Useful data can be collected from previous plays of a foe. The recorded matches provide information about popular opponent strategies. When enemy agents' behaviours and plans are recognized, it is possible to forecast their next actions and strategies. Machine learning approaches and statistical models are successfully applied for this task.

The planning process describes a method of achieving a set of goals by assigning tasks and searching a state space. A planner module takes into account a state of the environment and available information about states of agents. The estimated intentions of an opponent team provide additional knowledge that is used in strategy selection conditions. In fact, the search space is enormous, which is why plan building utilizes fragmentary plans. These plan components are represented by cooperation patterns or prepared strategies.

Growing skills of an agent team are achieved by application of learning methods. The requirement that agents learn during a match reduces the number of available approaches. The popular reinforcement learning method constantly updates world state rewards, which allows calculating the optimal plan. Another approach that accumulates experience is based on CBR. Each reusable case provides a solution rule that can include conditions related to the knowledge about the world and an opponent. Nevertheless, it is possible to join the both approaches to obtain new solutions.

The adversarial arrangement of powers, compared to pure cooperative problems, is a specific case and it has a relatively limited application in business. It might seem that the initiation of RoboCup project will stimulate development of the systems with opposing agent teams, but it disrupted a balance of an allocation of solutions in the considered domain. A large part of the solutions is dedicated to robotic soccer area forgetting about other fields of a potential application. These fields are computer games, military, and IT infrastructure defense systems.

The survey about the adversarial systems suggests that they are at the beginning of its development. Despite the fact that they successfully utilize solutions dedicated to other group of problems, there are still unmet requirements. The large part of research should be allocated in the opponent analysis. Even more important task is to achieve a learning quality that allows agents effectively learn from experience, because an opponent tactics are unknown and sometimes unpredictable. Other issues are largely determined by computational limitations which are the matter of a destination platform. Currently, the most challenging goal is to achieve a state of development of these systems that would enable a team of agents to win with teams controlled by skilled human players.

References

1. Uhrmacher, A., Weyns, D.: Multi-Agent Systems: Simulation and Applications. Taylor and Francis Group, CRC Press (2009)
2. Veloso, M., Stone, P.: Individual and collaborative behaviors in a team of homogeneous robotic soccer agents. In: International Conference on Multi Agent Systems, pp. 309–316 (1998)
3. Hugel, V., Bonnin, P., Blazevic, P.: Reactive and adaptive control architecture designed for the Sony legged robots league in RoboCup 1999. In: International Conference on Intelligent Robots and Systems, vol. 2, pp. 1032–1037 (2000)
4. Bredenfeld, A., Indiveri, G.: Robot behavior engineering using DD-Designer. In: IEEE International Conference on Robotics and Automation, vol. 1, pp. 205–210 (2001)
5. Shi, L., Jiang, C., Zhen, Y., Zengqi, S.: Learning competition in robot soccer game based on an adapted neuro-fuzzy inference system. In: Proceedings of the 2001 IEEE International Symposium on Intelligent Control, pp. 195–199 (2001)
6. Zhang, B., Chen, X., Liu, L.: Agent Architecture: A Survey on RoboCup 1999 Simulator Teams. In: Proceedings of the 3rd World Congress on Intelligent Control and Automation, pp. 194–198 (2000)
7. Tan, A., Ng, G.: A Biologically-Inspired Cognitive Agent Model Integrating Declarative Knowledge and Reinforcement Learning. In: International Conference on Web Intelligence and Intelligent Agent Technology, vol. 2, pp. 248–251 (2010)
8. Tan, A., Carpenter, G., Grossberg, S.: Intelligence through interaction: Towards a unified theory for learning. In: International Symposium on Neural Networks, pp. 1098–1107 (2007)
9. Sun, Y., Bo, W.: Agent Hybrid Architecture and its Decision Processes. In: Proceedings of the Fifth International Conference on Machine Learning and Cybernetics, pp. 641–644 (2006)
10. Munoz-Hernandez, S., Wiguna, W.S.: Fuzzy Prolog as Cognitive Layer in RoboCupSoccer. In: IEEE Symposium on Computational Intelligence and Games, pp. 340–345 (2007)
11. Li, S., Ye, Z., Sun, Z.: A New Agent Architecture for RoboCup Tournament: Cognitive Architecture. In: Proceedings of the 3rd World Congress on Intelligent Control and Automation, pp. 199–202 (2000)
12. Dunin-Keplicz, B., Verbrugge, R.: Teamwork in Multi-Agent Systems – A Formal Approach. Wiley Series in Agent Technology. John Wiley and Sons Ltd. (2010)

13. Wang, P.: A Brief Survey on Cooperation in Multi-agent System. In: 2010 International Conference On Computer Design and Appliations, vol. 2, pp. 39–43 (2010)
14. Ferber, J.: Multi-Agent Systems – An Introduction to Distributed Artifical Intelligence. Addison Wesley Longman (1999)
15. Heintz, F.: FCFoo – a Short Description. In: RoboCup 1999 Team Description: Simulation League (1999)
16. Girault, F., Stinckwich, S.: Footux Team Description: A Hybrid recursive based agent architecture. In: RoboCup 1999 Team Description: Simulation League (1999)
17. Fathzadeh, R., Mokhtari, V., Mousakhani, M., Mahmoudi, F.: Mining Opponent Behavior: A Champion of RoboCup Coach Competition. In: IEEE 3rd Latin American Robotics Symposium, pp. 80–83 (2006)
18. Chelberg, D., Welch, L., Lakshmikumar, A., Gillen, M., Zhou, Q.: Meta-reasoning for a distributed agent architecture. In: Proceedings of the 33rd Southeastern Symposium on System Theory, pp. 377–381 (2001)
19. Sharifi, M., Mousavian, H., Aavani, A.: Predicting the future state of the RoboCup simulation environment: heuristic and neural networks approaches. In: IEEE International Conference on Systems, Man and Cybernetics, vol. 1, pp. 32–37 (2003)
20. Chohra, A., Scholl, P., Kobialka, H.-U., Hermes, J., Bredenfeld, A.: Behavior learning to predict using neural networks (NN): Towards a fast, cooperative and adversarial robot team (RoboCup). In: Proceedings of the Second International Workshop on Robot Motion and Control, pp. 79–84 (2001)
21. Camilleri, G.: A generic formal plan recognition theory. In: International Conference on Information Intelligence and Systems, pp. 540–547 (1999)
22. Weber, B.G., Mateas, M.: A data mining approach to strategy prediction. In: IEEE Symposium on Computational Intelligence and Games, pp. 140–147 (2009)
23. Han, K., Veloso, M.: Automated Robot Behavior Recognition Applied to Robotic Soccer. In: Robotics Research: 9th International Symposium, pp. 199–204 (2000)
24. Rabiner, L.: A tutorial on Hidden Markov Models and selected applications in speech recognition. Proceedings of the IEEE 77, 86–257 (1989)
25. Lopez, R., Jimenez, A.: Hybridization of cognitive models using evolutionary strategies. In: IEEE Congress on Evolutionary Computation, pp. 3213–3218 (2009)
26. Javier, O., Lopez, R.: Self-Organized and Evolvable Cognitive Architecture for Intelligent Agents and Multi-agent Systems. In: Second International Conference on Computer Engineering and Applications, vol. 1, pp. 417–421 (2010)
27. Faria, B.M., Reis, L.P., Lau, N., Castillo, G.: Machine Learning algorithms applied to the classification of robotic soccer formations and opponent teams. In: IEEE Conference on Cybernetics and Intelligent Systems, pp. 344–349 (2010)
28. Devaney, M., Ram, A.: Needles in a Haystack: Plan Recognition in Large Spatial Domains Involving Multiple Agents. In: Proceedings of AAAI 1998, pp. 942–947 (1998)
29. Laird, J.E.: It knows what you're going to do: Adding anticipation to a Quakebot. In: Proceedings of the Fifth International Conference on Autonomous Agents, pp. 385–392 (2001)
30. Gu, W., Zhou, J.: A Hostile Plan Recognition based on Plan Semantic Tree-Graph. In: IEEE International Conference on Control and Automation, pp. 2411–2416 (2007)
31. Gu, W., Ren, H., Li, B., Liu, Y., Liu, S.: Adversarial Plan Recognition and Opposition Based Tactical Plan Recognition. In: International Conference on Machine Learning and Cybernetics, pp. 499–504 (2006)

32. Li, W., Wang, W.: Multi-Agent Oriented Tactical Plan Recognition Method with Uncertainty. In: Fourth International Conference on Natural Computation, vol. 6, pp. 54–58 (2008)
33. Suzic, R., Svenson, P.: Capabilities-based plan recognition. In: 9th International Conference on Information Fusion, pp. 1–7 (2006)
34. Li, W.S., Wang, W.X.: A Hybrid Tactical Plan Recognition Method Base on Planning System. In: Third International Conference on Natural Computation, vol. 2, pp. 126–130 (2007)
35. Han, Y., Yin, M., Chen, J., Gu, W.: An Algorithm for Domain Axiom Plan Recognition based on Extended Goal Graph. In: Proceedings of 2005 International Conference on Machine Learning and Cybernetics, vol. 1, pp. 260–264 (2005)
36. Snoeck, N., van Kranenburg, H., Eertink, H.: Plan recognition in smart environments. In: 2nd International Conference on Digital Information Management, vol. 2, pp. 713–716 (2007)
37. Zhang, J., Cai, Z., Gan, Y., Zhang, B., He, L.: A New Algorithm for Predicting Future Actions in Plan Recognition. In: International Conference on Computational Intelligence and Security Workshops, pp. 140–143 (2007)
38. Gu, W., Yin, J.: The Recognition and Opposition to Multiagent Adversarial Planning. In: International Conference on Machine Learning and Cybernetics, pp. 2759–2764 (2006)
39. Ruiz, M.A., Uresti, J.R.: Team Agent Behavior Architecture in Robot Soccer. In: IEEE Latin American Robotic Symposium, pp. 20–25 (2008)
40. Riyaz, S., Basir, O.: Intelligent Planning and Execution of Tasks Using Hybrid Agents. In: International Conference on Artificial Intelligence and Computational Intelligence, vol. 1, pp. 277–282 (2009)
41. Bonissone, P., Dutta, S., Wood, N.: Merging strategic and tactical planning in dynamic and uncertain environments. IEEE Transactions on Systems, Man and Cybernetics 24(6), 841–862 (1994)
42. She, Y., Grogono, P.: An Approach of Real-Time Team Behavior Control in Games. In: 21st International Conference on Tools with Artificial Intelligence, pp. 546–550 (2009)
43. Siebra, C., Tate, A.: An Investigation into the Use of Collaborative Concepts for Planning in Disaster Response Coalitions. In: IEEE Workshop on Distributed Intelligent Systems: Collective Intelligence and Its Applications, pp. 253–258 (2006)
44. Mota, L., Lau, N., Reis, L.: Co-ordination in RoboCup's 2D simulation league: Setplays as flexible, multi-robot plans. In: IEEE Conference on Robotics Automation and Mechatronics, pp. 362–367 (2010)
45. Ehsaei, M., Heydarzadeh, Y., Aslani, S., Haghighat, A.: Pattern-Based Planning System (PBPS): A novel approach for uncertain dynamic multi-agent environments. In: 3rd International Symposium on Wireless Pervasive Computing, pp. 524–528 (2008)
46. Riedmiller, M., Gabel, T.: On Experiences in a Complex and Competitive Gaming Domain: Reinforcement Learning Meets RoboCup. In: IEEE Symposium on Computational Intelligence and Games, pp. 17–23 (2007)
47. Junyuan, T., Desheng, L.: An Optimal Strategy Learning for RoboCup in Continuous State Space. In: Proceedings of the 2006 IEEE International Conference on Mechatronics and Automation, pp. 301–305 (2006)
48. Kuo, J., Lin, H.: Cooperative RoboCup agents using genetic case-based reasoning. In: IEEE International Conference on Systems, Man and Cybernetics, pp. 613–618 (2008)

49. Kuo, J., Cheng, H.: Applying assimilation and accommodation for cooperative learning of RoboCup agent. In: International Conference on Machine Learning and Cybernetics, vol. 6, pp. 3234–3239 (2010)
50. Srinivasan, T., Aarthi, K., Aishwarya Meenakshi, S., Kausalya, M.: CBRRoboSoc: An Efficient Planning Strategy for Robotic Soccer Using Case Based Reasoning. In: International Conference on Computational Intelligence for Modelling, Control and Automation, p. 113 (2006)
51. Xiong, L., Wei, C., Jing, G., Zhenkun, Z., Zekai, H.: A New Passing Strategy Based on Q-Learning Algorithm in RoboCup. In: 2008 International Conference on Computer Science and Software Engineering, pp. 524–527 (2008)
52. Kuo, J., Ou, Y.: An Evolutionary Fuzzy Behaviour Controller using Genetic Algorithm in RoboCup Soccer Game. In: 2009 Ninth International Conference on Hybrid Intelligent Systems, pp. 281–286 (2009)
53. Shi, L., Jinyi, Y., Zhen, Y., Zengqi, S.: Multiple Rewards Fuzzy Reinforcement Learning Algorithm in RoboCup Environment. In: Proceedings of the 2001 IEEE International Conference on Control Applications, pp. 317–322 (2001)
54. Siebra, C., Tate, A.: An Investigation into the Use of Collaborative Concepts for Planning in Disaster Response Coalitions. In: IEEE Workshop on Distributed Intelligent Systems: Collective Intelligence and Its Applications, pp. 253–258 (2006)
55. Carbone, A., Finzi, A., Orlandini, A., Pirri, F., Ugazio, G.: Augmenting situation awareness via model-based control in rescue robots. In: International Conference on Intelligent Robots and Systems, pp. 3699–3705 (2005)
56. Takahashi, T., Takeuchi, I., Matsuno, F., Tadokoro, S.: Rescue simulation project and comprehensive disaster simulator architecture. In: International Conference on Intelligent Robots and Systems, vol. 3, pp. 1894–1899 (2000)
57. Tadokoro, S., Kitano, H.: The RoboCup-Rescue project: a robotic approach to the disaster mitigation problem. In: IEEE International Conference on Robotics and Automation, vol. 4, pp. 4089–4094 (2000)
58. Takahashi, T., Tadokoro, S.: Working with robots in disasters. IEEE Robotics and Automation Magazine 9(3), 34–39 (2002)
59. An, A., Li, X., Xie, X.: Multi-agent interactions centric virtual battlefield simulation model. In: 2nd International Conference on Advanced Computer Control, vol. 3, pp. 315–319 (2010)
60. Li, X., Dang, S., Li, K., Liu, Q.: Multi-agent-based battlefield reconnaissance simulation by novel task decompositionand allocation. In: 5th International Conference on Computer Science and Education, pp. 1410–1414 (2010)
61. Li, Y., Wang, W., Ji, L., Zhu, J.: Research on Muti-Agent simulation and emulation in battlefield based on NETLOGO. In: International Conference on Computer Application and System Modeling, vol. 6, pp. 131–135 (2010)
62. Yu, Y., Zhao, G.: Virtual battlefield and combat simulation based on artificial life theory. In: Sixth International Conference on Natural Computation, vol. 6, pp. 2820–2825 (2010)
63. Huang, Y., Lu, C., Han, S.: Combat description framework of the naval systems based on Multi- Agent. In: IEEE International Conference on Advanced Management Science, vol. 2, pp. 591–594 (2010)
64. Parker, G.B., Probst, M.H.: Using evolution strategies for the real-time learning of controllers for autonomous agents in Xpilot-AI. In: IEEE Congress on Evolutionary Computation, pp. 1–7 (2010)

65. Parker, G.B., Parker, M.: Evolving Parameters for Xpilot Combat Agents. In: IEEE Symposium on Computational Intelligence and Games, pp. 238–243 (2007)
66. Cil, I., Mala, M.: MABSIM: A multi agent based simulation model of military unit combat. In: Second International Conference on the Applications of Digital Information and Web Technologies, pp. 731–736 (2009)
67. Liu, Y., Zhang, A.: Multi-Agent System and Its Application in Combat Simulation. In: International Symposium on Computational Intelligence and Design, vol. 1, pp. 448–452 (2008)
68. Liu, J., Zhao, C., Zhao, D., Gao, J.: Self-Organization Behaviors of Intelligent Antagonism Target Team of Air Combat Based on Pi-Calculus. In: International Workshop on Intelligent Systems and Applications, pp. 1–4 (2009)
69. Liu, J., Zhao, D., Zhao, C., Gao, J.: Study on mental attribution of decisions of multi-aircrafts cooperative combat command control. In: International Conference on Machine Learning and Cybernetics, vol. 4, pp. 2002–2005 (2009)

On Pricing Strategies of Boundedly Rational Telecommunication Operators

Bogumil Kaminski[1] and Maciej Latek[2]

[1] Decision Support and Analysis Division,
Warsaw School of Economics, Al. Niepodleglosci 162, Warsaw, Poland
bkamins@sgh.waw.pl
[2] Department of Computational Social Science,
George Mason University, 4400 University Dr., Fairfax, Virginia, U.S.A.
mlatek@gmu.edu

Abstract. We analyze a multiagent model of a pre-paid telecommunication market and illustrate how the topology of the call graph among customers influences long-run market prices. Verifying the robustness of our results by controlling for telecommunication operators' levels of rationality and price elasticity of customer demand for airtime, we show that operators' rationality levels influence the market's rate of convergence to long-run price levels while the price elasticity of demand significantly influences the relation between on- and off-network prices. In particular, increasing the price elasticity of demand leads to more price differentiation among customers regardless of call graph topology.

1 Introduction

We investigate a multiagent simulation of a pre-paid telecommunication market under the calling-party-pays (CPP) pricing regime. A key issue in theoretical studies of such markets is whether telecommunication operators can lessen competition by price discrimination between on- and off-network calls and between customers with different calls volumes [8,10]. On the empirical side, [4] have shown evidence of lower prices for on-network calls compared with off-network calls in the Turkish telecommunication market.

The standard approach for analyzing prices in CPP markets is based on the works of [2,14,15], and is now known in the literature as the A-LRT framework. Critically, A-LRT models forego the analysis of customers' call graph topology and telecommunication operators' computational or cognitive capacity constraints. In this paper we address this problem with a multiagent simulation model based on the framework presented in [12]. Our analysis extends those results by studying the effects of changing the telecommunication operators' levels of rationality and by allowing customer demand to react to prices.

[3,14,15] note that price discrimination between on- and off-network calls may lead to emergent coordination of operators' choices among customers, possibly resulting in a larger proportion of on-network calls than off-network calls in total traffic. Current studies of this effect such as [5,6,9,20] share the implicit

N.T. Nguyen (Ed.): Transactions on CCI VI, LNCS 7190, pp. 170–180, 2012.

assumption that calls graphs are fully connected and each customer proxies the share of his peers using a given operator with the overall market shares. This approach guarantees the models analytical tractability. However, as [1,11,19] show, this assumption is not met in practice. An alternative to homogenous representation of call graphs, based on the small world network topology (SWN) [18], was found to better represent country-scale call graphs.

A model taking into account the SWN topology of calls graph was proposed in [12] where they showed that under irregular topologies, as opposed to the A-LRT topology, price discrimination patterns between on- and off-network calls emerge that resemble real-life data. However, they assumed that (*a*) telecommunication operators' pricing strategies are limited to the myopic best response and (*b*) customers' demands for calls do not depend on prices. In this work we remove these limitations.

2 A Model of Pre-paid Market

In this section we briefly describe the model proposed by [12] and outline extensions implemented in this paper.

In the model, we identify three types of entities: services, clients and operators. A service is a voice number that is used by clients to make calls. Services are connected through a directed and weighted call graph. Weights on the edges of the graph change depending on prices. A client can own more than one service. Each client minimizes the total cost of calling by choosing operators for his services. Operators represent profit-maximizing telecommunication companies that strategically choose on- and off-network call prices under the CCP regime and face marginal costs for on-network calls and interconnection costs for off-network calls. We assume that the marginal cost of an on-network call is 1 and the marginal cost of an off-network call is equal to 0.5 for both operators involved in the call. In the second case, an interconnection fee equal to 0.5 is charged by the receiving operator to the operator from whose network the call originated.

We implemented the model as a discrete event, multiagent simulation using the MASON toolkit developed by [17]. The model architecture is presented on Figure 1. Three main modules of the simulation are (1) the representation of the call graph, (2) decision rule for choosing operators by clients and (3) the strategic price setting procedure for operators.

2.1 Call Graph Module

The procedure generating the initial call graph between services and a method that assigns services to customers is described in detail in [12]. In short, it can generate both SWN and fully-connected (A-LRT type) call graphs, accounting for the presence of client-service relations.

Initial weights on call graphs encode the intensity of communication between pairs of services, expressed in total call-time per tick of the model. During the runtime, the baseline demand is dynamically updated depending on the unit

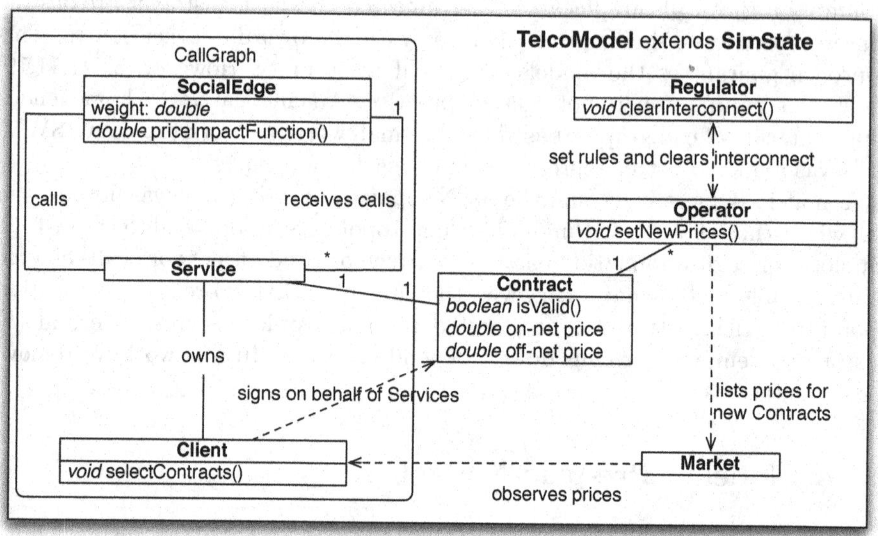

Fig. 1. UML class diagram of the structure of our model. SimState is MASON's base simulation class. Instances of Client, Service and Operator classes are treated as agents.

price associated with making a particular call. We define a demand multiplier as the following truncated linear function:

$$\eta(p) = \min\left(2, \max\left(\frac{1}{10}, 1 + a\,(1-p)\right)\right) \tag{1}$$

where a is the slope parameter. The value of $\eta(p)$ is used to multiply the initial weight in the call graph to obtain calling intensity for a given price p. This approach allows us to model how call intensity responds to changes in prices. We were unable to find empirical research that would allow deriving the functional form of the demand multiplier. Therefore we have chosen a simple function that at the same time shows the details of the effects of this choice, as presented in the Simulation Results section.

If a is not very far from 0, network weights do not respond to prices, similar to what one would expect for small price changes on realistic, mature pre-paid markets. For example, [7] reports that price elasticities for post-paid customers in the Austrian mobile market range from 1.1 to 0.47 and that pre-paid household customers have much lower elasticities.

2.2 Client's Decision Rule for Choice of Operator

We assume that client's choice of operators for his services is driven by minimizing the average calling cost per minute. This deviates from an assumption made by [12] where the total cost of calling was minimized. Such a change reflects the fact that under dynamic call volumes, the increased cost might be driven by a higher demand - not necessarily higher prices. We assume that in each time step every client chooses his allocation of services to operators.

Clients apply myopic best response to make decisions. Therefore a client coordinates his subscription choices between his services but assumes that the operator choices of neighbors will remain constant. This is akin to modeling the joint decision on the best operator by a group of friends by assuming that they are one client. Algorithm 1 presents the procedure used by clients to calculate the average cost of an allocation of services to operators.

Algorithm 1. Calculation of the average cost of usage for a postulated service allocation $\mathbf{o}_c$ for client c given the network neighbourhood and the call volume demand η. Variables p^a_{on} and p^a_{off} are on- and off-net prices of operator a.

```
Query current on- and off-net prices stored in vector p
Query current subscription choices of all peers o_{-c}
Set Cost(o_c) = 0
Set Volume(o_c) = 0
for all services A belonging to the client c do
  Get the proposed operator a = o_c(A)
  for all outgoing edges of service A do
    Get the destination service B
    Get the baseline edge weight w = w(A, B)
    if B belongs to client c then
      Get B's proposed operator, b = o_c(B)
    else
      Set b to the current operator used by B, b = o_{-c}(B)
    end if
    if a = b then
      Cost(o_c) += p^a_on η(p^a_on) w
      Volume(o_c) += η(p^a_on) w
    else
      Cost(o_c) += p^a_off η(p^a_off) w
      Volume(o_c) += η(p^a_off) w
    end if
  end for
end for
return Cost(o_c) / Volume(o_c)
```

2.3 Operators' Procedure for Setting Prices

Operators maximize profits. Algorithm 2 outlines how operators calculate profits for any given allocation of services to operators and any price scenario. The procedure deviates from [12] by accounting for how prices affect total call volumes.

Algorithm 2. Calculation of revenues of operators for a given network and set of choices of clients, price vector $\mathbf{p}$ and the call volume demand function η. Marginal cost $m = 1$ is shared equally in case of network-crossing calls. Variables p^a_{on} and p^a_{off} are on- and off-net prices offered by operator a.

Initialize revenue vector $\mathbf{r} = 0,\ \|\mathbf{r}\| = \texttt{numOperators}$
Query on- and off-network prices stored in vector $\mathbf{p}$
for all edges in the call graph **do**
  Get source service A and destination service B and operators they use, a and b
  Get the baseline edge weight $w = w(A, B)$
  if $a = b$ **then**
    $\mathbf{r}(a) \mathrel{+}= (p^a_{\text{on}} - m)\, \eta\, (p^a_{\text{on}})\, w$
  else
    $\mathbf{r}(a) \mathrel{+}= \left(p^a_{\text{off}} - k(a,b) - \frac{m}{2}\right) \eta\, (p^a_{\text{off}})\, w$
    $\mathbf{r}(b) \mathrel{+}= \left(k(a,b) - \frac{m}{2}\right) \eta\, (p^a_{\text{off}})\, w$
  end if
end for
return $\mathbf{r}$

We assume that operators use n^{th} order rationality to interact strategically. Details of this algorithm are described in [16]. In short, the algorithm calculates an operator's expected stream of future profits conditional on its pricing decisions, building scenarios of future pricing of its competitors and changes in clients' choices simultaneously. The algorithm achieves this by recursive simulation: operators simulate the environment forward in a *cloned* simulation to determine the outcomes of hypothetical pricing scenarios. The cloned simulation is initialized with the current state of the call graph and follows the same rules of behavior as the original one.

The algorithm has two parameters d and h. Parameter d represents the sophistication of operators' decision making. Setting $d = 0$ means that the operator will repeat its last pricing choice while $d = 1$ means that it will choose the best response prices assuming that all other operators set their prices using $d = 0$. This definition is inductive - an operator at d^{th} sophistication level assumes that all other operators are at level $d - 1^{th}$ when setting prices. In this sense increasing d increases the computational complexity of operators' reasoning, but also increases their strategic sophistication. In simple game-theoretic problems, increasing rationality level d makes players' choices move towards Nash equilibrium. Parameter h represents the number of periods in the future that are taken into account in optimization. An operator with $h = 1$ optimizes its choices only for the next period of simulation, if $h = 2$ it aggregates profits for two periods. All decisions are made with the full knowledge of the past pricings of all operators and the current state of the call graph, including allocations of services.

Table 1. Simulation parameters used during experiment

Parameter	Scenario value		Meaning
	A-LRT	SWN	
`averageDegree`	1000	4—6	Average degree of services on call graph
`rewireProb`	0	0.5	Rewiring probability used by the call graph generation algorithm
`servicePerClient`	1	5	Upper bounds of the client size distribution
`numOperators`	$\{2, 3, 4\}$		Number of operators
`numServices`	1000		Number of services
`connectionVariance`	20		Correlation between call destinations of services belonging to the same client
`m`	1		Marginal cost, shared equally among operators for off-network calls
`(d, h)`	$(1, 1)$		n-th order rationality parameters
`a`	$0, 0.5$		Slope of the call volume demand function η

3 Simulation Results

We compare the long-run pricing strategies of operators between A-LRT and SWN topologies by running experiments outlined in Table 1. For each parameter set, we run 10 simulation repetitions, each lasting for 70 iterations. The long-run statistics are computed for periods 50 to 70. This setting extends [12] by varying (d, h) parameters and allowing the slope a of the demand function to differ from 0.

[12] have shown that for $a = 0$ and $(d, h) = (1, 1)$ average markups per call are higher for SWN graphs than A-LRT ones. Additionally, they have demonstrated that increasing the number of operators influences SWN markets less than A-LRT markets. Finally, off-network prices are higher than on-network prices only for SWN markets, a situation that aligns well with observations of real telecommunication markets [4]. Using the extended model, we perform three types of robustness tests of the original results by (a) varying rationality levels of operators, (b) varying the slope a of the call volume demand multiplier η and (c) sweeping a wider range of possible call graph topologies.

First we have relaxed the assumption that total call volumes remain nearly constant. Figure 2 plots the long-run on- and off-network prices as a function of a of the demand multiplier function η. For small values of $a < 0.25$, the pattern of price discrimination remains unchanged. If the total call demand is highly elastic, price discrimination strengthens for SWN networks and persists for A-LRT networks. As we have indicated earlier, the functional form of the demand multiplier was chosen without docking with empirical studies but to show that a

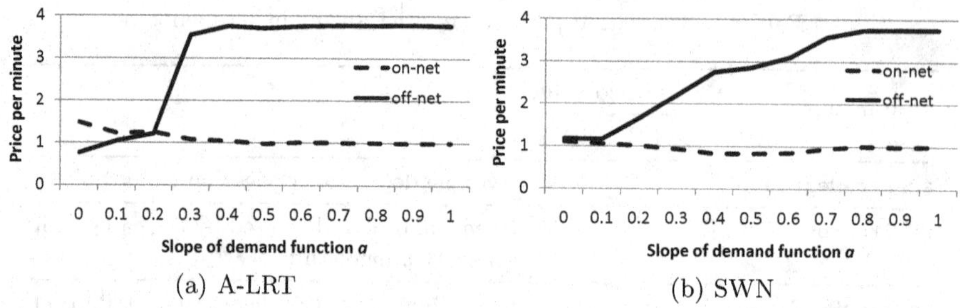

Fig. 2. Sensitivity of the long-run on- and off-network prices to the slope parameter a of the call volume demand function η. We set $(d, h) = (1, 1)$.

Table 2. Long-run average margins, on- and off-network prices per call in A-LRT and SWN topologies in triopoly, conditional on operators' planning horizons, rationality levels and the slope of the call volume demand function

Slope a	Rationality level d	Horizon h	On-net price		Off-net price		Margin	
			A-LRT	SWN	A-LRT	SWN	A-LRT	SWN
0	1	1	1.50	1.09	0.77	1.15	0.05	0.11
		2	1.61	1.12	0.82	1.18	0.12	0.14
	2	1	1.50	1.10	0.78	1.25	0.07	0.14
		2	1.54	1.06	0.79	1.27	0.09	0.13
0.5	1	1	1.03	0.84	3.74	2.52	0.53	0.69
		2	1.13	0.87	3.78	2.54	0.64	0.71
	2	1	0.87	0.81	3.63	3.81	0.31	0.75
		2	0.76	0.76	3.68	3.86	0.23	0.71

changing relationship between on-net and off-network prices can emerge without changing the call graph. This result implies that customer demand price elasticity, combined with the topology of the call graph, is an important factor in the analysis of the long-run pricing policies in telecommunication markets and both should be backed by empirical data.

Next we perform a sensitivity analysis on operators' decision making parameters. Table 2 presents the influence of altering planning horizons and rationality levels on the long-run margins and prices for triopoly markets. For all parameterizations with inelastic demand, the results are consistent with [12]. Figure 3 presents average margins as a function of time. Observe that while increasing rationality level and planning horizon may increase the rate of convergence and affect short-run market dynamics, the steady state remains roughly the same.

So far we have looked at only two alternative parameterizations of the topology of call graphs. In Table 3 we have summarized results of a continuous sweep

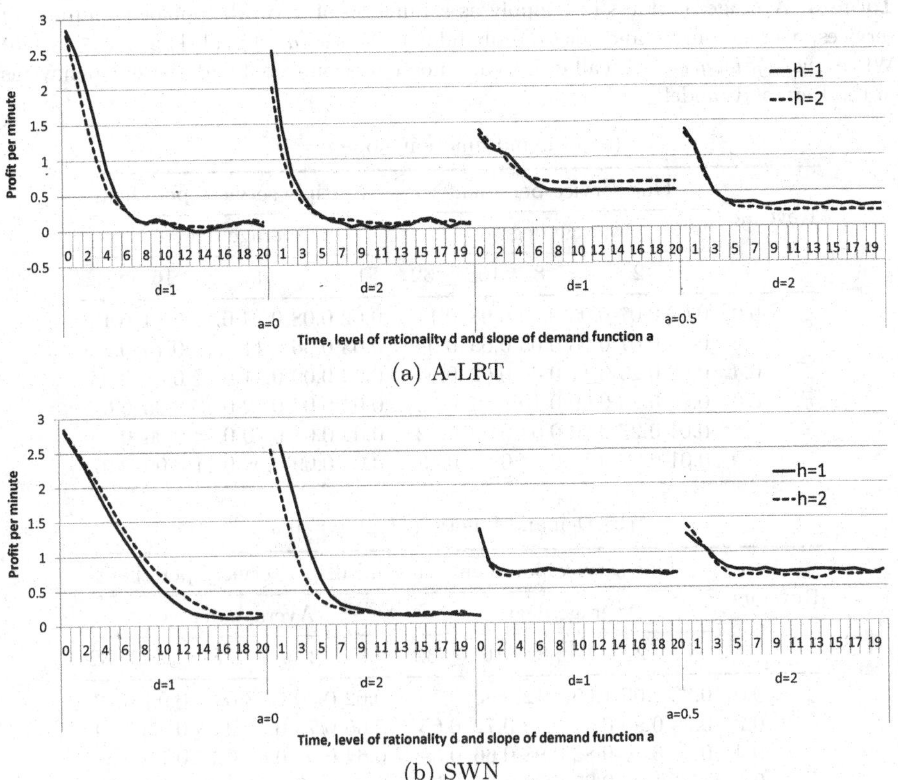

(a) A-LRT

(b) SWN

Fig. 3. Dynamics of average margins in A-LRT and SWN markets as a function of time and operators' rationality levels and planning horizons. We set $a \in \{0, 0.5\}$.

over a wide range call graph topology parameters using average markups. The topology of call graph is a function of the average degree of the graph and the rewire probability. For definitions of those parameters consult [13].

We notice that increasing network density, characterized by larger average degree, decreases markups. On the other hand, increasing network randomness, characterized by higher rewire probability, increases markups. However, the influence of network density dominates. A notable exception is the case of a very low density of call graph where the graph is composed of many disconnected clusters. In such a case, the network effects disappear and the competition changes to the standard Bertrand mode, resulting in prices nearly equal to marginal costs.

Additional simulation experiments in more complex settings and all codes used to produce our results can be accessed at `http://www.assembla.com/wiki/show/telcoMarket`.

Table 3. Average markups in triopoly as a function of network topology (number of services, average degree and rewire probability). We set $(d, h) = (1, 1)$ and $a \in (0, 0.5)$ When $averageDegree = 1$, call graphs are mostly disconnected and markets behave as in the Bertrand model.

(a) Demand function slope $a = 0$

Revenue		One service per client						Multiple services per client					
		Average degree						Average degree					
		1	2	4	8	16	≥ 32	1	2	4	8	16	≥ 32
Rewire prob	0.0	0.02	0.07	0.05	0.05	0.08	0.11	0.02	0.08	0.14	0.16	0.14	0.10
	0.2	0.03	0.07	0.08	0.05	0.05	0.02	0.03	0.06	0.11	0.19	0.10	0.05
	0.4	0.02	0.23	0.11	0.06	0.02	0.00	0.03	0.09	0.11	0.22	0.06	0.05
	0.6	0.01	0.25	0.09	0.10	0.04	0.03	0.04	0.07	0.12	0.13	0.08	0.06
	0.8	0.01	0.27	0.20	0.03	0.02	0.02	0.02	0.08	0.10	0.14	0.06	0.05
	1.0	0.01	0.32	0.15	0.02	0.05	0.03	0.03	0.09	0.08	0.11	0.09	0.07

(b) Demand function slope $a = 0.5$

Revenue		One service per client						Multiple services per client					
		Average degree						Average degree					
		1	2	4	8	16	≥ 32	1	2	4	8	16	≥ 32
Rewire prob	0.0	0.83	1.05	1.05	1.12	0.83	0.78	0.62	0.70	0.78	0.81	0.90	0.73
	0.2	0.89	0.90	0.97	0.99	0.72	0.65	0.65	0.76	0.72	0.63	0.80	0.64
	0.4	0.89	0.86	0.82	0.98	0.66	0.59	0.64	0.67	0.64	0.72	0.75	0.59
	0.6	0.91	1.04	0.95	0.79	0.68	0.56	0.69	0.63	0.67	0.68	0.70	0.59
	0.8	0.93	0.93	0.69	0.70	0.63	0.57	0.58	0.60	0.63	0.65	0.70	0.55
	1.0	0.87	0.72	0.71	0.65	0.64	0.53	0.65	0.66	0.63	0.78	0.66	0.59

4 Conclusions

In this paper we presented a computational model of pre-paid mobile telecommunication markets. Unlike classic A-LRT models, our model can account for local heterogeneity in call destinations. The analysis performed is a robustness check of results obtained by [12] with respect to parameterization of call graph topology, operators' rationality levels and price elasticities of call volume demand.

We have confirmed that using the baseline parameterization of [12], the SWN topology of call graphs offers operators higher profit margins than A-LRT networks. We have found that if the price elasticity of demand is introduced, price discrimination increases across all possible topologies. However, the last result depends on the choice of the functional form of the call volume demand function that was not validated empirically. Therefore we can conclude that the functional form of clients' price elasticity function is important and should be docked with the real-life data in applied research.

Second, we have stress-tested the model with different parameterizations of operators' decision making and found that the results remain stable, with the only difference being the rate of convergence to the steady state.

Finally we showed that for single component graphs, increasing the density of the call network decreases operators' margins, similarly to increasing the randomness of the call graph. We have also found that in extreme, for highly disconnected graphs it is possible to reduce the competition to the Bertrand model.

Acknowledgements. Useful comments by two anonymous referees are gratefully acknowledged. This research was supported by Warsaw School of Economics Research Grant number 03/S/0025/10.

References

1. Aiello, W., Chung, F., Lu, L.: A Random Graph Model for Massive Graphs. In: Proceedings of the Thirty-second Annual ACM Symposium on Theory Of Computing, pp. 171–180. ACM (2000)
2. Armstrong, M.: Network Interconnection in Telecommunications. Economic Journal 108, 545–564 (1998)
3. Armstrong, M., Wright, J.: Mobile Call Termination. Economic Journal 119, 270–307 (2009)
4. Atiyas, I., Dogan, P.: When good intentions are not enough: Sequential entry and competition in the Turkish mobile industry. Telecommunications Policy 31, 502–523 (2007)
5. Birke, D., Swann, P.: Network Effects in Mobile Telecommunications: an Empirical Analysis. Technical report, University of Nottingham (2004)
6. Blonski, M.: Network Externalities and Two-Part Tariffs in Telecommunication Markets. Information Economics and Policy 14, 95–109 (2002)
7. Dewenter, R., Haucap, J.: Demand Elasticities for Mobile Telecommunications in Austria. Journal of Economics and Statistics (Jahrbuecher fuer Nationaloekonomie und Statistik) 228, 49–63 (2008)
8. Dessein, W.: Network Competition in Nonlinear Pricing. RAND Journal of Economics 34, 593–611 (2003)
9. Grajek, M.: Estimating Network Effects and Compatibility in Mobile Telecommunications. ESMT Research Working Papers ESMT-07-001, ESMT European School of Management and Technology (2007)
10. Hahn, J.H.: Network Competition and Interconnection with Heterogeneous Subscribers. International Journal of Industrial Organization 22, 611–631 (2004)
11. Hidalgo, C., Rodriguez-Sickert, C.: Persistence, Topology and Sociodemographics of a Mobile Phone Network. Technical report, Center for Complex Network Research, Department of Physics, University of Notre Dame (2007)
12. Kaminski, B., Latek, M.: The Influence of Call Graph Topology on the Dynamics of Telecommunication Markets. In: Jędrzejowicz, P., Nguyen, N.T., Howlet, R.J., Jain, L.C. (eds.) KES-AMSTA 2010, Part I. LNCS (LNAI), vol. 6070, pp. 263–272. Springer, Heidelberg (2010)

13. Kleinberg, J.: The Small-World Phenomenon: An Algorithmic Perspective. In: Proc. of the 32nd Symposium on Theory of Computing, pp. 163–170. ACM (2000)
14. Laffont, J.J., Rey, P., Tirole, J.: Network Competition: I. Overview and Nondiscriminatory Pricing. RAND Journal of Economics 29, 1–37 (1998)
15. Laffont, J.J., Rey, P., Tirole, J.: Network Competition: II. Price Discrimination. RAND Journal of Economics 29, 38–56 (1998)
16. Latek, M., Axtell, R., Kaminski, B.: Bounded Rationality via Recursion. In: Proceedings of the Eighth International Conference on Autonomous Agents and Multiagent Systems, vol. 1, pp. 457–464. IFAAMAS (2009)
17. Luke, S., Cioffi-Revilla, C., Panait, L., Sullivan, K., Balan, G.: MASON: A Multi-Agent Simulation Environment. Simulation 81, 517–527 (2005)
18. Newman, M.: The Structure and Function of Complex Networks. SIAM Review 45, 167–256 (2003)
19. Onnela, J., Saramaki, J., Hyvonen, J., Szabo, G., Lazer, D., Kaski, K., Kertesz, J., Barabasi, A.: Structure and Tie Strengths in Mobile Communication Networks. Proc. Natl. Acad Sci. USA 104, 7332–7336 (2007)
20. Park, S.-H., Yeon, S.-J., Kim, S.-W., Kim, D.-H., Ha, W.-G.: The Dynamic Effects of Government Policies on Korean Telecommunication Services Market. In: Kennedy, M., Winch, G., Langer, R., Rowe, J., Yanni, J. (eds.) Proceedings of the 22nd Systems Dynamics Society Conference (2005), `http://www.systemdynamics.org/conferences/2005/proceed/papers/PARK426.pdf`

Reasoning about Time-Dependent Multi-agents: Foundations of Theorem Proving and Model Checking*

Norihiro Kamide

Waseda Institute for Advanced Study,
Waseda University,
1-6-1 Nishi Waseda, Shinjuku-ku, Tokyo 169-8050, Japan
drnkamide08@kpd.biglobe.ne.jp

Abstract. Firstly, an extension of linear-time temporal logic (LTL), called an agents-indexed linear-time temporal logic (ALTL), is introduced as a Gentzen-type sequent calculus. ALTL is intended to appropriately express reasoning about time-dependent multi-agents within a proof system. The cut-elimination and completeness theorems for ALTL are shown. Secondly, an extension of computation tree logic (CTL), called an agents-indexed computation tree logic (ACTL), is introduced as a Kripke-type semantics. ACTL is intended to appropriately formalize reasoning about time-dependent multi-agents within an executable temporal logic by model checking. The model-checking, validity and satisfiability problems for ACTL are shown to be decidable.

Keywords: Agents-indexed linear-time temporal logic, agents-indexed computation tree logic, time-dependent multi-agent, sequent calculus, model checking, completeness theorem.

1 Introduction

1.1 Linear-Time Temporal Logic versus Computation Tree Logic

Verifying and specifying time-dependent multi-agent systems are of growing importance in Computer Science since computer systems are generally used by or composed of time-dependent multi-agents. It is known that *linear-time temporal logic* (LTL) [4,17] and *computation tree logic* (CTL) [2] are one of the most useful temporal logics for verifying and specifying time-dependent and concurrent systems by *model checking* [3]. Indeed, LTL and CTL have been rivaled each other. LTL can express almost all important temporal properties, but LTL has no feasible model-checking algorithms. CTL has some feasible model-checking

* This paper is an extension of the presentation [9] in the track "Agent and multi-agent systems" of the conference KES 2010. Section 3 includes a new result (concerning ACTL) which is presented in this paper. In [9], the results for ACTL were not included.

N.T. Nguyen (Ed.): Transactions on CCI VI, LNCS 7190, pp. 181–201, 2012.

algorithms, but CTL cannot express some important temporal properties such as strong fairness. LTL has some simple proof systems such as Gentzen-type sequent calculus, but CTL has no such a simple proof system. By this fact, LTL is suitable for constructing a multi-agent extension of temporal proof systems.

In this paper, two multi-agent extensions of LTL and CTL are introduced and studied. The first one is an extension of LTL, called an *agents-indexed linear-time temporal logic* (ALTL). ALTL is introduced as a *Gentzen-type sequent calculus*, which is known to be a useful proof system for automated theorem proving. The second one is an extension of CTL, called an *agents-indexed computation tree logic* (ACTL). ACTL is introduced as a Kripke -type semantics, which is known to be a useful basis for model checking.[1]

1.2 Agents-Indexed Linear-Time Temporal Logic: A Basis for Theorem Proving

ALTL has some temporal, agent and fixpoint operators. By using these operators, reasoning about time-dependent multi-agents can appropriately be expressed. The proposed fixpoint operator in ALTL can express common knowledge (or information) of multi-agents. ALTL is also regarded as a combination of LTL and a *fixpoint logic*. The cut-elimination and completeness theorems for ALTL are shown as a main result of this paper. These theorems show that ALTL is attractive as a theoretical basis for automated theorem proving about time-dependent multi-agents.

The original contribution of ALTL is the result of the cut-elimination and completeness theorems for ALTL. Such a theoretical result was not obtained for other proposals for multi-agent temporal logics, although there were some results that include only one of these theorems.

Fixpoint logics (or fixed point logics) are regarded as logics with a *fixpoint* (or *fixed point*) operator. Typical examples of fixpoint logics are *propositional μ-calculus* [14], which is more expressive than temporal logics, and *common knowledge logic* [5], which is an extension of multi-agent epistemic logic. It is known that fixpoint logics are useful for representing temporal and knowledge-based reasoning. Combining LTL and a fixpoint logic is thus an attractive issue for representing time-dependent multi-agent systems. Indeed, a model checking (i.e. model-theoretic) approach to combine LTL and a common knowledge operator has been studied successfully [19].

A cut-free and complete Gentzen-type sequent calculus for combining LTL and a fixpoint logic has been required for providing a theoretical basis for automated theorem proving. However, a Gentzen-type sequent calculus for such a temporal fixpoint logic has not yet been studied. A reason may be that proving the cut-elimination and completeness theorems for such a combined logic is difficult since the traditional formulations of fixpoint operators are rather complex. This paper tries to overcome such a difficulty by introducing a new simple formulation of a fixpoint operator and by using an embedding-based proof method.

[1] We can also see that ACTL is an agent-based specialization of CTL.

In the following, we roughly explain the proposed formulation of the fixpoint operator. The symbol ω is used to represent the set of natural numbers. The symbol K is used to represent the set $\{\heartsuit_i \mid i \in \omega\}$ of agent modal operators, and the symbol K^* is used to represent the set of all words of finite length of the alphabet K. Greek lower-case letters ι and κ are used to represent any members of K^*. The characteristic inference rules for a fixpoint operator $\heartsuit_c$ are as follows:

$$\frac{\iota\kappa\alpha, \Gamma \Rightarrow \Delta}{\iota\heartsuit_c\alpha, \Gamma \Rightarrow \Delta}\ (\heartsuit_c\text{left}) \qquad \frac{\{\ \Gamma \Rightarrow \Delta, \iota\kappa\alpha \mid \kappa \in K^*\ \}}{\Gamma \Rightarrow \Delta, \iota\heartsuit_c\alpha}\ (\heartsuit_c\text{right}).$$

These inference rules are intended to imply the following axiom scheme:

$$\heartsuit_c\alpha \leftrightarrow \bigwedge\{\iota\alpha \mid \iota \in K^*\}.$$

This axiom scheme corresponds to the so-called iterative interpretation of common knowledge. Indeed, if we can read $\heartsuit_i\alpha$ as "agent i knows α," then we can understand $\heartsuit_c\alpha$ as "α is common knowledge of agents." Suppose that for any formula α, f_α is a mapping on the set of formulas such that

$$f_\alpha(x) := \bigwedge\{\heartsuit_i(x \wedge \alpha) \mid i \in \omega\}.$$

Then, $\heartsuit_c\alpha$ becomes a fixpoint of f_α.

1.3 Agents-Indexed Computation Tree Logic: A Basis for Model Checking

ACTL has a bounded version $\heartsuit_b$ of the fixpoint operator $\heartsuit_c$ of ALTL. The bounded fixpoint operator $\heartsuit_b$ is for obtaining the decidability of the model-checking problem for ACTL. Although such a bounded operator can also be adopted to the proposed semantics for ALTL, we consider only to adopt $\heartsuit_b$ in ACTL. A reason for introducing $\heartsuit_b$ in ACTL is that as mentioned before, the base logic CTL is also known to be an important temporal logic for model checking. We thus consider ACTL having $\heartsuit_b$. It is remarked that the unbounded fixpoint operator $\heartsuit_c$ can also be adopted to CTL, but a cut-free Gentzen-type sequent calculus for such an extended logic with $\heartsuit_c$ may be difficult to obtain. It is also remarked that constructing an LTL-based cut-free sequent calculus with $\heartsuit_b$ has not yet been succeeded.

The original contribution of ACTL is the simple and intuitive formalization of the fixpoint operator that can imply the decidability of the model-checking problem. On the other hand, we do not know the clear advantage for other proposals for temporal multi-agent model-checking frameworks (see Section 4). To investigate some detailed model-checking algorithms for ACTL is remained as a future work.

In the following, we explain the formulation of $\heartsuit_b$. The symbol K^m is used to represent the set of all words of at most "m-length" of the alphabet K. Note that K^m is a subset of K^*, and is also finite. This finiteness condition on K^m is critical for obtaining an embedding theorem of ACTL into CTL. Then, the characteristic axiom scheme for $\heartsuit_i$ and $\heartsuit_b$ is:

$$\heartsuit_b\alpha \leftrightarrow \bigwedge\{\iota\alpha \mid \iota \in K^m\}.$$

This axiom scheme corresponds to a "m-bounded" version of the iterative interpretation of common knowledge, which is obtained from the m-bounded version by replacing K^m with K^*. If we read $\heartsuit_i\alpha$ as "agent i has information α," then we can understand $\heartsuit_b\alpha$ as "α is finitely approximated common (or group) information of agents." In order to formalize these operators, we need to introduce an *agents-indexed Kripke structure*, which has agents-indexed satisfaction relations $\models^\iota$ $(\iota \in K^*)$.

A merit for introducing the m-bounded operator $\heartsuit_b$ is that we can obtain the decidability results of the model-checking, satisfiability and validity problems for ACTL. It may be difficult to obtain these decidability results for the extended CTL with the unbounded operator $\heartsuit_c$, since the extended logic cannot be embedded into CTL.

1.4 Small Motivating Examples

The fields of model-checking and theorem-proving based on temporal logics have been extended to cover verification and specification of multi-agent systems [21], which have become a topic of very active research. Some contributions have focused on extending such systems to the model checking tools and techniques usually employed for verification of reactive systems [18,19,20]. These obtain the validity of formula representing a property of interest in the model representing all the computations of the multi-agent system under consideration.

We now consider a simple coffee machine example which is a small modification of an example presented in [13] by Konikowska and Penczek. In the following example, we use the temporal operators G (globally in the future), F (eventually in the future) and the path quantifiers A (all computation paths), E (some computation path). It is remarked that in ACTL, the temporal operators G and F cannot occur without being preceded by a path quantifier A or E, i.e., pairs of symbols like AG and EF are indivisible. The coffee machine can be operated by several agents. Then, the following properties can be specified in ALTL and ACTL.

1. Coffee is always delivered in a cup:
   $\mathrm{G}(coffee{\rightarrow}cup)$ (in ALTL)
   $\mathrm{AG}(coffee{\rightarrow}cup)$ (in ACTL).
2. Always when coffee is delivered, the agent i knows that he is drinking:
   $\mathrm{G}(coffee{\rightarrow}\heartsuit_i drinking)$ (in ALTL)
   $\mathrm{AG}(coffee{\rightarrow}\heartsuit_i drinking)$ (in ACTL).
3. Always when an agent is thirsty, he will eventually drink coffee:
   $\mathrm{G}(thirsty{\rightarrow}\mathrm{F}drinking)$ (in ALTL)
   $\mathrm{AG}(thirsty{\rightarrow}\mathrm{EF}drinking)$ (in ACTL).
4. Always when there is no coffee, the agent i knows that he is not drinking:
   $\mathrm{G}(\neg coffee{\rightarrow}\heartsuit_i\neg drinking)$ (in ALTL)
   $\mathrm{AG}(\neg coffee{\rightarrow}\heartsuit_i\neg drinking)$ (in ACTL).

In this example, it is noted that we do not need to use the common knowledge operator $\heartsuit_c$ in ALTL and the bounded common knowledge operator $\heartsuit_b$ in ACTL. The next example will be required to use the operators $\heartsuit_c$ and $\heartsuit_b$.

Before to illustrate the next example, the notion of common knowledge is briefly explained below. The notion of common knowledge was probably first introduced by Lewis [15]. Let I be a fixed set of agents and α be an idea. Suppose α belongs to the common knowledge of I, and i and j are some members of I. Then, we have the facts "both i and j know α", "i knows that j knows α" and "j knows that i knows α". Moreover, we also have the facts "i knows that j knows that i knows α", and vice versa. Then, these nesting structures develop an infinite hierarchy as a result.

Based upon the interpretations (of $\heartsuit_c$ and $\heartsuit_b$) explained in Sections 1.2 and 1.3, ALTL and ACTL have some useful descriptions for a situation of computer login. An example of such situation is:

> "If the login password of a computer is regarded as common information in the group $A := \{1, 2, ..., n\}$ of agents, then an agent i in A will eventually be able to login the computer."

We can specify this situation as follows:

$$\mathrm{G}(\heartsuit_c\, \mathit{password} \to \heartsuit_i \mathrm{F}\, \mathit{login}) \quad \text{(in ALTL)},$$
$$\mathrm{AG}(\heartsuit_b\, \mathit{password} \to \heartsuit_i \mathrm{EF}\, \mathit{login}) \quad \text{(in ACTL)}.$$

1.5 Summary of This Paper

The contents of this paper is then summarized as follows.

In Section 2, ALTL is introduced as a Gentzen-type sequent calculus. The cut-elimination theorem for ALTL is proved using a theorem for syntactically embedding ALTL into a sequent calculus LK_ω for infinitary logic. Moreover, an *agent-time indexed semantics*, which is an extension of a semantics for LTL, is introduced for ALTL, and the completeness theorem with respect to this semantics is proved by combining two theorems for syntactically and semantically embedding ALTL into LK_ω.

In Section 3, ACTL is introduced as a Kripke-type semantics. By using a theorem for semantically embedding ACTL into CTL, the model-checking, validity and satisfiability problems for ACTL are shown to be decidable.

In Section 4, this paper is concluded and some related works are briefly addressed.

2 Agents-Indexed Linear-Time Temporal Logic

2.1 Sequent Calculus and Cut-Elimination

Let n be a fixed positive integer. Then, the symbol A is used to represent the set $\{1, 2, ..., n\}$ of agents. The following list is adopted for the language $\mathcal{L}$ of the underlying logic: (countable) propositional variables, $\rightarrow$ (implication), $\neg$ (negation), $\wedge$ (conjunction), $\vee$ (disjunction), $\heartsuit_i$ ($i \in A$) (agent i knows), $\heartsuit_c$ (least fixpoint or common knowledge), $\heartsuit_d$ (greatest fixpoint), X (next-time), G (globally in the future) and F (eventually in the future). Small letters $p, q, ...$ are used to denote propositional variables, Greek lower-case letters $\alpha, \beta, ...$ are used to denote formulas, and Greek capital letters $\Gamma, \Delta, ...$ are used to represent finite (possibly empty) sets of formulas. An expression $\circ\Gamma$ where $\circ \in \{\heartsuit_i\ (i \in A), \heartsuit_c, \heartsuit_d, \mathrm{X}, \mathrm{G}, \mathrm{F}\}$ is used to denote the set $\{\circ\gamma \mid \gamma \in \Gamma\}$. An expression $B \equiv C$ denotes the syntactical identity between B and C. The symbol ω is used to represent the set of natural numbers. The symbol K is used to represent the set $\{\heartsuit_i \mid i \in A\}$, and the symbol K^* is used to represent the set of all words of finite length of the alphabet K. Remark that K^* includes $\emptyset$ and hence $\{\iota\alpha \mid \iota \in K^*\}$ includes α. Greek lower-case letters ι and κ are used to denote any members of K^*. Lower-case letters i, j and k are sometimes used to denote any natural number. An expression $\mathrm{X}^i\alpha$ for any $i \in \omega$ is defined inductively by $\mathrm{X}^0\alpha \equiv \alpha$ and $\mathrm{X}^{n+1}\alpha \equiv \mathrm{X}\mathrm{X}^n\alpha$. Let T be $K \cup \{\mathrm{X}\}$. Then, T^* is used to represent the set of all words of finite length of the alphabet T. For example, $\mathrm{X}^i\iota\mathrm{X}^j\kappa$ is in T^*. An expression $\sharp$ (or $\sharp_i$) is used to represent an arbitrary member of T^*. $\sharp_1$ ($\in T^*$) is called a *permutation* of $\sharp$ ($\in T^*$) if $\sharp_1$ is obtained from $\sharp$ by shifting the places of the occurrences of X. For example, $\mathrm{X}^i\iota\mathrm{X}^j\kappa$ is a permutation of $\mathrm{X}^{i+j}\iota\kappa$. Remark that $\sharp$ itself is a permutation of $\sharp$. An expression of the form $\Gamma \Rightarrow \Delta$ is called a *sequent*. An expression $L \vdash S$ or $\vdash S$ is used to denote the fact that a sequent S is provable in a sequent calculus L. A rule R of inference is said to be *admissible* in a sequent calculus L if the following condition is satisfied: for any instance

$$\frac{S_1 \cdots S_n}{S}$$

of R, if $L \vdash S_i$ for all i, then $L \vdash S$.

A sequent calculus ALTL is introduced below.

Definition 1 (ALTL). *The initial sequents of* ALTL *are of the form: for any propositional variable p,*

$$\sharp p \Rightarrow \sharp p$$

The structural inference rules of ALTL *are of the form:*

$$\frac{\Gamma \Rightarrow \Delta, \alpha \quad \alpha, \Sigma \Rightarrow \Pi}{\Gamma, \Sigma \Rightarrow \Delta, \Pi}\ (\mathrm{cut}) \qquad \frac{\Gamma \Rightarrow \Delta}{\Sigma, \Gamma \Rightarrow \Delta, \Pi}\ (\mathrm{we}).$$

The logical inference rules of ALTL *are of the form: for any $m \in A$,*

$$\frac{\Gamma \Rightarrow \Delta, \sharp\alpha \quad \sharp\beta, \Sigma \Rightarrow \Pi}{\sharp(\alpha\rightarrow\beta), \Gamma, \Sigma \Rightarrow \Delta, \Pi}\ (\rightarrow\mathrm{left}) \qquad \frac{\sharp\alpha, \Gamma \Rightarrow \Delta, \sharp\beta}{\Gamma \Rightarrow \Delta, \sharp(\alpha\rightarrow\beta)}\ (\rightarrow\mathrm{right})$$

$$\frac{\sharp\alpha, \sharp\beta, \Gamma \Rightarrow \Delta}{\sharp(\alpha \wedge \beta), \Gamma \Rightarrow \Delta}\ (\wedge\mathrm{left}) \qquad \frac{\Gamma \Rightarrow \Delta, \sharp\alpha \quad \Gamma \Rightarrow \Delta, \sharp\beta}{\Gamma \Rightarrow \Delta, \sharp(\alpha \wedge \beta)}\ (\wedge\mathrm{right})$$

$$\frac{\sharp\alpha, \Gamma \Rightarrow \Delta \quad \sharp\beta, \Gamma \Rightarrow \Delta}{\sharp(\alpha \vee \beta), \Gamma \Rightarrow \Delta} \ (\vee\text{left}) \qquad \frac{\Gamma \Rightarrow \Delta, \sharp\alpha, \sharp\beta}{\Gamma \Rightarrow \Delta, \sharp(\alpha \vee \beta)} \ (\vee\text{right})$$

$$\frac{\Gamma \Rightarrow \Delta, \sharp\alpha}{\sharp\neg\alpha, \Gamma \Rightarrow \Delta} \ (\neg\text{left}) \qquad \frac{\sharp\alpha, \Gamma \Rightarrow \Delta}{\Gamma \Rightarrow \Delta, \sharp\neg\alpha} \ (\neg\text{right})$$

$$\frac{\sharp\heartsuit_m \mathrm{X}\alpha, \Gamma \Rightarrow \Delta}{\sharp\mathrm{X}\heartsuit_m\alpha, \Gamma \Rightarrow \Delta} \ (\mathrm{X}\heartsuit\text{left}) \qquad \frac{\Gamma \Rightarrow \Delta, \sharp\heartsuit_m \mathrm{X}\alpha}{\Gamma \Rightarrow \Delta, \sharp\mathrm{X}\heartsuit_m\alpha} \ (\mathrm{X}\heartsuit\text{right})$$

$$\frac{\sharp\mathrm{X}^k\alpha, \Gamma \Rightarrow \Delta}{\sharp\mathrm{G}\alpha, \Gamma \Rightarrow \Delta} \ (\mathrm{G}\text{left}) \qquad \frac{\{\ \Gamma \Rightarrow \Delta, \sharp\mathrm{X}^j\alpha \mid j \in \omega\ \}}{\Gamma \Rightarrow \Delta, \sharp\mathrm{G}\alpha} \ (\mathrm{G}\text{right})$$

$$\frac{\{\ \sharp\mathrm{X}^j\alpha, \Gamma \Rightarrow \Delta \mid j \in \omega\ \}}{\sharp\mathrm{F}\alpha, \Gamma \Rightarrow \Delta} \ (\mathrm{F}\text{left}) \qquad \frac{\Gamma \Rightarrow \Delta, \sharp\mathrm{X}^k\alpha}{\Gamma \Rightarrow \Delta, \sharp\mathrm{F}\alpha} \ (\mathrm{F}\text{right})$$

$$\frac{\sharp\kappa\alpha, \Gamma \Rightarrow \Delta \quad (\kappa \in K^*)}{\sharp\heartsuit_c\alpha, \Gamma \Rightarrow \Delta} \ (\heartsuit_c\text{left}) \qquad \frac{\{\ \Gamma \Rightarrow \Delta, \sharp\kappa\alpha \mid \kappa \in K^*\ \}}{\Gamma \Rightarrow \Delta, \sharp\heartsuit_c\alpha} \ (\heartsuit_c\text{right})$$

$$\frac{\{\ \sharp\kappa\alpha, \Gamma \Rightarrow \Delta \mid \kappa \in K^*\ \}}{\sharp\heartsuit_d\alpha, \Gamma \Rightarrow \Delta} \ (\heartsuit_d\text{left}) \qquad \frac{\Gamma \Rightarrow \Delta, \sharp\kappa\alpha \quad (\kappa \in K^*)}{\Gamma \Rightarrow \Delta, \sharp\heartsuit_d\alpha} \ (\heartsuit_d\text{right}).$$

Note that (Gright), (Fleft), ($\heartsuit_c$right) and ($\heartsuit_d$left) have infinite premises. Remark that Gentzen's sequent calculus LK for classical logic and Kawai's sequent calculus LT_ω [11] for LTL are subsystems of ALTL.

Remark that the sequents of the form $\sharp\alpha \Rightarrow \sharp\alpha$ for any formula α are provable in cut-free ALTL. This fact can be proved by induction on α.

An expression $\alpha \Leftrightarrow \beta$ represents two sequents $\alpha \Rightarrow \beta$ and $\beta \Rightarrow \alpha$.

Proposition 2. *The following sequents concerning $\heartsuit_i$ and $\heartsuit_c$ are provable in cut-free* ALTL*: for any $i \in A$,*

1. $\heartsuit_i(\alpha \rightarrow \beta) \Rightarrow \heartsuit_i\alpha \rightarrow \heartsuit_i\beta$,
2. $\heartsuit_c\alpha \Rightarrow \heartsuit_i\alpha$,
3. $\heartsuit_c\alpha \Rightarrow \kappa\alpha$ *for any* $\kappa \in K^*$,
4. $\heartsuit_c\alpha \Rightarrow \heartsuit_i\heartsuit_c\alpha$,
5. $\heartsuit_i\mathrm{X}\alpha \Leftrightarrow \mathrm{X}\heartsuit_i\alpha$.

Proof. We show only the following cases.

(1):

$$\dfrac{\dfrac{\begin{matrix}\vdots & & \vdots \\ \heartsuit_i\alpha \Rightarrow \heartsuit_i\alpha & & \heartsuit_i\beta \Rightarrow \heartsuit_i\beta\end{matrix}}{\heartsuit_i\alpha, \heartsuit_i(\alpha \rightarrow \beta) \Rightarrow \heartsuit_i\beta} \ (\rightarrow\text{left})}{\heartsuit_i(\alpha \rightarrow \beta) \Rightarrow \heartsuit_i\alpha \rightarrow \heartsuit_i\beta} \ (\rightarrow\text{right})$$

(4):

$$\dfrac{\dfrac{\begin{matrix}\vdots \\ \{\ \heartsuit_i\kappa\alpha \Rightarrow \heartsuit_i\kappa\alpha \mid \kappa \in K^*\}\end{matrix}}{\{\ \heartsuit_c\alpha \Rightarrow \heartsuit_i\kappa\alpha \mid \kappa \in K^*\}} \ (\heartsuit_c\text{left})}{\heartsuit_c\alpha \Rightarrow \heartsuit_i\heartsuit_c\alpha} \ (\heartsuit_c\text{right}).$$

(5): We have the fact $\vdash \heartsuit_i X\alpha \Leftrightarrow \heartsuit_i X\alpha$. This fact is proved by induction on α. Then, applying (X♡left) and (X♡right) to $\heartsuit_i X\alpha \Leftrightarrow \heartsuit_i X\alpha$, we obtain the required fact $\vdash \heartsuit_i X\alpha \Leftrightarrow X\heartsuit_i\alpha$. **Q.E.D.**

Proposition 3. *The rules of the form: for any* $i, m \in A$,

$$\frac{\Gamma \Rightarrow \Delta}{\heartsuit_i\Gamma \Rightarrow \heartsuit_i\Delta}\ (\heartsuit\text{regu})$$

$$\frac{\sharp X\heartsuit_m\alpha, \Gamma \Rightarrow \Delta}{\sharp\heartsuit_m X\alpha, \Gamma \Rightarrow \Delta}\ (X\heartsuit\text{left}^{-1}) \qquad \frac{\Gamma \Rightarrow \Delta, \sharp X\heartsuit_m\alpha}{\Gamma \Rightarrow \Delta, \sharp\heartsuit_m X\alpha}\ (X\heartsuit\text{right}^{-1})$$

are admissible in cut-free ALTL.

Proof. We show only the case for (♡regu). By induction on the proofs P of $\Gamma \Rightarrow \Delta$ in cut-free ALTL. We distinguish the cases according to the last inference of P. We show some cases.

Case (→left): The last inference of P is of the form:

$$\frac{\Gamma_1 \Rightarrow \Delta_1, \sharp\alpha \quad \sharp\beta, \Gamma_2 \Rightarrow \Delta_2}{\sharp(\alpha\to\beta), \Gamma_1, \Gamma_2 \Rightarrow \Delta_1, \Delta_2}\ (\to\text{left}).$$

By induction hypothesis, we have ALTL – (cut) $\vdash \heartsuit_i\Gamma_1 \Rightarrow \heartsuit_i\Delta_1, \heartsuit_i\sharp\alpha$ and ALTL – (cut) $\vdash \heartsuit_i\sharp\beta, \heartsuit_i\Gamma_2 \Rightarrow \heartsuit_i\Delta_2$. Then, we obtain the required fact:

$$\frac{\begin{array}{c}\vdots\\ \heartsuit_i\Gamma_1 \Rightarrow \heartsuit_i\Delta_1, \heartsuit_i\sharp\alpha\end{array} \quad \begin{array}{c}\vdots\\ \heartsuit_i\sharp\beta, \heartsuit_i\Gamma_2 \Rightarrow \heartsuit_i\Delta_2\end{array}}{\heartsuit_i\sharp(\alpha\to\beta), \heartsuit_i\Gamma_1, \heartsuit_i\Gamma_2 \Rightarrow \heartsuit_i\Delta_1, \heartsuit_i\Delta_2}\ (\to\text{left}).$$

Case ($\heartsuit_c$right): The last inference of P is of the form:

$$\frac{\{\ \Gamma \Rightarrow \Delta', \sharp\kappa\alpha \mid \kappa \in K^*\ \}}{\Gamma \Rightarrow \Delta', \sharp\heartsuit_c\alpha}\ (\heartsuit_c\text{right}).$$

By induction hypothesis, we have ALTL – (cut) $\vdash \heartsuit_i\Gamma \Rightarrow \heartsuit_i\Delta', \heartsuit_i\sharp\kappa\alpha$ for all $\kappa \in K^*$. Then, we obtain the required fact:

$$\frac{\begin{array}{c}\vdots\\ \{\ \heartsuit_i\Gamma \Rightarrow \heartsuit_i\Delta', \heartsuit_i\sharp\kappa\alpha \mid \kappa \in K^*\ \}\end{array}}{\heartsuit_i\Gamma \Rightarrow \heartsuit_i\Delta', \heartsuit_i\sharp\heartsuit_c\alpha}\ (\heartsuit_c\text{right}).$$

Q.E.D.

Remark that the rule (♡regu) is more expressive than the following standard inference rules for the normal modal logics K and KD:

$$\frac{\Gamma \Rightarrow \alpha}{\heartsuit_i\Gamma \Rightarrow \heartsuit_i\alpha} \qquad \frac{\Gamma \Rightarrow \gamma}{\heartsuit_i\Gamma \Rightarrow \heartsuit_i\gamma}$$

where γ can be empty. Thus, the operator $\heartsuit_i$ in ALTL is stronger than those in K and KD. $\heartsuit_i$ may thus be used for an alternative to the operators in K and KD.

Next, we consider a sequent calculus LK_ω for infinitary logic in order to show the syntactical embedding theorem of ALTL into LK_ω. A language of LK_ω is obtained from the language $\mathcal{L}$ of ALTL by deleting $\mathrm{X}, \mathrm{G}, \mathrm{F}, \heartsuit_i$ $(i \in A), \heartsuit_c$ and $\heartsuit_d$ and adding $\bigwedge$ (infinitary conjunction) and $\bigvee$ (infinitary disjunction). For $\bigwedge$ and $\bigvee$, if Θ is a countable nonempty set of formulas, then $\bigwedge\Theta$ and $\bigvee\Theta$ are also formulas. Expressions $\bigwedge\{\alpha\}$ and $\bigvee\{\alpha\}$ are equivalent to α. The standard binary connectives $\wedge$ and $\vee$ are regarded as special cases of $\bigwedge$ and $\bigvee$, respectively.

A sequent calculus LK_ω for infinitary logic is then presented below.

Definition 4 ($\mathbf{LK}_\omega$). *The initial sequents of* LK_ω *are of the form: for any propositional variable* p,

$$p \Rightarrow p.$$

The structural rules of LK_ω *are* (cut) *and* (we) *presented in Definition 1. The logical inference rules of* LK_ω *are of the form:*

$$\frac{\Gamma \Rightarrow \Sigma, \alpha \quad \beta, \Delta \Rightarrow \Pi}{\alpha{\rightarrow}\beta, \Gamma, \Delta \Rightarrow \Sigma, \Pi}\ (\rightarrow\mathrm{left}^{\emptyset}) \qquad \frac{\alpha, \Gamma \Rightarrow \Delta, \beta}{\Gamma \Rightarrow \Delta, \alpha{\rightarrow}\beta}\ (\rightarrow\mathrm{right}^{\emptyset})$$

$$\frac{\Gamma \Rightarrow \Delta, \alpha}{\neg\alpha, \Gamma \Rightarrow \Delta}\ (\neg\mathrm{left}^{\emptyset}) \qquad \frac{\alpha, \Gamma \Rightarrow \Delta}{\Gamma \Rightarrow \Delta, \neg\alpha}\ (\neg\mathrm{right}^{\emptyset})$$

$$\frac{\alpha, \Gamma \Rightarrow \Delta \quad (\alpha \in \Theta)}{\bigwedge\Theta, \Gamma \Rightarrow \Delta}\ (\textstyle\bigwedge\mathrm{left}) \qquad \frac{\{\, \Gamma \Rightarrow \Delta, \alpha \mid \alpha \in \Theta \,\}}{\Gamma \Rightarrow \Delta, \bigwedge\Theta}\ (\textstyle\bigwedge\mathrm{right})$$

$$\frac{\{\, \alpha, \Gamma \Rightarrow \Delta \mid \alpha \in \Theta \,\}}{\bigvee\Theta, \Gamma \Rightarrow \Delta}\ (\textstyle\bigvee\mathrm{left}) \qquad \frac{\Gamma \Rightarrow \Delta, \alpha \quad (\alpha \in \Theta)}{\Gamma \Rightarrow \Delta, \bigvee\Theta}\ (\textstyle\bigvee\mathrm{right})$$

where Θ *is a countable nonempty set of formulas.*

The superscript "$\emptyset$" in the rule names in LK_ω means that these rules are the special cases of the corresponding rules of ALTL, i.e., the case that $\sharp$ is $\emptyset$. The sequents of the form $\alpha \Rightarrow \alpha$ for any formula α are provable in cut-free LK_ω. As well-known, LK_ω enjoys cut-elimination.

The following definition of an embedding function is a modified extension of the embedding function of LTL into infinitary logic, which was proposed in [8] and was further studied in [10].

Definition 5. *Fix a countable non-empty set* Φ *of propositional variables, and define the sets* $\Phi_\sharp := \{p_\sharp \mid p \in \Phi\}$ $(\sharp \in T^*)$ *of propositional variables with* $p_\emptyset := p$ *(i.e.,* $\Phi_\emptyset := \Phi$*). The language* $\mathcal{L}^t$ *(or the set of formulas) of* ALTL *is defined using* $\Phi, \rightarrow, \neg, \wedge, \vee, \heartsuit_i$ $(i \in A)$, $\heartsuit_c$, $\heartsuit_d$, X, G *and* F. *The language* $\mathcal{L}^i$ *of* LK_ω *is defined using* $\bigcup_{\sharp \in T^*} \Phi_\sharp, \rightarrow, \neg, \bigwedge$ *and* $\bigvee$. *The binary versions of* $\bigwedge$ *and* $\bigvee$ *are also denoted as* $\wedge$ *and* $\vee$*, respectively, and these binary symbols are assumed to be included in* $\mathcal{L}^i$. *Moreover, we assume the following condition: for any permutations* $\sharp_1$ *and* $\sharp_2$ *of* $\sharp$ $(\in T^*)$ *and any* $p \in \Phi$, $p_{\sharp_1} = p_{\sharp_2}$*, i.e.,* $\Phi_{\sharp_1} = \Phi_{\sharp_2}$.

A mapping f *from* $\mathcal{L}^t$ *to* $\mathcal{L}^i$ *is defined as follows.*

1. *for any* $p \in \Phi$, $f(\sharp p) := p_\sharp \in \Phi_\sharp$ $(\sharp \in T^*)$, *esp.*, $f(p) := p \in \Phi_\emptyset$,
2. $f(\sharp(\alpha \circ \beta)) := f(\sharp\alpha) \circ f(\sharp\beta)$ *where* $\circ \in \{\rightarrow, \wedge, \vee\}$,
3. $f(\sharp\neg\alpha) := \neg f(\sharp\alpha)$,
4. $f(\sharp\heartsuit_c\alpha) := \bigwedge\{f(\sharp\kappa\alpha) \mid \kappa \in K^*\}$,
5. $f(\sharp\heartsuit_d\alpha) := \bigvee\{f(\sharp\kappa\alpha) \mid \kappa \in K^*\}$,
6. $f(\sharp \mathrm{G}\alpha) := \bigwedge\{f(\sharp \mathrm{X}^j\alpha) \mid j \in \omega\}$,
7. $f(\sharp \mathrm{F}\alpha) := \bigvee\{f(\sharp \mathrm{X}^j\alpha) \mid j \in \omega\}$,
8. $f(\sharp\heartsuit_i \mathrm{X}\alpha) := f(\sharp \mathrm{X}\heartsuit_i\alpha)$.

An expression $f(\Gamma)$ denotes the result of replacing every occurrence of a formula α in Γ by an occurrence of $f(\alpha)$.

Theorem 6 (Syntactical embedding). *Let* Γ *and* Δ *be sets of formulas in* $\mathcal{L}^t$, *and* f *be the mapping defined in Definition 5. Then:*

1. *if* ALTL $\vdash \Gamma \Rightarrow \Delta$, *then* $\mathrm{LK}_\omega \vdash f(\Gamma) \Rightarrow f(\Delta)$.
2. *if* LK_ω – (cut) $\vdash f(\Gamma) \Rightarrow f(\Delta)$, *then* ALTL – (cut) $\vdash \Gamma \Rightarrow \Delta$.

Proof. • (1) : By induction on the proofs P of $\Gamma \Rightarrow \Delta$ in ALTL. We distinguish the cases according to the last inference of P. We show only the following cases.

Case ($\sharp p \Rightarrow \sharp p$): The last inference of P is of the form: $\sharp p \Rightarrow \sharp p$. In this case, we obtain $\mathrm{LK}_\omega \vdash f(\sharp p) \Rightarrow f(\sharp p)$, i.e., $\mathrm{LK}_\omega \vdash p_\sharp \Rightarrow p_\sharp$ $(p_\sharp \in \Phi_\sharp)$ by the definition of f.

Case ($\rightarrow$left): The last inference of P is of the form:

$$\frac{\Gamma \Rightarrow \Sigma, \sharp\alpha \quad \sharp\beta, \Delta \Rightarrow \Pi}{\sharp(\alpha\rightarrow\beta), \Gamma, \Delta \Rightarrow \Sigma, \Pi}\ (\rightarrow\text{left}).$$

By induction hypothesis, we have $\mathrm{LK}_\omega \vdash f(\Gamma) \Rightarrow f(\Sigma), f(\sharp\alpha)$ and $\mathrm{LK}_\omega \vdash f(\sharp\beta), f(\Delta) \Rightarrow f(\Pi)$. Then, we obtain the required fact:

$$\frac{\begin{array}{c}\vdots \\ f(\Gamma) \Rightarrow f(\Sigma), f(\sharp\alpha)\end{array} \quad \begin{array}{c}\vdots \\ f(\sharp\beta), f(\Delta) \Rightarrow f(\Pi)\end{array}}{f(\sharp\alpha)\rightarrow f(\sharp\beta), f(\Gamma), f(\Delta) \Rightarrow f(\Sigma), f(\Pi)}\ (\rightarrow\text{left}^\emptyset)$$

where $f(\sharp\alpha)\rightarrow f(\sharp\beta)$ coincides with $f(\sharp(\alpha\rightarrow\beta))$ by the definition of f.

Case ($\heartsuit_c$left): The last inference of P is of the form:

$$\frac{\sharp\kappa\alpha, \Gamma \Rightarrow \Delta \quad (\kappa \in K^*)}{\sharp\heartsuit_c\alpha, \Gamma \Rightarrow \Delta}\ (\heartsuit_c\text{left}).$$

By induction hypothesis, we have $\mathrm{LK}_\omega \vdash f(\sharp\kappa\alpha), f(\Gamma) \Rightarrow f(\Delta)$, and hence obtain the required fact:

$$\frac{\begin{array}{c}\vdots \\ f(\sharp\kappa\alpha), f(\Gamma) \Rightarrow f(\Delta) \quad (f(\sharp\kappa\alpha) \in \{f(\sharp\kappa\alpha) \mid \kappa \in K^*\})\end{array}}{\bigwedge\{f(\sharp\kappa\alpha) \mid \kappa \in K^*\}, f(\Gamma) \Rightarrow f(\Delta)}\ (\textstyle\bigwedge\text{left})$$

where $\bigwedge\{f(\sharp\kappa\alpha) \mid \kappa \in K^*\}$ coincides with $f(\sharp\heartsuit_c\alpha)$ by the definition of f.

Case ($\heartsuit_c$right): The last inference of P is of the form:

$$\frac{\{\ \Gamma \Rightarrow \Delta, \sharp\kappa\alpha \mid \kappa \in K^*\ \}}{\Gamma \Rightarrow \Delta, \sharp\heartsuit_c\alpha}\ (\heartsuit_c\text{right}).$$

By induction hypothesis, we have $\mathrm{LK}_\omega \vdash f(\Gamma) \Rightarrow f(\Delta), f(\sharp\kappa\alpha)$ for all $\kappa \in K^*$. Let Φ be $\{f(\sharp\kappa\alpha) \mid \kappa \in K^*\}$. We obtain the required fact:

$$\frac{\begin{array}{c}\vdots\\ \{\ f(\Gamma) \Rightarrow f(\Delta), f(\sharp\kappa\alpha) \mid f(\sharp\kappa\alpha) \in \Phi\ \}\end{array}}{f(\Gamma) \Rightarrow f(\Delta), \bigwedge\Phi}\ (\bigwedge\text{right})$$

where $\bigwedge\Phi$ coincides with $f(\sharp\heartsuit_c\alpha)$ by the definition of f.

Case (X$\heartsuit$left): The last inference of P is of the form:

$$\frac{\sharp\heartsuit_m \mathrm{X}\alpha, \Gamma \Rightarrow \Delta}{\sharp\mathrm{X}\heartsuit_m\alpha, \Gamma \Rightarrow \Delta}\ (\mathrm{X}\heartsuit\text{left}).$$

By induction hypothesis, we have $\mathrm{LK}_\omega \vdash f(\sharp\heartsuit_m\mathrm{X}\alpha), f(\Gamma) \Rightarrow f(\Delta)$ and hence obtain the required fact $\mathrm{LK}_\omega \vdash f(\sharp\mathrm{X}\heartsuit_m\alpha), f(\Gamma) \Rightarrow f(\Delta)$, since $f(\sharp\mathrm{X}\heartsuit_m\alpha)$ coincides with $f(\sharp\heartsuit_m\mathrm{X}\alpha)$ by the definition of f.

• (2) : By induction on the proofs Q of $f(\Gamma) \Rightarrow f(\Delta)$ in LK_ω. We distinguish the cases according to the last inference of Q. We show only the following case. The last inference of Q is of the form:

$$\frac{\{\ f(\Gamma) \Rightarrow f(\Delta), f(\sharp\kappa\alpha) \mid f(\sharp\kappa\alpha) \in \Phi\ \}}{f(\Gamma) \Rightarrow f(\Delta), \bigwedge\Phi}\ (\bigwedge\text{right})$$

where $\Phi = \{f(\sharp\kappa\alpha) \mid \kappa \in K^*\}$, and $\bigwedge\Phi$ coincides with $f(\sharp\heartsuit_c\alpha)$ by the definition of f. By induction hypothesis, we have $\mathrm{ALTL} \vdash \Gamma \Rightarrow \Delta, \sharp\kappa\alpha$ for all $\kappa \in K^*$. We thus obtain the required fact:

$$\frac{\begin{array}{c}\vdots\\ \{\ \Gamma \Rightarrow \Delta, \sharp\kappa\alpha \mid \kappa \in K^*\ \}\end{array}}{\Gamma \Rightarrow \Delta, \sharp\heartsuit_c\alpha}\ (\heartsuit_c\text{right}).$$

Q.E.D.

Theorem 7 (Cut-elimination). *The rule* (cut) *is admissible in cut-free* ALTL.

Proof. Suppose $\mathrm{ALTL} \vdash \Gamma \Rightarrow \Delta$. Then, we have $\mathrm{LK}_\omega \vdash f(\Gamma) \Rightarrow f(\Delta)$ by Theorem 6 (1), and hence $\mathrm{LK}_\omega - (\mathrm{cut}) \vdash f(\Gamma) \Rightarrow f(\Delta)$ by the cut-elimination theorem for LK_ω. By Theorem 6 (2), we obtain $\mathrm{ALTL} - (\mathrm{cut}) \vdash \Gamma \Rightarrow \Delta$. **Q.E.D.**

Remark that by Theorem 7, we can strengthen the statements of Theorem 6 by replacing "if then" with "iff". This fact will be used to prove the completeness theorem for ALTL.

2.2 Semantics and Completeness

Let Γ be a set $\{\alpha_1, ..., \alpha_m\}$ $(m \geq 0)$ of formulas. Then, Γ^* represents $\alpha_1 \vee \cdots \vee \alpha_m$ if $m \geq 1$, and otherwise $\neg(p \rightarrow p)$ where p is a fixed propositional variable. Also Γ_* represents $\alpha_1 \wedge \cdots \wedge \alpha_m$ if $m \geq 1$, and otherwise $p \rightarrow p$ where p is a fixed propositional variable. The symbol $\geq$ or $\leq$ is used to represent a linear order on ω.

The semantics for ALTL is defined below.

Definition 8. *Agent-time indexed valuations* $I^{\iota;i}$ $(\iota \in K^*, i \in \omega)$ *are mappings from the set of all propositional variables to the set* $\{t, f\}$ *of truth values. Then, agent-time indexed satisfaction relations* $\models_{\iota;i} \alpha$ $(\iota \in K^*, i \in \omega)$ *for any formula* α *are defined inductively by:*

1. *for any propositional variable* p, $\models_{\iota;i} p$ *iff* $I^{\iota;i}(p) = t$,
2. $\models_{\iota;i} \alpha \wedge \beta$ *iff* $\models_{\iota;i} \alpha$ *and* $\models_{\iota;i} \beta$,
3. $\models_{\iota;i} \alpha \vee \beta$ *iff* $\models_{\iota;i} \alpha$ *or* $\models_{\iota;i} \beta$,
4. $\models_{\iota;i} \alpha \rightarrow \beta$ *iff not-*$(\models_{\iota;i} \alpha)$ *or* $\models_{\iota;i} \beta$,
5. $\models_{\iota;i} \neg\alpha$ *iff not-*$(\models_{\iota;i} \alpha)$,
6. *for any* $k \in A$, $\models_{\iota;i} \heartsuit_k \alpha$ *iff* $\models_{\iota\heartsuit_k;i} \alpha$,
7. $\models_{\iota;i} \heartsuit_c \alpha$ *iff* $\models_{\iota\kappa;i} \alpha$ *for all* $\kappa \in K^*$,
8. $\models_{\iota;i} \heartsuit_d \alpha$ *iff* $\models_{\iota\kappa;i} \alpha$ *for some* $\kappa \in K^*$,
9. $\models_{\iota;i} \mathrm{X}\alpha$ *iff* $\models_{\iota;i+1} \alpha$,
10. $\models_{\iota;i} \mathrm{G}\alpha$ *iff* $\models_{\iota;j} \alpha$ *for any* $j \geq i$,
11. $\models_{\iota;i} \mathrm{F}\alpha$ *iff* $\models_{\iota;j} \alpha$ *for some* $j \geq i$.

A formula α *is called* ALTL-valid *if* $\models_{\emptyset;0} \alpha$ *holds for any agent-time indexed satisfaction relations* $\models_{\iota;i}$ $(\iota \in K^*, i \in \omega)$. *A sequent* $\Gamma \Rightarrow \Delta$ *is called ALTL-valid if so is the formula* $\Gamma_* \rightarrow \Delta^*$.

Note that the following clause holds for any agent-time indexed satisfaction relation $\models_{\iota;i}$, any formula α, any $i \in \omega$ and any $\kappa \in K^*$,

$$\models_{\iota;i} \kappa\alpha \text{ iff } \models_{\iota\kappa;i} \alpha.$$

Next, the semantics for LK_ω is defined below.

Definition 9. *Let* Θ *be a countable nonempty set of formulas. A valuation* I *is a mapping from the set of all propositional variables to the set* $\{t, f\}$ *of truth values. A satisfaction relation* $\models \alpha$ *for any formula* α *is defined inductively by:*

1. $\models p$ *iff* $I(p) = t$ *for any propositional variable* p,
2. $\models \bigwedge\Theta$ *iff* $\models \alpha$ *for any* $\alpha \in \Theta$,
3. $\models \bigvee\Theta$ *iff* $\models \alpha$ *for some* $\alpha \in \Theta$,
4. $\models \alpha \rightarrow \beta$ *iff not-*$(\models \alpha)$ *or* $\models \beta$,
5. $\models \neg\alpha$ *iff not-*$(\models \alpha)$.

A formula α *is called* LK_ω-valid *if* $\models \alpha$ *holds for any satisfaction relation* $\models$. *A sequent* $\Gamma \Rightarrow \Delta$ *is called* LK_ω*-valid if so is the formula* $\Gamma_* \rightarrow \Delta^*$.

As it is well known, the following completeness theorem holds for LK_ω: For any sequent S,

$$\mathrm{LK}_\omega \vdash S \text{ iff } S \text{ is } \mathrm{LK}_\omega\text{-valid}.$$

Lemma 10. *Let f be the mapping defined in Definition 5. For any agent-time indexed satisfaction relation $\models_{\iota;i}$ ($\iota \in K^*, i \in \omega$), we can construct a satisfaction relation $\models$ such that for any formula α in $\mathcal{L}^t$,*

$$\models_{\iota;i} \alpha \textit{ iff } \models f(\iota \mathrm{X}^i \alpha).$$

Proof. Let Φ be a set of propositional variables and $\Phi_\sharp$ be the set $\{p_\sharp \mid p \in \Phi\}$ of propositional variables with $p_\emptyset := p$. Suppose that $I^{\iota;i}$ ($\iota \in K^*, i \in \omega$) are mappings from Φ to $\{t, f\}$. Suppose that I is a mapping from $\bigcup_{\sharp \in T^*} \Phi_\sharp$ to $\{t, f\}$. Suppose moreover that $I^{\iota;i}(p) = t$ iff $I(p_{\iota \mathrm{X}^i}) = t$. Then the lemma is proved by induction on the complexity of α.

- Base step:

Case ($\alpha \equiv p \in \Phi$): $\models_{\iota;i} p$ iff $I^{\iota;i}(p) = t$ iff $I(p_{\iota \mathrm{X}^i}) = t$ iff $\models p_{\iota \mathrm{X}^i}$ iff $\models f(\iota \mathrm{X}^i p)$ (by the definition of f).

- Induction step:

Case ($\alpha \equiv \alpha_1 \to \alpha_2$): $\models_{\iota;i} \alpha_1 \to \alpha_2$ iff not-($\models_{\iota;i} \alpha_1$) or $\models_{\iota;i} \alpha_2$ iff not-($\models f(\iota \mathrm{X}^i \alpha_1)$) or $\models f(\iota \mathrm{X}^i \alpha_2)$ (by induction hypothesis) iff $\models f(\iota \mathrm{X}^i \alpha_1) \to f(\iota \mathrm{X}^i \alpha_2)$ iff $\models f(\iota \mathrm{X}^i (\alpha_1 \to \alpha_2))$ (by the definition of f).

Cases ($\alpha \equiv \alpha_1 \wedge \alpha_2$ and $\alpha \equiv \alpha_1 \vee \alpha_2$): Similar to Case ($\alpha \equiv \alpha_1 \to \alpha_2$).

Case ($\alpha \equiv \neg\beta$): $\models_{\iota;i} \neg\beta$ iff not-($\models_{\iota;i} \beta$) iff not-($\models f(\iota \mathrm{X}^i \beta)$) (by induction hypothesis) iff $\models \neg f(\iota \mathrm{X}^i \beta)$ iff $\models f(\iota \mathrm{X}^i \neg\beta)$ (by the definition of f).

Case ($\alpha \equiv \heartsuit_k \beta$): $\models_{\iota;i} \heartsuit_k \beta$ iff $\models_{\iota \heartsuit_k;i} \beta$ iff $\models f(\iota \heartsuit_k \mathrm{X}^i \beta)$ (by induction hypothesis) iff $\models f(\iota \mathrm{X}^i \heartsuit_k \beta)$ (by the definition fo f).

Case ($\alpha \equiv \heartsuit_c \beta$): $\models_{\iota;i} \heartsuit_c \beta$ iff $\models_{\iota\kappa;i} \beta$ for any $\kappa \in K^*$ iff $\models f(\iota\kappa \mathrm{X}^i \beta)$ for any $\kappa \in K^*$ (by induction hypothesis) iff $\models f(\iota \mathrm{X}^i \kappa \beta)$ for any $\kappa \in K^*$ (by the definition of f) iff $\models \bigwedge\{f(\iota \mathrm{X}^i \kappa \beta) \mid \kappa \in K^*\}$ iff $\models f(\iota \mathrm{X}^i \heartsuit_c \beta)$ (by the definition of f).

Case ($\alpha \equiv \heartsuit_d \beta$): Similar to Case ($\alpha \equiv \heartsuit_c \beta$).

Case ($\alpha \equiv \mathrm{X}\beta$): $\models_{\iota;i} \mathrm{X}\beta$ iff $\models_{\iota;i+1} \beta$ iff $\models f(\iota \mathrm{X}^{i+1} \beta)$ (by induction hypothesis) iff $\models f(\iota \mathrm{X}^i \mathrm{X}\beta)$.

Case ($\alpha \equiv \mathrm{G}\beta$): $\models_{\iota;i} \mathrm{G}\beta$ iff $\models_{\iota;j} \beta$ for any $j \geq i$ iff $\models f(\iota \mathrm{X}^j \beta)$ for any $j \geq i$ (by induction hypothesis) iff $\forall k \in \omega\ [\models f(\iota \mathrm{X}^{i+k} \beta)]$ iff $\models \gamma$ for any $\gamma \in \{f(\iota \mathrm{X}^{i+k} \beta) \mid k \in \omega\}$ iff $\models \bigwedge\{f(\iota \mathrm{X}^{i+k} \beta) \mid k \in \omega\}$ iff $\models f(\iota \mathrm{X}^i \mathrm{G}\beta)$ (by the definition of f).

Case ($\alpha \equiv \mathrm{F}\beta$): Similar to Case ($\alpha \equiv \mathrm{G}\beta$). **Q.E.D.**

Lemma 11. *Let f be the mapping defined in Definition 5. For any satisfaction relation $\models$, we can construct an agent-time indexed satisfaction relation $\models_{\iota;i}$ such that for any formula α in $\mathcal{L}^t$,*

$$\models f(\iota \mathrm{X}^i \alpha) \textit{ iff } \models_{\iota;i} \alpha.$$

Proof. Similar to the proof of Lemma 10. **Q.E.D.**

Theorem 12 (Semantical embedding). *Let f be the mapping defined in Definition 5. For any formula α in $\mathcal{L}^t$,*

α *is ALTL-valid iff* $f(\alpha)$ *is* LK_ω*-valid.*

Proof. By Lemmas 10 and 11. We take 0 for i and take $\emptyset$ for ι. **Q.E.D.**

Theorem 13 (Completeness). *For any sequent S,*

ALTL $\vdash S$ *iff* S *is ALTL-valid.*

Proof. Let $\Gamma \Rightarrow \Delta$ be S and α be $\Gamma_* \to \Delta^*$. It is sufficient to show that ALTL $\vdash \Rightarrow \alpha$ iff α is ALTL-valid. We show this as follows. ALTL $\vdash \Rightarrow \alpha$ iff $\mathrm{LK}_\omega \vdash \Rightarrow f(\alpha)$ (by Theorems 6 and 7) iff $f(\alpha)$ is LK_ω-valid (by the completeness theorem for LK_ω) iff α is ALTL-valid (by Theorem 12). **Q.E.D.**

3 Agents-Indexed Computation Tree Logic

In this section, similar notions and notations as in the previous section are adopted. *Formulas* of ACTL are constructed from (countable) propositional variables, $\to$, $\wedge$, $\vee$, $\neg$, $\heartsuit_i$ $(i \in A)$, $\heartsuit_b$ (bounded-depth common information or knowledge), X, G, F, U (until), A (all computation paths) and E (some computation path). The symbols X, G, F and U are called *temporal operators*, and the symbols A and E are called *path quantifiers*. The symbol ATOM is used to denote the set of propositional variables.

Definition 14. *Formulas α are defined by the following grammar, assuming $p \in$ ATOM and $i \in A$:*

$$\alpha ::= p \mid \alpha{\to}\alpha \mid \alpha\wedge\alpha \mid \alpha\vee\alpha \mid \neg\alpha \mid \heartsuit_i\alpha \mid \heartsuit_b\alpha \mid \mathrm{AX}\alpha \mid \mathrm{EX}\alpha \mid \mathrm{AG}\alpha \mid \mathrm{EG}\alpha \mid \mathrm{AF}\alpha \mid \mathrm{EF}\alpha \mid \mathrm{A}(\alpha\mathrm{U}\alpha) \mid \mathrm{E}(\alpha\mathrm{U}\alpha).$$

Note that pairs of symbols like AG and EU are indivisible, and that the symbols X, G, F and U cannot occur without being preceded by an A or an E. Similarly, every A or E must have one of X, G, F and U to accompany it. Some operators are redundant as those in CTL, because some operators can be obtained by the other operators (e.g., $\mathrm{AG}\alpha := \neg\mathrm{EF}\neg\alpha$).

Recall that the symbol K is used to represent the set $\{\heartsuit_i \mid i \in A\}$, and that the symbol K^* is used to represent the set of all words of finite length of the alphabet K. Recall also that Greek lower-case letters ι and κ are used to denote any members of K^*. The symbol K^m is used to represent the set of all words of at most *m-length* of the alphabet K. Note that K^m is finite. In the following discussion, the number m of K^m is fixed as a certain positive integer.

Definition 15. *A structure $\langle S, S_0, R, \{L^\iota\}_{\iota\in K^*}\rangle$ is called an* agents-indexed Kripke structure *if:*

1. *S is the set of states,*
2. *S_0 is a set of initial states and $S_0 \subseteq S$,*
3. *R is a binary relation on S which satisfies the condition: $\forall s \in S\ \exists s' \in S\ [(s, s') \in R]$,*
4. *L^ι ($\iota \in K^*$) are functions from S to the power set of a nonempty subset* AT *of* ATOM.

A path *in an agents-indexed Kripke structure is an infinite sequence of states, $\pi = s_0, s_1, s_2, ...$ such that $\forall i \geq 0\ [(s_i, s_{i+1}) \in R]$.*

The logic ACTL is then defined based on an agents-indexed Kripke structure with satisfaction relations $\models^\iota$ ($\iota \in K^*$).

Definition 16 (ACTL). *Let* AT *be a nonempty subset of* ATOM. Satisfaction relations *$\models^\iota$ ($\iota \in K^*$) on an agents-indexed Kripke structure $M = \langle S, S_0, R, \{L^\iota\}_{\iota \in K^*}\rangle$ are defined as follows (s represents a state in S):*

1. *for any $p \in \mathrm{AT}$, $M, s \models^\iota p$ iff $p \in L^\iota(s)$,*
2. *$M, s \models^\iota \alpha_1 \rightarrow \alpha_2$ iff $M, s \models^\iota \alpha_1$ implies $M, s \models^\iota \alpha_2$,*
3. *$M, s \models^\iota \alpha_1 \wedge \alpha_2$ iff $M, s \models^\iota \alpha_1$ and $M, s \models^\iota \alpha_2$,*
4. *$M, s \models^\iota \alpha_1 \vee \alpha_2$ iff $M, s \models^\iota \alpha_1$ or $M, s \models^\iota \alpha_2$,*
5. *$M, s \models^\iota \neg\alpha_1$ iff not-$[M, s \models^\iota \alpha_1]$,*
6. *for any $i \in A$, $M, s \models^\iota \heartsuit_i\alpha$ iff $M, s \models^{\iota\heartsuit_i} \alpha$,*
7. *$M, s \models^\iota \heartsuit_b\alpha$ iff $M, s \models^{\iota\kappa} \alpha$ for all $\kappa \in K^m$,*
8. *$M, s \models^\iota \mathrm{AX}\alpha$ iff $\forall s_1 \in S\ \ [(s, s_1) \in R$ implies $M, s_1 \models^\iota \alpha]$,*
9. *$M, s \models^\iota \mathrm{EX}\alpha$ iff $\exists s_1 \in S\ \ [(s, s_1) \in R$ and $M, s_1 \models^\iota \alpha]$,*
10. *$M, s \models^\iota \mathrm{AG}\alpha$ iff for all paths $\pi \equiv s_0, s_1, s_2, ...$, where $s \equiv s_0$, and all states s_i along π, we have $M, s_i \models^\iota \alpha$,*
11. *$M, s \models^\iota \mathrm{EG}\alpha$ iff there is a path $\pi \equiv s_0, s_1, s_2, ...$, where $s \equiv s_0$, and for all states s_i along π, we have $M, s_i \models^\iota \alpha$,*
12. *$M, s \models^\iota \mathrm{AF}\alpha$ iff for all paths $\pi \equiv s_0, s_1, s_2, ...$, where $s \equiv s_0$, there is a state s_i along π such that $M, s_i \models^\iota \alpha$,*
13. *$M, s \models^\iota \mathrm{EF}\alpha$ iff there is a path $\pi \equiv s_0, s_1, s_2, ...$, where $s \equiv s_0$, and for some state s_i along π, we have $M, s_i \models^\iota \alpha$,*
14. *$M, s \models^\iota \mathrm{A}(\alpha_1 \mathrm{U} \alpha_2)$ iff for all paths $\pi \equiv s_0, s_1, s_2, ...$, where $s \equiv s_0$, there is a state s_k along π such that $[(M, s_k \models^\iota \alpha_2)$ and $\forall j\ (0 \leq j < k$ implies $M, s_j \models^\iota \alpha_1)]$,*
15. *$M, s \models^\iota \mathrm{E}(\alpha_1 \mathrm{U} \alpha_2)$ iff there is a path $\pi \equiv s_0, s_1, s_2, ...$, where $s \equiv s_0$, and for some state s_k along π, we have $[(M, s_k \models^\iota \alpha_2)$ and $\forall j\ (0 \leq j < k$ implies $M, s_j \models^\iota \alpha_1)]$.*

We can naturally consider the unbounded version ACTL_ω which is obtained from ACTL by replacing the condition 7 by:

7′. $M, s \models^\iota \heartsuit_c\alpha$ iff $M, s \models^{\iota\kappa} \alpha$ for all $\kappa \in K^*$.

However, the decidability of validity, satisfiability and model-checking problems for ACTL_ω cannot be shown using the proposed embedding-based method.

ACTL_ω is embeddable into the infinitary version CTL_ω which is obtained from CTL by adding an infinitary conjunction connective $\bigwedge$. But, logics with $\bigwedge$ are known as undecidable, and hence such an embedding result cannot imply the decidability. Thus, the decidability or undecidability of ACTL_ω has not been clarified yet.

Definition 17. *A formula α is* valid *(*satisfiable*) in* ACTL *if and only if*

> *$M, s \models^{\emptyset} \alpha$ holds for any (some) agents-indexed Kripke structure $M = \langle S, S_0, R, \{L^{\iota}\}_{\iota \in K^*}\rangle$, any (some) $s \in S$, and any (some) satisfaction relations $\models^{\iota}$ $(\iota \in K^*)$ on M.*

Definition 18. *Let M be an agents-indexed Kripke structure $\langle S, S_0, R, \{L^{\iota}\}_{\iota \in K^*}\rangle$ for* ACTL*, and $\models^{\iota}$ $(\iota \in K^*)$ be satisfaction relations on M. Then, the* model checking problem *of* ACTL *is defined by: for any formula α, find the set $\{s \in S \mid M, s \models^{\emptyset} \alpha\}$.*

Let C be a finite set of formulas. Then, an expression $\bigwedge C$ represents the conjunction of all elements of C.

Proposition 19. *The following formulas concerning $\heartsuit_i$ and $\heartsuit_b$ are valid in* ACTL*: for any formulas α and β,*

1. *$\heartsuit_b\alpha \to \kappa\alpha$ for any $\kappa \in K^m$,*
2. *$\heartsuit_b\alpha \to \heartsuit_i\heartsuit_b\alpha$,*
3. *$\heartsuit_b\alpha \leftrightarrow \bigwedge\{\iota\alpha \mid \iota \in K^m\}$.*

Proof. We show only (3) below. Let M be an agents-indexed Kripke structure $M = \langle S, S_0, R, \{L^{\iota}\}_{\iota \in K^*}\rangle$. Then we obtain: for any $s \in S$ and $\models^{\iota}$ $(\iota \in K^*)$ on M,

$$\begin{aligned} & M, s \models^{\emptyset} \heartsuit_b\alpha \\ \text{iff } & M, s \models^{\kappa} \alpha \text{ for all } \kappa \in K^m, \\ \text{iff } & M, s \models^{\emptyset} \kappa\alpha \text{ for all } \kappa \in K^m, \\ \text{iff } & M, s \models^{\emptyset} \textstyle\bigwedge\{\kappa \mid \kappa \in K^m\}. \end{aligned}$$

Q.E.D.

Note that the formula 3 in Proposition 19 is a finite approximation of the well-known iterative interpretation of common knowledge.

In order to define the translation of ACTL into CTL, CTL is defined below.

Definition 20 (CTL). *A* Kripke structure *for* CTL *is a structure $\langle S, S_0, R, L\rangle$ such that*

1. *S, S_0 and R have the same conditions as in Definition 15*
2. *L is a function from S to the power set of a nonempty subset* AT *of* ATOM.

A satisfaction relation $\models$ *on a Kripke structure $M = \langle S, S_0, R, L\rangle$ for* CTL *is defined by the same conditions 1–5 and 8–15 as in Definition 16 by deleting the superscript ι. The validity, satisfiability and model-checking problems for* CTL *are defined as usual.*

Remark that $\models^{\emptyset}$ of ACTL includes $\models$ of CTL, and hence ACTL is an extension of CTL.

Definition 21. *Let* AT *be a non-empty subset of* ATOM, *and* AT^{ι} $(\iota \in K^*)$ *be the sets* $\{p^{\iota} \mid p \in \mathrm{AT}^{\iota}\}$ *of propositional variables where* $p^{\emptyset} := p$ *(i.e.,* $\mathrm{AT}^{\emptyset} := \mathrm{AT}$*). The language* $\mathcal{L}^A$ *(the set of formulas) of* ACTL *is defined using* AT, $\heartsuit_i$ $(i \in A)$, $\heartsuit_b$, $\neg, \rightarrow, \wedge, \vee$, X, F, G, U, A *and* E. *The language* $\mathcal{L}$ *of* CTL *is obtained from* $\mathcal{L}^A$ *by adding* $\bigcup_{\iota \in K^*} \mathrm{AT}^{\iota}$ *and deleting* $\{\heartsuit_i, \heartsuit_b\}$. *A mapping* f *from* $\mathcal{L}^A$ *to* $\mathcal{L}$ *is defined by:*

1. *for any* $p \in \mathrm{AT}$, $f(\iota p) := p^{\iota} \in \mathrm{AT}^{\iota}$, *esp.,* $f(p) := p$,
2. $f(\iota(\alpha \circ \beta)) := f(\iota\alpha) \circ f(\iota\beta)$ *where* $\circ \in \{\wedge, \vee, \rightarrow\}$,
3. $f(\iota\dagger\alpha) := \dagger f(\iota\alpha)$ *where* $\dagger \in \{\neg, \mathrm{AX}, \mathrm{EX}, \mathrm{AG}, \mathrm{EG}, \mathrm{AF}, \mathrm{EF}\}$,
4. $f(\iota\dagger(\alpha \mathrm{U} \beta))) := \dagger(f(\iota\alpha)\mathrm{U}f(\iota\beta))$ *where* $\dagger \in \{\mathrm{A}, \mathrm{E}\}$,
5. $f(\iota\heartsuit_b\alpha) := \bigwedge\{f(\iota\kappa\alpha) \mid \kappa \in K^m\}$.

Lemma 22. *Let* f *be the mapping defined in Definition 21. For any agents-indexed Kripke structure* $M := \langle S, S_0, R, \{L^{\iota}\}_{\iota \in K^*}\rangle$ *for* ACTL, *and any satisfaction relations* $\models^{\iota}$ $(\iota \in K^*)$ *on* M, *we can construct a Kripke structure* $N := \langle S, S_0, R, L\rangle$ *for* CTL *and a satisfaction relation* $\models$ *on* N *such that for any formula* α *in* $\mathcal{L}^A$ *and any state* s *in* S,

$$M, s \models^{\iota} \alpha \textit{ iff } N, s \models f(\iota\alpha).$$

Proof. Let AT be a nonempty subset of ATOM, and AT^{ι} be the sets $\{p^{\iota} \mid p \in \mathrm{AT}\}$ of propositional variables. Suppose that M is an agents-indexed Kripke structure $\langle S, S_0, R, \{L^{\iota}\}_{\iota \in K^*}\rangle$ such that

L^{ι} $(\iota \in K^*)$ are functions from S to the power set of AT.

Suppose that N is a Kripke structure $\langle S, S_0, R, L\rangle$ such that

L is a function from S to the power set of $\bigcup_{\iota \in K^*} \mathrm{AT}^{\iota}$.

Suppose moreover that for any $s \in S$ and any $p \in \mathrm{AT}$,

$p \in L^{\iota}(s)$ iff $p^{\iota} \in L(s)$.

Then, the claim is proved by induction on the complexity of α.

• Base step:

Case $\alpha \equiv p \in \mathrm{AT}$: We obtain: $M, s \models^{\iota} p$ iff $p \in L^{\iota}(s)$ iff $p^{\iota} \in L(s)$ iff $N, s \models p^{\iota}$ iff $N, s \models f(\iota p)$ (by the definition of f).

• Induction step:

Case $\alpha \equiv \beta \wedge \gamma$: We obtain: $M, s \models^{\iota} \beta \wedge \gamma$ iff $M, s \models^{\iota} \beta$ and $M, s \models^{\iota} \gamma$ iff $N, s \models f(\iota\beta)$ and $N, s \models f(\iota\gamma)$ (by induction hypothesis) iff $N, s \models f(\iota\beta) \wedge f(\iota\gamma)$ iff $N, s \models f(\iota(\beta \wedge \gamma))$ (by the definition of f).

Case $\alpha \equiv \beta \vee \gamma$: Similar to Case $\alpha \equiv \beta \wedge \gamma$.

Case $\alpha \equiv \beta{\to}\gamma$: We obtain: $M, s \models^{\iota} \beta{\to}\gamma$ iff $M, s \models^{\iota} \beta$ implies $M, s \models^{\iota} \gamma$ iff $N, s \models f(\iota\beta)$ implies $N, s \models f(\iota\gamma)$ (by induction hypothesis) iff $N, s \models f(\iota\beta){\to}f(\iota\gamma)$ iff $N, s \models f(\iota(\beta{\to}\gamma))$ (by the definition of f).

Case $\alpha \equiv \neg\beta$: We obtain: $M, s \models^{\iota} \neg\beta$ iff not-$[M, s \models^{\iota} \beta]$ iff not-$[N, s \models f(\iota\beta)]$ (by induction hypothesis) iff $N, s \models \neg f(\iota\beta)$ iff $N, s \models f(\iota\neg\beta)$ (by the definition of f).

Case $\alpha \equiv \heartsuit_i\beta$: We obtain: $M, s \models^{\iota} \heartsuit_i\beta$ iff $M, s \models^{\iota\heartsuit_i} \beta$ iff $N, s \models f(\iota\heartsuit_i\beta)$ (by induction hypothesis).

Case $\alpha \equiv \heartsuit_b\beta$: We obtain: $M, s \models^{\iota} \heartsuit_b\beta$ iff $M, s \models^{\iota\kappa} \beta$ for any $\kappa \in K^m$ iff $N, s \models f(\iota\kappa\beta)$ for any $\kappa \in K^m$ (by induction hypothesis) iff $N, s \models \bigwedge\{f(\iota\kappa\beta) \mid \kappa \in K^m\}$ iff $N, s \models f(\iota\heartsuit_b\beta)$ (by the definition of f).

Case $\alpha \equiv \mathrm{AX}\beta$: We obtain: $M, s \models^{\iota} \mathrm{AX}\beta$ iff $\forall s_1 \in S$ $[(s, s_1) \in R$ implies $M, s_1 \models^{\iota} \beta]$ iff $\forall s_1 \in S$ $[(s, s_1) \in R$ implies $N, s_1 \models f(\iota\beta)]$ (by induction hypothesis) iff $N, s \models \mathrm{AX}f(\iota\beta)$ iff $N, s \models f(\iota\mathrm{AX}\beta)$ (by the definition of f).

Case $\alpha \equiv \mathrm{EX}\beta$: Similar to Case $\alpha \equiv \mathrm{AX}\beta$.

Case $\alpha \equiv \mathrm{AG}\beta$: We obtain:

$M, s \models^{\iota} \mathrm{AG}\beta$
iff for all paths $\pi \equiv s_0, s_1, s_2, ...$, where $s \equiv s_0$, and all states s_i along π, we have $M, s_i \models^{\iota} \beta$
iff for all paths $\pi \equiv s_0, s_1, s_2, ...$, where $s \equiv s_0$, and all states s_i along π, we have $N, s_i \models f(\iota\beta)$ (by induction hypothesis)
iff $N, s \models \mathrm{AG}f(\iota\beta)$
iff $N, s \models f(\iota\mathrm{AG}\beta)$ (by the definition of f).

Cases $\alpha \equiv \mathrm{EG}\beta$, $\alpha \equiv \mathrm{AF}\beta$ and $\alpha \equiv \mathrm{EF}\beta$: Similar to Case $\alpha \equiv \mathrm{AG}\beta$.

Case $\alpha \equiv \mathrm{A}(\beta\mathrm{U}\gamma)$: We obtain:

$M, s \models^{\iota} \mathrm{A}(\beta\mathrm{U}\gamma)$
iff for all paths $\pi \equiv s_0, s_1, s_2, ...$, where $s \equiv s_0$, there is a state s_k along π such that $[M, s_k \models^{\iota} \gamma$ and $\forall j[i \leq j < k$ implies $M, s_j \models^{\iota} \beta]$
iff for all paths $\pi \equiv s_0, s_1, s_2, ...$, where $s \equiv s_0$, there is a state s_k along π such that $[N, s_k \models f(\iota\gamma)$ and $\forall j[i \leq j < k$ implies $N, s_j \models f(\iota\beta)]$ (by induction hypothesis)
iff $N, s \models \mathrm{A}(f(\iota\beta)\mathrm{U}f(\iota\gamma))$
iff $N, s \models f(\iota\mathrm{A}(\beta\mathrm{U}\gamma))$ (by the definition of f).

Case $\alpha \equiv \mathrm{E}(\beta\mathrm{U}\gamma)$: Similar to Case $\alpha \equiv \mathrm{A}(\beta\mathrm{U}\gamma)$. **Q.E.D.**

Lemma 23. *Let f be the mapping defined in Definition 21. For any Kripke structure $N := \langle S, S_0, R, L\rangle$ for* CTL, *and any satisfaction relation $\models$ on N, we can construct an agents-indexed Kripke structure $M := \langle S, S_0, R, \{L^{\iota}\}_{\iota \in K^*}\rangle$ for* ACTL *and satisfaction relations $\models^{\iota}$ $(\iota \in K^*)$ on M such that for any formula α in $\mathcal{L}^A$ and any state s in S,*

$N, s \models f(\iota\alpha)$ *iff* $M, s \models^{\iota} \alpha$.

Proof. Similar to the proof of Lemma 22. **Q.E.D.**

Theorem 24 (Semantical embedding). *Let f be the mapping defined in Definition 21. For any formula α in $\mathcal{L}^A$,*

α *is* ACTL*-valid iff* $f(\alpha)$ *is* CTL*-valid.*

Proof. By Lemmas 22 and 23. **Q.E.D.**

Theorem 25 (Decidability). *The model-checking, validity and satisfiability problems of* ACTL *are decidable.*

Proof. By the mapping f defined in Definition 21, a formula α of ACTL can finitely be transformed into the corresponding formula $f(\alpha)$ of CTL. By Lemmas 22 and 23 and Theorem 24, the model-checking, validity and satisfiability problems for ACTL can be transformed into those of CTL. Since the model checking, validity and satisfiability problems for CTL are decidable, the problems for ACTL are also decidable. **Q.E.D.**

4 Concluding Remarks

Firstly, in this paper, the logic ALTL (agents-indexed linear-time temporal logic) was introduced as a Gentzen-type sequent calculus. ALTL was intended to appropriately represent reasoning about time-dependent multi-agents within a proof system. As a main result of this paper, the cut-elimination and completeness theorems for ALTL were shown by combining two theorems for syntactically and semantically embedding ALTL into infinitary logic. It was thus shown that ALTL is attractive as a theoretical basis for automated theorem proving about time-dependent multi-agents.

Secondly, the logic ACTL (agents-indexed computation tree logic) was introduced as a Kripke-type semantics. ACTL was intended to appropriately represent reasoning about time-dependent multi-agents within an executable temporal logic by model checking. As a main result of this paper, the decidability of the model-checking, validity and satisfiability problems for ACTL was shown. It was thus shown that ACTL is attractive as a theoretical basis for model checking about time-dependent multi-agents.

Some related works are reviewed below. There are some agents-based or knowledge-based approaches to model checking. Some agents-based model checkers have successfully been developed [19,6,16,7]. For example, an approach to model checking for the *modal logic of knowledge and linear-time in distributed systems with perfect recall* was established by van der Meyden and Shilov [19]. They showed that some model checking problems with or without a common knowledge operator are undecidable or PSPACE-complete. A model checker for real-time and multi-agent systems, called *VerICS*, has been developed by Kacprzak et al. [7]. They focused on SAT-based model checking for multi-agent systems and several extensions and implementations to real-time systems' verification. Although ALTL is intended to provide a useful proof theory, the proposed semantics for ALTL may also be applicable to model checking, satisfiability checking and validity checking for time-dependent multi-agent systems.

There are some approaches to cooperate CTL with knowledge or multi-agent operators. A multi-agent extension ALT of CTL was introduced by Alur et al. [1], and an epistemic extension ATEL of ALT was studied by van der Hoek and Wooldridge [18]. Some epistemic extensions of CTL were studied by van der Meyden and Wong [20]. In particular, the model checking complexity for the logic CKB_m, which has a similar bounded setting to the common knowledge operator in ACTL, was shown to be EXPTIME-complete at least for systems without perfect recall.

There is an approach for formalizing multi-valued logic of knowledge and time. A multi-valued μK calculus (mv μK-calculus), an expressive logic to specify knowledge and time in multi-agent systems, was introduced and studied by Konikowska and Penczek [13]. They showed that the general method of translation [12] from multi-valued to two-valued De Morgan algebras can be extended to mv μK-calculus model checking. This way can reduce the model checking problem for mv μK-calculus to several instances of the model checking problem for two-valued μK-calculus. The mv μK-calculus can be regarded as a multi-valued μ-calculus combined with knowledge modalities. Hence, the mv μK-calculus is more expressive than the logics CTL, LTL and μ-calculus.

Acknowledgments. I would like to thank the referees for their valuable comments and suggestions. This work was partially supported by the Japanese Ministry of Education, Culture, Sports, Science and Technology, Grant-in-Aid for Young Scientists (B) 20700015.

References

1. Alur, R., Henzinger, T.A., Kupferman, O.: Alternating-time temporal logic. Journal of the ACM 49(5), 672–713 (2002)
2. Clarke, E.M., Emerson, E.A.: Design and Synthesis of Synchronization Skeletons using Branching Time Temporal Logic. In: Kozen, D. (ed.) Logic of Programs 1981. LNCS, vol. 131, pp. 52–71. Springer, Heidelberg (1982)
3. Clarke, E.M., Grumberg, O., Peled, D.A.: Model checking. The MIT Press (1999)
4. Emerson, E.A.: Temporal and modal logic. In: van Leeuwen, J. (ed.) Handbook of Theoretical Computer Science, Formal Models and Semantics (B), pp. 995–1072. Elsevier, MIT Press (1990)
5. Fagin, R., Halpern, J.Y., Moses, Y., Vardi, M.Y.: Reasoning about knowledge. MIT Press (1995)
6. Gammie, P., van der Meyden, R.: MCK: Model Checking the Logic of Knowledge. In: Alur, R., Peled, D.A. (eds.) CAV 2004. LNCS, vol. 3114, pp. 479–483. Springer, Heidelberg (2004)
7. Kacprzak, M., Nabialek, W., Niewiadomski, A., Penczek, W., Polroa, A., Szreter, M., Wozawa, B., Zbrzezny, A.: VerICS 2007: A model checker for real-time and multi-agent systems. Fundamenta Informaticae 85(1-4), 313–328 (2008)
8. Kamide, N.: Embedding Linear-Time Temporal Logic into Infinitary Logic: Application to Cut-Elimination for Multi-agent Infinitary Epistemic Linear-Time Temporal Logic. In: Fisher, M., Sadri, F., Thielscher, M. (eds.) CLIMA IX. LNCS (LNAI), vol. 5405, pp. 57–76. Springer, Heidelberg (2009)

9. Kamide, N.: A Proof System for Time-dependent Multi-agents. In: Setchi, R., Jordanov, I., Howlett, R.J., Jain, L.C. (eds.) KES 2010. LNCS (LNAI), vol. 6276, pp. 178–187. Springer, Heidelberg (2010)
10. Kamide, N., Wansing, H.: Combining linear-time temporal logic with constructiveness and paraconsistency. Journal of Applied Logic 8, 33–61 (2010)
11. Kawai, H.: Sequential calculus for a first order infinitary temporal logic. Zeitschrift für Mathematische Logik und Grundlagen der Mathematik 33, 423–432 (1987)
12. Konikowska, B., Penczek, W.: Model checking for multi-valued computation tree logics. In: Fitting, M., Orłowska, E. (eds.) Beyond Two: Theory and Applications of Multiple Valued Logic, pp. 193–210. Physica-Verlag (2003)
13. Konikowska, B., Penczek, W.: Model checking for multivalued logic knowledge and time. In: Proceedings of the 5th International Conference on Autonomous Agent and Multiagent Systems (AAMAS 2006), pp. 169–176. ACM (2006)
14. Kozen, D.: Results on the propositional mu-calculus. Theoretical Computer Science 27, 333–354 (1983)
15. Lewis, D.K.: Convention: A philosophical study. Harvard University Press (1969)
16. Lomuscio, A., Raimondi, F.: MCMAS: A Model Checker for Multi-agent Systems. In: Hermanns, H. (ed.) TACAS 2006. LNCS, vol. 3920, pp. 450–454. Springer, Heidelberg (2006)
17. Pnueli, A.: The temporal logic of programs. In: Proceedings of the 18th IEEE Symposium on Foundations of Computer Science, pp. 46–57 (1977)
18. van der Hoek, W., Wooldridge, M.: Cooperation, knowledge, and time: Alternating-time temporal epistemic logic and its applications. Studia Logica 75(1), 125–157 (2003)
19. van der Meyden, R., Shilov, N.V.: Model Checking Knowledge and Time in Systems with Perfect Recall (Extended Abstract). In: Pandu Rangan, C., Raman, V., Sarukkai, S. (eds.) FST TCS 1999. LNCS, vol. 1738, pp. 432–445. Springer, Heidelberg (1999)
20. van der Meyden, R., Wong, K.-S.: Complete axiomatizations for reasoning about knowledge and branching time. Studia Logica 75(1), 93–123 (2003)
21. Wooldridge, M.: An introduction to multiagent systems. John Wiley and Sons Ltd. (2002)

Learning Predictive Models for Financial Time Series by Using Agent Based Simulations

Filippo Neri

Dept. of Computer Science, University of Naples, Naples 80125, Italy
filippo.neri@unina.it

Abstract. In this work, we discuss a computational technique to model financial time series combining a learning component with a simulation one. An agent based model of the financial market is used to simulate how the market will evolve in the short term while the learning component based on evolutionary computation is used to optimize the simulation parameters. Our experimentations on the DJIA and SP500 time series show the effectiveness of our learning simulation system in their modeling. Also we test its robustness under several experimental conditions and we compare the predictions made by our system to those obtained by other approaches. Our results show that our system is as good as, if not better than, alternative approaches to modeling financial time series. Moreover we show that our approach requires a simple input, the time series for which a model has to be learned, versus the complex and feature rich input to be given to other systems thanks to the ability of our system to adjust its parameters by learning.

Keywords: Agent based modeling, Simulated annealing, Differential evolution, Financial time series, Prediction of the SP500 and DJIA time series.

1 Introduction

The investigation of financial markets, and their time series, is a challenging research task for scientists of many fields including Economics, Statistics, and Computer Science. Computer scientists have recently developed computational approaches to the study of complex systems, like Agent Based Modeling (ABM) [1,2,3,4] and Agent-based Computational Economics (ACE) [5,6,7], which could also be used to study financial time series. The research philosophy of ABM and ACE consists of building computational models of a system's elementary components (agents) and of their relative interactions and then empirically evaluate their capability to simulate directly or indirectly the phenomena object of investigation. However, as financial markets still remain unpredictable, research contributions on modeling their behavior keep being sought for.

In this paper, we describe and empirically evaluate a learning simulation system able to learn an agent based model (the simulation component) of financial time series by exploiting evolutionary computation (the learning component).

N.T. Nguyen (Ed.): Transactions on CCI VI, LNCS 7190, pp. 202–221, 2012.

Research perspectives when modeling financial markets in the artificial intelligence community usually fall into one of the following:

a) evaluating or learning trading strategies for some financial instruments (commodities, bonds, shares, derivatives, etc.);
b) developing artificial markets, whose internal dynamics can be controlled, in order to study which "features" of the markets are responsible for the formation of notable phenomena (price bubble, for instance) that are observable in real markets;
c) and modeling the time series of the values/prices for some financial assets.

With the only intent to provide some examples of the listed research approaches and without claiming to be exhaustive, we mention some papers that fall into the previous categorization. In [8], a society of trading agents uses genetic algorithms to learn trading strategies. Genetic algorithms are used to learn which of the many input parameters, derived from financial technical analysis [9], are useful in identifying profitable investment decisions. As the research focuses on trading, the paper does not report information about how well the trading agents can approximate the financial time series that have been traded. So there is no way to know how good is their system in estimating or tracking a specific asset. A similar research approach is followed in [10], where a multi agent system based on learning classifiers can discover trading strategies that outperform simple investing strategies like "buy and hold" or "keeping the money in a saving account". With a similar philosophy, in [11] neural networks are used to learn trading strategies. In these works, as well, no information is given on how well the system can forecast the value of a financial asset.

In the second category of works, artificial markets are used to investigate how different interaction policies among the agents would produce phenomena that are also observable in real markets. In [12], an agent based artificial market allows to experiment with investment strategies, guiding each agent, in order to observe how they affect the values of financial assets. One of their findings is that over confident investors contribute in making the market efficient. A market is said efficient if any change in the fundamental drivers of an asset value are quickly incorporated into the asset price. In plain words: the arrival of any good or bad news affecting an asset value produces an appropriate and rapid variation in the trading price of the asset. In [13], an artificial market, the Santa Fe Institute (SFI) Artificial Stock Market, is used to empirically test hypothesis about how investors adapt their expectations in time and how their adjustments affect those of the other traders. As a last example of this type of research, in [7], investors, modeled into an agent based market, use either a trading strategy based on trend expectation for a given stock or a trading strategy based on basic fundamental analysis of the stock value. The resulting artificial market displays volatility clustering phenomena similar to those observed in real financial markets. The works following this research perspective, report no application of their systems to the approximation of time series of real financial assets.

Finally, the last group of works aim to closely approximate the time series of real assets. This approach involves evaluating how good some equation models or computational models are in estimating some target time series. The models can be either developed by the researcher by hand or automatically built by exploiting maybe machine learning algorithms. Some instances of this approach are: [14] where an agent based market tries to explain the behavior of the SP500 index in a short period of time; the exploited model is manually built. In [15], neural networks and genetic algorithms are used to learn and predict the time series of the DJIA index. While in [16], a manually determined equation model, based on inflation indexes, is used to explain the behavior of stock prices.

The research reported in this paper belongs to the last category of investigation: we will describe how a Learning Financial Agent Based Simulator (L-FABS) can approximate the time series of the DJIA and SP500 indexes over extended periods of time and under many experimental settings. We will also compare its performances with respect to other approaches in order to assess the effectiveness of different computational techniques in modeling financial time series.

The rest of the paper is organized as follows: Sections from 2 to 5 describe the components of our system: a simple financial agent, how a time series can be simulated by a group of simple financial agents, and how a learning techniques can enable a group of simple financial agents to learn a model for a given time series. In Section 6 and 7, the experimental evaluation of our system is reported, while in Section 8 alternative modeling approaches are compared to our system. Finally, in Section 9, the conclusions are drawn.

2 The Simple Financial Agent Based Simulator

Before describing the architecture of our system, we want to point out two main assumptions that we have made about the economic behavior of the individual investor. We hypothesized that each investment decision depends on two main drivers:

a) the propensity to take some risks today, by buying a financial asset, in exchange for a future uncertain reward, when selling the asset. Indeed any investor has to decide if it is good for her/him to buy, for instance, a Treasury Bond (very safe, but low return), a corporate obligation (not safe as a treasury bond, giving a discrete return), or a company share (no guarantee on the capital as the company may fail, but good return). The investment decision is made according to the investor's risk/reward profile which we will model as a risk/reward propensity rate in the system.
b) the common and public consensus about the future behavior of the asset. Public knowledge about the economic outlook diffused by financial news, economic reports, etc. will influence the investment decision of every one operating in the market. If the economic outlook is negative, on average people will tend to sell some of their assets. If the economic future looks positive, investors tend buy more assets. In the paper, we call market sentiment, market mood, or just sentiment, the common perception for the economy outlook and we will model it accordingly in our system.

We can now start describing the main component of our simulator: the FinancialAgent. A FinancialAgent implements the decision making process underlying the investment decision of buying, selling or holding an asset. In details, a FinancialAgent will decide to buy some asset with probability P(X<BuyThreshold), it will hold to its assets with probability P(BuyThreshold<X<SellThreshold), and it will sell some of its assets with probability P(X>SellThreshold). The abstract algorithm for a FinancialAgent is:

```
FinancialAgent(AgentId, Sentiment)
  TotAssets = TotalAssetsF(AgentId)
  InvAssets = InvestedAssetsF(AgentId)
  RiskRewardRate = RiskRewardPropensityF(AgentId)
  BuyThreshold= RiskRewardRate × Sentiment
  SellThreshold = (1 - ((1 - BuyThreshold) / 2))
  randomNum = random(1)
  // random(1) returns a random number in the interval (0,1)
  if (randomNum < BuyThreshold) then
    // buy some assets
    InvAssets = InvAssets + 2% × TotAssets
  endif
  if (randomNum > SellThreshold) then
    // sell some assets
    InvAssets = InvAssets - 2% × TotAssets
  endif
  UpdateAssets(AgentId)
```

As it can be seen in the algorithm, the probabilities to buy/sell/hold are dependent on the current level of sentiment about the economy. In fact the probability to buy assets increases along with the sentiment, while the probability to sell assets decreases when the sentiment is raising and vice versa. Also the amount of assets to be bought or sold is set to 2% of the total assets of the investors. The value 2% has been chosen as it represents twice the average daily variation of the studied time series. We verified empirically in an earlier work [14] that it provides reasonable simulation results and has been kept constant since then. It might be changed in case the time series under investigation displays an average daily variation higher than 1%.

Given the code for a FinancialAgent, the simulation of the entire financial market can be obtained by implementing the system architecture shown in Fig. 1, thus realizing the Simple Financial Agent Based Simulator S-FABS. In Fig. 1, several instances of FinancialAgent are created, each one with its own status in terms of own assets, invested assets and risk/reward propensity. Then an investment round is performed during which each agent decides if buying, selling, or holding taking into account the Sentiment value for the round. At the end of the round, it is possible to measure the percentage of invested assets. This percentage is used as an

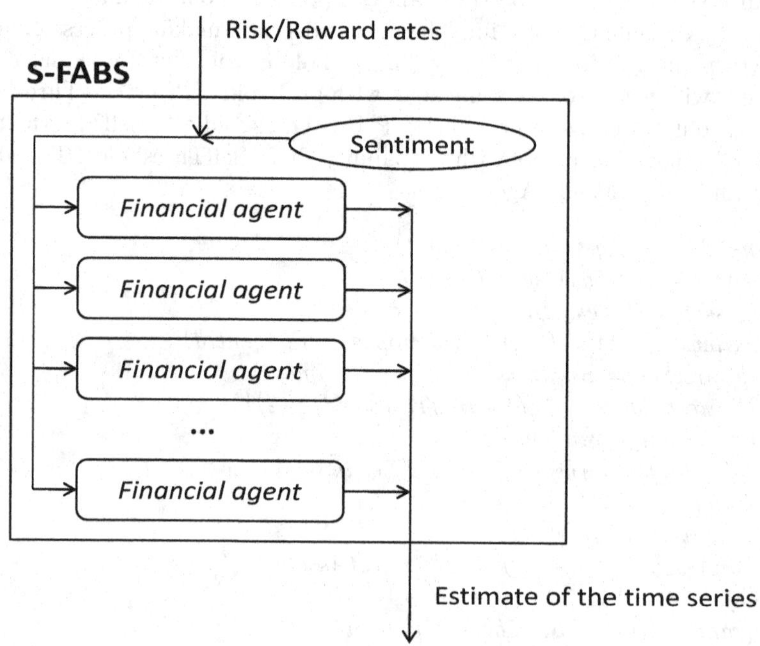

Fig. 1. The architecture of S-FABS showing the relationships between the simulated investors, *FinancialAgent(s)*, the input (the vector of risk/reward rates), and the output (the estimate for the time series) of the system

estimate for one data point of the target time series. If the investment round is repeated n times, the output will represent an estimate for an n-length time series.

As shown in Fig. 1, S-FABS takes as input the vector of risk/rewards propensity rates for each Financial Agent. During each round, the risk/rewards propensity rates are used in combination with the current value of the economic sentiment by each Financial Agent to take an investment decision. We will comment on the Sentiment function in the experimental section of the paper as it will be subject of learning under some of the experimental set ups.

A final point about the Financial Agents in S-FABS. In our study, we employ four types or classes of Financial Agents to capture the richness in investment decisions and in size of financial transactions that occur in real financial markets. The four types of investors we model are: individual investors (and the likes), banks (and the likes), hedge funds (and the likes), and central banks (and the likes). They differ in term of the size of the assets they can invest in financial markets and for their risk/reward appetite. In addition, their numerical presence is also different. Here are the values we used during our simulations:

Investor type	Total Assets (in millions)	Percentage over 100 Investors
Individual	0.1	30
Funds	100	20
Banks	1000	49
Central Banks	10000	1

The figures in the table are to be read only as a rough approximation for the average composition of the investors operating in the financial markets. Specific reasons for choosing four types of investors and for setting their parameters include: common view about who operates in the markets, the desire to keep the model simple while showing how it can preserve the diversity of the investors, and personal conversations with investment managers [17].

3 The Complete Learning Simulator L-FABS: Adding a Learning Capability to S-FABS

In this section, we comment on the architecture of the complete learning simulator L-FABS that results from the integration of S-FABS with a learning algorithm. In Fig. 2, the architecture of L-FABS is appearing. The picture shows how a learning algorithm can be use to find the vector of risk/reward propensity rates (plus any possible additional parameter object of experimentation) given as input to S-FABS for approximating the target time series.

The chosen architecture of L-FABS allows for decoupling the learning phase from the simulation phase thus making it possible to select as learning system any machine learning algorithm able to find a vector of values that minimizes a given error function. Examples of suitable machine learning algorithms include: genetic algorithms [18,19], decision trees [20], neural networks [21], simulated annealing [22], and differential evolution [23]. Given the possibility to select any of these learning methods, we decided to use simulated annealing and differential evolution because the author has research experience in evolutionary computation and he is aware that evolutionary learning produces good results even when little or any domain knowledge is available [19].

For the error function to be minimized, we need to select one that can evaluate how well two time series are similar: the Mean Average Percentage Error (MAPE) is a suitable choice. The MAPE measure is commonly used in Statistics when two data samplings have to be compared in term of a non dimensional measure. The Mean Average Percentage Error is defined as:

$$MAPE(X,Y) = \frac{1}{N}\sum_{i=1}^{N}\left|\frac{x_i - y_i}{x_i}\right|$$

In the formula, X and Y are two time series, x_i and y_i are the i-th elements of the time series, and N is the length of the time series. Given two time series X and Y, the lower their MAPE value, the closer the two are. The MAPE value

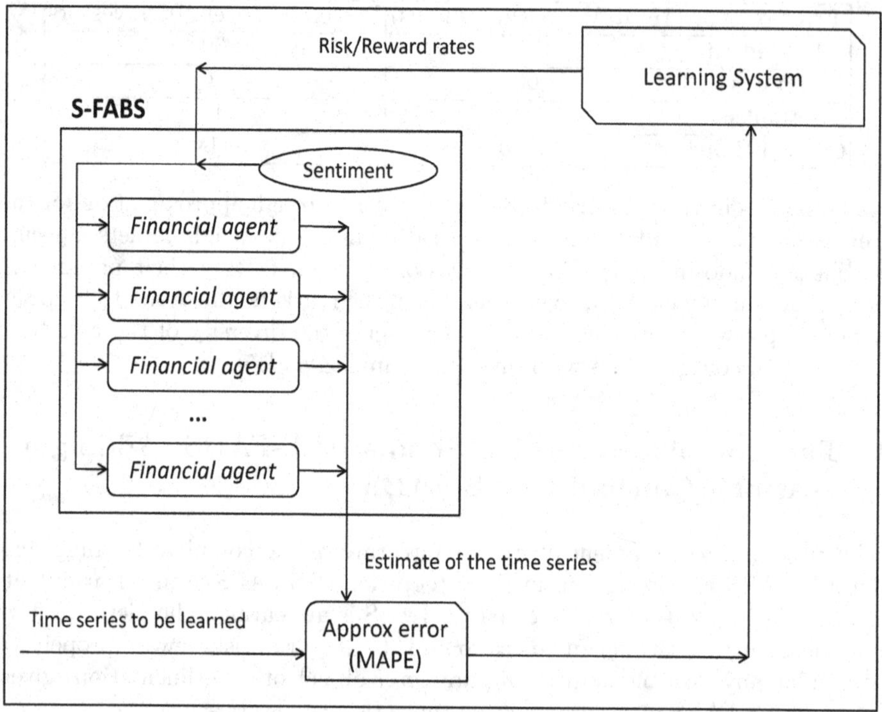

Fig. 2. The architecture of L-FABS showing the relationships between S-FABS, the simulated individual investors (*FinancialAgent(s)*), the approximation function, and the learning algorithm. All together, these algorithms result in the L-FABS system.

can provide a useful indication of how well a learning system has been able to approximate a target time series thus it can be used as a measure of the learning error.

4 Exploiting Simulated Annealing in L-FABS

Simulated Annealing is one of the machine learning algorithm that can be used as learning system in L-FABS. Simulated annealing [22] iteratively searches for the minimum of a given function E (the Error function) by generating at each step random candidate points for the minimum in the proximity of the current candidate minimum point which represents the "center" of exploration. At the end of each step, Simulated Annealing may move the center of exploration at a newly generated point with a given probability. The domain of the Error function can be thought as a space to be search, thus the name *search space.* Simulated Annealing, as a search process, can also be interpreted as walking along a stochastic trajectory from one point in the domain of the Error function

E to another point in search for the function minimum while the probability of changing the exploration center is reducing.

In our integration of Simulated Annealing in L-FABS, a point s in the search space is a vector of numbers, representing the risk/reward propensity rates that are provided as input to S-FABS, plus any additional parameters that have to be learned according to the experimental set up. The Error function E to be minimized is defined as the MAPE function.

All the other parameters of Simulated Annealing are set according to Kirkpatrick et al. [22], the work that introduced Simulated Annealing, as we are not interested in this paper in studying their impact on the annealing process. Finally, we recall that adapting Simulated Annealing, or any other evolutionary learning techniques, to a specific learning task is similar to the need of defining a domain specific fitness function and task oriented cross over operators when using genetic algorithms as shown for instance in [18,24].

5 Using Differential Evolution in L-FABS

As discussed for simulated annealing, Differential Evolution can be used as well as learning technique in L-FABS. Differential Evolution is a population based evolutionary computation method that proved effective in searching the domain of complex continuous functions to be minimized [23]. Differential Evolution[1] is based on the idea of producing a novel candidate solution by adding to a population individual (a vector) the weighted difference among two population individuals. Being the population individuals represented as vectors, the Differential Equation algorithm can be easily adapted to search for those parameter vectors for S-FABS that results in low approximation errors.

Differential Evolution, code below, operates through the following steps:

a) Initialization Step - an individual $p[i]$ is selected from the current population and assigned to the variable *tmp*
b) Crossover Step - some components of a newly created individual (for instance the n-th component of a translated individual $p[r1][n] + F * (p[r2][n] - p[r3][n])$) may be randomly added to the original individual in *tmp*. As output from the crossover operator, the resulting trial individual, now in *tmp*, contains some components coming from an individual in the current population $p[i]$ and some taken from a translated individual.
c) Selection Step - the trial individual *tmp* is evaluated, with respect to the function to be minimized, and if its evaluation is lower than the original individual $p[i]$, then it is added to the population of the following generation, possibly the best solution found so far is also changed to *tmp*. Otherwise the trial individual is discarded and $p[i]$ is added to the next generation population. A possible template for the described Differential Evolution algorithm, as appearing in [23], is:

[1] The code for Differential Evolution algorithm used in the experimental session is based on the source files available at
`http://www.icsi.berkeley.edu/storn/code.html`

//Definitions of the input parameters
//D, a constant dependent on the problem at hand. It is equal to the number of parameters to be learned
//NP, number of individuals in the population
//genmax, the generation number
//CR, the probability that a novel component ends up in the trial individual tmp
//F, the weight of the difference among two population individuals during the crossover operation
//Strategy, the selected crossover strategy

```
DifferentialEvolution(D, NP, genmax, CR, F, Strategy)
  count = 0
  while(count++ < genmax)do
     r1 = random() * NP; r2 = random() * NP
     r3 = random() * NP; r4 = random() * NP
     for(i = 0; i < NP, i++){
        cost[i] = evaluate(p[i])}
     for(i = 0; i < NP, i++)
        //INITIALIZATION step
        tmp = p[i];
        n = (int)(random() * D);
        //CROSSOVER step
        if(Strategy == 0) //Best individual policy
           L = 0;
           do
              tmp[n] = best[n] + F * (p[r2][n] - p[r3][n])
              n = (n + 1)%D
              L++
           while(random() < CR)and(L < D));
        endif
        if(Strategy == 1) //Random individual policy
           for(L = 0; L < D; L++)
              if((random() < CR)||L == (D - 1))
                 tmp[n] = p[r1][n] + F * (p[r2][n] - p[r3][n])
              endif
              n = (n + 1)%D
           endfor
        endif
        //SELECTION step
        trialCost = evaluate(tmp)
        if(trialCost <= cost[i])
           cost[i] = trialCost;
           pnew[i] = tmp;
           if(trialCost < bestCost)
```

```
                bestCost = trialCost;
                best = tmp;
            endif
        endif
        elsepnew[i] = p[i]
    endfor
    // INSERT NEW individual in the population
    copyPopulation(pnew, p)
endwhile
return(best)
```

In the Differential Evolution algorithm, two crossover strategies have been considered, among those studied in [23]: we call them *Best individual crossover* and *Random individual crossover*, they differ by how they select the individual/solution from which they build the translated individual. The Best individual crossover selects the best individual found so far, while the Random individual crossover selects a random element of the current population. Both crossover policies are known for providing good results across several problems [23].

Our research objective in this paper is not to find the best configuration for Differential Evolution, we accept from the literature that it works and produces good results so we use the parameter settings suggested by their inventors when exploiting them in L-FABS. When applying Differential Evolution its input parameters D, NP, genmax, CR, F, Strategy are assigned as follows. D is set equal to the number of risk/rewards rates to be learned; NP, CR and F have been set to 40, 0.5 and 0.9 respectively, according to the suggestions made by the inventors; genmax has been set to 40 because the Differential Evolution can converge and solve our task in less than 40 generations; this has been verified on sample runs with random parameter settings.

As a difference between Simulated Annealing and Differential Evolution, we may note that the Differential Evolution is based on evolving a population of trial solutions for the minimization problem, while Simulated Annealing relies on evolving a single candidate solution round over round. One may perhaps expect that a population based method is more effective in finding a function minimum because at each round it can exploit a sample of n points in the function domain, while an individual based method, like Simulated Annealing, can rely only on one data point per round. We will see in the experimental section how the two methods compare in finding a solution for our domain.

6 Research Methodology to Evaluate L-FABS

One of the research objective of this paper is to perform an empirical evaluation of L-FABS on modeling and predicting financial time series. We will then proceed as follows to undertake our goal:

a) first we will select some publicly available financial time series that represent the behavior of financial markets,
b) then we choose a definition for the Sentiment function to estimate the market mood
c) finally we will select a variety of experimental conditions, described in the following section, under which to measure the performances of L-FABS.

The selected time series selected are:

Dataset DJIA - learning set: DJIA from 3 Jan 1994 to 17 Dec 2003 and test set: DJIA from 18 Dec 2003 to 23 Oct 2006.
Dataset SP500 - learning set: SP500 from 3 Jan 1994 to 17 Dec 2003 and test set: SP500 from 18 Dec 2003 to 23 Oct 2006.

The DJIA and SP500 time series represent an aggregate measure of the USA stock markets and they represent the behavior of the stocks of the highest capitalized public companies quoted in the USA stock markets. These time series are also known as market indexes by financial operators. An additional reason for selecting the two datasets is that they have been used to test other learning algorithms and are therefore useful to compare our system with other ones. All the datasets contain the daily closing values of the indexes and have been freely acquired from the finance section of yahoo.com. As usual with learning systems, we will train L-FABS on a part of the dataset, the learning set, and then we will use the remaining part of the dataset as test set to assess the performances of the learned model.

In the performed experiments, we will evaluate L-FABS when estimating either the next value of the time series (the value of the next trading day) or the seven days ahead value of the time series. The seven days ahead prediction has been selected as it is the most far ahead prediction made by other learning systems and thus can serve as an interesting comparison data.

Moving to the definition of the Sentiment function for determining the market mood, we want to stress that our approach does not impose any restriction on how the market mood is determined. For our experiments, we implemented the Sentiment function as follows to keep it as simple and as general as possible:

```
function Sentiment(time, mavgDays)
  begin=time-1
  end=time-mavgDays
  if (MAVG(PredictedData, begin, end) <
     MAVG(RealData, begin, end))
     then return(α)
     else return(β)
```

The variables RealData and PredictedData give access to the time series of the real and predicted values. The Moving AVeraGe function (MAVG) returns the average of the latest n values in a time series up to the current time t. The MAVG function is defined as:

$$\text{MAVG(TimeSeries,t,n)} = \frac{\sum_{k=0}^{n-1} TimeSeries(t-k)}{n}$$

where TimeSeries is an array of the values of the time series to be used, and t and n are indexes for the values to be used in the calculation of the moving average. According to our definition of the Sentiment function, the outlook of the real market is considered bullish if the moving average (MAVG) of the predicted time serie is lower than the moving average of the real data. If this is the case, the Sentiment value is set to an high value so that a bullish mood is communicated to the Financial Agents in S-FABS. The opposite happens if the predictions of the system have been higher than the real data. The values α and β will assume the constant values of 0.65 and 0.30 in a set of experiments, while will be determined by the learning algorithm in another set of experiments.

In our experiments, we will invoke the Sentiment function as either Sentiment(CurrentTime,1), case identified in the following with S1, or Sentiment(CurrentTime,5), case identified with S2. In case S1, only the values of the previous day of the two time series are used, while in case S2, the averaged value of the latest previous five days are used to estimate the market mood.

7 Experimental Settings and Evaluation of L-FABS

We are now ready to discuss our experiments. We begin by describing how the tables reporting the empirical findings are structured. In the following tables, each row represents an experimental set up. Column "values for α and β" indicates the values for the α and β parameters to be used in the Sentiment function; column "Sentiment" indicates if the Sentiment value is calculated with modality S1 or S5; column "Day to predict" indicates the number of days ahead for which a prediction of the time serie is made; and, finally, column "MAPE" indicates the MAPE values measured on the test set. The MAPE errors are obtained as the average over 10 runs of the same experimental setup.

Moreover each table is divided in two parts: the first four rows are experiments with constant values for the α and β parameters, while the last four rows represent experiments where α and β are learned by the learning algorithm together with the risk/reward propensity rates. This means that the experimental set up in row one is similar to the experimental setting of row five with the difference that the learning task in row one consists of finding the vector of risk/reward propensity rates, whereas in row five the learning task is to find the vector of risk/reward propensity rates plus the values for the α and β parameters.

In Tables from 1 to 4, we report the prediction errors obtained by L-FABS when simulated annealing has run for 200 and 400 rounds. From the experimental findings, it appears that predicting the next day value of the time series is easier than predicting the seven days ahead value. This finding confirms the intuitive experience that the farther a prediction is moved into the future, the less accurate it will be. Also it emerges that using only the previous day close for estimating the market mood, Sentiment S1, tends to be as good as using the moving average

Table 1. Experimental results on dataset DJIA using 200 rounds of simulated annealing

values for α and β	Sentiment	Day to predict	MAPE %
constant values			
0.65, 0.30	S1	1	0.76
0.65, 0.30	S5	1	0.74
0.65, 0.30	S1	7	1.48
0.65, 0.30	S5	7	1.51
learned values			
0.40, 0.31	S1	1	0.62
0.31, 0.29	S5	1	0.67
0.51, 0.47	S1	7	1.35
0.43, 0.44	S5	7	1.52

Table 2. Experimental results on dataset DJIA using 400 rounds of simulated annealing

values for α and β	Sentiment	Day to predict	MAPE %
constant values			
0.65, 0.30	S1	1	0.74
0.65, 0.30	S5	1	0.69
0.65, 0.30	S1	7	1.48
0.65, 0.30	S5	7	1.47
learned values			
0.55, 0.48	S1	1	0.57
0.51, 0.48	S5	1	0.58
0.50, 0.43	S1	7	1.39
0.53, 0.43	S5	7	1.45

Table 3. Experimental results on dataset SP500 using 200 rounds of simulated annealing

values for α and β	Sentiment	Day to predict	MAPE %
constant values			
0.65, 0.30	S1	1	0.76
0.65, 0.30	S5	1	0.70
0.65, 0.30	S1	7	1.47
0.65, 0.30	S5	7	1.52
learned values			
0.69, 0.99	S1	1	0.73
0.81, 0.48	S5	1	0.68
0.23, 0.17	S1	7	1.44
0.47, 0.19	S5	7	1.57

Table 4. Experimental results on dataset SP500 using 400 rounds of simulated annealing

values for α and β	Sentiment	Day to predict	MAPE %
constant values			
0.65, 0.30	S1	1	0.73
0.65, 0.30	S5	1	0.70
0.65, 0.30	S1	7	1.47
0.65, 0.30	S5	7	1.54
learned values			
0.51, 0.50	S1	1	0.58
0.54, 0.49	S5	1	0.63
0.88, 0.91	S1	7	1.35
0.86, 0.68	S5	7	1.33

Table 5. Experimental results on dataset DJIA using 40 rounds of Differential Evolution

Crossover	values for α and β	Sentiment	Day to predict	MAPE %
	constant values			
best	0.65, 0.30	S1	1	0.74
best	0.65, 0.30	S5	1	0.70
best	0.65, 0.30	S1	7	1.57
best	0.65, 0.30	S5	7	1.50
	learned values			
best	0.48, 0.40	S1	1	0.58
best	0.87, 0.74	S5	1	0.58
best	0.45, 0.42	S1	7	1.37
best	0.45, 0.44	S5	7	1.36

Table 6. Experimental results on dataset DJIA using 40 rounds of Differential Evolution

Crossover	values for α and β	Sentiment	Day to predict	MAPE %
	constant values			
random	0.65, 0.30	S1	1	0.69
random	0.65, 0.30	S5	1	0.71
random	0.65, 0.30	S1	7	1.48
random	0.65, 0.30	S5	7	1.54
	learned values			
random	0.52, 0.43	S1	1	0.59
random	0.60, 0.55	S5	1	0.58
random	0.73, 0.69	S1	7	1.39
random	0.46, 0.41	S5	7	1.39

Table 7. Experimental results on dataset SP500 using 40 rounds of Differential Evolution

Crossover	values for α and β	Sentiment	Day to predict	MAPE %
	constant values			
best	0.65, 0.30	S1	1	0.74
best	0.65, 0.30	S5	1	0.69
best	0.65, 0.30	S1	7	1.47
best	0.65, 0.30	S5	7	1.44
	learned values			
best	0.52 , 0.52	S1	1	0.62
best	0.55 , 0.53	S5	1	0.63
best	0.43 , 0.40	S1	7	1.57
best	0.59 , 0.53	S5	7	1.59

Table 8. Experimental results on dataset SP500 using 40 rounds of Differential Evolution

Crossover	values for α and β	Sentiment	Day to predict	MAPE %
	constant values			
random	0.65, 0.30	S1	1	0.75
random	0.65, 0.30	S5	1	0.69
random	0.65, 0.30	S1	7	1.46
random	0.65, 0.30	S5	7	1.46
	learned values			
random	0.51, 0.49	S1	1	0.64
random	0.39, 0.36	S5	1	0.59
random	0.46, 0.42	S1	7	1.52
random	0.44, 0.42	S5	7	1.60

of the latest five days, case S5. Comparing the results in the first four rows with the latter four rows in the table, it is also evident that when the system is let to learn the parameters α and β as well, L-FABS is able to produce slightly better forecasts.

Let us consider now the results in Tables 5 to 8, here L-FABS is exploiting Differential Evolution as learning algorithm. For this set of experiments, we run Differential Evolution selecting either the "Random individual" or the "Best individual" crossover policy. Quite interestingly, the measured prediction errors under these experimental set ups are very similar to those observed when using simulated annealing as learning method. Even under these configurations, L-FABS shows the ability to better predict the one day forward value for a time series over the seven days ahead value. Also L-FABS displays a lower prediction error when learning is also applied to the α and β parameters thus letting L-FABS model with more precision the given time series. Moreover the two crossover strategies display similar prediction effectiveness. Finally, the obtained errors are quite close for similar experimental set ups, compare the MAPE values across the Tables from 5 to 8.

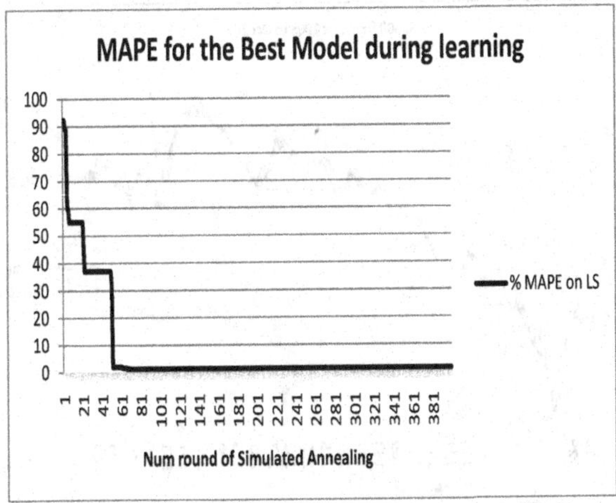

Fig. 3. Convergence curve of the learning algorithm in L-FABS reporting the MAPE error for the best model found at any given cycle of simulation annealing

Our conclusion is that both an individual based evolutionary learning method, such as simulated annealing, and a population based evolutionary learning method, such as differential evolution, are able to solve the learning task with a limited and acceptable amount of computational resources and that none of the two appears to be a better learner over the other for our domain.

We also like to observe that the MAPE errors, for the same experimental setup across tables from 1 to 8, tend to be very close. This behavior is an important positive characteristic of a learning system and it is called *robustness* that is the ability to display a consistently good behavior across a range of different configurations.

For completeness, we add few comments on the convergence behavior of the selected learning methods. If we consider how quickly simulated annealing is able to find a good solution, Fig. 3, it is evident that, in about 100 rounds, it is able to discover a quite acceptable solution. Fig. 3 shows the curve of convergence of the simulated annealing by reporting for each round of annealing the MAPE error of the best model found so far measured on the training set. A similar behavior is observed when differential evolution is used as learning algorithm. Finally, just as an example, we show the graph of a time series predicted by L-FABS and the target SP500 time series in Fig. 4. The reported graph is an exemplar of the typical behavior of L-FABS under many experimental settings. As it can be seen from the graph, the dotted line (target) and the solid line (predicted) are very close confirming the error figures that have been reported in the tables.

8 Experimental Comparison of L-FABS to Other Systems

For providing an exhaustive evaluation of L-FBAS, we will compare its performances with respect to those obtained on the same datasets by alternative

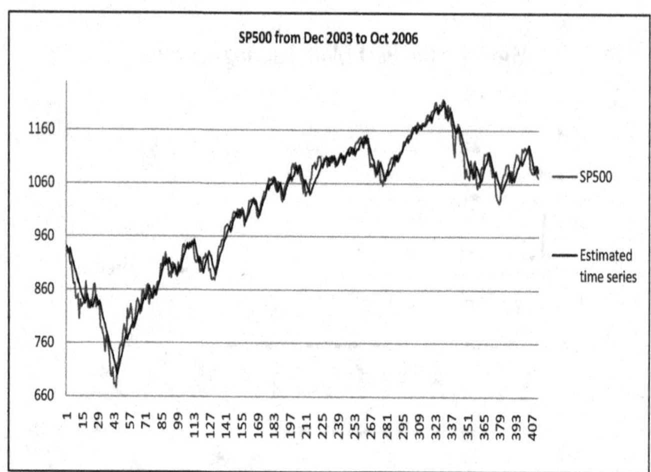

Fig. 4. The actual and predicted SP500 time series when testing L-FABS with settings: α=0.60, β=0.30, S1, and Day to predict 1

Table 9. Experimental results, averaged over 10 runs, for Dataset DJIA and Dataset SP500

Dataset	Day to predict	PSO MAPE %	MLP MAPE %	L-FABS MAPE %
DJIA	1	0.65	1.06	0.57
DJIA	7	1.47	5.64	1.39
SP500	1	0.66	1.00	0.58
SP500	7	1.47	3.11	1.35

approaches for which enough implementation details have been given in the literature [15]. In Table 9, we compare L-FABS, a Particle Swarm Optimization algorithm (PSO) [25] and a Multi-Layer Perceptron (MLP) [26], whose parameters have been set up as in [15], when operating on datasets DJIA and SP500. The results for L-FABS are relative to the configuration: α and β are learned, Sentiment set to S1, and 400 rounds of simulated annealing. This is just a subjective choice by the author as equally good results can be observed under different experimental set ups in the tables described in the previous section.

We also note that any learning/prediction made by PSO or MLP requires: the value of the target time series at the current time plus a number of financial technical indicators such as: EMA10, EMEA20, EMEA30, ADO, and some others. Financial technical indicators are useful in forecasting financial time series according to the philosophy of financial technical analysis used by technical traders. For a primer on technical analysis and indicators, any introductory book on the topic will do: for instance [9]. As an example of technical indicator, EMA10 stands for the Exponential Moving Average calculated over 10 previous periods and is defined as EMA(t,j=10) = value(t-1) x a + EMA(t-1,j-1)*(1-a) where value(t) is the value at time t of the time series under consideration and the smoothing factor a is defined as a = 2 / (j + 1).

On the contrary the input to L-FABS is only the time series of the data for which a model has to be learned and the system itself will adjust its parameters by learning.

The results in Table 9 show that the forecasting errors of L-FABS are better than those obtained by of PSO and MLP. Moreover, it is evident, as observed in the previous section, that the forecasting error increases when farther into the future the prediction is to be made. And this holds for all the systems. This finding is also in line with what we expect to happen in real financial markets.

9 Conclusions

In this paper, we discussed how the learning simulator L-FABS, an agent based simulator with evolutionary learning, could learn the models of some target financial time series extracted from the historical data of the SP500 and DJIA indexes. Moreover we evaluated the modeling performances of L-FABS under several experimental settings and by comparison with the results obtained by other learning systems. The main findings of our work are that:

a) the learning simulator L-FABS can model well the studied SP500 and DJIA time series. We believe that the experimental results support the research hypothesis that combining an agent based simulator with a learning system by means of a simple system architecture results in a learning simulator able to approximate the financial time series under study.
b) the approximation errors of L-FABS, observed in the experiments, are comparable with, if not lower of, those obtained by learners based on particle swarm optimization or neural networks. An advantage of using L-FABS over the other systems is that L-FABS works directly over the data of the target financial time series whereas the other learners require a manual pre-processing of the data to introduce information rich attributes such as EMA, ADO, etc. which are derived from financial technical indicators.
c) finally, both simulated annealing and differential evolution proved to be robust when applied to our learning task: they were able to learn models for the financial time series under investigation with low prediction errors under several experimental conditions. The learning algorithms used in the experiment where run using their classical parameter settings as provided in the research papers that introduced them. Then no specific tuning for the learning component has been used to obtain the observed results, yet quite good approximations for the financial time series have been observed under a variety of experimental settings. Low approximation errors could be obtained both when trying to predict the next day close value of the time series and the seven days ahead one. Those empirical findings support the hypothesis that information about the near future behavior of the time series could be extrapolated by the preceding points up to the current time.

References

1. Bonabeau, E.: Agent-based modeling: Methods and techniques for simulating human systems. Proceedings of the National Academy of Sciences 99, 7280–7287 (2002)
2. Epstein, J.M., Axtell, R.: Growing artificial societies: social science from the bottom up. The Brookings Institution, Washington, DC, USA (1996)
3. Neri, F.: Software agents as a simulation tool to study aggregate consumers' behavior in market places. IASR Journal of Advanced Research in Computer Science 1, 32–43 (2009)
4. Neri, F.: PIRR: a methodology for distributed network management in mobile networks. WSEAS Transaction on Information Science and Applications 5, 306–311 (2008)
5. Lebaron, B.: Agent based computational finance: Suggested readings and early research. Journal of Economic Dynamics and Control 24, 679–702 (1998)
6. Tesfatsion, L.: Agent-based computational economics: Growing economies from the bottom up. Artif. Life 8, 55–82 (2002)
7. Hoffmann, A.O.I., Delre, S.A., von Eije, J.H., Jager, W.: Artificial multi-agent stock markets: Simple strategies, complex outcomes. In: Advances in Artificial Economics. Lecture Notes in Economics and Mathematical Systems, vol. 584, pp. 167–176. Springer, Heidelberg (2006)
8. Kendall, G., Su, Y.: A multi-agent based simulated stock market - testing on different types of stocks. In: Congress on Evolutionary Computation CEC 2003, pp. 2298–2305 (2003)
9. Kirkpatrick, C., Dahlquist, J.: Technical Analysis: The Complete Resource for Financial Market Technicians. FT Press (2006)
10. Schulenburg, S., Ross, P.: An Adaptive Agent Based Economic Model. In: Lanzi, P.L., Stolzmann, W., Wilson, S.W. (eds.) IWLCS 1999. LNCS (LNAI), vol. 1813, pp. 263–284. Springer, Heidelberg (2000)
11. Dempster, M.A.H., Payne, T.W., Romahi, Y., Thompson, G.W.P.: Computational learning techniques for intraday fx trading using popular technical indicators. IEEE Transactions on Neural Networks 12, 744–754 (2001)
12. Takahashi, H., Terano, T.: Analyzing the Influence of Overconfident Investors on Financial Markets through Agent-based Model. In: Yin, H., Tino, P., Corchado, E., Byrne, W., Yao, X. (eds.) IDEAL 2007. LNCS, vol. 4881, pp. 1042–1052. Springer, Heidelberg (2007)
13. Arthur, W.B., Holland, J.H., LeBaron, B., Palmer, R., Taylorm, P.: Asset pricing under endogenous expectation in an artificial stock market. In: The Economy as an Evolving Complex System II. Santa Fe Institute Studies in the Sciences of Complexity Lecture Notes, pp. 15–44 (1997)
14. Neri, F.: Using software agents to simulate how investors' greed and fear emotions explain the behavior of a financial market. In: WSEAS Conference ICOSSE 2009, Genoa, Italy, pp. 241–245 (2009)
15. Majhi, R., Sahoo, G., Panda, A., Choubey, A.: Prediction of sp500 and djia stock indices using particle swarm optimization techniques. In: Congress on Evolutionary Computation 2008, pp. 1276–1282. IEEE Press (2008)
16. Kitov, I.: Predicting conocophillips and exxon mobil stock price. Journal of Applied Research in Finance 2, 129–134 (2009)
17. Cesa, A.: Discussion about how financial markets work: an investment manager perspective. Personal correspondance with the author (2009)

18. Goldberg, D.: Genetic Algorithms in Search, Optimization, and Machine Learning. Addison-Wesley, Reading (1989)
19. Neri, F.: Traffic packet based intrusion detection: decision trees and generic based learning evaluation. WSEAS Transaction on Computers 4, 1017–1024 (2005)
20. Quinlan, J.R.: C4.5: Programs for Machine Learning. Morgan Kaufmann, California (1993)
21. Rumelhart, D.E., Hinton, G.E., Williams, R.J.: Learning internal representations by error propagation. In: Parallel Distributed Processing: Explorations in the Microstructure of Cognition. Foundations, vol. 1, pp. 318–362. MIT Press, Cambridge (1986)
22. Kirkpatrick, S., Gelatt, C.D., Vecchi, M.P.: Optimization by simulated annealing. Science 220, 671–680 (1983)
23. Storn, R., Price, K.: Differential evolution - a simple and efficient heuristic for global optimization over continuous spaces. Journal of Global Optimization 11, 341–359 (1997)
24. Neri, F., Saitta, L.: Exploring the power of genetic search in learning symbolic classifiers. IEEE Trans. on Pattern Analysis and Machine Intelligence PAMI-18, 1135–1142 (1996)
25. Kennedy, J., Eberhard, R.: Particle swarm optimization. In: Int. Conf. on Neural Networks, pp. 1942–1948. IEEE Press (1995)
26. Zirilli, J.: Financial prediction using Neural Networks. International Thompson Computer Press (1997)

Author Index